William Bartram on the Southeastern Indians

Travels of William Bartram

April 1773 – October 1776

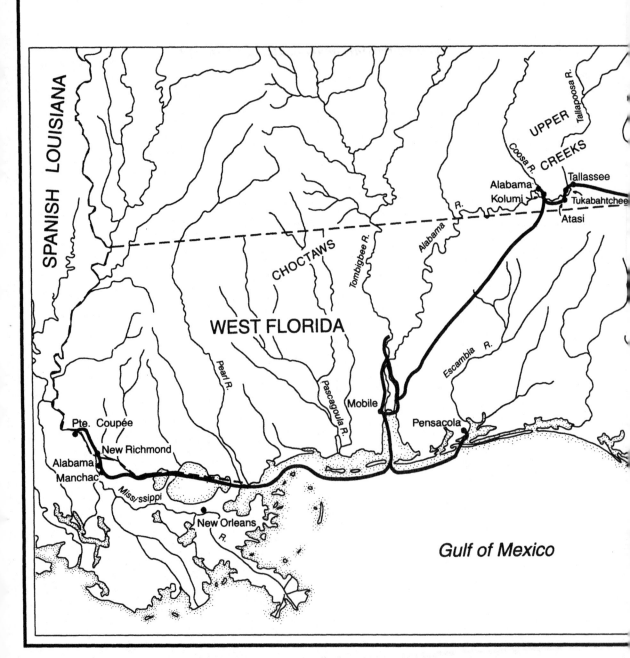

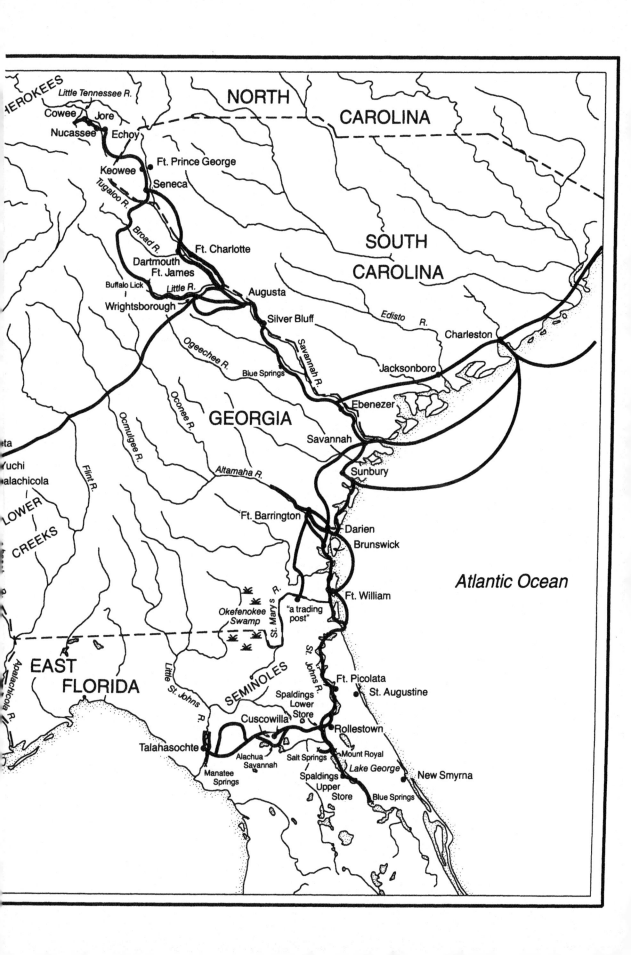

INDIANS OF THE SOUTHEAST

WILLIAM BARTRAM

on the Southeastern Indians

EDITED AND ANNOTATED BY GREGORY A. WASELKOV

AND KATHRYN E. HOLLAND BRAUND

University of Nebraska Press

Lincoln and London

∞

First Nebraska paperback printing: 2002

Library of Congress Cataloging-in-Publication Data
William Bartram on the Southeastern Indians / edited and annotated by
Gregory A. Waselkov and Kathryn E. Holland Braund.
p.   cm.—(Indians of the Southeast)
Includes bibliographical references and index.
ISBN 0-8032-4772-9 (cloth: alk. paper)
ISBN 0-8032-6205-1 (paper: alk. paper)
1. Southern States—Description and travel—Early works to 1800.
2. Indians of North America—Southern States.   3. Bartram, William,
1739–1823—Journeys—Southern States.   I. Waselkov, Gregory A.
II. Braund, Kathryn E. Holland, 1955–   .   III. Series.
F213.W713   1995
917.504′3—dc20
94-29756
CIP

Title page illustration: This sketch of a Quaker gentleman is found in an untitled
manuscript, written in William Bartram's hand, on the moral sensibility of animals;
Bartram Family Papers, vol. 1, p.83 (courtesy, Historical Society of Pennsylvania)

Contents

Illustrations

Series Editors' Introduction

For 200 years, people have been reading and enjoying William Bartram, a renowned naturalist. His vivid descriptions of the flora and fauna of the American Southeast captured a world that no longer exists. First published in 1791, Bartram's *Travels* has been reprinted many times, often carefully edited and annotated by students of natural history. But Bartram was interested in the human as well as the natural history of the Southeast and his writings include large sections devoted to the American Indians of the region. Thus Bartram's writings have also become important to students of Native American history. Along with James Adair, Bartram is the prime source on the life ways of the early Creeks and Seminoles. Recognizing this, Gregory Waselkov and Kathryn Holland Braund, experienced interpreters of early southeastern Indian history, have edited Bartram's writings to identify and present in one volume all of his Indian materials, both published and unpublished. We are pleased to offer this significant collection of Bartram as part of the Indians of the Southeast Series.

Theda Perdue   Michael D. Green

Preface

Like many other books, this one began with a small idea, when some interesting and informative documents came to our attention in the fall of 1988. They included a set of drawings of eighteenth-century, southeastern American Indian buildings and mounds, copies of lost originals by William Bartram. Few historians or anthropologists were aware of these important sketches, and another relatively unknown Bartram manuscript among the Henry Knox Papers also warranted identification and broader exposure. From this beginning the larger goal developed of identifying, editing, and publishing all of Bartram's known writings on Native Americans. We were already collaborating on an archaeological and ethnohistorical study of the eighteenth-century Upper Creek town of Fusihatchee, so a joint project on Bartram's Indian writings seemed a natural extension. Since biologists have dominated most previous research on Bartram, we feel our complementary backgrounds as an anthropological archaeologist (GAW) and a historian (KEHB) have given us a different perspective on this important early American naturalist and writer.

While one of us (GAW) concentrated on editing and analyzing Bartram's major published works, his *Travels* and "Observations," the other (KEHB) began an extensive search of manuscript repositories for new Bartram material. During the course of our research, we quickly realized that most published interpretations of Bartram's writings contain an amazing number of errors (which we have endeavored to correct in our notes). Some of these errors are attributable to a general unfamiliarity with works not published in Bartram's lifetime. To address this problem, all of his writings on the American Indians, apart from a few very minor documents (mostly brief notes with little factual content found among the Bartram Family Papers and the Benjamin Smith Barton Papers), are included in their entirety or quoted at length. Moreover, in the absence of a reliable biography of Bartram, we undertook research on that count too. Here also we encountered many errors of fact and interpretation. The story behind Bartram's unpublished papers is often as fascinating as the works themselves, so our introductory essays reconstruct the history of the Bartram documents. While this book has been a collaborative effort, and both authors have contributed to every part of the work, the opening chapter and the introductory essays for *Travels*, "Observations," and "Hints," as well as the annotations for "Hints," are primarily the work of Braund, while Waselkov was largely responsible for the annotations to *Travels* and "Observations" and for the concluding essay.

We have tried to be comprehensive and accurate in considering Bartram's contribution to the study of American Indians in the eighteenth-century Southeast. This effort at inclusiveness has inevitably led to some minimal repetition in our introductions and notes as we attempt to reconstruct the historical and scientific context of Bartram's writings.

In some cases, we have had to make a choice between alternative versions of Bartram's writings. Extracts from *Travels* were drawn from the original 1791 Philadelphia edition. Francis Harper's authoritative "naturalist's edition," published in 1958, closely followed this version. We made two editorial alterations to *Travels*. In the 1791 edition, the first word of each paragraph was capitalized; we have lowercased all except the initial letter. Bartram's footnotes have been placed at the bottom of the page where their point of reference occurs. Any missing letters or other editorial emendations, which are few, have been placed in brackets. Page references to *Travels* cite the 1791 edition, indicated here by bracketed page numbers in the text.

A lengthy search of more than three dozen manuscript repositories failed to unearth the original manuscript copy of Bartram's "Observations on the Creek and Cherokee Indians." Perhaps this publication will lead to its discovery, if it still exists. The sole published version, which appeared in 1853, was heavily edited by Ephraim G. Squier. Of the two surviving manuscript copies, we think the one transcribed by John Howard Payne is the most accurate. Our transcription follows the Payne copy of the original manuscript as closely as possible. Capitalizations and the intended locations of paragraph breaks are often questionable in this copy, and some idiosyncratic footnote marks have been altered to simplify printing. The other manuscript copy was made by Edwin H. Davis. Although the Davis text is less reliable than the Payne copy, we believe that it does contain more accurate representations of Bartram's original accompanying sketches, since Davis copied many of them on tracing paper. When available, reproductions made by Payne, Davis, and Squier are reprinted here for comparison.

The previously unpublished document, entitled "Some Hints & Observations," is not written in Bartram's hand, and the original of this, too, has apparently been lost. Our transcription of this document follows the manuscript precisely, although, once again, capitalization and paragraph breaks are problematic throughout.

In our notes, quotations from other documents follow the editorial conventions discussed above. When reliable published versions exist, these, too, are referenced.

Acknowledgments

The following repositories responded kindly to our written and telephone inquiries regarding William Bartram and his writings on the southeastern American Indians: American Antiquarian Society, Worcester, Massachusetts; Ethnography Department of the British Museum (Museum of Mankind), London; British Museum (Natural History), London; Free Library of Philadelphia; Huntington Library, San Marino, California; Illinois Historical Society, Urbana; Indiana Historical Society, Indianapolis; John Carter Brown Library, Providence, Rhode Island; Latin American Library, Tulane University, New Orleans; Massachusetts Historical Society, Boston; Maryland Historical Society, Baltimore; Newberry Library, Chicago; Ross County Historical Society, Chillicothe, Ohio; Southwest Museum, Los Angeles; Thomas Gilcrease Museum, Tulsa, Oklahoma; University of Cincinnati Library, Cincinnati, Ohio; Special Collections, University of Kansas Libraries, Lawrence; Western Reserve Historical Society, Cleveland, Ohio; William L. Clements Library, University of Michigan, Ann Arbor; and the University of Pennsylvania Library, Philadelphia.

We especially thank the following manuscript repositories that provided us with documents and illustrations from among their collections: the Historical Society of Pennsylvania, the American Philosophical Society Library, the Academy of Natural Sciences, all in Philadelphia; the New York Historical Society and the Pierpont Morgan Library, New York City; New England Historic and Genealogical Society, Boston; National Anthropological Archives, Smithsonian Institution, and the Manuscript Division of Library of Congress, Washington, D.C.; the Gray Herbarium Archives, Harvard University, Cambridge, Massachusetts; the British Museum, London; the British Public Record Office, Kew, England; and the Earl of Derby's Estate, Knowsley Hall, Prescot, Merseyside, England.

Several individuals have offered advice and assistance along the way. We especially appreciate the help of the many manuscript curators and li-

xviii

*Acknowledg-
ments*

brarians who graciously handled our requests for information and pho-
tocopies, particularly Beth Carroll-Horrocks of the American Philosophical
Society Library and Ellen Slack and Toby Gearhart of the Historical Society
of Pennsylvania. Dana Brumbelow, of the Auburn Public Library, Auburn,
Alabama, graciously and promptly handled many of our interlibrary loan
requests. Many Bartram scholars, including Charlotte Porter, Gainesville,
Florida, and Ralph S. Palmer, Tenants Harbor, Maine, provided enthusias-
tic support and shared their thoughts with us.

We particularly want to thank Steve Thomas, Craig Sheldon, Linda
Waselkov, Kyle G. Braund, and Stephen Williams for their insightful comments on portions of this book in manuscript, and Peter Wood and Tom
Hatley, who generously provided us with primary and secondary sources
they had discovered. Hilda Cruthirds helped assemble the index and generally assisted us during the last phases of editing.

Grants to one of us (GAW) from the National Science Foundation
(BNS-8718934 and BNS-8907700) and the National Endowment for the
Humanities (RO-22030), independent federal agencies, helped support
this project.

William Bartram on the Southeastern Indians

CHAPTER ONE
William Bartram and
the Southeastern Indians:
An Introduction

William Bartram's writings are among the most valuable primary historical sources on the Muscogulges—commonly known as the Creeks and Seminoles—and the Cherokees. In addition to his famous *Travels Through North & South Carolina, Georgia, East & West Florida . . .* , Bartram wrote several other important works that deal with the southeastern American Indians, particularly the manuscript report to Dr. John Fothergill (drawn from the field journals on which *Travels,* too, was based) and his "Observations on the Creek and Cherokee Indians."[1] A third manuscript, "Some Hints & Observations, concerning the civilization, of the Indians, or Aborigines of America," probably written prior to 1790, contains Bartram's advice regarding the direction of American Indian policy.[2] Taken together, these works complement other travelers' accounts and government documents and provide a broad base of ethnographic knowledge about southeastern Native Americans in the late eighteenth century. Bartram's passionate regard for the natural world, his relative impartiality, and his keen scientist's eye make his writings unique and valuable resources. They offer an intimate and enlightening view of the southeastern Indians and their world during the late colonial and revolutionary eras.

This volume draws together all William Bartram's important writings on Indians, including extensive extracts from *Travels* and the complete texts of "Observations" and "Some Hints." Additional material from the "Report to Fothergill," personal letters, and other documents, as well as selected passages from a work by his father, John Bartram—"Diary of a Journey Through the Carolinas, Georgia, and Florida, 1765–66"[3]—are also quoted at length. The intent is to produce a volume of William Bartram's writings that conveys the scope of his contributions to southeastern Indian anthropology, archaeology, and ethnohistory. Most modern scholarly studies of Bartram have concentrated either on his writings viewed as literature or on his accomplishments in the botanical and zoological realms of natural history, depending on each scholar's personal interests and range of knowledge. Bartram's anthropological significance, while widely acknowledged, has received relatively little critical review. By focusing on the large body of his writings principally concerned with southeastern Indians, perhaps we can achieve a better balance in our appreciation of Bartram as an important figure in American Enlightenment science. Humans were as much a part of his natural world as were plants and animals.

Bartram could have led a life of scientific detachment, remaining contentedly aloof in his botanical garden without ever concerning himself with his distant Indian neighbors. But, from an early age, he demonstrated an independence of thought and a tolerance for other ways of life that set him apart from most of his colonial contemporaries.

William and his twin sister, Elizabeth, were born April 9, 1739, at Kingsessing, John and Ann Bartram's farm along the Schuylkill River, on the outskirts of Philadelphia. He received a liberal upbringing in his parents' free-thinking Quaker household and a classical education at the Philadelphia Academy. Young William exhibited a remarkable talent for sketching plants and animals.[4] According to his father, "Botany & drawing is his darling delight." John Bartram recognized his son's extraordinary talent but was worried that William would not be able to "get A handsom livelyhood by it."[5] In the spring of 1755, the concerned parent confided to his friend and correspondent, the wealthy English wool merchant and gardener Peter Collinson, "I want to put him to some business by which he may with care & industry get A temperate resonable liveing I am afraid Botany & drawing will not afford him one & hard labour does not agree with him."[6] In his quest to secure a "liveing" for his son, John repeated his concerns to many of his well-placed friends, seeking their patronage for "Billy."[7]

John Bartram considered a wide range of vocations for his son. After first proposing surveying, he offered "to put him to A doctor to learn Phisick & surgery," encouraged him to take up printing, and passed along Benjamin Franklin's suggestion that William consider the craft of engraving.[8] None of these occupations appealed to the young man, who preferred to sketch animals and plants. Moreover, none seemed to offer a secure future. In an attempt to direct William toward a more promising career, a frustrated John Bartram apprenticed his son briefly to a Philadelphia merchant in 1756–57. In 1761, William went to live with his father's half-brother, Col. William Bartram, a prosperous planter, merchant, and member of the North Carolina General Assembly.[9] After a rough passage by sea, William arrived at heavily flooded Wilmington "to a bad Markett, a wrong Season of the Year." Nevertheless, William set to work as a merchant on the Cape Fear River.[10] For four years, William lived as a member of his uncle's household and dutifully tried his hand at storekeeping, but the mercantile life held little fascination for him. By 1764, John Bartram lamented to his friend Collinson that William "will be ruined in Carolina every thing goes rong with him there."[11]

By the terms of the 1763 Treaty of Paris, which ended the Seven Years' War, Great Britain acquired all the North American territory claimed by France and Spain east of the Mississippi River except New Orleans. These new British lands were organized into the colonies of East Florida and West Florida. John Bartram was eager to visit Britain's newly acquired colonies to search out new plants and acquire botanical specimens, and he expressed those sentiments to Collinson.[12] In the fall of 1764, John pointedly asked his friend, "could not thay be prevailed upon to enable me to travail A year or two through our kings new acquisitions to make A thorow natural & vegitable search either by publick authority or private subscription." He named only two conditions: he must have "one to accompany me" and a "sufficient" allowance to pay expenses.[13] Due to Collinson's influence at court, the elder Bartram, best-known gardener and plant taxonomist in Britain's North American colonies and a correspondent of Linnaeus, received instructions from George III in 1765 to identify and describe the flora of the newest colonies, East and West Florida.[14]

The position did carry a minor stipend, but John's exact title remained unclear. In the letter Peter Collinson sent to John Bartram informing him that "my Repeated Solicitations have not been in Vain," Collinson wrote that the King "appointed thee His Botanist."[15] An elated John Bartram wrote to his son William on May 19, 1765, that "Ld Bute & ye Earl of northumberland declared that it was nessessary that ye floridase should be searched & that I was ye Properest person to do it." He also informed William of other "very generous offers" he had received from Lord Adam Gordon and General Bouquet for expense-paid travel to Quebec and Pensacola. But having received a royal appointment, he was forced to turn them down. He mused, "I should rather chuse ye last & now cant Comply with it." In the same letter, he reassured William that he had just written Collinson that "I must have A Companion."[16] Perhaps John saw in the royal appointment a way finally to secure a position not only for himself but also for his son.

At the time, William, then aged twenty-six, still worked as a merchant in North Carolina. But the younger man had already indicated to his father his wish to visit the Floridas. In June, John wrote his son, "our friend Peter ordered me to take my son or A servant with me & as thee wrote to me last winter & seemed so very desirous to go there: now thee hath A fair opertunity so pray let me know as soon as possible." Since John Bartram was certain his son would join him, his letter of invitation included advice on how William could most efficiently settle his business affairs.[17] Thus, William joined the expedition as companion and artist, roles he had played on his father's travels since the age of twelve.[18] Like his father, William was an ardent admirer of the natural world. Moreover, the younger Bartram had already gained some recognition as an artist when several of his drawings of birds and turtles had been published in England.[19]

The journey was to have a profound impact on William's life, since it was during this expedition that he fell under the spell of Florida and had his first direct encounter with southeastern Indians. Charleston was the pair's initial destination, where they obtained assistance and advice from Henry Laurens and Dr. Alexander Garden, which would soon prove invaluable during their journey to the colony of East Florida. A distinguished South Carolinian, Laurens eventually served as president of the Continental Congress and was a member of the American peace delegation to Paris in 1782. Garden, a physician, was a graduate of the University of Edinburgh, a fellow of the Royal Society, and a long-time friend and correspondent of John Bartram.[20] Father and son were also introduced to John Stuart, who had recently been appointed Superintendent of Indian Affairs for the Southern Department, in which capacity he was able to provide the Bartrams with information and introductions.[21] From Charleston, John and William traveled up the Savannah River to Silver Bluff, home of George Galphin, the most successful trader with the Creeks and Cherokees. Later they would meet James Spalding, another prominent trader. By introducing William to these members of the southern colonial elite, the 1765 expedition with his father laid the groundwork for his later independent travels in the southeastern backcountry.

Upon their arrival in East Florida in October 1765, the Bartrams met Gov. James Grant. According to the governor, the elder Bartram "informed me that he was appointed Botanist to his Majesty for the Floridas, he had no Commission or Instructions to produce but as he seemed to be a plain Man, I took it upon his word, and shewed him every Civility in my Power." Further, Grant provided the Bartram party with "a Boat, a Tent, attendents and with other things as appeared to me, to be necessary for the accommodation of the old man."[22]

In addition to investigating the flora and fauna of East Florida, the Bartrams attended the Congress of Picolata in November 1765, which brought together leaders of the Muscogulges (both Creeks and Seminoles) and

John Stuart and James Grant, representing British interests.[23] John Bartram's account of the congress site and proceedings supplements the official British record of the event and provides important details on Indian custom, including the easternmost record of the calumet ceremony.[24]

Before leaving East Florida, John Bartram provided Grant with a copy of his journal. Grant believed Bartram's portrait of his colony was not as favorable as it could have been, but he rationalized that since William intended to settle in the colony, "the account he gives in the Northern Provinces, will be to the advantage of this Colony."[25] Unfortunately, the copy of Bartram's journal forwarded to the British Board of Trade by Grant was published in England by William Stork in 1766 without John's permission. Stork dubbed John Bartram the "Botanist to His Majesty for the Floridas," as Grant had recorded in his letter, and as John had been led to believe by Peter Collinson. But Collinson was outraged and wrote to John Bartram, "If Thou hadst Intended to Lett Stork puff off his Book with thy Journal to publish thy Fame as Kings Botanist to the World which by the way is a Title thou assumes without the Kings Leave or License which is makeing very free with Majesty it is posible for this undue Liberty they annuity may be withdrawn but I hope Not because thou Well Deserves It."[26]

Illness forced John Bartram to abandon his hopes of visiting the colony of West Florida, but the environment, people, and way of life in the southernmost colonies appealed immensely to William. Faced with the prospect of resuming his tedious and unprofitable mercantile ventures, he decided to remain behind in East Florida as a planter when his father departed.

Exactly when and why William decided to become a settler in East Florida is unclear. Given that he had expressed a desire to visit the colony prior to the journey with his father, settling there may have been his intention all along. In any case, on February 17, 1766, the East Florida Council granted him a warrant to survey 500 acres of land.[27] Although John assisted his son in the endeavor and purchased the necessary tools — and slaves — essential for a rice and indigo planter, he did so with apprehension.

In addition to procuring provisions for his son, John sought, received, and passed along advice from leading South Carolinians on such varied subjects as clearing pine lands, rice cultivation, slave management, and attracting mullets into canoes by the use of torches. His letter recounting the numerous articles he had sent southward for William's plantation contained, along with helpful hints, ominous tones: "thee hath had sufficient warning." John was convinced the effort was wasted. To his friend Peter Collinson he confided, "I am afraid all will be threwed away upon him he is so whimsical & so unhappy as not to take any of his friends advice."[28]

William Gerard De Brahm, the royal surveyor for the southern colonies, had offered William a place on his staff. According to John Bartram, "mr. De Bram wanted him to go with him to draw draughts for him in his survey of florida but Billy would not tho by that Journey he would have had ye finest opertunity of seeing ye countrey & its productions[.]"[29] John further lamented to his friend and patron Peter Collinson in June of 1766, "nothing will do with him now but he will be A planter upon St Johns river about 24 mile from Augustine & 6 from ye fort of Picolata[.] this frolick of his hath & our maintenance drove me to great straits. . . ."[30]

His father's concern proved well founded, and bad news soon reached Philadelphia. William's quick failure strained the relationship between father and son. In July 1766, after learning that William's initial crop of rice had withered, John sent a stinging letter to his son: "I sent thee two guineas which the doth not mention nor ye grindstone & millstones nor ye tools & other things I sent which I suppose they usual ingratitude would not suffer the to mention: thay cost me dear & so much that I am still in debt for them." Profuse advice followed, and John concluded the letter with a sober observation: "I am not against finding thee real nessesaries this year but thee must expect to suffer ye first year as all do in new settlements."[31]

William's problems, however, were not all of his own making. Henry Laurens, who visited William in July 1766, found his plantation situated in "the least agreeable of all the places that I have seen."[32] In fact, William's clearing sat on the edge of a swamp, and he had built his dwelling — "or rather hovel," in Laurens's terms — in a darkly shaded location along a stagnant stretch of the river. The six slaves his father had provided were uncooperative, and the rebellious threats of one frightened him. Mosquitoes, heat, and humidity sapped his energy. By the time Laurens arrived, William was sick, lonely, low on provisions, and ready to return home.[33] Laurens promised William he would inform John Bartram of his son's "wretched & forlorn" state. After receiving Henry Laurens's bleak account of William's circumstances, John wrote to Laurens recommending that his son sell his holdings and return home. He also agreed to pay for the provisions that Laurens had indicated were desperately needed by William. In September 1766, Laurens bluntly noted in his correspondence to William, "if he writes the same to you [to come home] and you do not not follow his advice you can't reasonably expect his further aid." In addition, Laurens suggested that William obtain a better piece of land and try lumbering and the production of cypress shingles as well as rice cultivation to earn his way. In the meantime, Laurens vowed he would send "any little necessaries from this place which I will do on your own account and wait for payment till convenient." Despite the timely arrival of Laurens's provisions, William decided to abandon the effort.[34]

Although William's next actions are not precisely known, by the end of the year he had left his holding and retreated to St. Augustine.[35] William once again met De Brahm, who apparently persuaded him to participate briefly in the East Florida survey, and De Brahm entered Bartram's name on his list of employees as a draftsman.[36] Bartram left St. Augustine in November 1766 and spent the early part of 1767 with members of De Brahm's team charged with exploring and charting Florida south of St. Augustine along the Mosquito River, particularly the future site of New Smyrna. Bartram recorded in *Travels,* "I was there [at New Smyrna] about ten years ago, when the surveyor run the lines or precincts of the colony, when there was neither habitation nor cleared field. . . . It was then a famous Orange grove," and Bartram was especially interested in the "spacious Indian mount and avenue," similar to the Mount Royal earthworks that he later depicted in his "Observations."[37] When De Brahm reported to mutual friends in Charleston that Bartram had been shipwrecked after leaving St. Augustine and had not been heard from for some time, many assumed the worst. The shipwreck occurred off the coast, almost directly east of New Smyrna, and Bartram noted the location in the map he drew to illustrate *Travels* (figure 1). By late April 1767, he was again writing family and friends from St. Augustine. Perhaps Bartram had joined the survey to scout out a better location for a new plantation. In any case, he neither applied for another land grant nor did he continue with the survey crew. Instead, he returned to Philadelphia.[38] Once home, William helped his father prepare a map of St. Augustine at the request of Collinson, who was pleased with the effort.[39]

After his return to Philadelphia, William again entered the mercantile business. In his spare time, he wrote vivid descriptions of what he had seen during his Florida stint, and he continued to provide Collinson with "Elegant" drawings of plants, butterflies, and insects, which Collinson proudly displayed to his friends.[40] Collinson confided to John Bartram in mid-1767 that he had "for years past been looking out for [William] but no opening has offered."[41] Now Collinson's continued efforts on William's behalf proved invaluable. Among the notables to view the products of William's "Inimitable Pensil" were Daniel Solander, a student of Linnaeus and one of the leading botanists associated with the British Museum; George Ehret, a well-known horticultural illustrator; and Margaret Cavendish Bentinck, the Duchess of Portland, an avid conchologist and owner of the finest shell collection in England. All were impressed, especially the Duchess of Portland, who commissioned William to provide her with drawings of "all [American] Land, River, & your Sea Shells *from the very least to the greatest.*"[42]

However, the most important connection provided by Collinson proved

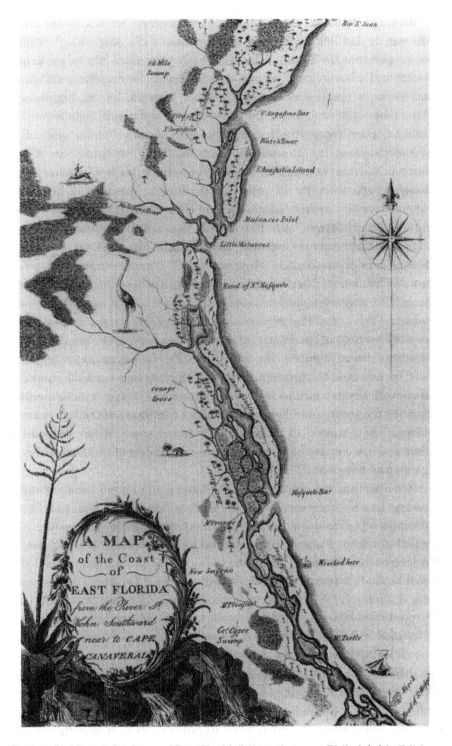

Figure 1. "A Map of the Coast of East Florida" from the 1791 Philadelphia Edition of *Travels*

to be Dr. John Fothergill, a prominent London physician and horticultural-ist who had created the largest private botanical garden in England, filled with exotic plants from all over the world. No eccentric plant collector, Dr. Fothergill was a hard-headed businessman and highly respected member of the international scientific community. Like the Bartrams and Peter Collinson, he belonged to the Society of Friends, or Quakers.

Though Bartram's prospects as an artist and illustrator appeared to be improving, business and financial disaster continued to dog him. By 1770, he was deeply in debt. In desperation, and without telling his family, he fled his creditors in Philadelphia and returned to North Carolina, where he hoped to collect on debts due him since his merchant days there in the 1760s.[43] He finally wrote to his father proposing to return to East Florida, but the elder Bartram was shocked and informed his son: "we are surprised at thy wild notion of going to Augustine; indeed I don't intend to have any more of my Estate spent there or to ye southerd upon any pretense what-ever[.] I think it much better for the to come home & dwell amongst thy relations & friends who I doubt not will endeavour to put thee in A way of profitable business if thee will take their advice & be industrious and care-full."[44]

Having failed to secure his father's support, William Bartram, by then in Charleston, hit upon a course of action that would send him back to Florida — not as a planter or surveyor, but as an explorer, artist, and natural-ist. In 1772, with uncharacteristic boldness, he wrote to Dr. John Fothergill. After the death of John Bartram's patron Collinson in 1770, Fothergill had accepted the responsibility of encouraging and supporting the Philadel-phia botanist, from whom he intermittently received shipments of seeds, cuttings, and drawings of plants. Now William turned to his father's friend. In a letter to Fothergill, he explained his situation and asked support for his own expedition to study the natural flora and fauna of the southern colo-nies.[45]

William had reason to hope for a favorable response to his proposal, for in 1768 Fothergill had written John Bartram praising some "exquisite drawings" of William's that Collinson had shown him. At that time, he had commissioned William to draw various American land turtles and compile data about them. Moreover, the generous Fothergill had offered twenty guineas for the work, but noted, "I will not restrict him to this sum. Let him take his own time. Send me a drawing or two as time and opportunities offer."[46] For the next four years, William obliged and, slowly, drawings were forwarded to Fothergill.[47] Indeed, William's request for support for a southern tour was accompanied by additional drawings.[48]

On October 22, 1772, Fothergill accepted the plan and offered his patronage, obligingly allowing William to "suggest what terms might be agree-able" to Dr. Lionel Chalmers of Charleston, whom Fothergill asked to supervise the venture. Fothergill could not have known at the time that he was sponsoring the creation of an American literary masterpiece, but he reiterated his high aspirations for William's artistic abilities. "In drawing thy hand is a good one, and by attention and care may become excellent."[49]

John Bartram learned of his son's scheme from Fothergill, who explained, "For his sake, as well as thine, I should be glad to assist him. He draws neatly, has a strong relish for natural history, and it is a pity that such a genius should sink under distress."[50] The elder Bartram doubted the practicality of William's plan, but nonetheless provided a character reference for his son. Fothergill was convinced that William's plan had merit and believed that the expedition might prove to be the springboard for a thriving horticultural business. He wrote to John Bartram, "He may perhaps in the space of two or three years, if his life is spared[,] get into a good livelihood by sending boxes of plants and seeds to Europe from those less frequented parts of America."[51] At last, William Bartram had found his niche.

Fothergill provided ten guineas immediately for necessary provisions, and instructed Lionel Chalmers "to allow him any other sum not exceeding 50 £ per annum for two years certain," plus any "extraordinary expenses" incurred in packing and shipping botanical specimens to London, as well as an "allowance for his drawings, proportionate to their accuracy."[52] In return, William was to keep a "little journal, marking the soil, situation, plants in general, remarkable animals, where found, and the several particulars relative to them as they cast up. Land and river shells will be acceptable, as also any rare insects."[53] In addition to various instructions regarding preparation of specimens and the like, Dr. Fothergill provided the aspiring naturalist with spiritual guidance.

> But in the midst of all these attentions, forget not the one thing needfull. In studying nature forget not its author. Study to be gratefull to that hand which has endowed thee with a capacity to distinguish thyself as an artist. Avoid useless or improper company. Be much alone, and learn to trust in the help and protection of him who has formed us and everything. Fear him, and he will raise thee friend, and keep thy foot from sliding.[54]

As his writings prove, Friend William did not forget his mentor's advice. In the course of these travels, Bartram — keen, rational observer and believing man — matured and prospered, in a metaphysical if not material sense.

With his confidence bolstered by such prestigious patronage, William
Bartram, now aged thirty-three, returned home briefly, but triumphantly,
to set his personal affairs in order. He left Philadelphia on March 20, 1773,
beginning a journey that would last nearly four years.

Once in the South, he disregarded Fothergill's exhortation to "confine
his rambles within narrower bounds."[55] Instead he toured the entire southeastern backcountry, gathering impressions of the Native Americans of the
region as he sketched and collected botanical specimens. He ventured up
the Savannah River, into Cherokee territory, and traveled through all three
major divisions of the Muscogulges: the Seminole villages located in the
vicinity of present-day Gainesville, Florida; the Lower Creek towns scattered
along the Chattahoochee River; and the Upper Creek towns situated along
the Coosa and Tallapoosa rivers in what is now central Alabama. Farther
west, Bartram visited Choctaw and Alabama villages on an excursion to the
Mississippi River.

Fothergill directed Bartram to procure seeds and bulbs that might thrive
in the temperate climate of England and the European continent, where
he had found lucrative markets for his exotic plants. Therefore, he was
particularly insistent that William devote the majority of his time to seeking
plants native to the cooler, upland country of the Cherokees, rather than
the sultry Florida colonies. Though the surviving record does not relate
whether Fothergill had any interest in the Indians themselves, his instructions did provide an excuse for Bartram's trip to the Indian country. "I am
pleased," Fothergill explained in a letter of September 4, 1773, "that so
favourable a pasage has been open'd into the Cherokee country by the
asistance of my worthy Frd. Dr. Chalmers and Commissioner Stuart, to
whom I am not quite unknown, and to whom for this instance of his Friendship I think myself under great obligations."[56] Still, Bartram's patron was
more interested in plants than in the Cherokees, and directed him to seek
out

a young man from England, engaged in the service of a company at
Charlestown; he travels into the Cherokee country, and though unacquainted
with Botany has sent me many rare seeds, and some plants packed up with
much judgement, which are now recovering from that voyage. It may not be
improper at some time to go with him, as he will be able to point out things
which he has not been able to collect.[57]

Perhaps Fothergill instructed Bartram, in a letter that has not survived,
to carefully observe the Indians he encountered in order to judge their

fitness for "civilizing." Fothergill had previously helped sponsor a young Quaker missionary (whose identity remains a mystery) to the southern Indians. In 1765, Fothergill wrote:

> A person of liberal sentiments and education, patient of labour and able to bear much, has found himself engaged as by a sense of duty to attempt the civilizing of some Indians if he can. He is gone to South Carolina and proposes to make a beginning among the Creeks or Cherokees, as he shall find it most proper. He proposes to live among them, teach their children to read, the men agriculture, if they are willing to learn, and cure a few if possible of their wandering life to make them civil, social creatures. He is supported by a few persons here, chiefly Friends, who think him as equal to the task as most, as he engages from principle in the work. . . .[58]

Whether or not at Fothergill's prompting, Bartram made the study of the southern Indians one of his primary goals and quickly progressed far beyond his patron's inaccurate views of Native Americans. Unlike most of his contemporaries, Bartram did not simply assume that the "white" way was best, nor did he presume that the Indians were inferior intellectually or morally. He was one of the few to ask what the Indians' view of "civilization" might be, when, in *Travels*, he wrote:

> In the consideration of this important subject it will be necessary to enquire, whether they were inclined to adopt the European modes of civil society? whether such a reformation could be obtained, without using coercive or violent means? and lastly, whether such a revolution would be productive of real benefit to them . . . ?[59]

Bartram sailed into Charleston harbor on March 31, 1773, and from there proceeded to Savannah. He arrived in Georgia in time to witness one of the most important events of the era for the eighteenth-century Creeks and Cherokees — the New Purchase Cession, by which the two tribes were coerced into ceding over 2 million acres of land to the colony of Georgia in return for cancellation of their trade debts (figure 2). Indian Superintendent John Stuart had encouraged Bartram to attend the conference, where he could introduce the naturalist to the assembled tribal leaders and explain the purpose of Bartram's intended travels through their country. Following the conference, despite Superintendent Stuart's warning that it might not be "alltogether safe" to enter the Indian country at that time, Bartram accompanied one of the surveying parties as the cession boundaries were laid out. It is unclear whether or not Bartram helped prepare the

Figure 2. Map of the Northern Part of the New Purchase Cession (courtesy, British Public Record Office, CO5/662 [MPG2])

map of the cession. Since official British records of the conference have yet to be located, Bartram's account provides the only firsthand glimpse of the controversial negotiations and survey of the ceded lands.[60]

After the survey, Bartram returned to Savannah and readied the botanical specimens he had secured on that segment of his journey for shipment. Evidently he intended then to visit the Cherokee country, as Fothergill had requested, but on Christmas Day, 1773, a number of Creek warriors raided the Georgia frontier, killing fifteen white settlers and two black slaves who were clearing lands in the New Purchase. In the journal he was keeping at Fothergill's request, Bartram wrote, "Soon after my return . . . to Savanah the country was alarmed by an express from Augusta, that the Indians were for war, & had actually murdered Several Families not far from Augusta; upon this I was advised not to venture amongst them but as the lower Creeks in east Florida were not openly concerned in the mischief I imagined I might with safety turn my discoveries in that quarter[.]"[61] Bartram's memory of the incident mellowed with time, and in *Travels* he simply noted that the "Cherokees and their confederates being yet discontented, and on bad terms with the white people, it was unsafe to pursue my travels into the north western regions of Carolina."[62] In fact, the Cherokees, mindful of their humiliation at the hands of the Creeks during the New Purchase conference, quickly sided with Georgia against the Creek raiders, and they promised to aid the colony if the Creeks declared all-out war.

The hostilities, known in Georgia as the White-Sherrill murders, were settled in relatively short order by negotiations between the Lower Creeks and Georgia. But the frontier troubles provided Bartram with an excuse to forsake the Cherokee country for East Florida, home of the Lower Creeks and Seminoles — the very tribes from which the raiders had come.[63] Bartram, who clearly preferred Florida to Carolina, had found a pretext to leave the piedmont.

When he reached Florida, he found even the Lower Creek–Seminole territory safe for white travelers, since, at the first news of the attacks against the Georgia frontier, leading Creek headmen immediately sent word to the colony disavowing the renegade warriors and promising to make amends for the murders. At a conference held in April 1774, at Savannah, Gov. James Wright of Georgia imposed an interdict on Creek and Seminole trade until the leaders of the war faction were executed, according to the terms of various treaties.[64] When a vessel from Frederica, in June 1774, delivered cloth, rum, rifles, and ammunition to the Lower Trading Store of James Spalding and Company on the St. Johns River, the governor of East Florida immediately seized the weapons. Although a guest of Spalding at the time, Bartram made no mention of this affair in his report or book.[65]

Perhaps the most memorable scenes from Bartram's *Travels* recount his tour of the Alachua savanna with a company of deerskin traders.[66] At Cuscowilla, Bartram met Cowkeeper of Alachua, who bestowed on the peripatetic naturalist the honorary title "PUC PUGGY or the Flower hunter" in the Muskogee language. During his Florida sojourn, he also visited with Long Warrior, leading warrior of Cuscowilla, whom he had first met in 1765 at the Congress of Picolata. Bartram had several opportunities to observe him, including a dramatic exchange between Long Warrior and trader Charles McLatchy over credit terms. In addition to his prowess as a war leader, Long Warrior "was acknowledged by the Indians to have communion with powerful invisible beings or spirits, and on that account esteemed worthy of homage and great respect."[67] He also presented a striking appearance, and Bartram's sketch of Long Warrior serves as the frontispiece for *Travels*.

Following his Florida sojourn, Bartram made a two-month-long foray in the late spring of 1775 into the Appalachian Mountains to visit the Lower and Middle Cherokee towns he had missed earlier; then he began his tour of the Creek country.[68] In his field report, and later in *Travels* and in his "Observations" manuscript, Bartram provided numerous details about Cherokee and Creek culture, including agricultural practices and food preparation, gender roles, manufactures, town organization and government, art and architecture, the origin of specific towns, and the institution of slavery among the Creeks and Seminoles.

Bartram also commented extensively on colonial traders, British officials, and Indian leaders. He observed all aspects of the commercial hunting economy that had developed among the southeastern Indians by the late eighteenth century. Deerskin traders were Bartram's guides and companions almost everywhere he traveled in Florida and in Creek and Cherokee towns elsewhere. He visited trading stores and warehouses both in Florida and Georgia and in the Indian villages, where he witnessed the exchange of goods. His account is especially valuable when one considers his impeccable credentials for impartial reporting, for Bartram was a complete outsider — neither government official nor deerskin trader, not southern colonist or land speculator — with no direct interest in the trade.[69]

The deerskin trade was the driving force in southeastern Indian culture change during this period. Bartram carefully noted how the demands of the trading economy had transformed Native society, and he enumerated the effects of imported goods on their way of life. Conflicts with neighboring Indian societies over hunting grounds frequently led to intertribal warfare. During the time Bartram traveled among the Creeks, they were involved in a bloody struggle with the Choctaws for control of hunting territory north of Pensacola, between the Alabama and Escambia rivers, which he vividly described as "a solitary, uninhabited wilderness, the bloody field of Schambe, where those contending bands of American bravos, Creeks and Chactaws, often meet in dire conflict."[70]

Alcohol abuse was the great evil of the trade, and Bartram described not only the ill effects but also the efforts of the Indians to curtail the rum traffic. On his journey from West Florida to the Creek towns, Bartram met two traders from Pensacola who were illegally transporting forty kegs of Jamaican rum into the Upper Creek country. According to the usual practice of "dashing," or diluting the rum with water, the pair would have been able to sell at least eighty kegs to the Indians. But the traders were overtaken by a party of Creek warriors, "who discovering their species of merchandize, they forthwith struck their tomahawks into every keg, giving the liquor to the thirsty sand, not tasting a drop of it themselves, and they [the traders] had enough to do to keep the tomahawks from their own skulls."[71]

The rapid transformation from a self-sufficient subsistence economy to one based on commercial hunting and trade worked to remake Creek society in numerous ways. Bartram wrote that the Muscogulges "wage eternal war against deer and bear, to procure food and clothing, and other necessaries and conveniences; which is indeed carried to an unreasonable and perhaps criminal excess, since the white people have dazzled their senses with foreign superfluities."[72] At the same time, the strength and adaptability of their culture sustained individual Creeks and provided ways to meet the challenges presented by the deerskin traders, the new market mentality, and the influx of manufactured products. Hospitality and sharing of available goods, always important in Creek life, remained so despite a new emphasis on material goods. Bartram, though he decried the excesses of the trade, also recognized and appreciated the Muscogulges' enduring tradition of generosity:

> . . . I know that a Creek Indian would not only receive in his house a Traveler or Sojourner of whatever Nation, Colour or Language, (without distinction of rank, or any other exception of person) and here treat him as a Brother or his own Child, as long as he pleases to Stay, and this without the least hope or thought of interest or reward, but serves you with the best of every thing his ability can afford; — he would divide with you the last grain of corn, or piece of flesh, — offer you the most valuable things in his possession that he imagines would be acceptable — nay, would part with every thing rather than contend, or let a Stranger remain or go away necessitous.[73]

Most of Bartram's contemporaries — due to ignorance and prejudice — held Native American societies in low repute. Even John Bartram harbored strong prejudices about Indian societies, an unusual attitude for a Quaker. In a letter to Peter Collinson written near the end of the Seven Years' War in

1763, John Bartram argued that "ye most probable & only method to establish A lasting peace with ye barbarous Indians is to bang them stoutly & make them sensible that we are men whom thay for many years despised as women."[74] In 1711, William's grandfather had been killed, and his step-grandmother, aunt, and uncle taken captive by Tuscaroras, from whom they were later ransomed.[75] Perhaps it was this tragic incident that embittered William's father toward all Indians. John's subsequent dealings with them did not change his views, and on one of his botanical explorations "far beyond our mountains," he was accosted by an Indian who "pulled off my hat in a great pashion & chewed it all round[,] I suppose to shew me that they would eat me if I came in that countrey again." The stout Quaker, far from being intimidated, resolutely "steped up to him & twisted it out of his hands & ran after him."[76]

Although William must have heard these stories many times, he did not share his father's antipathy toward Indians. Perhaps his open-minded approach to American Indian societies developed subconsciously in opposition to the overt mistrust of all Indians frequently proclaimed by his outspoken, domineering father. Doubtless, his Quaker background had much to do with his more enlightened views.[77] Indeed, William Bartram demonstrated an unusual ability to overcome many of his society's ethnocentric biases in his portrayal of American Indian cultures. On the other hand, he unquestionably endeavored in his writings to present Native Americans in a way that his readers would find appealing and morally correct, especially in regard to practices that white society found reprehensible. In his mind, a society should be judged, at least initially, by its own standards. For instance, while most whites were appalled by the widespread Native American practice of burning captives, Bartram attempted to understand the tradition and judge it in light of the Muscogulge law of retaliation. He wrote: "If we consider them with respect to their private character or in a moral view, they must, I think, claim our approbation, if we divest ourselves of prejudice and think freely. As moral men they certainly stand in no need of European civilization."[78] In Bartram's "ultra-indulgent attitude toward the Indians," to borrow Francis Harper's apt characterization, critics have identified a bias in Bartram's writings, which he acknowledged and which should not be ignored.[79] But Bartram was also an exceptionally tolerant man, far ahead of his time in his advocacy of such concepts as cultural relativism, environmental appreciation and preservation, and animal rights.

As N. Bryllion Fagin wrote in *William Bartram, Interpreter of the American Landscape:*

Bartram's exuberant style, his enthusiasm for nature and primitive simplicity, may have led him to ascribe to his Indians "fanciful" soliloquies, but these "romantic" tendencies do not invalidate the facts he presents of the lives of the Indian tribes he came in contact with; while in his conclusion and judgements, based on these facts, he observes a rational restraint thoroughly "unromantic."[80]

War interrupted Bartram's southern tour. By 1775, the growing conflict between Britain and her colonies had sorely divided the inhabitants of South Carolina, Georgia, and East Florida. John Stuart, who had provided Bartram with so much early assistance, was chased first from Charleston, then Savannah, by angry rebel mobs. By late June, he was attempting to direct Indian affairs for the British from the relative safety of St. Augustine, in East Florida, where James Spalding and his employees, including many of Bartram's travel companions, had declared their loyalty to the king. Aligned against them were George Galphin, who now supervised southern Indian policy for the Americans, and Lachlan McIntosh, Bartram's Georgia host, whom he regarded as a father figure.[81]

Fothergill, a political moderate who still hoped that all-out war could be averted, was unaware of the situation in the South. On May 6, 1776, he wrote to John Bartram, "I have heard nothing from William in a long time. Nor know any News where he is. The Floridas keep an open communication with England from thence he might pass any News. I have wrote both to him and Dr. Chalmers by every opportunity, requesting him, to confine himself to a limited district — search it carefully, and collect into some small spot, the rare plants he may meet with and cultivate them till better times occur."[82]

Although he might have wished to divorce himself from the fierce conflict roiling around him, Bartram could not keep the war at bay. Reportedly, he briefly joined a regiment for the defense of Georgia called up by Lachlan McIntosh, who was now in charge of the rebels' military forces in that quarter. This must have been during the early part of 1776. By midyear, intense border fighting had rendered the southern backcountry unsafe for further exploration. With the Georgia–East Florida border in turmoil, there seemed little choice but for Bartram to end his travels. In November 1776, William set out from Savannah for Philadelphia.[83]

During his extended journey, Bartram had supplied John Fothergill not only with sporadic reports but also with 209 botanical specimens, many of which were new to the scientific community. In addition, Bartram had sent his patron numerous drawings of plants and animals of the American Southeast, and he completed other botanical drawings after his return to Philadelphia.[84]

He arrived at his father's home in January 1777.[85] John Bartram died just eight months later, on September 22, 1777, after bequeathing his house, garden, and nursery business to his son John (figure 3).[86] William's legacy had been the failed plantation in East Florida. Now, with no source of income, he was forced to rely on his brother for support. For the remainder of the war, the entire Bartram family actively supported the rebel cause, and in August 1778, William voluntarily took the "Affirmation of Allegiance and Fidelity," as required by Pennsylvania's Revolutionary General Assembly (figure 4).[87]

William Bartram spent the years following his father's death helping his brother, and later his niece, manage the family business. After Dr. Fothergill died in 1780, the numerous specimens and extraordinary sketches he had sent to England were unappreciated by Fothergill's heirs and brought Bartram neither fame nor fortune.[88] Even so, he retained copies of his field journals. Some of his "Books, Specimens, & Paper" were left in the care of friends in Charleston and returned to him at the conclusion of the war.[89] From these—and from memory—he crafted his monumental work, *Travels*, which was published in 1791.

There is little evidence that Bartram ever left the family home again, despite many opportunities for teaching and exploration that came his way. Failing health seems to have been the main reason for this, particularly his deteriorating eyesight.[90] Moreover, Bartram suffered a "violent fracture" of his right leg as the result of a fall from a tree in his garden in 1786. The accident left him bedridden "for near 12 Months."[91] According to his own account, he fell "near 20 feet from a Cypress Tree in the garden where I was gathering seeds." By late 1787, he reported that the fall had nearly proved fatal, but that he had recovered sufficiently "so as to be able to walk about pretty well tho it being a compound fracture & as near as possible to the Ankle joint, which is Yet stiff & troublesom after much walking."[92]

These physical ailments affected Bartram's mental outlook, and in March 1791, just prior to the publication of *Travels*, he mused to his friend Benjamin Smith Barton, the Philadelphia physician and author-naturalist, "And 'tho I am comparitively like an Old Saw, or Auger; or Ax, worn out, Rusty, & cast away as useless, yet even these rejected instruments, after being new Steeled, & repared, may again be prefere'd to some useful purpose or other."[93]

In time, many useful purposes presented themselves. Bartram illustrated several volumes for Barton and provided "observations" on natural history subjects that were included in many of Barton's works.[94] In the years following the publication of *Travels*, he was generally revered by the budding scientific and intellectual community in Philadelphia, which, in December 1812, unanimously elected him to the Academy of Natural Science of Philadelphia.[95] Although there is no record that Bartram regularly attended

Figure 3. William Bartram's Drawing of His Father's House and Garden (private collection; copyright reserved)

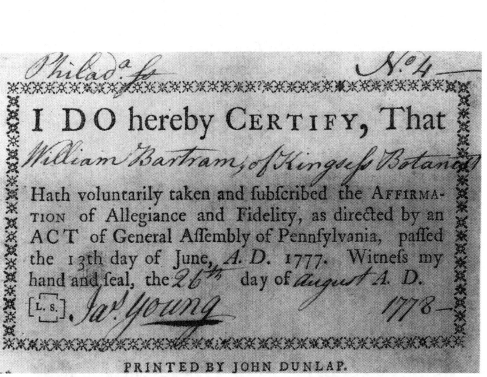

Figure 4. William Bartram's "Affirmation of Allegiance and Fidelity" (courtesy, Library of Congress)

academy meetings or participated in Philadelphia social life, he did correspond with a number of prominent scientists and politicians and kept busy in his garden, studying plants, observing the migration of birds, and recording weather data. His work and meditations were frequently interrupted, for his admirers refused to grant him the life of a recluse.

William — and his father's garden — attracted the attention of many prominent people. A number of delegates to the Constitutional Convention, held in Philadelphia in 1787, visited the garden, among them Alexander Hamilton and James Madison. George Washington made the trip to Kingsessing at least twice. Other famous visitors to Bartram's garden were André Michaux, the renowned French botanist; Alexander Wilson, the preeminent ornithologist who resided with Bartram for a time; and Dr. Benjamin Smith Barton, who frequently took his botany classes to visit Bartram in his garden. Charles Willson Peale, the great artist of the early Republic, painted Bartram's portrait (figure 5).[96] One visitor to Bartram's garden, around 1797, described the naturalist as "an old man who, with a rake in his hand, was breaking the clods of earth in a tulip bed. His hat was old and flapped over his face, his coarse shirt was seen near his neck, as he wore no cravat or kerchief; his waistcoat and breeches were both of leather,

Figure 5. Portrait of William Bartram by Charles Willson Peale (courtesy, Independence National Historical Park)

and his shoes were tied with leather strings. . . . This was the botanist, traveller, and philosopher we had come to see."[97]

In addition to his reputation as a naturalist and explorer, as one who had lived among the Indians and who had observed their customs and traditions firsthand, Bartram was also one of the few experts on Indian affairs in the new republic. Thomas Jefferson, who lived across the Schuylkill River from Bartram for brief periods when the new U.S. government was seated chunk_0in Philadelphia in the 1790s, visited the Kingsessing garden to discuss horticulture and natural history with Bartram. It is most probable the two discussed the southern Indians as well. During Jefferson's presidency, Bartram was mentioned as a prospective member of the Red River exploratory expedition. Bartram was informed of the president's offer by his friend Dr. Barton, who noted that Bartram's "friends and the friends of science" in Philadelphia would raise at least $600 as remuneration, in addition to the government's compensation, should he accept the offer.[98] William Bartram was undoubtedly flattered, and he quickly informed Barton, "I think if the Plann of the Expedition is such that a person of my age could be likely to perform I willinly consent to it." Accordingly, Bartram was briefed about the proposed expedition by the president's representative and by Barton.[99] But Bartram eventually declined, citing "advanced Age & consequent infirmities."[100]

One visitor welcomed most heartily by the aging naturalist was young Lachlan McIntosh, the nephew of Gen. Lachlan McIntosh, Bartram's old friend from Georgia. Following the young man's visit, Bartram wrote a nostalgic letter to the elder McIntosh, recalling his southern travels and the days spent with the McIntosh family. According to Bartram, his years in the South "left permanent impressions on my Mind, never to be effaced, scarcely an object or occurrence, that has happened to me since, fails of recalling to my view those happy Scenes, happy hours, which I injoyed in Your Family." Appropriately, Bartram signed his letter "Pug puggy, The Flower hunter."[101]

Though some of his colonial and European contemporaries might have failed to realize Bartram's genius and the monumental character of his work, the Native Americans among whom he traveled were more astute. To them, Puc Puggy appeared a fair and tolerant observer of their land and their customs. They welcomed him into their towns and into their homes. They recognized his honesty, endured his curious gaze, accepted his botanical researches, and patiently answered his questions. Although it was not the original purpose of his travels, one can argue that William Bartram's greatest contribution was neither his botanical discoveries nor his graceful drawings, but his consummate portrait of the eighteenth-century Southeast and its inhabitants.

William Bartram died on July 22, 1823, on the edge of his garden, at the age of eighty-five.[102]

CHAPTER TWO
Travels Through North & South Carolina, Georgia, East & West Florida . . .

INTRODUCTION

William Bartram's *Travels* has been dubbed "the most astounding verbal artifact of the early republic."[1] Indeed, Bartram's work, which "presents itself at various times as a travel journal, a naturalist's notebook, a moral and religious effusion, an ethnographic essay, and a polemic on behalf of the cultural institutions and the rights of American Indians," is a true classic of American literature.[2] *Travels* is based on Bartram's field notes, journals, and remembrances that accrued during his tour of the southern backcountry, from 1773 to 1777. The time when Bartram decided to polish his diaries and produce a publishable account of his journey is not known—perhaps he conceived the notion very early, while still in the South. In any case, he must have begun editing his rough notes soon after his return to Philadelphia, in early 1777. By 1783 he had produced a manuscript, which he showed to several interested visitors.[3] In 1786, a Philadelphia publisher, Enoch Story, attempted to raise subscribers for the work and even went so far as to notify Benjamin Franklin that Bartram wished to dedicate the proposed volume to him.[4] But Story did not publish Bartram's book.

The failure of this first publishing attempt appears to be at least partially attributable to the interference of Benjamin Smith Barton, a young Philadelphian who recognized Bartram's genius and befriended the older man, while continually exploiting him for information on the natural world and the American Indians. Bartram's publisher charged Barton, who was about to leave America for study in Scotland, with plotting to have Bartram's manuscript published abroad, to the detriment of his profit. Barton denied any such intent and, through deft persuasion, he managed to salvage his relationship with Bartram as the proposed venture with Story foundered.

Barton was bold enough to write to Bartram from Edinburgh, in August 1787, that he had mentioned the manuscript to "many other learned and worthy men: they all seem anxious to see it in print; and I am very certain the work, especially if illustrated with plates, would sell very well." Further, he proposed that Bartram allow him to edit the journal, add material of his own, and have it printed under both their names at his own expense.[5]

Barton wrote to Bartram again on February 19, 1788, urging him to proceed with publication of his journal. Again, he maintained that his interest arose "almost wholly from a desire to rescue from obscurity (you will pardon the phrase)" a valuable contribution to science. Barton reassured Bartram there was a market for the work: "I need hardly inform you again that Natural History and Botany are the fashionable and the favourite studies of the polite as well as of the learned parts of Europe."[6] Bartram tactfully deflected Barton's offer to publish jointly, and the two men remained on good terms. In the years that followed, Barton incorporated Bartram's expertise on natural history into his own books, and usually gave Bartram proper credit for his contributions. Though historians have sometimes castigated Barton for "pilfering" Bartram's work, the younger man's enthusiasm and encouragement doubtless served as a catalyst, prompting the more retiring older man to proceed with the publication of his manuscript.[7]

Many scholars have puzzled over the fact that Bartram's book did not appear until fourteen years after his return from the South. Although Story had advertised the proposed book in 1786, Bartram was still polishing the manuscript and adding material at that time. In a 1787 letter, in answer to Barton's inquiries from Edinburgh, Bartram wrote that he had still not decided on publication and that his manuscript "remains yet in improper Embryo." Moreover, Bartram suffered from nagging doubts as to the value of his own work: "I am doubtful of its consiquence in respect to publick benefit[.] The Narative might afford some amusement & serve to kill time with the Inquisitive of all Denominations." Bartram further noted that he had given some thoughts to retracing his southern tour and thereby gaining additional material, but was prevented by his long convalescence following his fall from a cypress tree.[8]

Another reason for the delay in publication was that Bartram was awaiting species identifications from the trained botanists in England whom Fothergill had charged with classifying the botanical specimens Bartram sent to London. Unfortunately, those who had been entrusted with overseeing the task were soon diverted from their job by the even more spectacular specimens then coming from Australia and the tropical Pacific.[9] Perhaps the arrival of a trunk of his sent to him from Charleston in the summer of 1786 by Mary Lamboll Thomas facilitated Bartram's efforts to complete his manuscript. Mrs. Thomas, the daughter of Thomas Lamboll, had received Bartram into her home during his time in Charleston. Bartram had left his trunk in her care when he left Charleston in late 1776. The war, and the consequent disruption of shipping, had prevented its return until ten years later. Bartram was surprised to find that the books, papers, and botanical specimens stored for a decade in the trunk looked "nearly as well" as they had when he had consigned them to her care in 1776.[10] Their unexpected resurrection may have inspired renewed activity on the manuscript.

In time, the manuscript was finally finished, and in 1790, the Philadelphia publishing firm of James and Johnson began soliciting subscribers for *Travels*. Robert Parrish, a fellow Quaker, directed the subscription efforts and traveled to New York, the temporary seat of the U.S. government under the recently adopted Constitution, to promote the forthcoming work. In June, he wrote to Bartram: "I find the disposition of the Inhabitants of this City much more favourable to the work than I heretofore apprehended, they not being that unenlightened set of People which they are frequently represented to be." Moreover, Parrish urged Bartram to provide more illustrations to enhance the book's marketability. According to Parrish, while the sketches of birds that Bartram had provided were "very much admired," he believed that if Bartram would send him "the head of the Indian Chief & Some other drawings I think it would be of still greater advantage, nay Numbers of Persons wish to have the Indian in full stature & dress. If thee could recollect clear enough to draw him I am inclined to believe that I could procure a number of Subscribers from the St. Tamminy's Society here who are extremely fond of anything that resembles an Indian—at any rate I think it best to forward me his Head as soon as possible."[11]

Parrish was correct in his assessment of the St. Tammany's Society. When a Creek treaty delegation visited New York City later in the year, the society invited the entire delegation, as well as many prominent members of the government, to a banquet. The timely journey of the Creeks from their homeland to New York undoubtedly inspired many subscriptions to Bartram's work. Advertisements for *Travels* appeared that summer in the *Pennsylvania Packet and Daily Advertiser,* usually accompanied by extracts from the text relating to the Seminole village of Cuscowilla.[12] In the summer of 1791, the book finally appeared.[13]

One of Bartram's main goals was to describe the new plants he had discovered during his journey, but in *Travels* he accomplished much more. Far more than a catalog of plants and their habitats, the book included graphic accounts of the landscapes, animals, and peoples he had encountered. Thus, to credit Bartram merely with the discovery of a few new plant species is not sufficient, for he presented to his contemporaries a well-rounded picture of relatively unknown lands, and he preserved for posterity a picture of the eighteenth-century southeastern environment prior to extensive change and disruption by white settlement.

The book consists of four major parts. Part 1, which contains five chapters, covers the first stage of Bartram's journey (figure 6). It details the author's first exploration of the Georgia coast, his attendance at the New Purchase Cession with the Creeks and Cherokees, held in Augusta, Georgia, and his participation in the survey of the ceded Indian lands. Part 1 concludes with an account of a trip up the Altamaha River, including Bartram's account of Indian mounds and the Creek migration legend. Events in the first four chapters of part 1 occurred principally in 1773, but the last chapter, judging from internal evidence, is placed out of sequence. Francis Harper speculated that this Altamaha voyage actually took place in 1776.[14]

Part 2 describes Bartram's travels through East Florida and the Seminole towns (figure 7), which mostly occurred in 1774, including his famous account of the Alachua savanna and the Indian town of Cuscowilla, although here, too, Bartram rearranged the sequence of his various excursions.[15] Part 3 presents his travels among the Cherokee villages, his momen-

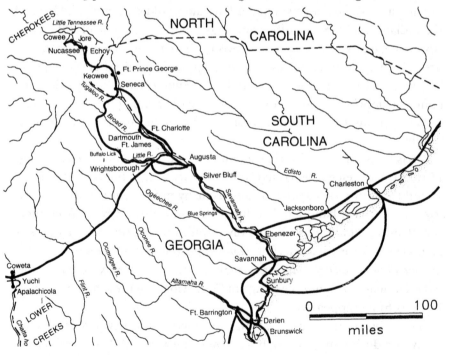

Figure 6. William Bartram's Travels in Georgia and the Cherokee Country

tous journeys on horseback through the Creek country, and boat trips in West Florida and on the Mississippi River (figure 8). It ends with descriptions of his last months in Georgia and his return to Philadelphia.

Part 4, which contains six chapters and carries its own title page, may have been intended for separate publication. With this section, entitled "An Account of the Persons, Manners, Customs and Government of the Muscogulges or Creeks, Cherokees, Chactaws, &c., Aborigines of the Continent of North America," Bartram provided us with one of the finest ethnographic accounts of the southeastern Indians written in the eighteenth century.

Whatever else may be said of Bartram's work, it is certainly not a precisely dated travel diary. Indeed, scarcely a date can be trusted in the entire volume. Francis Harper, who devoted much of his professional career to studying Bartram's writings and retracing Bartram's route, noted that the traveler "suffered either from a faulty memory or from an indifference to dates — if not from both!"[16] Part of Bartram's problem was the very nature of his adventure, for he, like the Indians and the traders who lived among them, was relatively free from the constraints of the Western world's rigid calendar. Thus, Bartram recorded the passage of time, as did the Indians, by the rhythms of nature. He found no need to be precise: he stays a week

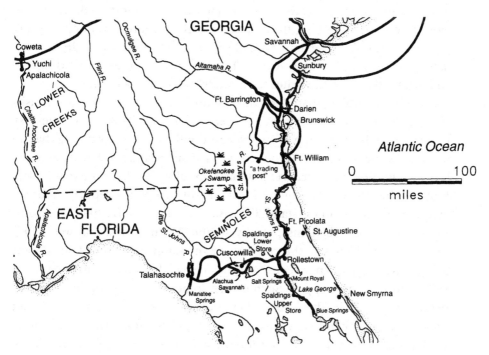

Figure 7. William Bartram's Travels in East Florida and the Seminole Country

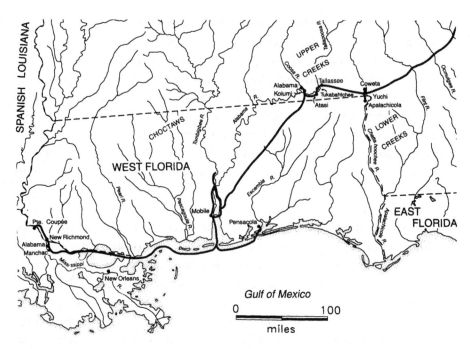

Figure 8. William Bartram's Travels in the Creek Country and West Florida

or two at one location, travels several days to reach another. Bartram was more intent on describing the wonders he encountered and enjoying his sojourn to the fullest extent possible than on achieving exactitude with dates. It was simply not his priority. The modern reader must be indulgent, and most will forgive the writer for literally "losing track of time."

But more troubling than Bartram's failure to record precise dates consistently is his apparent carelessness when he did supply dates. In the first report sent to his English patron, Dr. Fothergill, he began by stating that he departed Philadelphia on March 20, 1774 — one year later than he actually left that city. One may surmise that Bartram substituted, for the year he left Philadelphia, the year in which he was actually writing the report, but other errors are harder to understand. For instance, a letter to Lachlan McIntosh, in which he described his journey to the Alachua savanna, was dated July 15, 1775. However, the contents of the letter and other known facts about Bartram's journey seem to indicate that the letter must have been written in 1774, not 1775.[17] Such errors, some of even greater magnitude, occur frequently in the *Travels*. Many of these are printers' errors, not Bartram's, but taken together, such mistakes make it nearly impossible to reconstruct an accurately dated itinerary for Bartram, though many have tried.[18] There is evidence to suggest that Bartram did not see the proofs of

the completed work, which may explain the many typographical errors and
some of the incorrect dates.

Following publication of *Travels*, the *Universal Asylum and Columbia Magazine* ran excerpts from the work, including much of part 4 and parts of the Cuscowilla journey narrative. While the magazine's reviewer generally credited Bartram with providing much useful information regarding the natural sciences, he disapproved "of the garb in which they appear," calling Bartram's "rhapsodical effusions . . . [and] style so very incorrect and disgustingly pompous." The reviewer also could not "help thinking that he magnifies the virtues of the Indians, and views their vices through too friendly a medium."[19] Other magazines were likewise critical of Bartram's melodramatic prose but were generally complimentary of his contribution to natural history. The reviewer for the *Massachusetts Magazine* believed that Bartram's "botanical researches are more copious than any other writers" and noted that even "the Aboriginals . . . [have not] escaped the minutiae of attention." The reviewer found Bartram's descriptions "rather too luxuriant and florid," but declared "a thousand of these trivia faults, the effect of a poetical imagination, are amply compensated for, by a rich vein of piety, blended with the purest morality."[20]

However, many doubted the validity of Bartram's most original observations, particularly his vivid account of alligator behavior. Later observers proved his observations, almost without exception, to have been correct, but Bartram must have been mortified to see his veracity questioned so publicly. Considering the overall lack of praise the work received, Francis Harper concluded: "The generally indifferent reception accorded his maximum effort must have been vastly discouraging. . . . Is it any wonder that the contributions from his pen during the next 31 years were so meager?"[21]

Apart from a few brief articles, Bartram wrote little during the remainder of his life. In addition to lingering memories of reviewers' disparagements, Bartram's failing eyesight and generally poor health, and the fact that he never traveled again, contributed to his lack of interest in writing for the public. Though he published little, he remained active, observing nature in his garden, collaborating with and serving as a mentor for numerous young scientists, as well as undertaking illustrative work for his friend Barton.

The book fared well abroad, and several editions promptly appeared in England, Ireland, Germany, Austria, and France.[22] There, the unrestrained classical imagery in Bartram's writings, and what Thomas Carlyle labeled his "wondrous kind of floundering eloquence," inspired a generation of European romantic writers.[23] Samuel Taylor Coleridge drew on Bartram's dreamlike descriptions of the lush Florida landscape for his own works, notably "The Rime of the Ancient Mariner" and "Kubla Khan." *Travels* provided inspiration for William Wordsworth, who fancifully envisioned Bartram, in his poem "Ruth," as "a youth from Georgia's shore" who attempts to win a young woman's affection. Likewise, the French writer François René de Chateaubriand drew on Bartram's images in his "Atala."[24] For these writers, Bartram's Indians were symbols of humanity untarnished by the hypocrisy of Western civilization. In America itself, Henry David Thoreau, in his classic essay *Walden,* cited Bartram's description of the Creek "busk," or annual renewal ceremony, in which the Indians destroyed worn-out domestic articles and clothing, as an appropriate remedy for American materialism.[25] The wide popularity of Bartram's work continues to the present, and the book has seen numerous reprintings, including the authoritative *Naturalist's Edition* by Francis Harper, published in 1958.

While the Indian references in *Travels,* excerpted here, are a critical and voluminous segment of Bartram's Indian writings, and must, therefore, be included in a volume that claims to be comprehensive in its coverage of that subject, we are also acutely aware that presenting extracts from that book distorts the author's holistic portrayal of the American South. We recognize Bartram's *Travels* as a masterpiece of literature and natural history, and we vigorously encourage everyone with an interest in the region to read his book in its entirety, preferably Francis Harper's ably annotated version, which faithfully reproduces the original Philadelphia edition of 1791.

Travels Through North & South Carolina, Georgia, East & West Florida, the Cherokee Country, the Extensive Territories of the Muscogulges, or Creek Confederacy, and the Country of the Chactaws; Containing an Account of the Soil and Natural Productions of Those Regions, Together with Observations on the Manners of the Indians

(Extracts from the book by William Bartram, published by James & Johnson, Philadelphia, 1791)

"[1] At the request of Dr. Fothergill, of London, to search the Floridas, and the western parts of Carolina and Georgia, for the discovery of rare and useful productions of nature, chiefly in the vegetable kingdom; in April, 1773, I embarked for Charleston, South-Carolina, on board the brigantine Charleston Packet. . . ." Thus begins William Bartram's *Travels,* a lively, detailed account of his observations on the natural history—the flora, fauna, and human inhabitants—of the southern colonies of British North America and neighboring Indian lands. In his introduction, Bartram explained his philosophical and scientific interests in the southern Indians.

[xxxiii] I shall now offer such observations as must necessarily occur, from such a careful attention to, and investigation of the manners of the Indian nations; being induced, while travelling among them, to associate with them, that I might judge for myself whether they were deserving of the severe censure, which prevailed against them among the white people, that they were incapable of civilization.

In the consideration of this important subject it will be necessary to enquire, whether they were inclined to adopt the European modes of civil society? whether such a reformation could be obtained, without using coercive or violent means? and lastly, whether such a revolution would be productive of real benefit to them, and consequently beneficial to the public? I was satisfied in discovering that they were desirous of becoming united with us, in civil and religious society.

It may, therefore, not be foreign to the subject, to point out the propriety of sending men of ability and virtue, under the authority of government, as friendly visitors, into their towns; let these men be instructed to learn perfectly their languages, and by a liberal and friendly intimacy, become acquainted with their customs and usages, religious and civil; their system of legislation and police, as well as their most ancient and present traditions and history. These men thus enlightened and instructed, would be qualified to judge equitably, and when returned to us, to make true and just reports, which might assist the legislature of the United States to form, and offer to them a judicious plan, for their civilization and union with us.

But I presume not to dictate in these high concerns of government, and I am fully convinced that such important matters are far above my ability; the duty and respect we owe to religion and rectitude, the most acceptable incense we can offer to the Almighty, as an atonement for our negligence, in the care of the present and future well being of our Indian brethren, induces me to mention this matter, though perhaps of greater concernment than we generally are aware of.

Bartram began his southward journey in March 1773 (note the first of many erroneous dates in the book),[1] arriving in Charleston on the last day of the month. He sailed on to Savannah, Georgia, where he purchased a horse and immediately began his overland travels. On Colonel's Island, Bartram discovered a prehistoric shell midden site.

[5] The surface and vegetable mould here is generally a loose sand, not very fertile, except some spots bordering on the sound and inlets, where are found heaps or mounds of sea-shell, either formerly brought there, by the Indians, who inhabited the island, or which were perhaps thrown up in ridges, by the beating surface of the sea: possibly both these circumstances may have contributed to their formation. . . . [6] I observed, amongst the shells of the conical mounds, fragments of earthen vessels, and of other utensils, the manufacture of the ancients: about the centre of one of them, the rim of an earthen pot appeared amongst the shells and earth, which I carefully removed, and drew it out, almost whole: this pot was curiously wrought all over the outside, representing basket work, and was undoubtedly esteemed a very ingenious performance, by the people, at the age of its construction.[2]

During his earlier stay in Charleston, Bartram had met John Stuart, Indian Superintendent for the Southern District.[3] Stuart had offered, "[9] in order to facilitate my travels in the Indian territories," to "introduce my business to the chiefs of the Cherokees, Creeks, and other nations, and recommend me to their friendship and protection" if Bartram would attend the forthcoming treaty negotiations in Augusta in about a month. To occupy his time in the interim, Bartram set out for Florida. At Darien, Georgia, he stopped at the home of Lachlan McIntosh, who offered to send along his son John to serve as guide to the Augusta conference and the Indian country; he proved "[15] a very agreeable companion through a long and toilsome journey of near a thousand miles." Continuing to Fort Barrington, on the Altamaha River, Bartram arrived at a ferry.

[16] Here is a considerable height and bluff on the river, and evident [17] vestiges of an ancient Indian town may be seen, such as old extensive fields, and conical mounds, or artificial heaps of earth. I here crossed the river, which is about five hundred yards over, in a good large boat, rowed by a Creek Indian, who was married to a white woman; he seemed an active, civil, and sensible man.

While riding horseback on the trail to a trading house that was located across the St. Marys River in Florida, Bartram encountered a Seminole warrior. This episode may have actually occurred in the summer of 1776.[4]

[20] . . . when, on a sudden, an Indian appeared crossing the path, at a considerable distance before me. On perceiving that he was armed with a rifle, the first sight of him startled me, and I endeavoured to elude his sight, by stopping my pace, and keeping large trees between us; but he espied me, and turning short a-[21]bout, sat spurs to his horse, and came up on full gallop. I never before this was afraid at the sight of an Indian, but at this time, I must own that my spirits were very much agitated: I saw at once, that being unarmed, I was in his power, and having now but a few moments to prepare, I resigned myself entirely to the will of the Almighty, trusting to his mercies for my preservation; my mind then became tranquil, and I resolved to meet the dreaded foe with resolution and chearful confidence. The intrepid Siminole stopped suddenly, three or four yards before me, and silently viewed me, his countenance angry and fierce, shifting his rifle from shoulder to shoulder, and looking about instantly on all sides. I advanced towards him, and with an air of confidence offered him my hand, hailing him, brother; at this he hastily jerked back his arm, with a look of malice, rage and disdain, seeming every way disconcerted; when again looking at me more attentively, he instantly spurred up to me, and, with dignity in his look and action, gave me his hand. Possibly the silent language of his soul, during the moment of suspense (for I believe his design was to kill me when he first came up) was after this manner: "White man, thou art my enemy, and thou and thy brethren may have killed mine; yet it may not

be so, and even were that the case, thou art now alone, and in my power. Live; the Great Spirit forbids me to touch thy life; go to thy brethren, tell them thou sawest an Indian in the forests, who knew how to be humane and compassionate." In fine, we shook hands, and parted in a friendly manner, in the midst of a dreary wilderness; and he informed me of the course and distance to the trading-house, where I found he had been extremely ill treated the day before.

[22] I now sat forward again, and after eight or ten miles riding, arrived at the banks of St. Mary's, opposite the stores, and got safe over before dark. The river is here about one hundred yards across, has ten feet water, and, following its course, about sixty miles to the sea, though but about twenty miles by land. The trading company here received and treated me with great civility. On relating my adventures on the road, particularly the last with the Indian, the chief replied, with a countenance that at once bespoke surprise and pleasure, "My friend, consider yourself a fortunate man: that fellow," said he, "is one of the greatest villains on earth, a noted murderer, and outlawed by his countrymen. Last evening he was here, we took his gun from him, broke it in pieces, and gave him a severe drubbing: he, however, made his escape, carrying off a new rifle gun, with which, he said, going off, he would kill the first white man he met."

On seriously contemplating the behaviour of this Indian towards me, so soon after his ill treatment, the following train of sentiments insensibly crouded in upon my mind.

Can it be denied, but that the moral principle, which directs the savages to virtuous and praiseworthy actions, is natural or innate? It is certain they have not the assistance of letters, or those means of education in the schools of philosophy, where the virtuous sentiments and actions of the most illustrious characters are recorded, and carefully laid before the youth of civilized nations: therefore this moral principle must be innate, or they must be under the immediate influence and guidance of a more divine and powerful preceptor, [23] who, on these occasions, instantly inspires them, and as with a ray of divine light, points out to them at once the dignity, propriety, and beauty of virtue.

[24] The river St. Mary has its source from a vast lake, or marsh, called Ouaquaphenogaw,[5] which lies [25] between Flint and Oakmulge rivers, and occupies a space of near three hundred miles in circuit. This vast accumulation of waters, in the wet season, appears as a lake, and contains some large islands or knolls, of rich high land; one of which the present generation of the Creeks represent to be a most blissful spot of the earth: they say it is inhabited by a peculiar race of Indians, whose women are incomparably beautiful; they also tell you, that this terrestrial paradise has been seen by some of their enterprising

hunters, when in pursuit of game, who being lost in inextricable swamps and bogs, and on the point of perishing, were unexpectedly relieved by a company of beautiful women, whom they call daughters of the sun, who kindly gave them such provisions as they had with them, which were chiefly fruit, oranges, dates, &c. and some corn cakes, and then enjoined them to fly for safety to their own country; for that their husbands were fierce men, and cruel to strangers: they further say, that these hunters had a view of their settlements, situated on the elevated banks of an island, or promontory, in a beautiful lake; but that in their endeavours to approach it, they were involved in perpetual labyrinths, and, like inchanted land, still as they imagined they had just gained it, it seemed to fly before them, alternately appearing and disappearing. They resolved, at length, to leave the delusive pursuit, and to return; which, after a number of inexpressible difficulties, they effected. When they reported their adventures to their countrymen, their young warriors were enflamed with an irresistable desire to invade, and make a conquest of, so charming a country; but all their attempts have hitherto proved abortive, [26] never having been able again to find that enchanting spot, nor even any road or pathway to it; yet they say that they frequently meet with certain signs of its being inhabited, as the building of canoes, footsteps of men, &c. They tell another story concerning the inhabitants of this sequestered country, which seems probable enough, which is, that they are the posterity of a fugitive remnant of the ancient Yamases, who escaped massacre after a bloody and decisive conflict between them and the Creek nation (who, it is certain, conquered, and nearly exterminated, that once powerful people) and here found an asylum, remote and secure from the fury of their proud conquerors.[6]

Bartram returned to Darien and soon set off with John McIntosh for the Indian congress at Augusta, which he attended between May 14 and June 3, 1773.[7]

[33] A few days after our arrival at Augusta, the chiefs and warriors of the Creeks and Cherokees being arrived, the Congress and the business of the treaty came on, and the negociations continued undetermined many days; the merchants of Georgia demanding at least two millions of acres of land from the Indians, as a discharge of their debts, due, and of long standing; the Creeks, on the other hand, being a powerful and proud spirited people, their young warriors were unwilling to submit to so large a demand, and their conduct evidently betrayed a disposition to dispute the ground by force of arms, and they could not at first be brought to listen to reason and amicable terms; however, at length, the cool and deliberate counsels of the ancient venerable chiefs, enforced by liberal presents of suitable goods, were too powerful

inducements for them any longer to resist, and finally prevailed. The treaty concluded in unanimity, peace, and good order; and the honorable Superintendant, not forgetting his promise to me, at the conclusion, mentioned my business, and recommended me to the protection of the Indian chiefs and warriors. The presents being distributed amongst the Indians, they departed, returning home to their towns.

Superintendent John Stuart, who had opposed the cession, noted the thinly veiled hostility of the Creeks and Cherokees at the congress and warned Bartram that he believed it was not wise for the naturalist to enter the Indian country alone at that time. So Bartram joined the survey party charged with demarcating the boundary of the northern portion of the cession.[8]

[33] A company of sur-[34]veyors were appointed, by the Governor and Council, to ascertain the boundaries of the new purchase; they were to be attended by chiefs of the Indians, selected and delegated by their countrymen, to assist, and be witnesses that the articles of the treaty were fulfilled, as agreed to by both parties in Congress.

Col. Barnet, who was chosen to conduct this business on the part of the Georgians, a gentleman every way qualified for that important trust, in a very friendly and obliging manner, gave me an invitation to accompany him on this tour.

The survey party included "[35] surveyors, astronomers, artisans, chain-carriers, markers, guides, and hunters, besides a very respectable number of gentlemen, who joined us, in order to speculate in the lands, together with ten or twelve Indians. . . ." The group followed the lower trading path to the Ogeechee River and proceeded on to Little River, where Bartram noted evidence of a Mississippian archaeological site.

[37] Not far distant from the terrace, or eminence, overlooking the low grounds of the river, many very magnificent monuments of the power and industry of the ancient inhabitants of these lands are visible. I observed a stupendous conical pyramid, or artificial mount of earth, vast tetragon terraces, and a large sunken area, of a cubical form, encompassed with banks of earth; and certain traces of a large Indian town, the work of a powerful nation, whose period of grandeur perhaps long preceded the discovery of this continent.[9]

[38] After about seven miles progress through this forest of gigantic Black Oaks, we enter on territories which exhibit more varied scenes: the land rises almost insensibly by gentle ascents, exhibiting desert plains, high forests,

gravelly and stony ridges, ever in sight of rapid rivulets; the soil, as already described. We then passed over large rich savannas, or natural meadows, wide-spreading cane swamps, and frequently old Indian settlements, now deserted and overgrown with forests. These are always on or near the banks of rivers, or great swamps, the artificial mounts and terraces elevating them above the surrounding groves. I observed, in the antient cultivated fields, 1. Diospyros, 2. Gleditsia triacanthos, 3. Prunus Chicasaw,* 4. Callicarpa, 5. Morus rubra, 6. Juglans exaltata, 7. Juglans nigra,[10] which inform us, that these trees were cultivated by the ancients, on account of their fruit, as being wholesome and nourishing food. Tho' these are natives of the forest, yet they thrive better, and are more fruitful, in cultivated plantations, and the fruit is in great estimation with the present generation of Indians, particularly Juglans exaltata* commonly called shell-barked hiccory; the Creeks store up the latter in their towns. I have seen above an hundred bushels of these nuts belonging to one family. They pound them to pieces, and then cast them into boiling water, which, after passing through fine strainers, preserves the most oily part of the liquid: this they call by a name which signifies Hiccory milk; it is as sweet and rich as fresh cream, and is an ingredient in most of their cookery, especially homony and corn cakes.[11]

Native Americans frequently assisted European explorers and surveyors in their mapmaking endeavors. As a consequence, many of the best maps of the colonial Southeast incorporate considerable Indian content, usually unacknowledged. The following dispute occurred at a "Buffalo Lick" near the headwaters of Little River.[12]

[39] We were detained at this place one day, in adjusting and planning the several branches of the survey. A circumstance occurred during this time, which was a remarkable instance of Indian sagacity, and had nearly disconcerted all our plans, and put an end to the business. The surveyor having fixed his compass on the staff, and about to ascertain the course from our place of departure, which was to strike Savanna river at the confluence of a [40] certain river, about seventy miles distance from us; just as he had determined upon the point, the Indian Chief came up, and observing the course he had fixed upon, spoke, and said it was not right; but that the course to the place was so and so, holding up his hand, and pointing. The surveyor replied, that he himself was certainly right, adding, that that little instrument (pointing to the compass) told him so, which, he said, could not err. The Indian answered, he knew better,

* The Chicasaw plumb I think must be excepted, for though certainly a native of America, yet I never saw it wild in the forests, but always in old deserted Indian plantations: I suppose it to have been brought from the S.W. beyond the Missisippi, by the Chicasaws.

and that the little wicked instrument was a liar; and he would not acquiesce in its decisions, since it would wrong the Indians out of their land. This mistake (the surveyor proving to be in the wrong) displeased the Indians; the dispute arose to that height, that the Chief and his party had determined to break up the business, and return the shortest way home, and forbad the surveyors to proceed any farther: however, after some delay, the complaisance and prudent conduct of the Colonel made them change their resolution; the Chief became reconciled, upon condition that the compass should be discarded, and rendered incapable of serving on this business; that the Chief himself should lead the survey; and, moreover, receive an order for a very considerable quantity of goods.[13]

Following the course determined by the headman, the survey party proceeded north to the headwaters of Broad River. There Bartram observed a plant,

[41] . . . the Physic-nut, or Indian Olive. . . . The Indians, when they go in pursuit of deer, carry this fruit with them, supposing that it has the power of charming or drawing that creature to them; from whence, with the traders, it has obtained the name of the Physic-nut, which means, with them, charming, conjuring, or fascinating [figure 9].[14]

[44] One of our Indian young men, this evening, caught a very large salmon trout, weighing about fifteen pounds, which he presented to the Col. who ordered it to be served up for supper. The Indian struck this fish, with a reed harpoon, pointed very sharp, barbed, and hardened by the fire. The fish lay close under the steep bank, which the Indian discovered and struck with his reed; instantly the fish darted off with it, whilst the Indian pursued, without extracting the harpoon, and with repeated thrusts drowned it, and then dragged it to shore.[15]

With the survey concluded, Bartram and McIntosh returned to Darien. From July 1773 to March 1774, Bartram's movements seem to have been limited to the Altamaha River valley. That river is formed by the confluence of the Ocmulgee and Oconee rivers.

[53] About seventy or eighty [54] miles above the confluence of the Oakmulge and Ocone, the trading path, from Augusta to the Creek nation, crosses these fine rivers, which are there forty miles apart. On the east banks of the Oakmulge, this trading road runs nearly two miles through ancient Indian

Figure 9. William Bartram's Drawing of the "Physic-nut" and an Unidentified Bird
(courtesy, British Museum of Natural History)

fields, which are called the Oakmulge fields: they are the rich low lands of the river. On the heights of these low grounds are yet visible monuments, or traces, of an ancient town, such as artificial mounts or terraces, squares and banks, encircling considerable areas. Their old fields and planting land extend up and down the river, fifteen or twenty miles from this site.[16]

And, if we are to give credit to the account the Creeks give of themselves, this place is remarkable for being the first town or settlement, when they sat down (as they term it) or established themselves, after their emigration from the west, beyond the Missisippi, their original native country. On this long journey they suffered great and innumerable difficulties, encountering and vanquishing numerous and valiant tribes of Indians, who opposed and retarded their march. Having crossed the river, still pushing eastward, they were obliged to make a stand, and fortify themselves in this place, as their only remaining hope, being to the last degree persecuted and weakened by their surrounding foes. Having formed for themselves this retreat, and driven off the inhabitants by degrees, they recovered their spirits, and again faced their enemies, when they came off victorious in a memorable and decisive battle. They afterwards gradually subdued their surrounding enemies, strengthening themselves by taking into confederacy the vanquished tribes.[17]

[55] And they say, also, that about this period the English were establishing the colony of Carolina, and the Creeks, understanding that they were a powerful, warlike people, sent deputies to Charleston, their capital, offering them their friendship and alliance, which was accepted, and, in consequence thereof, a treaty took place between them, which has remained inviolable to this day: they never ceased war against the numerous and potent bands of Indians, who then surrounded and cramped the English plantations, as the Savannas, Ogeeches, Wapoos, Santees, Yamasees, Utinas, Icosans, Paticas, and others, until they had extirpated them. The Yamasees and their adherents sheltering themselves under the power and protection of the Spaniards of East Florida, they pursued them to the very gates of St. Augustine, and the Spaniards refusing to deliver them up, these faithful intrepid allies had the courage to declare war against them, and incessantly persecuted them, until they entirely broke up and ruined their settlements, driving them before them, till at length they were obliged to retire within the walls of St. Augustine and a few inferior fortified posts on the sea coast.[18]

After a few days, I returned to Broughton Island. The Cherokees and their confederates being yet discontented, and on bad terms with the white people, it was unsafe to pursue my travels into the north western regions of Carolina; . . .[19]

In March 1774, Bartram met James Spalding,[20] owner of several trading houses on the St. Johns River in Florida, who offered him assistance if his travels should carry him in that direction. Bartram promptly set sail from Spalding's home on St. Simons Island, bound for Florida. On Amelia Island, he noted another large Indian mound site.

[65] On [66] Egmont estate, are several very large Indian tumuli, which are called Ogeeche mounts, so named from that nation of Indians, who took shelter here, after being driven from their native settlements on the main near Ogeeche river. Here they were constantly harrassed by the Carolinians and Creeks, and at length slain by their conquerors, and their bones intombed in these heaps of earth and shells.[21]

Bartram continued on to the St. Johns, and up that river.

[75] I had not left sight of my encampment, following a winding path through a grove of Live Oak, Laurel (Magn. grandiflora) and Sapindus, before an Indian stepped out of a thicket and crossed the path just before me, having a large turkey cock, flung across his shoulders, he saw me and stepping up and smiling, spoke to me in English, bidding me good-morning. I saluted him with "Its well brother," led him to my camp, and treated him with a dram. This friendly Indian informed me that he lived at the next plantation, employed as a hunter, I asked him how far it was to the house; he answered about half a mile by land, and invited me to go there, telling me that his master was a very good, kind man, and would be glad to see me.[22]

After spending one day at the Marshall plantation, Bartram sailed to another plantation, where he was told of recent meetings at St. Augustine between the Seminoles and Governor Tonyn.[23]

Bartram idiosyncratically applied the name "Lower Creeks" to Indians living in Florida who were known to everyone else as Seminoles. Other English-speakers reserved the name "Lower Creeks" for inhabitants of the Muscogulge towns clustered around the middle Chattahoochee River, and "Upper Creeks" for those living along the Tallapoosa, Coosa, and Alabama rivers. Bartram referred to both these designated groups collectively as "Upper Creeks," "the Muscogulge," or "the Nation." During the period under discussion, the British and the Creeks themselves considered the Seminole towns part of the Lower Creek Nation, not a separate tribal entity.[24]

[78] . . . there had, but a few days since, been a counsel held at St. Augustine, between the governor of East Florida, and the chiefs of the Lower Creeks. They had been delegated by their [79] towns, to make enquiry, concerning the late alarm and depredations, committed by the Indians upon the traders, which the

nation being apprised of, recommended these deputies to be chosen and sent, as soon as possible, in order to make reasonable concessions, before the flame, already kindled, should spread into a general war. The parties accordingly met in St. Augustine, and the affair was amicably adjusted, to the satisfaction of both parties. The chiefs of the delinquent bands, whose young warriors had committed the mischief, promised to indemnify the traders for the loss of their goods, and requested that they might return to their store-houses, with goods as usual, and that they should be safe in their persons and property, The traders at this time, were actually preparing to return. It appeared upon a strict investigation of facts, that the affair had taken its rise from the licentious conduct of a few vagrant young hunters of the Siminole nation, who, imagining themselves to have been ill treated, in their dealings, with the traders (which by the bye was likely enough to be true) took this violent method of doing themselves justice. The culprits however endeavoured to exculpate themselves, by asserting, that they had no design or intention of robbing the traders of their effects, but meant it only as a threat, and that the traders, from a consciousness of their dishonesty, had been terrified and fled, leaving their stores, which they took possession of, to prevent their being totally lost.

Bartram sailed on to Fort Picolata,[25] an abandoned Spanish structure, passing by the unhappy site of his failed indigo and rice plantation. Continuing his ascent of the river, Bartram made camp for the night under some live oaks. Regarding that species, he noted that "[85] It bears a prodigious quantity of fruit; the acorn is small, but sweet and agreeable to the taste when roasted, and is food for almost all animals. The Indians obtain from it a sweet oil, which they use in the cooking of hommony, rice, &c. and they also roast them in hot embers, eating them as we do chesnuts."[26] Farther upstream he kept along the western or "Indian shore" of the St. Johns.

[92] As I continued coasting the Indian shore of this bay, on doubling a promontory, I suddenly saw before me an Indian settlement, or village. It was a fine situation, the bank rising gradually from the water. There were eight or ten habitations, in a row, or street, fronting the water, and about fifty yards distance from it. Some of the youth were naked, up their hips in the water, fishing with rods and lines, whilst others, younger, were diverting themselves in shooting frogs with bows and arrows. On my near approach, the little children took to their heels, and ran to some women, who were hoeing corn; but the stouter youth stood their ground, and, smiling, called to me. As I passed along, I observed some elderly people reclined on skins spread on the ground, under the cool shade of spreading Oaks and Palms, that were ranged in front of their

houses; they arose, and eyed me as I passed, but perceiving that I kept on,
without stopping, they resumed their former position. They were civil, and
appeared happy in their situation.

There was a large Orange grove at the upper [93] end of their village; the
trees were large, carefully pruned, and the ground under them clean, open,
and airy. There seemed to be several hundred acres of cleared land, about the
village; a considerable portion of which was planted, chiefly with corn (Zea) [,]
Batatas, Beans, Pompions, Squashes, (Cucurbita verrucosa) [,] Melons
(Cucurbita citrullus) [,] Tobacco (Nicotiana) [,] &c. abundantly sufficient for
the inhabitants of the village.[27]

Bartram next visited the mostly abandoned English settlement of Charlotia, founded by Denys Rolle in 1764.[28] The town was built on an earlier
Indian site, along the east shore of the river.

[94] I saw many fragments of the earthen ware of the ancient inhabitants, and
bones of animals, amongst the shells, and mixed with the earth, to a great
depth. This high shelly bank continues, by gentle parallel ridges, near a quarter
of a mile back from the river. . . . [95] The aborigines of America, had a very
great town in this place, as appears from the great tumuli, and conical mounts
of earth and shells, and other traces of a settlement which yet remain. There
grew in the old fields on these heights great quantities of Callicarpa. . . .[29]

Bartram soon arrived at Spalding's Lower Store. This trading house
served as his home base while he explored the surrounding region, accompanied by one of the traders.[30] On one of these short excursions he
revisited Mount Royal, overlooking Lake George (an embayment of the
St. Johns River), which he had first seen in 1766 with his father, John
Bartram.[31]

[99] At about fifty yards distance from the landing place, stands a
magnificent Indian mount. About fifteen years ago I visited this place, at which
time there were no settlements of white people, but all appeared wild and
savage; yet in that uncultivated state, it possessed an almost inexpressible air of
grandeur, which was now entirely changed. At that time there was a very
considerable extent of old fields, round about the mount; there was also a large
Orange grove, together with Palms and Live Oaks, extending from near the
mount, along the banks, downwards, all of which has since been cleared away to
make room for planting ground. But what greatly contributed towards
compleating the magnificence of the scene, was a noble Indian highway, which
led from the great mount, on a strait line, three quarters of a mile, first through

a point or wing of the Orange grove, and continuing thence through an awful forest, of Live Oaks, it was terminated by Palms and Laurel Magnolias, on the verge of an oblong artificial lake, which was on the edge of an extensive green level savanna. This grand highway was about fifty yards wide, sunk a little below the common level, and the earth thrown up on each side, making a bank of about two feet high.[32]

Another archaeological site was found at the southern end of Drayton's Island in Lake George.[33]

[102] This island appears, from obvious vestiges, to have been once the chosen residence of an Indian prince, there being to this day, evident remains of [103] a large town of the Aborigines. It was situated on an eminence, near the banks of the lake, and commanded a comprehensive and charming prospect of the waters, islands, East and West shores of the lake, the capes, the bay and Mount Royal, and to the South the view is in a manner infinite, where the skies and waters seem to unite. On the site of this ancient town, stands a very pompous Indian mount, or conical pyramid of earth, from which runs in a strait line, a grand avenue or Indian highway, through a magnificent grove of Magnolias, Live Oaks, Palms and Orange trees, terminating at the verge of a large green level savanna. This island appears to have been well inhabited, as is very evident, from the quantities of fragments of Indian earthen-ware, bones of animals and other remains, particularly in the shelly heights and ridges, all over the island.

Sailing on, Bartram made camp at the head of Lake George, near "[107] some almost unlimited savannas and plains, which were absolutely enchanting; they had been lately burnt by the Indian hunters, and had just now recovered their vernal verdure and gaiety." Another day's travel brought him to Spalding's Upper Store.[34]

[111] On our arrival at the upper store, we found it occupied by a white trader, who had for a companion, a very handsome Siminole young woman. Her father, who was a prince, by the name of the White Captain, was an old chief of the Siminoles, and with part of his family, to the number of ten or twelve, were encamped in an Orange grove near the stores, having lately come in from a hunt.

This white trader, soon after our arrival, delivered up the goods and storehouses to my companion, and joined his father-in-law's camp, and soon after went away into the forests on hunting and trading amongst the flying camps of Siminoles.

He is at this time, unhappy in his connections with his beautiful savage. It is but a few years since he came here, I think from North Carolina, a stout genteel well-bred man, active, and of a heroic and amiable disposition, and by his industry, honesty, and engaging manners, had gained the affections of the Indians, and soon made a little for-[112]tune by traffic with the Siminoles: when, unfortunately, meeting with this little charmer, they were married in the Indian manner. He loves her sincerely, as she possesses every perfection in her person to render a man happy. Her features are beautiful, and manners engaging. Innocence, modesty, and love, appear to a stranger in every action and movement; and these powerful graces she has so artfully played upon her beguiled and vanquished lover, and unhappy slave, as to have already drained him of all his possessions, which she dishonestly distributes amongst her savage relations. He is now poor, emaciated, and half distracted, often threatening to shoot her, and afterwards put an end to his own life; yet he has not resolution even to leave her; but now endeavours to drown and forget his sorrows, in deep draughts of brandy. Her father condemns her dishonest and cruel conduct.

These particulars were related to me by my old friend the trader, directly after a long conference which he had with the White Captain on the subject, his son in law being present. The scene was affecting; they both shed tears plentifully. My reasons for mentioning this affair, so foreign to my business, was to exhibit an instance of the power of beauty in a savage, and their art and finesse in improving it to their private ends. It is, however, but doing justice to the virtue and moral conduct of the Siminoles, and American Aborigines in general, to observe, that the character of this woman is condemned and detested by her own people, of both sexes; and if her husband should turn her away, according to the customs and usages of these people, she would not get a husband again, as a divorce seldom takes place but in consequence of a [113] deliberate impartial trial, and public condemnation, and then she would be looked upon as a harlot.

Such is the virtue of these u[n]tutored savages: but I am afraid this is a common phrase epithet, having no meaning, or at least improperly applied; for these people are both well tutored and civil; and it is apparent to an impartial observer, who resides but a little time amongst them, that it is from the most delicate sense of the honour and reputation of their tribes and families, that their laws and customs receive their force and energy. This is the divine principle which influences their moral conduct, and solely preserves their constitution and civil government in that purity in which they are found to prevail amongst them.

[114] Being desirous of continuing my travels and observations, higher up the river, and having an invitation from a gentleman who was agent for, and

resident at a large plantation, the property of an English gentleman, about sixty miles higher up, I resolved to pursue my researches to that place; and having engaged in my service a young Indian, nephew to the White Captain, he agreed to assist me in working my vessel up as high as a certain bluff, where I was, by agreement, to land him, on the West or Indian shore, whence he designed to go in quest of the camp of the White Trader, his relation.

Only a few miles into the voyage, at an Orange grove on the western shore,

[115] . . . my Indian companion requested me to set him on shore, being already tired of rowing under a fervid sun, and having for some time intimated a dislike to his situation, I readily complied with his desire, knowing the impossibility of compelling an Indian against his own inclinations, or even prevailing upon him by reasonable arguments, when labour is in the question; before my vessel reached the shore, he sprang out of her and landed, when uttering a shrill and terrible whoop, he bounded off like a roebuck, and I lost sight of him. I at first apprehended that as he took his gun with him, he intended to hunt for some game and return to me in the evening. The day being excessively hot and sultry, I concluded to take up my quarters here until next morning.

The Indian not returning this morning, I sat sail alone.[35]

Bartram continued his canoe journey up the St. Johns River, eventually reaching a shell midden site at St. Francis, between Lakes Dexter and Beresford.

[138] This was a high perpendicular bluff, fronting more than one hundred yards on the river, the earth black, loose and fertile, it is a composition of river-shells, sand, &c. back of it from the river, were open Pine forests and savannas. I met with a circumstance here, that, with some, may be reckoned worthy of mentioning, since it regards the monuments of the ancients; as I have already observed, when I landed it was quite dark, and in collecting [139] wood for my fire, stroling in the dark about the groves, I found the surface of the ground very uneven, by means of little mounts and ridges; in the morning I found I had taken up my lodging on the border of an ancient burying ground; sepulchres or tumuli of the Yamasees, who were here slain by the Creeks in the last decisive battle, the Creeks having driven them into this point, between the doubling of the river, where few of them escaped the fury of the conquerors. These graves occupied the whole grove, consisting of two or three acres of ground; there were near thirty of these cemeteries of the dead, nearly of an equal size and

form, they were oblong, twenty feet in length, ten or twelve feet in width and
three or four feet high, now overgrown with Orange trees, Live Oaks, Laurel
Magnolias, Red bays and other trees and shrubs, composing dark and solemn
shades.[36]

Several more days' travel brought him to the Beresford plantation, situated about thirty miles west of the Greek and Minorcan settlement of New
Smyrna. On an earlier visit to the St. Johns, in 1766 or 1767, Bartram had

[145] . . . observed then, near when New-Smyrna now stands, a spacious Indian
mount and avenue, which stood near the banks of the river; the avenue ran on a
strait line back, through the groves, across the ridge, and terminated at the
verge of natural savannas and ponds.[37]

Bartram soon reached the southernmost limits of his travels and began
to descend the St. Johns.[38] He interjected the following passage in a description of crows and vultures.

[151] The Creeks or Muscogulges construct their royal standard of the tail
feather of this bird, which is called by a name signifying the eagle's tail; this they
carry with them when they go to battle, but then it is painted with a zone of red
within the brown tips; and in peaceable negociations it is displayed new, clean
and white, this standard is held most sacred by them on all occasions; and is
constructed and ornamented with great ingenuity. These birds seldom appear
but when the deserts are set on fire (which happens almost every day
throughout the year, in [152] some part or other, by the Indians, for the
purpose of rousing the game, as also by the lightning:) when they are seen at a
distance soaring on the wing, gathering from every quarter, and gradually
approaching the burnt plains, where they alight upon the ground yet smoking
with hot embers; they gather up the roasted serpents, frogs and lizards; filling
their sacks with them; at this time a person may shoot them at pleasure, they not
being willing to quit the feast, and indeed seem to brave all danger.[39]

Farther on, Bartram camped in an orange grove, which was "[154] . . .
narrow, betwixt the river banks and ancient Indian fields, where there are
evident traces of the habitations of the ancients. . . ."[40] At Spalding's Upper
Store, Bartram found "[156] a small party of Indians here, who had lately
arrived with their hunts to purchase goods." Continuing on his way, he
camped one evening at "[160] an ancient landing place, which is a sloping
ascent to a level grassy plain, an old Indian field." Upon reaching Spalding's Lower Store in late April 1774,[41] Bartram joined a group of traders

(probably led by Job Wiggens) heading west to Alachua "[170] to treat with the Cowkeeper and other chiefs of Cuscowilla, on the subject of re-establishing the trade, &c. agreeable to the late treaty of St. Augustine." Among his observations along the path to Cuscowilla, he included a digression on the "brown spotted gar."

[176] The Indians make use of their sharp teeth to scratch or bleed themselves with, and their pointed scales to arm their arrows.[42] This fish is sometimes eaten, and to prepare them for food, they cover them whole in hot embers, where they bake them, the skin with the scales easily peel off, leaving the meat white and tender.

[184] Continuing eight or nine miles through this sublime forest, we entered on an open forest of lofty Pines and Oaks, on gently swelling sand hills, and presently saw the lake, its waters sparkling through the open groves. Near the path was a large artificial mound of earth, on a most charming, high situation, supposed to be the work of the ancient Floridans or Yamasees, with other traces of an Indian town; here were three or four Indian habitations, the women and children saluted us with chearfulness and complaisance.[43] After riding near a mile farther we arrived at Cuscowilla, near the banks: a pretty brook of water ran through the town, and entered the lake just by.

We were welcomed to the town, and conducted by the young men and maidens to the chief's house, which stood on an eminence, and was distinguished from the rest by its superior magnitude, a large flag being hoisted on a high staff at one corner. We immediately alighted; the chief, who is called the Cowkeeper,[44] attended by several ancient men, came to us, and in a very free and sociable manner, shook our hands (or rather arms) a form of salutation peculiar to the American Indians, saying at the same time, "You are come." We followed him to an apartment prepared for the reception of their guests.[45]

The pipe being filled, it is handed around, after which a large bowl, with what they call "Thin drink,"[46] is brought in and set down on a small low table; in this bowl is a great wooden ladle; each person takes up in it as much as he pleases, and after drinking until satisfied, returns it again into the bowl, pushing the handle towards the [next] person in the circle, and so it goes round.

[185] After the usual compliments and enquiries relative to our adventures, &c. the chief trader informed the Cowkeeper, in the presence of his council or attendants, the purport of our business, with which he expressed his satisfaction. He was then informed what the nature of my errand was, and he received me with complaisance, giving me unlimited permission to travel over the country for the purpose of collecting flowers, medicinal plants, &c. saluting me by the name of PUC PUGGY or the Flower hunter, recommending me to the friendship and protection of his people.

Figure 10. William Bartram's Drawing of "The Great Alachua-Savana" (courtesy, American Philosophical Society)

The next day being agreed on to hold a council and transact the business of our embassy, we acquainted the chief with our intention of making our encampment on the borders of the great ALACHUA SAVANNA [figures 10 and 11],[47] and to return at the time appointed to town, to attend the council according to agreement.

Soon after we had fixed on the time and manner of proceeding on the further settlement of the treaty, a considerable number of Indians assembled around their chief, when the conversation turned to common and familiar topics.

The chief is a tall well made man, very affable and cheerful, about sixty years of age, his eyes lively and full of fire, his countenance manly and placid, yet ferocious, or what we call savage; his nose aquiline, his dress extremely simple, but his head trimmed and ornamented in the true Creek mode. He has been a great warrior, having then attending him as slaves, many Yamasee captives, taken by himself when young. They were dressed better [186] than he, served and waited upon him with signs of the most abject fear. The manners and

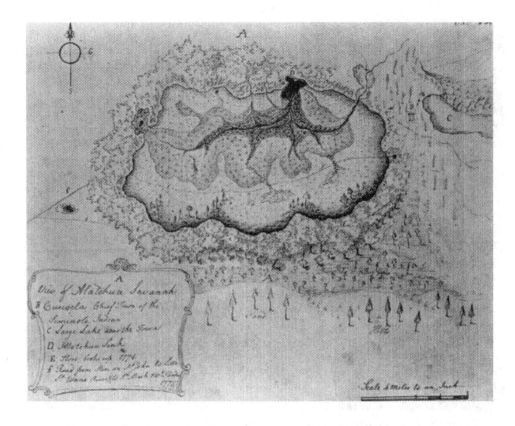

Figure 11. William Bartram's "View of Alatchua Savanah" (courtesy, British Museum of Natural History)

customs of the Alachuas, and most of the lower Creeks or Siminoles, appear evidently tinctured with Spanish civilization. Their religious and civil usages manifest a predilection for the Spanish customs. There are several Christians among them, many of whom wear little silver crucifixes, affixed to a wampum collar round their necks, or suspended by a small chain upon their breast. These are said to be baptized, and notwithstanding most of them speak and understand Spanish, yet they have been the most bitter and formidable Indian enemies the Spaniards ever had. The slaves, both male and female, are permitted to marry amongst them: their children are free, and considered in every respect equal to themselves, but the parents continue in a state of slavery as long as they live.

In observing these slaves, we behold at once, in their countenance and manners, the striking contrast betwixt a state of freedom and slavery. They are the tamest, the most abject creatures that we can possibly imagine: mild, peaceable and tractable, they seem to have no will or power to act but as directed by their masters; whilst the free Indians, on the contrary, are bold, active and clamorous. They differ as widely from each other as the bull from the ox.[48]

The repast is now brought in, consisting of venison, stewed with bear's oil, fresh corn cakes, milk and homony, and our drink honey and water, very cool and agreeable. After partaking of this banquet, we took leave and departed for the great savanna.

[190] Soon after sun-rise, a party of Indians on horse-back, appeared upon the savanna, to collect together several herds of cattle which they drove along near our camp, towards the town. One of the party came up and informed us the cattle belonged to the chief of Cuscowilla, that he had ordered some of the best steers of his droves to be slaughtered for a general feast for the whole town, in compliment of our arrival, and pacific negotiations.[49]

The cattle were as large and fat as those of the rich grazing pastures of Moyomensing in Pennsylvania. The Indians drove off the lowing herds, and we soon followed them to town, in order to be at council at the appointed hours, leaving two young men of our party to protect our camp.

[191] Upon our arrival we repaired to the public square or council-house, where the chiefs and senators were already convened, the warriors and young men assembled soon after, the business being transacted in public. As it was no more than a ratification of the late treaty of St. Augustine, with some particular commercial stipulations, with respect to the citizens of Alachua, the negociations soon terminated to the satisfaction of both parties.

The banquet succeeds; the ribs and choisest fat pieces of the bullocks, excellently well barbecued, are brought into the apartment of the public square, constructed and appointed for feasting; bowls and kettles of stewed flesh and broth are brought in for the next course, and with it a very singular dish, the traders call it tripe soup; it is made of the belly or paunch of the beef, not overcleansed of its contents, cut and minced pretty fine, and then made into a thin soup, seasoned well with salt and aromatic herbs; but the seasoning not quite strong enough to extinguish its original savour and scent. This dish is greatly esteemed by the Indians, but is, in my judgment, the least agreeable they have amongst them.

The town of Cuscowilla, which is the capital of the Alachua tribe, contains about thirty habitations, each of which consists of two houses nearly the same size, about thirty feet in length, twelve feet wide, and about the same in height; the door is placed midway on one side or in the front; this house is divided equally, across, into two apartments, one of which is the cook room[50] and common hall, and the other their lodging room. The other house is nearly of the same dimensions, standing about twenty yards from the dwelling house, its end fronting [192] the door; this building is two stories high, and constructed in a different manner, it is divided transversly, as the other, but the end next the dwelling house is open on three sides, supported by posts or pillars, it has an open loft or platform, the ascent to which, is by a portable stairs or ladder; this is a pleasant, cool, airy situation, and here the master or chief of the family, retires to repose in the hot seasons, and receives his guests or visitors: the other half of this building is closed on all sides by notched logs; the lowest or ground part is a potatoe house, and the upper story over it a granary for corn and other provisions. Their houses are constructed of a kind of frame; in the first place, strong corner pillars are fixed in the ground, with others somewhat less, ranging on a line between; these are strengthened by cross pieces of timber, and the whole with the roof is covered close with the bark of the Cypress tree. This dwelling stands near the middle of a square yard, encompassed by a low bank, formed with the earth taken out of the yard, which is always carefully swept.[51] Their towns are clean, the inhabitants being particular in laying their filth at a proper distance from their dwellings, which undoubtedly contributes to the healthiness of their habitations.

The town stands on the most pleasant situation, that could be well imagined or desired, in an inland country; upon a high swelling ridge of sand hills, within three or four hundred yards of a large and beautiful lake, . . . [193] At present the ground betwixt the town and the lake is adorned by an open grove of very tall Pine trees, which standing at a considerable distance from each other, admit a delightful prospect of the sparkling waters. The lake abounds with various excellent fish and wild fowl; there are incredible numbers of the latter, especially in the winter season, when they arrive here from the North to winter.

The Indians abdicated the ancient Alachua town on the borders of the savanna, and built here, calling the new town Cuscowilla; their reasons for removing their habitation were on account of its unhealthiness, occasioned, as they say, by the stench of the putrid fish and reptiles in the summer and autumn, driven on shore by the alligators, and the exhalations from marshes of the savanna, together with the persecution of the musquitoes.

They plant but little here about the town, only a small garden spot at each habitation, consisting of a little Corn, Beans, Tobacco[,] Citruls, &c. their plantations which supply them with the chief of their vegetable provisions, such as Zea, Convolvulus batata, Cucurbita citrulus, Cuc. laginaria, Cuc. pepo, Cuc. melopepo, Cuc. verrucosa, Dolichos varieties, &c.[52] lies on the rich prolific lands bordering on the great Alachua savanna, about two miles distance, which plantation is one common in-[194]closure, and is worked and tended by the whole community; yet every family has its particular part, according to its own appointment, marked off when planted, and this portion receives the common labour and assistance until ripe, when each family gathers and deposits in its granary its own proper share, setting apart a small gift or contribution for the public granary, which stands in the centre of the plantation.[53]

The youth, under the supervisal of some of their ancient people, are daily stationed in their fields, who are continually whooping and hallooing, to chase away crows, jackdaws, black-birds and such predatory animals, and the lads are armed with bows and arrows, who, being trained up to it from their early youth, are sure at a mark, and in the course of the day load themselves with squirrels, birds, &c. The men in turn patrole the Corn fields at night, to protect their provisions from the depredations of night rovers, as bears, raccoons and deer; the two former being immoderately fond of young Corn, when the grain is filled with a rich milk, as sweet and nourishing as cream, and the deer are as fond of the Potatoe vines.

After the feast was over, we returned to our encampment on the great savanna, towards the evening. Our companions, whom we left at the camp, were impatient for our return, having been out horse hunting in the plains and groves during our absence. They soon left us, on a visit to the town, having there some female friends, with whom they were anxious to renew their acquaintance. The Siminole girls are by no means destitute of charms to please the rougher sex: the white traders, are fully sensible how greatly it is for their advantage [195] to gain their affections and friendship in matters of trade and commerce; and if their love and esteem for each other is sincere, and upon principles of reciprocity, there are but few instances of their neglecting or betraying the interests and views of their temporary husbands; they labour and watch constantly to promote their private interests, and detect and prevent any plots or evil designs which may threaten their persons, or operate against their trade or business.

Bartram, accompanied by the "old trader," continued his circuit of the Alachua savanna.

[198] Passing through a great extent of ancient Indian fields, now grown over with forests of stately trees, Orange groves and luxuriant herbage. The old trader, my associate, informed me it was the ancient Alachua, the capital of that famous and powerful tribe, who peopled the hills surrounding the savanna, when, in days of old, they could assemble by thousands at ball play and other juvenile diversions and athletic exercises, over those, then, happy fields and green plains; and there is no reason to doubt of his account being true, as almost every step we take over those fertile heights, discovers remains and traces of ancient human habitations and cultivation.

The last evening on the Alachua savanna, Bartram and the trader were rejoined by their traveling companions, who brought with them

[207] . . . some Indians, who were merry, agreeable guests as long as they staid;

they were in full dress and painted, but before dark they mounted their horses, which were of the true Siminole breed, set spurs to them, uttering all at once a shrill whoop, and went off for Cuscowilla.

The travelers followed a branch of the "[208] old Spanish highway"[54] back to Spalding's Lower Store.

[209] Passed by an Indian village situated on this high, airy sand ridge, consisting of four or five habitations; none of the people were at home, they were out at their hunting camps; we observed plenty of corn in their cribs.[55] Following a hunting path eight or nine miles, through a vast Pine forest and grassy savanna, well timbered, the ground covered with a charming carpet of various flowering plants, came to a large creek of excellent water, and here we found the encampment of the Indians, the inhabitants of the little town we had passed; we saw their women and children, the men being out hunting. The women presented themselves to our view as we came up, at the door of their tents, veiled in their mantle, modestly shewing their faces when we saluted them.

[210] At this time the talks (or messages between the Indians and white people) were perfectly peaceable and friendly, both with the Lower Creeks and the Nation or Upper Creeks;[56] parties of Indians were coming in every day with their hunts: indeed the Muscogulges or Upper Creeks very seldom disturb us. Bad talks from the Nation is always a very serious affair, and to the utmost degree alarming to the white inhabitants.

The Muscogulges are under a more strict government or regular civilization than the Indians in general. They lie near their potent and declared enemy, the Chactaws; their country having a vast frontier, naturally accessible and open to the incursions of their enemies on all sides, they find themselves under the necessity of associating in large, populous towns, and these towns as near together as convenient that they may be enabled to succour and defend one another in case of sudden invasion; this consequently occasions dear and bear to be scarce and difficult to procure, which obliges them to be vigilent and industrious; this naturally begets care and serious attention, which we may suppose in some degree forms their natural disposition and manners, and gives them that air of dignified gravity, so strikingly characteristic in their aged people, and that steadiness, just and chearful reverence in the middle aged and youth, which sits so easy upon them, and appears so natural: for however strange it may appear to us, the same moral duties which with us form the amiable, virtuous character, and is so diffi-[211]cult to maintain, there, without compulsion or visible restraint, operates like instinct, with a surprising harmony and natural ease, insomuch that it seems impossible for them to act out of the common high-road to virtue.

We will now take a view of the Lower Creeks or Siminoles, and the natural disposition which characterises this people, when, from the striking contrast, the philosopher may approve or disapprove, as he may think proper, from the judgment and opinion given by different men.

The Siminoles, but a weak people, with respect to numbers, all of them I suppose would not be sufficient to people one of the towns in the Muscogulge (for instance, the Uches on the main branch of the Apalachucla river, which alone contains near two thousand inhabitants.)[57] Yet this handful of people possesses a vast territory, all East Florida and the greatest part of West Florida, which being naturally cut and divided into thousands of islets, knolls and eminences, by the innumerable rivers, lakes, swamps, vast savannas and ponds, form so many secure retreats and temporary dwelling places, that effectually guard them from any sudden invasions or attacks from their enemies; and being such a swampy, hommocky country, furnishes such a plenty and variety of supplies for the nourishment of varieties of animals, that I can venture to assert, that no part of the globe so abounds with wild game or creatures fit for the food of man.

Thus they enjoy a superabundance of the necessaries and conveniencies of life, with the security of person and property, the two great concerns of mankind. The hides of deer, bears, tigers and [212] wolves,[58] together with honey, wax and other productions of the country, purchase their cloathing, equipage and domestic utensils from the whites. They seem to be free from want or desires. No cruel enemy to dread; nothing to give them disquietude, but the gradual encroachments of the white people. Thus contented and undisturbed, they appear as blithe and free as the birds of the air, and like them as volatile and active, tuneful and vociferous. The visage, action and deportment of a Siminole, being the most striking picture of happiness in this life; joy, contentment, love and friendship, without guile or affectation, seem inherent in them, or predominant in their vital principle, for it leaves them but with the last breath of life. It even seems imposing a constraint upon their ancient chiefs and senators, to maintain a necessary decorum and solemnity, in their public councils; not even the debility and decrepitude of extreme old age, is sufficient to erase from their visages, this youthful, joyous simplicity; but like the grey eve of a serene and calm day, a gladdening, cheering blush remains on the Western horizon after the sun is set.

I doubt not but some of my countrymen who may read these accounts of the Indians, which I have endeavoured to relate according to truth, at least as they appeared to me, will charge me with partiality or prejudice in their favour.

I will, however, now endeavour to exhibit their vices, immoralities and imperfections, from my own observations and knowledge, as well as accounts from the white traders, who reside amongst them.

[213] The Indians make war against, kill and destroy their own species, and their motives spring from the same erroneous source as it does in all other nations of mankind; that is, the ambition of exhibiting to their fellows, a superior character of personal and national valour, and thereby immortalize themselves, by transmitting their names with honour and lustre to posterity; or in revenge of their enemy, for public or personal insults; or lastly, to extend the borders and boundaries of their territories: but I cannot find upon the strictest enquiry, that their bloody contests, at this day are marked with deeper stains of inhumanity or savage cruelty, than what may be observed amongst the most civilized nations: they do indeed scalp their slain enemy, but they do not kill the females or children of either sex: the most ancient traders, both in the Lower and Upper Creeks, assured me they never saw an instance of either burning or tormenting their male captives; though it is said they used to do it formerly. I saw in every town in the Nation and Siminoles that I visited, more or less male captives, some extremely aged, who were free and in as good circumstances as their masters; and all slaves have their freedom when they ma[rr]y, which is permitted and encouraged; when they and their offspring, are every way upon an equality with their conquerors; they are given to adultery and fornication, but I suppose in no greater excess than other nations of men. They punish the delinquents, male and female, equally alike, by taking off their ears. This is the punishment for adultery.[59] Infamy and disgrace is supposed to be a sufficient punishment for fornication, in either sex.

They are fond of games and gambling, and a-[214]muse themselves like children, in relating extravagant stories, to cause surprise and mirth.

They wage eternal war against deer and bear, to procure food and clothing, and other necessaries and conveniences; which is indeed carried to an unreasonable and perhaps criminal excess, since the white people have dazzled their senses with foreign superfluities.[60]

From mid-June to mid-July 1774, Bartram made another excursion with a party of traders from Spalding's Lower Store to visit "Talahasochte or White King's Town" on the Suwanee River.[61]

[215] The trading company for Talahasochte being now in readiness to proceed for that quarter, under the direction of our chief trader, in the cool of the morning we sat off, each of us having a good horse to ride, besides having in our caravan several pack horses laden with provisions, camp equipage and other necessaries; a young man from St. Augustine, in the service of the governor of East Florida accompanied us, commissioned to purchase of the Indians and

traders, some Siminole horses. They are the most beautiful and sprightly species of that noble creature, perhaps any where to be seen; but are of a small breed, and as delicately formed as the American roe buck. A horse in the Creek or Mus-[216]cogulge tongue is echoclucco, that is the great deer (echo is a deer and clucco is big:) the Siminole horses are said to descend originally from the Andalusian breed, brought here by the Spaniards when they first established the colony of East Florida. From the forehead to their nose is a little arched or aquiline, and so are the fine Chactaw horses among the Upper Creeks, which are said to have been brought thither from New-Mexico across Mississippi, by those nations of Indians who emigrated from the West, beyond the river. These horses are every way like the Siminole breed, only being larger, and perhaps not so lively and capricious. It is a matter of conjecture and enquiry, whether or not the different soil and situation of the country, may have contributed in some measure, in forming and establishing the difference in size and other qualities betwixt them. I have observed the horses and other animals in the high hilly country of Carolina, Georgia, Virginia and all along our shores, are of a much larger and stronger make, than those which are bred in the flat country next the sea coast; a buck-skin of the Upper Creeks and Cherokees will weigh twice as heavy as those of the Siminoles or Lower Creeks, and those bred in the low flat country of Carolina.[62]

Skirting the Alachua savanna, the travelers passed herds of grazing Seminole horses on the savannas near Talahasochte.

[222] In this extensive lawn were several troops of horse, and our company had the satisfaction of observing several belonging to themselves. One occurrance, remarkable here, was a troop of horse under the controul and care of a single black dog, which seemed to differ in no respect from the wolf of Florida, except his being able to bark as the common dog. He was very careful and industrious in keeping them toge-[223]ther, and if any one strolled from the rest at too great a distance, the dog would spring up, head the horse and bring him back to the company. The proprietor of these horses is an Indian in Talahasochte, about ten miles distance from this place, who, out of humour and experiment, trained his dog up from a puppy to this business; he follows his master's horses only, keeping them in a separate company where they range, and when he is hungry or wants to see his master, in the evening he returns to town, but never stays at home a night.[63]

[226] On our arrival at Talahasochte,[64] in the evening we repaired to the trading house formerly belonging to our chief, where were a family of Indians, who immediately and complaisantly moved out to accommodate us. The White

60
―――――
Travels
Through
North
&
South
Carolina

King with most of the male inhabitants were out hunting or tending their Corn plantations.

The town is delightfully situated on the elevated East banks of the river, the ground level to near the river, when it descends suddenly to the water; [227] I suppose the perpendicular elevation of the ground may be twenty or thirty feet. There are near thirty habitations constructed after the mode of Cuscowilla; but here is a more spacious and neat council-house.

These Indians have large handsome canoes, which they form out of the trunks of Cypress trees (Cupressus disticha) some of them commodious enough to accomodate twenty or thirty warriors. In these large canoes they descend the river on trading and hunting expeditions on the sea coast, neighbouring islands and keys, quite to the point of Florida, and sometimes cross the gulph, extending their navigations to the Bahama islands and even to Cuba: a crew of these adventurers had just arrived, having returned from Cuba but a few days before our arrival, with a cargo of spirituous liquors, Coffee, Sugar and Tobacco. One of them politely presented me with a choice piece of Tobacco, which he told me he had received from the governor of Cuba.[65]

They deal in the way of barter, carrying with them deer skins, furs, dry fish, bees-wax, honey, bear's oil and some other articles. They say the Spaniards receive them very friendly, and treat them with the best spirituous liquors.

The Spaniards of Cuba likewise trade here or at St. Marks, and other sea ports on the West coast of the isthmus in small sloops; particularly at the bay of Calos, where are excellent fishing banks and grounds; not far from which is a considerable town of the Siminoles, where they take great quantities of fish, which they salt and cure on shore, and barter with the Indians and traders for skins, furs, &c. and return with their cargoes to Cuba.[66]

[228] The trader of the town of Talahasochte informed me, that he had, when trading in that town, large supplies of goods, from these Spanish trading vessels, suitable for that trade; and some very essential articles, on more advantageous terms than he could purchase at Indian stores either in Georgia or St. Augustine.

Towards the evening after the sultry heats were past, a young man of our company, having previously procured the loan of a canoe from an Indian, proposed to me a fishing excursion for trout with the bob. We sat off down the river, and before we had passed two miles caught enough for our hous[e]hold: he was an excellent hand at this kind of diversion; some of the fish were so large and strong in their element, as to shake his arms stoutly and dragged us with the canoe over the floods before we got them in. It is in the eddy coves, under the points and turnings of the river, where the surface of the waters for some acres is covered with the leaves of the Nymphea, Pistia and other amphibious herbs and grass, where the haunts and retreats of this famous fish are, as well as others of various tribes.

Observing a fishing canoe of Indians turning a point below and coming towards us, who hailing us, we waited their coming up; they were cheerful merry fellows, and insisted on our accepting of part of their fish, they having a greater quantity and variety, especially of the bream my favourite fish; we exchanged some of our trout with them.

Our chief being engaged with the chiefs of the town in commercial concerns, and others of our company, out in the forests with the Indians, hunt-[229]ing up horses belonging to the trading company; the young interpreter, my companion, who was obliging to me and whom our chief previously recommended to me as an associate; proposed to me another little voyage down the river; this was agreeable to me, being desirous of increasing my observations during our continuance at Talahasochte; as when the White King should return to town (which was expected every hour) we intended after audience and treaty to leave them and encamp in the forests, about fifteen miles distance and nearer the range of their horses.

Bartram and the interpreter, a white trader, went to Manatee Spring, where they saw the skeleton of a manatee killed by the Indians the previous winter. According to the trader, "[231] . . . the flesh of this crea-[232]ture is counted wholesome and pleasant food; the Indians call them by a name which signifies the big beaver." They then rode westward,

[232] . . . sometimes falling into, and keeping for a time, the ancient Spanish high road to Pensacola, now almost obliterated: passed four or five miles through old Spanish fields.

[233] There are to be seen plain marks or vestiges of the old Spanish plantations and dwellings; as fence posts and wooden pillars of their houses, ditches and even Corn ridges and Batata hills. From the Indian accounts, the Spaniards had here a rich, well cultivated and populous settlement, and a strong fortified post, as they likewise had at the savanna and fields of Capola; but either of them far inferior to one they had some miles farther South-West towards the Apalachuchla River, now called the Apalachean Old Fields, where yet remain vast works and buildings, as fortifications, temples, some brass cannon, mortars, heavy church bells, &c.[67]

On their return to Talahasochte, they again crossed the "[234] . . . ancient Spanish high way" to Pensacola, "which is open like a magnificent avenue, and the Indians have a bad road or pathway on it."

[235] At length, towards evening, we turned about and came within sight of the river, where falling on the Indian trading path, we continued along it to the landing-place opposite the town, when hallooing and discharging our pieces, an Indian with a canoe came presently over and conducted us to the town before dark.

On our arrival at the trading house, our chief was visited by the head men of the town, when instantly the White King's arrival in town was anounced; a messenger had before been sent in to prepare a feast, the king and his retinue having killed several bears. A fire is now kindled in the [236] area of the public square; the royal standard is displayed, and the drum beats to give notice to the town of the royal feast.[68]

The ribs and the choice pieces of the three great fat bears already well barbecued or broiled, are brought to the banqueting house in the square, with hot bread; and honeyed water for drink.

When the feast was over in the square, (where only the chiefs and warriors were admitted, with the white people) the chief priest, attended by slaves, came with baskets and carried off the remainder of the victuals &c. which was distributed amongst the families of the town; the king then withdrew, repairing to the council house in the square, whither the chiefs and warriors, old and young, and such of the whites as chose, repaired also; the king, war-chief and several ancient chiefs and warriors were seated on the royal cabins, the rest of the head men and warriors, old and young, sat on the cabins on the right hand of the king's, and the cabins or seats on the left, and on the same elevation are always assigned for the white people, Indians of other towns, and such of their own people as chose.

Our chief, with the rest of the white people in town, took their seats according to order; Tobacco and pipes are brought, the calamut[69] is lighted and smoaked, circulating according to the usual forms and ceremony, and afterwards black drink[70] concluded the feast. The king conversed, drank Cassine and associated familiarly with his people and with us.

After the public entertainment was over, the young people began their music and dancing in the [237] square, whither the young of both sexes repaired, as well as the old and middle aged: this frolick continued all night.

The White King of Talahasochte is a middle aged man, of moderate stature, and though of a lofty and majestic countenance and deportment, yet I am convinced this dignity which really seems graceful, is not the effect of vain supercilious pride, for his smiling countenance and his cheerful familiarity bespeak magnanimity and benignity.

Next a council and treaty was held, they requested to have a trading house again established in the town, assuring us that every possible means should constantly be pursued to prevent any disturbance in future on their part; they informed us that the murderers of M'Gee * and his associates, were to be put to death, that two of them were already shot, and they were in pursuit of the other.

Our chief trader in answer, informed them that the re-establishment of friendship and trade was the chief object of his visit, and that he was happy to find his old friends of Talahasochte in the same good disposition, as they ever were towards him and the white people, that it was his wish to trade with them, and that he was now come to collect his pack-horses to bring them goods. The king and the chiefs having been already acquainted with my business and pursuits amongst them, received me very kindly; the king in particular complimented me, [238] saying that I was as one of his own children or people, and should be protected accordingly, while I remained with them, adding, "Our whole country is before you, where you may range about at pleasure, gather physic plants and flowers, and every other production," thus the treaty terminated friendly and peaceably.

The traders' packhorse caravan made camp outside Talahasochte, in preparation for the return trip to Spalding's Lower Store.

[241] Early in the morning our chief invited me with him on a visit to the town, to take a final leave of the White King. We were graciously received, and treated with the utmost civility and hospitality; there was a noble entertainment and repast provided against our arrival, consisting of bears ribs, venison, varieties of fish, roasted turkies (which they call the white man's dish) [,] hot corn cakes, and a very agreeable, cooling sort of jelly, which they call conte; this is prepared from the root of the China brier (Smilax pseudo China . . . ;) they chop the roots in pieces, which are afterwards well pounded in a wooden mortar, then being mixed with clean water, in a tray or trough, they strain it through baskets, the sediment, which settles to the bottom of the second vessel, is afterwards dried in the open air, and is then a very fine, reddish flour or meal; a small quantity of this mixed with warm water and sweetened with honey, when cool, becomes a beautiful, delicious jelly, very nourishing and wholesome; they also mix it with fine Corn flour, which being fried in fresh bear's oil makes very good hot cakes or fritters.[71]

On our taking leave of the king and head men, they intreated our chief to represent to the white people, their unfeigned desire to bury in oblivion the

---

* M'Gee was the leader of a family of white people from Georgia, destined across the isthmus, to the Mobile river; they travelled on horse-back as far as this town, where they procured canoes of the Indians, continuing their travels, descending the river and coasting the main S.W. but at night, when on shore hunting provisions, their camp was surprised and attacked by a predatory band of Indians, who slew M'Gee and the rest of the men and carried off the plunder and a woman to their towns.

late breach of amity and intermission of commerce, which they trusted would never be reflected on the people of Talahasochte; and lastly, [242] that we would speedily return with merchandize as heretofore; all which was cheerfully consented to, assuring them their wishes and sentiments fully coincided with ours.

[244] Soon after entering the forests, we were met in the path by a small company of Indians, smiling and beckoning to us long before we joined them; this was a family of Talahasochte who had been out on a hunt, and were returning home loaded with barbecued meat, hides and honey; their company consisted of the man, his wife and children, well mounted on fine horses, with a number of pack-horses; the man presently offered us a fawn-skin[72] of honey, which we gladly accepted, and at parting I presented him with some fish hooks, sewing needles, &c. For in my travels amongst the Indians, I always furnished myself with such useful and acceptable little articles of light carriage, for presents; we parted and before night rejoined our companions at the Long Pond.

On our return to camp in the evening, we were saluted by a party of young Indian warriors, who had pitched their camp on a green eminence near the lake, and at a small distance from our camp, under a little grove of Oaks and Palms. This company consisted of seven young Siminoles, under the conduct of a young prince or chief of Talahasochte, a town Southward in the isthmus, they were all dressed and painted with singular elegance, and richly ornamented with silver plates, chains, &c. after the Siminole mode, with waving plumes of feathers on their crests.[73] On our coming up to them they arose and shook hands; we alighted and sat awhile with them by their cheerful fire.

The young prince informed our chief, that he was in pursuit of a young fellow, who had fled from the town, carrying off with him one of his favourite young wives or concubines; he said merrily he would have the ears of both of them before [245] he returned; he was rather above the middle stature, and the most perfect human figure I ever saw; of an amiable engaging countenance, air and deportment; free and familiar in conversation, yet retaining a becoming gracefulness and dignity. We arose, took leave of them, and crossed a little vale covered with a charming green turf, already illumined by the soft light of the full moon.

Soon after joining our companions at camp, our neighbours the prince and his associates paid us a visit; we treated them with the best fare we had, having till this time preserved some of our spirituous liquors; they left us with perfect cordiality and cheerfulness, wishing us a good repose, and retired to their own camp, having a band of music with them, consisting of a drum, flutes and a rattle gourd, they entertained us during the night with their music, vocal and instrumental.

There is a languishing softness and melancholy air in the Indian convivial songs, especially of the amorous class, irresistibly moving, attractive, and exquisitely pleasing, especially in these solitary recesses when all nature is silent.

On the return trip, Bartram and his companions stopped to explore some sinkholes, descending into them with the assistance of "[247] . . . a long snagged sapling, called an Indian ladder. . . ." Upon arriving at the trading house, he immediately sailed up the St. Johns to explore Lake George again. He was back at Spalding's Lower Store by the end of July 1774.

[255] At the trading-house I found a very large party of the Lower Creeks encamped in a grove, just without the pallisadoes; this was a predatory band of the Siminoles, consisting of about forty warriors destined against the Chactaws of West Florida. They had just arrived here from St. Augustine, where they had been with a large troop of horses for sale, and furnished themselves with a very liberal supply of spirituous liquors, about twenty kegs, each containing five gallons.

These sons of Mars had the continence and fortitude to withstand the temptation of even tasting a drop of it until their arrival here, where they purposed to supply themselves with necessary articles to equip them for the expedition, and proceed on directly; but here meeting with our young traders and pack-horse men, they were soon prevailed on to broach their beloved nectar; which in the end caused some disturbance, and the consumption of most of their liquor, for after they had once got a smack of it, they never were sober for ten days, and by that time there was but little left.

In a few days this festival exhibited one of the most ludicrous bachanalian scenes that is possible to be conceived, white and red men and women without distinction, passed the day merrily with these jovial, amorous topers, and the nights in convivial songs, dances and sacrifices to Venus, as long as they could stand or move; for in these frolicks both sexes take those liberties with each other, and [256] act, without constraint or shame, such scenes as they would abhor when sober or in their senses; and would endanger their ears and even their lives; but at last their liquor running low, and being most of them sick through intoxication, they became more sober, and now the dejected lifeless sots would pawn every thing they were in possession of, for a mouthful of spirits to settle their stomachs, as they termed it. This was the time for the wenches to make their market, as they had the fortitude and subtilty by dissimulation and artifice to save their share of the liquor during the frolick, and that by a very singular stratagem, for, at these riots, every fellow who joins in the club, has his own quart bottle of rum in his hand, holding it by the neck so sure that he never looses hold of it day or night, drunk or sober, as long as the frolick continues, and with this, his beloved friend, he roves about continually, singing, roaring and reeling to and fro, either alone or arm in arm with a brother toper, presenting his bottle to every one, offering a drink, and is sure to meet his beloved female if he can, whom he complaisantly begs to drink with him, but the modest fair, veiling her face in a mantle, refuses (at the beginning of the frolick) but he presses and at last insists; she being furnished with an empty bottle, concealed in her mantle, at last consents, and taking a good long draught, blushes, drops her pretty face on her bosom and artfully discharges the rum into her bottle, and by repeating this artifice soon fills it; this she privately conveys to her secret store, and then returns to the jovial game, and so on during the festival; and when the comic farce is over, the wench retails this precious cordial to them at her own price.[74]

[257] There were a few of the chiefs, particularly the Long Warrior [figures 12 and 13] their leader, who had the prudence and fortitude to resist the alluring temptation during the whole farce; but though he was a powerful chief, a king and a very cunning man, he was not able to controul these madmen, although he was acknowledged by the Indians to have communion with powerful invisible beings or spirits, and on that account esteemed worthy of homage and great respect.

After the Indians became sober they began to prepare for their departure; in the morning early the Long Warrior and chiefs sent a messenger to Mr. M'Latche,[75] desiring to have a talk with him upon matters of moment; accordingly about noon they arrived; the conference was held in the piazza of the council house; the Long Warrior and chiefs who attended him, took their seats upon a long bench adjoining the side or front of the house, reaching the whole length of it, on one hand; and the principal white traders on the other, all on the same seat; I was admitted at this conference, Mr. M'Latche and the Long Warrior sat next to each other, my late companion, the old trader and myself sat next to him.

The Long Warrior spake, saying, that he and his companions were going to fight their enemies the Chactaws, and that some of his associates being in want of blankets, shirts and some other articles, which they declined supplying themselves with at St. Augustine, because they had rather stick close to their old friend Mr. Spalding, and bring their buckskins, furs and other produce of their country to his trading house, (which they knew [258] were acceptable) to purchase what they wanted; But not having the skins, &c. with them to pay for such things as they had occasion for, yet doubted not, but that on their return, they should bring with them sufficient not only to pay their debts, about to be contracted, but be able to make other considerable purchases, as the principal object of this expedition was hunting on the plentiful borders of the Chactaws.[76] Mr. M'Latche hesitating, and expressing some dissatisfaction at his request;

Figure 12. William Bartram's Drawing of "Mico-chlucco." On the reverse of the original drawing, Bartram made the following notation: "should be twelve feathers in the Eagle's Tail or ensigne." This correction is evident in the published version, which appeared as the Frontispiece for *Travels* in 1791 (fig. 13) (original drawing courtesy, American Philosophical Society, B. S. Barton-Delafield Collection)

Figure 13. Frontispiece for the 1791 Philadelphia Edition of *Travels*

particularly at the length of time and great uncertainty of obtaining pay for the goods, and moreover his being only an agent for Messrs. Spalding & Co. and the magnitude and unprecedented terms of the Long Warrior's demands, required the company's assent and directions before he could comply with their request.

This answer displeased the Indian chief, and I observed great agitation and tumult in his passions, from his actions, hurry and rapidity of speech and expression; the old interpreter who sat by asked me if I fully understood the debate, I answered that I apprehended the Long Warrior was displeased, he told me he was so, and then recapitulated what has been said respecting his questions and Mr. M'Latche's answer; adding that upon his hesitation he immediately replied, in seeming disgust and great expressions of anger, "Do you presume to refuse me credit; certainly you know who I am and what power I have; but perhaps you do not know that if the matter required it, and I pleased, that I could command and cause the terrible thunder * now rolling in the skies above, to descend [259] upon your head, in rapid fiery shafts, and lay you prostrate at my feet, and consume your stores, turning them instantly into dust and ashes." Mr. M'Latche calmly replied, that he was fully sensible that the Long Warrior was a great man, a powerful chief of the bands of the respectable Siminoles, that his name was terrible to his enemies, but still he doubted if any man upon earth had such power, but rather believed that thunder and lightning was under the direction of the Great Spirit, but however, since we are not disposed to deny your power, supernatural influence and intercourse with the elements and spiritual agents, or withhold the respect and homage due to so great a prince of the Siminoles, friends and allies to the white people; if you think fit now in the presence of us all here, command and cause yon terrible thunder with its rapid fiery shafts, to descend upon the top of that Live Oak † in front of us, rend it in pieces, scatter his brawny limbs on the earth and consume them to ashes before our eyes, we will then own your supernatural power and dread your displeasure.

After some silence the prince became more calm and easy, and returned for answer, that recollecting the former friendship and good understanding, which had ever subsisted betwixt the white people and red people of the Siminole bands, and in particular, the many acts of friendship and kindness received from Mr. M'Latche, he would look over this affront; he acknowledged his reasoning and expostulations to be just and manly, that he should suppress his resentment, and withhold his power and vengeance at present. Mr. M'Latche concluded, by saying that he was not [260] in the least intimidated by his threats of destroying him with thunder and lightning, neither was he disposed

---

* It thundered, lightened and rained in a violent manner during these debates.
† A large ancient Live Oak stood in the yard about fifty yards distance.

in any manner to displease the Siminoles, and should certainly comply with his requisitions, as far as he could proceed without the advice and directions of the company, and finally agreed to supply him and his followers with such things as they stood most in need of, such as shirts, blankets and some paints, one half to be paid for directly, and the remainder to stand on credit until their return from the expedition. This determination entirely satisfied the Indians. We broke up the conference in perfect amity and good humour, and they returned to their camp and in the evening, ratified it with feasting and dancing, which continued all next day with tolerable decorum. An occurrence happened this day, by which I had an opportunity of observing their extraordinary veneration or dread of the rattle snake; I was in the forenoon busy in my apartment in the council-house,[77] drawing some curious flowers; when, on a sudden, my attention was taken off by a tumult without, at the Indian camp; I stepped to the door opening to the piazza, where I met my friend the old interpreter, who informed me that there was a very large rattle snake in the Indian camp, which had taken possession of it, having driven the men, women and children out, and he heard them saying that they would send for Puc-Puggy (for that was the name which they had given me, signifying the Flower Hunter) to kill him or take him out of their camp; I answered that I desired to have nothing to do with him, apprehending some disagreeable consequences, and desired that the Indians might be acquainted that I was engaged in business that required application and quiet, and was determined to avoid it if [261] possible; my old friend turned about to carry my answer to the Indians, I presently heard them approaching and calling for Puc-Puggy; starting up to escape from their sight by a back door, a party consisting of three young fellows, richly dressed and ornamented, stepped in, and with a countenance and action of noble simplicity, amity and complaisance, requested me to accompany them to their encampment; I desired them to excuse me at this time; they plead and entreated me to go with them, in order to free them from a great rattle snake which had entered their camp, that none of them had freedom or courage to expel him, and understanding that it was my pleasure to collect all their animals and other natural productions of their land, desired that I would come with them and take him away, that I was welcome to him. I at length consented and attended on them to their encampment, where I beheld the Indians greatly disturbed indeed. The men with sticks and tomahawks, and the women and children collected together at a distance in affright and trepidation, whilst the dreaded and revered serpent leisurely traversed their camp, visiting the fire places from one to another, picking up fragments of their provisions and licking their platters. The men gathered around me, exciting me to remove him: being armed with a lightwood knot, I approached the reptile, who instantly collected himself in a vast coil (their attitude of defence) I cast my missile weapon at him, which luckily taking his head, dispatched him instantly, and laid him trembling at my feet; I took out my knife, severed his head from his body, then turning about, the Indians complimented me with every demonstration of satisfaction and approbation for my heroism, and friendship for them. I carried off [262] the head of the serpent bleeding in my hand as a trophy of victory, and taking out the mortal fangs, deposited them carefully amongst my collections. I had not been long retired to my apartment before I was again roused from it by a tumult in the yard, and hearing Puc-Puggy called on, I started up, when instantly the old interpreter met me again, and told me the Indians were approaching in order to scratch me; I asked him for what; he answered for killing the rattle snake within their camp. Before I could make any reply or effect my escape, three young fellows singing, arm in arm, came up to me; I observed one of the three was a young prince who had, on my first interview with him, declared himself my friend and protector, when he told me that if ever occasion should offer in his presence, he would risk his life to defend mine or my property. This young champion stood by his two associates, one on each side of him, the two affecting a countenance and air of displeasure and importance, instantly presenting their scratching instruments, and flourishing them, spoke boldly, and said that I was too heroic and violent, that it would be good for me to loose some of my blood to make me more mild and tame, and for that purpose they were come to scratch me; they gave me no time to expostulate or reply, but attempted to lay hold on me, which I resisted, and my friend, the young prince, interposed and pushed them off, saying that I was a brave warrior and his friend, that they should not insult me, when instantly they altered their countenance and behaviour; they all whooped in chorus, took me friendly by the hand, clapped me on the shoulder and laid their hands on their breasts in token of sincere friendship, and laughing aloud, said I was a sincere friend to the Siminoles, [263] a worthy and brave warrior, and that no one should hereafter attempt to injure me: they then all three joined arm in arm again and went off, shouting and proclaiming Puc-Puggy was their friend, &c. Thus it seemed that the whole was a ludicrous farce to satisfy their people and appease the manes * of the slain rattle snake.

The next day was employed by the Indians in preparations for their departure, such as taking up their goods from the trading house, collecting together their horses, making up their packs, &c. and the evening joyfully spent in songs and dances. The succeeding morning after exhibiting the war farce they decamped, proceeding on their expedition against their enemy.

[303] After the predatory band of Siminoles, under the conduct of the Long Warrior, had decamped, Mr. M'Latche invited me with him on a visit to an

---

* These people never kill the rattle snake or any other serpent, saying if they do so, the spirit of the killed snake will excite or influence his living kindred or relatives to revenge the injury or violence done to him when alive.[78]

Indian town, about twelve miles distance from the trading-house, to regale ourselves at a feast of Water mellons and Oranges, the Indians having brought a canoe load of them to the trading-house the day preceding, which they disposed of to the traders. This was a circumstance pretty extraordinary to me, it being late in September, a season of the year when the Citruel are ripe and gone in Georgia and Carolina, but here the weather yet continued hot and sultry, and consequently this cool, exhilerating fruit was still in high relish and estimation.

After breakfasting, having each of us a Siminole horse completely equipped, we sat off: the ride was agreeable and variously entertaining; we kept no road or pathway constantly, but as Indian hunting tracks, by chance suited our course, riding through high, open Pine forests, green lawns and flowery savannas in youthful verdure and gaity, having been lately burnt, but now overrun with a green enamelled carpet, checquered with hommocks of trees of dark green foliage, intersected with serpentine rivulets, their banks adorned with shrubberies of various tribes, as Andromeda formosissima, And. nitida, And. virides, And. calyculata, And. axilaris, Halmea spuria, Annona alba, &c. About noon we arrived at the town, the same little village [304] I passed by on my ascent of the river, on the banks of the little lake below Charlotia.[79]

We were received and entertained friendly by the Indians, the chief of the village conducting us to a grand, airy pavilion in the center of the village. It was four square; a range of pillars or posts on each side supporting a canopy composed of Palmetto leaves, woven or thatched together, which shaded a level platform in the center that was ascended to from each side, by two steps or flights, each about twelve inches high, and seven or eight feet in breadth, all covered with carpets or matts, curiously woven of split canes dyed of various colours; here being seated or reclining ourselves, after smoking tobacco, baskets of choicest fruits were brought and set before us.

The fields surrounding the town and groves were plentifully stored with Corn, Citruels, Pumpkins, Squashes, Beans, Peas, Potatoes, Peaches, Figs, Oranges, &c.

In mid-November 1774, Bartram departed by schooner for Frederica, Georgia, after giving his sailing bark to "[305] the old interpreter, Job Wiggens, often my travelling companion, friend and [306] benefactor. . . ." Having made his way eventually to Charleston, he set off, in April 1775,[80] for Silver Bluff, South Carolina, the home of the trader George Galphin. At Silver Bluff, Bartram once again noted "[315] old fields" and "various monuments and vestiges of the residence of the ancients, as Indian conical mounts, terraces, areas, &c. . . ."[81] From John Stuart, he obtained letters of recommendation to present to the British commissary to the Cherokees,

Alexander Cameron, and from George Galphin he obtained a letter of introduction addressed to traders living in the principal Creek towns. He then proceeded to Fort James, in the forks of the Savannah and Broad rivers.[82]

[324] I made a little excursion up the Savanna river, four or five miles above the fort, with the surgeon of the garrison, who was so polite as to attend me to shew me some remarkable Indian monuments, which are worthy of every travellers notice. These wonderful labours of the ancients stand in a level [325] plain, very near the bank of the river, now twenty or thirty yards from it; they consist of conical mounts of earth and four square terraces, &c. The great mount is in the form of a cone, about forty or fifty feet high, and the circumference of its base two or three hundred yards, entirely composed of the loamy rich earth of the low grounds; the top or apix is flat; a spiral path or track leading from the ground up to the top is still visible, where now grows a large, beautiful spreading Red Cedar (Juniperus Americana;) there appears four niches, excavated out of the sides of this hill, at different heights from the base, fronting the four cardinal points; these niches or sentry boxes are entered into from the winding path, and seem to have been ment for resting places or look-outs. The circumjacent level grounds are cleared and planted with Indian Corn at present, and I think the proprietor of these lands, who accompanied us to this place, said that the mount itself yielded above one hundred bushels in one season: the land hereabouts is indeed exceeding fertile and productive.

It is altogether unknown to us, what could have induced the Indians to raise such a heap of earth in this place, the ground for a great space around being subject to inundations, at least once a year, from which circumstance we may conclude they had no town or settled habitations here: some imagine these tumuli were constructed for look-out towers. It is reasonable to suppose, however, that they were to serve some important purpose in those days, as they were public works, and would have required the united labour and attention of a whole nation, circumstanced as they were, to have constructed one of them almost in an age. There are [326] several less ones round about the great one, with some very large tetragon terraces on each side, near one hundred yards in length, and their surface four, six, eight and ten feet above the ground on which they stand.

We may however hazard a conjecture, that as there is generally a narrow space or ridge in these low lands, immediately bordering on the rivers bank, which is eight or ten feet higher than the adjoining low grounds, that lie betwixt the stream and the heights of the adjacent main land, which, when the river overflows its banks, are many feet under water, when, at the same time, this ridge on the river bank is above water and dry, and at such inundations appears as an island in the river. Now these people might have had a town on this ridge, and this mount raised for a retreat and refuge in case of an inundation, which are unforeseen and surprise them very suddenly, spring and autumn.[83]

On the road to the Cherokee town of Keowee, Bartram stayed a few days at "Lough-abber," the plantation of Alexander Cameron, "[326] deputy commissary for Indian affairs for the Cherokee nation. . . ."[84] There, he observed "[327] Angelica lucido or Nondo"[85] growing in abundance; "it is in high estimation with the Indians as well as white inhabitants, and sells at a great price to the Southern Indians of Florida, who dwell near the sea coast where this never grows spontaneously." Bartram soon came to the first of the Lower Cherokee towns, Isu'nigu, or Seneca.

[329] The Cherokee town of Sinica is a very respectable settlement, situated on the East bank of the Keowe river, though the greatest number of Indian habitations are on the opposite shore, where likewise stands the council-house in a level plain betwixt the river and a range of beautiful lofty hills, which rise magnificently, and seem to bend over [330] the green plains and the river; but the chief's house, with those of the traders, and some Indian dwellings are seated on the ascent of the heights on the opposite shore; this situation in point of prospect far excels the other, as it overlooks the whole settlement, the extensive fruitful plains on the river above and below, and the plantations of the inhabitants, commanding a most comprehensive diversified view of the opposite elevations.

Sinica is a new town rebuilt since the late Indian war, when the Cherokees were vanquished and compelled to sue for peace, by general Middleton, commander of the Carolinian auxiliaries acting against them, when the lower and middle settlements were broken up:[86] the number of inhabitants are now estimated at about five hundred, and they are able to muster about one hundred warriors.[87]

Next day I left Sinica alone, and after riding about sixteen miles, chiefly through high forests of excellent land at a little distance from the river, arrived in the evening at fort Prince George Keowe.[88]

Keowe is a most charming situation, and the adjacent heights are naturally so formed and disposed, as with little expence of military architecture to be rendered almost impregnable; . . . .

[331] Abandoned as my situation now was, yet thank heaven many objects met together at this time, and conspired to conciliate, and in some degree compose my mind, heretofore somewhat dejected and unharmonized: all alone in a wild Indian country, a thousand miles from my native land, and a vast

distance from any settlements of white people. It is true, here were some of my own colour, yet they were strangers, and though friendly and hospitable, their manners and customs of living so different from what I had been accustomed to, administered but little to my consolation: some hundred miles yet to travel, the savage vindictive inhabitants lately ill-treated by the frontier Virginians, blood being spilt between them and the injury not yet wiped away by formal treaty; the Cherokees extremely jealous of white people travelling about their mountains, especially if they should be seen peeping in amongst the rocks or digging up their earth.[89]

The vale of Keowe is seven or eight miles in extent, that is from the little town of Kulsage * about a mile above, thence down the river six or seven miles, where a high ridge of hills on each side of the river almost terminates the vale, but opens again below the narrow ridge, and continues ten or twelve [332] miles down to Sinica, and in width one and two miles: this fertile vale within the remembrance of some old traders with whom I conversed, was one continued settlement, the swelling sides of the adjoining hills were then covered with habitations, and the rich level grounds beneath lying on the river, was cultivated and planted, which now exhibit a very different spectacle, humiliating indeed to the present generation, the posterity and feeble remains of the once potent and renowned Cherokees: the vestiges of the ancient Indian dwellings are yet visible on the feet of the hills bordering and fronting on the vale, such as posts or pillars of their habitations, &c.

There are several Indian mounts or tumuli, and terraces, monuments of the ancients, at the old site of Keowe, near the fort Prince George, but no Indian habitations at present; and here are several dwellings inhabited by white people concerned in the Indian trade; Mr. D. Homes is the principal trader here.

The old fort Prince George now bears no marks of a fortress, but serves for a trading house.

[333] I waited two or three days at this post expecting the return of an Indian, who was out hunting; this man was recommended to me as a suitable person for a protector and guide to the Indian settlements over the hills, but upon information that he would not be in shortly, and there being no other person suitable for the purpose, rather than be detained, and perhaps thereby frustrated in my purposes, determined to set off alone and run all risks.

From Keowee, about May 19, 1775, Bartram rode alone into the North Carolina mountains, passing numerous abandoned Lower and Middle Cherokee town sites and old fields.[90] The first he described simply as "[333] the remains of a town of the ancients, as [334] the tumuli, terraces,

* Sugar Town.

posts or pillars, old Peach and Plumb orchards, &c. sufficiently testify." Further on he came to the "[335] ruins of the Occonne town," and "[337] the ruins [338] of a town of the ancients," finally, simply noting that he "[338] observed frequently ruins of the habitations or villages of the ancients." After spending the night in an unoccupied "Indian hunting cabin," Bartram pressed on, passing

[345]. . . the ruins of the ancient famous town of Sticoe.[91] Here was a vast Indian mount or tumulus and great terrace, on which stood the council house, with banks encompassing their circus; here were also old Peach and Plumb orchards, some of the trees appeared yet thriving and fruitful. . . .

From this abundant evidence of abandoned Cherokee settlements, Bartram offered the following generalization.

[346] These swelling hills, the prolific beds on which the towering mountains repose, seem to have been the common situations of the towns of the a[n]cients, as appear from the remaining ruins of them yet to be seen; and the level rich vale and meadows in front, their planting grounds.

At one point along the trading path, where it crossed some rough, rocky ground,

[348] . . . I observed on each side of the road many vast heaps of these stones, Indian graves undoubtedly *.

Bartram then visited Echoe, Nucassi, Watauga, and Sticoe, some of the Middle Towns of the Cherokees.[93]

[349] Thus was my agreeable progress for about fifteen miles, since I came upon the sources of the Tanase,[94] at the head of this charming vale: in the evening espying a human habitation at the foot of the sloping green hills, beneath lofty forests of the mountains on the left hand, and at the same time observed a man crossing the river from the opposite shore in a canoe and coming towards me, I waited his approach, who hailing me, I answered I was for Cowe; he intreated me very civilly to call at his house, adding that he would presently come to me.

* At this place was fought a bloody and decisive battle between these Indians and the Carolinians, under the conduct of general Middleton, when a great number of Cherokee warriors were slain, which shook their power, terrified and humbled them, insomuch that they deserted most of their settlements in the low countries, and betook themselves to the mountains as less accessible to the regular forces of the white people.[92]

I was received and entertained here until next day with the most perfect civility. After I had dined, towards evening, a company of Indian girls, inhabitants of a village in the hills at a small distance, called, having baskets of strawberries; and this man, who kept here a trading-house, and being married to a Cherokee woman of family, was indulged to keep a stock of cattle, and his helpmate being an excellent house-wife and a very agreeable good woman, treated us with cream and strawberries.

Next morning after breakfasting on excellent coffee, relished with bucanned venison, hot corn cakes, excellent butter and cheese, sat forwards again for Cowe, which was about fifteen miles distance, keeping the trading path which coursed through the low lands between the hills and the river, now spacious and well beaten by travellers, [350] but somewhat intricate to a stranger, from the frequent colateral roads falling into it from villages or towns over the hills: after riding about four miles, mostly through fields and plantations, the soil incredibly fertile, arrived at the town of Echoe, consisting of many good houses, well inhabited; I passed through and continued three miles farther to Nucasse, and three miles more brought me to Whatoga: riding through this large town, the road carried me winding about through their little plantations of Corn, Beans, &c. up to the council-house, which was a very large dome or rotunda, situated on the top of an ancient artificial mount, and here my road terminated; all before me and on every side appeared little plantations of young Corn, Beans, &c. divided from each other by narrow strips or borders of grass, which marked the bounds of each one's property, their habitation standing in the midst: finding no common high road to lead me through the town, I was now at a stand how to proceed farther, when observing an Indian man at the door of his habitation, three or four hundred yards distance from me, beckoning to come to him, I ventured to ride through their lots, being careful to do no injury to the young plants, the rising hopes of their labour and industry, crossed a little grassy vale watered by a silver stream, which gently undulated through, then ascended a green hill to the house, where I was cheerfully welcomed at the door and led in by the chief, giving the care of my horse to two handsome youths, his sons. During my continuance here, about half an hour, I experienced the most perfect and agreeable hospitality conferred on me by these happy people; I mean happy in their dispositions, in their apprehensions of rectitude with regard to our social [351] or moral conduct: O divine simplicity and truth, friendship without fallacy or guile, hospitality disinterested, native, undefiled, unmodifyed by artificial refinements.

My venerable host gracefully and with an air of respect, led me into an airy, cool apartment, where being seated on cabins, his women brought in a refreshing repast, consisting of sodden venison, hot corn cakes, &c. with a pleasant cooling liquor made of hommony well boiled, mixed afterwards with milk; this is served up either before or after eating in a large bowl, with a very large spoon or ladle to sup it with.

After partaking of this simple but healthy and liberal collation and the dishes cleared off, Tobacco and pipes were brought, and the chief filling one of them, whose stem, about four feet long, was sheathed in a beautiful speckled snake skin, and adorned with feathers and strings of wampum, lights it and smoaks a few whiffs, puffing the smoak first towards the sun, then to the four cardinal points and lastly over my breast, hands it towards me, which I cheerfully received from him and smoaked, when we fell into conversation; he first enquired if I came from Charleston? if I knew John Stewart, Esq.? how long since I left Charleston? &c. Having satisfied him in my answers in the best manner I could, he was greatly pleased, which I was convinced of by his attention to me, his cheerful manners and his ordering my horse a plentiful bait of corn, which last instance of respect is conferred on those only to whom they manifest the highest esteem, saying that corn was given by the Great Spirit only for food to man.

[352] I acquainted this ancient prince and patriarch of the nature and design of my peregrinations, and that I was now for Cowe, but having lost my road in the town, requested that I might be informed. He cheerfully replied, that he was pleased I was come in their country, where I should meet with friendship and protection, and that he would himself lead me into the right path.

After ordering my horse to the door we went forth together, he on foot and I leading my horse by the bridle, thus walking together near two miles, we shook hands and parted, he returning home and I continuing my journey for Cowe.

This prince is the chief of Whatoga, a man universally beloved, and particularly esteemed by the whites for his pacific and equitable disposition, and revered by all for his exemplary virtues, just, moderate, magnanimous and intrepid.

He was tall and perfectly formed; his countenance cheerful and lofty and at the same time truly characteristic of the red men, that is, the brow ferocious and the eye active, piercing or fiery, as an eagle. He appeared to be about sixty years of age, yet upright and muscular, and his limbs active as youth.

After leaving my princely friend, I travelled about five miles through old plantations, now under grass, but appeared to have been planted the last season; the soil exceeding fertile, loose, black, deep and fat. I arrived at Cowe about noon; this settlement is esteemed the capital town; it is situated on the bases of the hills on both sides of the river, near to its bank, and here terminates the great vale [353] of Cowe, exhibiting one of the most charming natural mountainous landscapes perhaps any where to be seen; ridges of hills rising grand and sublimely one above and beyond another, some boldly and majestically advancing into the verdant plain, their feet bathed with the silver flood of the Tanase, whilst others far distant, veiled in blue mists, sublimely mount aloft, with yet greater majesty lift up their pompous crests and overlook vast regions.

The vale is closed at Cowe by a ridge of mighty hills, called the Jore mountain, said to be the highest land in the Cherokee country, which crosses the Tanase here.

On my arrival at this town I waited on the gentlemen to whom I was recommended by letter, and was received with respect and every demonstration of hospitality and friendship.

I took my residence with Mr. Galahan the chief trader here, an ancient respectable man who had been many years a trader in this country, and is esteemed and beloved by the Indians for his humanity, probity and equitable dealings with them, which to be just and candid I am obliged to observe (and blush for my countrymen at the recital) is somewhat of a prodigy, as it is a fact, I am afraid too true, that the white traders in their commerce with the Indians, give great and frequent occasions of complaint of their dishonesty and violence; but yet there are a few exceptions, as in the conduct of this gentleman, who furnishes a living instance of the truth of the old proverb, that "Honesty is the best policy," for this old honest Hibernian has often been protected by the Indians, when all others round [354] about him have been ruined, their property seized and themselves driven out of the country or slain by the injured, provoked natives.

Next day after my arrival I crossed the river in a canoe, on a visit to a trader who resided amongst the habitations on the other shore.

After dinner, on his mentioning some curious scenes amongst the hills, some miles distance from the river, we agreed to spend the afternoon in observations on the mountains.

After riding near two miles through Indian plantations of Corn, which was well cultivated, kept clean of weeds and was well advanced, being near eighteen inches in height, and the Beans planted at the Corn-hills were above ground; we leave the fields on our right, turning towards the mountains and ascending through a delightful green vale or lawn, which conducted us in amongst the pyramidal hills and crossing a brisk flowing creek, meandering through the meads which continued near two miles, dividing and branching in amongst the hills; we then mounted their steep ascents, rising gradually by ridges or steps one above another, frequently crossing narrow, fertile dales as we ascended; the air feels cool and animating, being charged with the fragrant breath of the mountain beauties, the blooming mountain cluster Rose, blushing Rhododendron and fair Lilly of the valley: having now attained the summit of this very elevated ridge, we enjoyed a fine prospect indeed; the enchanting Vale of Keowe, perhaps as celebrated for fertility, fruitfulness and beautiful prospects as the Fields of Pharsalia or the Vale of Tempe: the town, the elevated peeks of the Jore mountains, a very dis-[355]tant prospect of the Jore village in a beautiful lawn, lifted up many thousand feet higher than our present situation, besides a view of many other villages and settlements on the sides of the mountains, at various distances and elevations; the silver rivulets gliding by them and snow white cataracts glimmering on the sides of the lofty hills; the bold promontories of the Jore mountain stepping into the Tanase river, whilst his foaming waters rushed between them.

After viewing this very entertaining scene we began to descend the mountain on the other side, which exhibited the same order of gradations of ridges and vales as on our ascent, and at length rested on a very expansive, fertile plain, amidst the towering hills, over which we rode a long time, through magnificent high forests, extensive green fields, meadows and lawns. Here had formerly been a very flourishing settlement, but the Indians deserted it in search of fresh planting land, which they soon found in a rich vale but a few miles distance over a ridge of hills. Soon after entering on these charming, sequestered, prolific fields, we came to a fine little river, which crossing, and riding over fruitful strawberry beds and green lawns, on the sides of a circular ridge of hills in front of us, and going round the bases of this promontory, came to a fine meadow on an arm of the vale, through which meandered a brook, its humid vapours bedewing the fragrant strawberries which hung in heavy red clusters over the grassy verge; we crossed the rivulet, then rising a sloping, green, turfy ascent, alighted on the borders of a grand forest of stately trees, which we penetrated on foot a little distance to a horse-stamp, where was a large squadron of those [356] useful creatures, belonging to my friend and companion, the trader, on the sight of whom they assembled together from all quarters; some at a distance saluted him with shrill neighings of gratitude, or came prancing up to lick the salt out of his hand; whilst the younger and more timorous came galloping onward, but coyly wheeled off, and fetching a circuit stood aloof, but as soon as their lord and master strewed the chrystaline salty bait on the hard beaten ground, they all, old and young, docile and timorous, soon formed themselves in ranks and fell to licking up the delicious morsel.

It was a fine sight; more beautiful creatures I never saw; there were of them of all colours, sizes and dispositions. Every year as they become of age he sends off a troop of them down to Charleston, where they are sold to the highest bidder.

Having paid our attention to this useful part of the creation, who, if they are under our dominion, have consequently a right to our protection and favour. We returned to our trusty servants that were regaling themselves in the exuberant sweet pastures and strawberry fields in sight, and mounted again; proceeding on our return to town, continued through part of this high forest skirting on the meadows; began to ascend the hills of a ridge which we were under the necessity of crossing, and having gained its summit, enjoyed a most enchanting view, a vast expanse of green meadows and strawberry fields; a meandering river gliding through, saluting in its various turnings the swelling, green, turfy knolls, embellished with parterres of flowers and fruitful strawberry beds; flocks of turkies strolling about them; herds of deer prancing in the meads [357] or bounding over the hills; companies of young, innocent Cherokee virgins, some busily gathering the rich fragrant fruit, others having already filled their baskets, lay reclined under the shade of floriferous and fragrant native bowers of Magnolia, Azalea, Philadelphus, perfumed Calycanthus, sweet Yellow Jessamine and ceruliam Glycine frutescens, disclosing their beauties to the fluttering breeze, and bathing their limbs in the cool fleeting streams; whilst other parties, more gay and libertine, were yet collecting strawberries or wantonly chasing their companions, tantalising them, staining their lips and cheeks with the rich fruit.

This sylvan scene of primitive innocence was enchanting, and perhaps too enticing for hearty young men long to continue idle spectators.

In fine, nature prevailing over reason, we wished at least to have a more active part in their delicious sports. Thus precipitately resolving, we cautiously made our approaches, yet undiscovered, almost to the joyous scene of action. Now, although we meant no other than an innocent frolic with this gay assembly of hamadryades, we shall leave it to the person of feeling and sensibility to form an idea to what lengths our passions might have hurried us, thus warmed and excited, had it not been for the vigilance and care of some envious matrons who lay in ambush, and espying us gave the alarm, time enough for the nymphs to rally and assemble together; we however pursued and gained ground on a group of them, who had incautiously strolled to a greater distance from their guardians, and finding their retreat now like to be cut off, took shelter under cover of a little grove, but on perceiving themselves to be discovered by us, kept their stati-[358]on, peeping through the bushes; when observing our approaches, they confidently discovered themselves and decently advanced to meet us, half unveiling their blooming faces, incarnated with the modest maiden blush, and with native innocence and cheerfulness, presented their little baskets, merrily telling us their fruit was ripe and sound.

We accepted a basket, sat down and regaled ourselves on the delicious fruit, encircled by the whole assembly of the innocently jocose sylvan nymphs; by this time the several parties under the conduct of the elder matrons, had disposed themselves in companies on the green, turfy banks.

My young companion, the trader, by concessions and suitable apologies for the bold intrusion, having compromised the matter with them, engaged them to bring their collections to his house at a stipulated price, we parted friendly.

And now taking leave of these Elysian fields, we again mounted the hills, which we crossed, and traversing obliquely their flowery beds, arrived in town in the cool of the evening.

[359] After waiting two days at Cowe expecting a guide and protector to the Overhill towns, and at last being disappointed, I resolved to pursue the journey alone, though against the advice of the traders; the Overhill Indians being in an ill humour with the whites, in consequence of some late skirmishes between them and the frontier Virginians, most of the Overhill traders having left the nation.

Early in the morning I sat off attended by my worthy old friend Mr. Gallahan, who obligingly accompanied me near fifteen miles, we passed through the Jore village, which is pleasingly situated in a little vale on the side of the mountain, a pretty rivulet or creek winds about through the vale, just under the village; here I observed a little grove of the Casine yapon, which was the only place I had seen it grow in the Cherokee country,[95] the Indians call it the beloved tree, and are very careful to keep them pruned and cultivated, they drink a very strong infusion of the leaves, buds and tender branches of this plant, which is so celebrated, indeed venerated by the Creeks, and all the Southern maritime nations of Indians; then continued travelling down the vale about two miles, the road deviating, turning and winding about the hills, and through groves and lawns, watered by brooks and rivulets, rapidly rushing from the towering hill on [360] every side, and flowing into the Jore, which is a considerable branch of the Tanase.

Bartram attempted to visit the Overhill towns, across the Nantahala range of the Appalachian Mountains. On May 24, 1775, after riding a few miles,

[361] . . . I took out of my wallet some biscuit and cheese, and a piece of neat's tongue, composing myself to ease and refreshment; when suddenly appeared within a few yards, advancing towards me from behind the point, a stout likely young Indian fellow, armed with a rifle gun, and two dogs attending, [362] upon sight of me he stood, and seemed a little surprised, as I was very much; but instantly recollecting himself and assuming a countenance of benignity and cheerfulness, came briskly to me and shook hands heartily; and smilingly enquired from whence I came, and whither going, but speaking only in the Cherokee tongue, our conversation was not continued to a great length. I presented him with some choice Tobacco, which was accepted with courtesy and evident pleasure, and to my enquiries concerning the roads and dista[n]ce to the Overhill towns, he answered me with perfect cheerfulness and good temper; we then again shook hands and parted in friendship, he descended the hills, singing as he went.

[364] Soon after crossing this large branch of the Tanase, I observed descending the heights at some distance, a company of Indians, all well mounted on horse back; they came rapidly forward; on their nearer approach I observed a chief at the head of the carravan, and apprehending him to be the Little Carpenter, emperor or grand chief of the [365] Cherokees; as they came up I turned off from the path to make way, in token of respect, which compliment was accepted and gratefully and magnanimously returned, for his highness with a gracious and cheerful smile came up to me, and clapping his hand on his breast, offered it to me, saying, I am Ata-cul-culla, and heartily shook hands with me, and asked me if I knew it;[96] I answered that the Good Spirit who goes before me spoke to me, and said, that is the great Ata-cul-culla, and added that I was of the tribe of white men, of Pennsylvania, who esteem themselves brothers and friends to the red men, but particularly so to the Cherokees, and that notwithstanding we dwelt at so great a distance we were united in love and friendship, and that the name of Ata-cul-culla was dear to his white brothers of Pennsylvania.

After this compliment, which seemed to be acceptable, he enquired if I came lately from Charleston, and if John Stewart was well, saying that he was going to see him; I replied that I came lately from Charleston on a friendly visit to the Cherokees; that I had the honour of a personal acquaintance with the superintendant, the beloved man, who I saw well but the day before I sat off, and who, by letters to the principal white men in the nation, recommended me to the friendship and protection of the Cherokees: to which the great chief was pleased to answer very respectfully, that I was welcome in their country as a friend and brother; and then shaking hands heartily bid me farewell, and his retinue confirmed it by an united voice of assent. After giving my name to the chief, requesting my compliments to the superintendant, the emperor moved, continuing his journey for Charles-[366]ton, and I yet persisting in my intentions of visiting the Overhill towns continued on; leaving the great forest I mounted the high hills, descending them again on the other side and so on repeatedly for several miles, without observing any variation in the natural productions since passing the Jore; and observing the slow progress of vegetation in this mountainous, high country; and, upon serious consideration, it appeared very plainly that I could not, with entire safety, range the Overhill settlements until the treaty was over, which would not come on till late in June, I suddenly came to a resolution to defer these researches at this time, and leave them for the employment of another season and a more favourable opportunity, and return to Dartmouth in Georgia, to be ready to join a company of adventurers who were to set off in July for Mobile in West Florida. The leader of this company had been recommended to me as a fit person to assist me on so long and hazardous a journey, through the vast territories of the Creeks.

Therefore next day I turned about on my return, proceeding moderately, being engaged in noting such objects as appeared to be of any moment, and collecting specimens, and in the evening of next day arrived again at Cowe.

Next morning Mr. Galahan conducted me to the chief of Cowe, who during my absence had returned from the chace. The remainder of this day I spent in observations in and about the town, reviewing my specimens, &c.

The town of Cowe consists of about one hundred dwellings, near the banks of the Tanase, on both sides of the river.

[367] The Cherokees construct their habitations[97] on a different plan from the Creeks, that is but one oblong four square building, of one story high; the materials consisting of logs or trunks of trees, stripped of their bark, notched at their ends, fixed one upon another, and afterwards plaistered well, both inside and out, with clay well tempered with dry grass, and the whole covered or roofed with the bark of the Chesnut tree or long broad shingles. This building is however partitioned transversely, forming three apartments, which communicate with each other by inside doors;[98] each house or habitation has besides a little conical house, covered with dirt, which is called the winter or hot-house; this stands a few yards distance from the mansion-house, opposite the front door.

The council or town-house is a large rotunda, capable of accommodating several hundred people; it stands on the top of an ancient artificial mount of earth, of about twenty feet perpendicular, and the rotunda on the top of it being above thirty feet more, gives the whole fabric an elevation of about sixty feet from the common surface of the ground. But it may be proper to observe, that this mount on which the rotunda stands, is of a much ancienter date than the building, and perhaps was raised for another purpose. The Cherokees themselves are as ignorant as we are, by what people or for what purpose these artificial hills were raised; they have various stories concerning them, the best of which amounts to no more than mere conjecture, and leave us entirely in the dark; but they have a tradition common with the other nations of Indians, that they found them in much the same condition as they now appear, when their forefathers arrived [368] from the West and possessed themselves of the country, after vanquishing the nations of red men who then inhabited it, who themselves found these mounts when they took possession of the country, the former possessors delivering the same story concerning them: perhaps they were designed and apropriated by the people who constructed them, to some religious purpose, as great altars and temples similar to the high places and sacred groves anciently amongst the Canaanites and other nations of Palestine and Judea.

The rotunda is constructed after the following manner, they first fix in the ground a circular range of posts or trunks of trees, about six feet high, at equal distances, which are notched at top, to receive into them, from one to another, a range of beams or wall plates; within this is another circular order of very large and strong pillars, above twelve feet high, notched in like manner at top, to receive another range of wall plates, and within this is yet another or third range of stronger and higher pillars, but fewer in number, and standing at a greater distance from each other; and lastly, in the centre stands a very strong pillar, which forms the pinnacle of the building, and to which the rafters centre at top; these rafters are strengthened and bound together by cross beams and laths, which sustain the roof or covering, which is a layer of bark neatly placed, and tight enough to exclude the rain, and sometimes they cast a thin superficies of earth over all.[99] There is but one large door, which serves at the same time to admit light from without and the smoak to escape when a fire is kindled; but as there is but a small fire kept, sufficient to give light at night, and that fed with dry [369] small sound wood divested of its bark, there is but little smoak; all around the inside of the building, betwixt the second range of pillars and the wall, is a range of cabins or sophas, consisting of two or three steps, one above or behind the other, in theatrical order, where the assembly sit or lean down; these sophas are covered with matts or carpets, very curiously made of thin splints of Ash or Oak, woven or platted together; near the great pillar in the centre the fire is kindled for light, near which the musicians seat themselves, and round about this the performers exhibit their dances and other shews at public festivals, which happen almost every night throughout the year.

About the close of the evening I accompanied Mr. Galahan and other white traders to the rotunda, where was a grand festival, music and dancing. This assembly was held principally to rehearse the ball-play dance,[100] this town being challenged to play against another the next day.

The people being assembled and seated in order, and the musicians having taken their station, the ball opens, first with a long harangue or oration, spoken by an aged chief, in commendation of the manly exercise of ball-play, recounting the many and brilliant victories which the town of Cowe had gained over the other towns in the nation, not forgetting or neglecting to recite his own exploits, together with those of other aged men now present, coadjutors in the performance of these athletic games in their youthful days.

This oration was delivered with great spirit and eloquence, and was meant to influence the passions [370] of the young men present, excite them to emulation and inspire them with ambition.

This prologue being at an end, the musicians began, both vocal and instrumental, when presently a company of girls, hand in hand, dressed in clean white robes and ornamented with beads, bracelets and a profusion of gay ribbands, entering the door, immediately began to sing their responses in a gentle, low and sweet voice, and formed themselves in a semicircular file or line, in two ranks, back to back, facing the spectators and musicians, moving slowly round and round; this continued about a quarter of an hour, when we were surprised by a sudden very loud and shrill whoop, uttered at once by a company of young fellows, who came in briskly after one another, with rackets or hurls in one hand. These champions likewise were well dressed, painted and ornamented with silver bracelets, gorgets and wampum, neatly ornamented with moccasins and high waving plumes in their diadems, who immediately formed themselves in a semicircular rank also, in front of the girls, when these changed their order, and formed a single rank parallel to the men, raising their voices in responses to the tunes of the young champions, the semicircles continually moving round. There was something singular and diverting in their step and motions, and I imagine not to be learned to exactness but with great attention and perseverance; the step, if it can be so termed, was performed after the following manner, i.e. first, the motion began at one end of the semicircle, gently rising up and down upon their toes and heels alternately, when the first was up on tip-toe, the next began to raise the heel, and by the time the first rested again on the heel, the second was [371] on tip toe, thus from one end of the rank to the other, so that some were always up and some down, alternately and regularly, without the least baulk or confusion; and they at the same time, and in the same motion, moved on obliquely or sideways, so that the circle performed a double or complex motion in its progression, and at stated times exhibited a grand or universal movement, instantly and unexpectedly to the spectators, by each rank turning to right and left, taking each others places; the movements were managed with inconceivable alertness and address, and accompanied with an instantaneous and universal elevation of the voice and shrill short whoop.

The Cherokees besides the ball play dance, have a variety of others equally entertaining; the men especially exercise themselves with a variety of gesticulations and capers, some of which are ludicrous and diverting enough; and they have others which are of the martial order, and others of the chace; these seem to be somewhat of a tragical nature, wherein they exhibit astonishing feats of military prowess, masculine strength and activity. Indeed all their dances and musical entertainments seem to be theatrical exhibitions or plays, varied with comic and sometimes lascivious interludes; the women however conduct themselves with a very becoming grace and decency, insomuch that in amorous interludes, when their responses and gestures seem consenting to natural liberties, they veil themselves, just discovering a glance of their sparkling eyes and blushing faces, expressive of sensibility.

Next morning early I sat off on my return, and meeting with no material occurrences on the road, in two days arrived safe at Keowe, where I tarried two or three days, employed in augmenting my [372] collections of specimens, and waiting for Mr. Galahan who was to call on me here, to accompany him to Sinica, where he and other traders where to meet Mr. Cameron, the deputy commissary, who were to hold a congress at that town, with the chiefs of the

Lower Cherokees, to consult preliminaries introductory to a general congress
and treaty with these Indians, which was to be convened next June, and held in
the Overhill towns.

I observed in the environs of Keowe, on the bases of the rocky hills,
immediately ascending from the low grounds near the river bank, a great
number of very singular antiquities, the work of the ancients; they seem to me
to have been altars for sacrifice or sepulchres; they were constructed of four flat
stones, two set on an edge for the sides, one closed one end, a very large flat one
lay horizontally at top, so that the other end was open; this fabric was four or five
feet in length, two feet high and three in width. I enquired of the trader what
they were, who could not tell me certainly, but supposed them to be ancient
Indian ovens; the Indians can give no account of them: they are on the surface
of the ground and are of different dimensions.[101]

I accompanied the traders to Sinica, where we found the commissary and the
Indian chiefs convened in counsel; continued at Sinica sometime, employing
myself in observations and making collections of every thing worthy of notice;
and finding the Indians to be yet unsettled in their determination and not in a
good humour, I abandoned the project of visiting the regions beyond the
Cherokee mountains for this season; sat off for my return to fort James
Dartmouth, lodged this night in the [373] forests near the banks of a delightful
large creek, a branch of Keowe river, and next day arrived safe at Dartmouth.

List of the towns and villages in the Cherokee nation inhabited at this day, viz.

No. 1 Echoe
2 Nucasse   On the Tanase East of the Jore mountains.
3 Whatoga   4 towns.
4 Cowe

5 Ticoloosa
6 Jore   Inland on the branches of the Tanase.
7 Conisca   4 towns.
8 Nowe

9 Tomothle
10 Noewe
11 Tellico
12 Clennuse   On the Tanase over the Jore mountains.
13 Ocunnolufte   8 towns.
14 Chewe
15 Quanuse
16 Tellowe

17	Tellico	
18	Chatuga	Inland towns on the branches of the
19	Hiwasse	Tanase and other waters over the Jore
20	Chewase	mountains. 5 towns.
21	Nuanha	

22	Tallase	
23	Chelowe	
24	Sette	Overhill towns on the Tanase or
25	Chote great	Cherokee river. 6 towns.
26	Joco	
27	Tahasse	

[374]

28	Tamahle	
29	Tuskege	Overhill towns on the Tanase or Cherokee
30	——. Big Island	river.
31	Nilaque	5 towns.
32	Niowe	

Lower towns East of the mountains, viz.

No. 1	Sinica	
2	Keowe	On the Savanna or Keowe river.
3	Kulsage	

4	Tugilo	
5	Estotowe	On Tugilo river.

6	Qualatche	
7	Chote	On Flint river.

Towns on the waters of other rivers.
Estotowe great. Allagae. Jore. Nae oche.

In all forty-three towns.[102]

By mid-June 1775, Bartram had returned from the Cherokee country. At Fort Charlotte, on the Savannah River, he rendezvoused with a "[375] company of adventurers for West Florida"[103] that was soon joined by two groups of traders from Augusta, bound for the Creek country.

[377] I thought it worthy of taking notice of a singular method the traders make use of to reduce the wild young horses to their hard duty. When any one persists in refusing to receive his load, if threats, [378] the discipline of the whip and other common abuse prove insufficient, after being haltered, a pack-horseman catches the tip end of one of his ears betwixt his teeth and pinches it, when instantly the furious strong creature, trembling, stands perfectly still until he is loaded.[104]

The caravan made camp on the banks of the Oconee River, near "[379] an extensive, green, open, level plain, consisting of old Indian fields and plantations. . . ."

[380] Our encampment was fixed on the site of the old Ocone town,[105] which, about sixty years ago, was evacuated by the Indians, who finding their situation disagreeable from its vicinity to the white people, left it, moving upwards into the Nation or Upper Creeks, and there built a town, but that situation not suiting their roving disposition, they grew sickly and tired of it, and resolved to seek a habitation more agreeable to their minds; they all arose, directing their migration South-Eastward towards the sea coast, and in the course of their journey, observing the delightful appearance of the extensive plains of Alachua and the fertile hills environing it, they sat down and built a town on the banks of a spacious and beautiful lake, at a small distance from the plains, naming this new town Cuscowilla: this situation pleased them, the vast desarts, forests, lake and savannas around, affording unbounded range of the best hunting ground for bear and deer, their favourite game. But although this situation was healthy and delightful to the utmost degree, affording them variety and plenty of every desirable thing in their estimation, yet troubles and afflictions found them out. This territory, to the promontory of Florida, was then claimed by the Tomocos, Utinas, Calloosas, Yamases and other remnant tribes of the ancient Floridans and the more Northern refugees, driven away by the Carolinians, now in alliance and under the protection of the Spaniards, who assisting them, attacked the new settlement and for many years were very troublesome, but the Alachuas or Ocones being strengthened by other emigrants and fugitive bands from the Upper Creeks, with whom they were confederated, and who gradually established other towns in this low country, stretching a line of settlements [381] across the isthmus, extending from the Alatamaha to the bay of Apalache: these uniting were at length able to face their enemies and even attack them in their own settlements, and in the end, with the assistance of the Upper Creeks, their uncles, vanquished their enemies and destroyed them, and then fell upon the Spanish settlements, which they also entirely broke up. But having treated of these matters in the journal of my travels into East Florida, I end this digression and proceed again on my journey.

About forty miles farther, the travelers crossed the Ocmulgee River at present-day Macon.[106]

[381] . . . on the East bank of the river lies the famous Oakmulge fields, where are yet conspicuous very wonderful remains of the power and grandeur of the ancients of this part of America, in the ruins of a capital town and settlement, as vast artificial hills, terraces, &c. already particularly mentioned in my tour through the lower districts of Georgia.

Around the middle of July 1775, Bartram and his companions approached the Chattahoochee River and the first of the Creek settlements.[107]

[388] Next day after traversing a very delightful territory, exhibiting a charming rural scenery of primitive nature, gently descending and passing alternately easy declivities of magnificent terraces supporting sublime forests, almost endless grassy fields, detatched groves and green lawns for the distance of nine or ten miles, we arrived at the banks of the Chata Uche river opposite the Uche town, where after unloading our horses, the Indians came over to us in large canoes, by means of which, with the cheerful and liberal assistance of the Indians, ferried over their merchandize, and afterwards driving our horses altogether into the river swam them over: the river here is about three or four hundred yards wide, carries fifteen or twenty feet water and flows down with an active current; the water is clear, cool and salubrious.

The Uche town is situated in a vast plain, on the gradual ascent as we rise from a narrow strip of low ground immediately bordering on the river: it is the largest, most compact and best situated Indian town I ever saw; the habitations are large and neatly built; the walls of the houses are constructed of a wooden frame, then lathed and plaistered inside and out with a reddish well tempered clay or morter, which gives them the appearance of red brick walls, and these houses are neatly covered or roofed with Cypress bark or shingles of that tree. The town appeared to be populous and thriving, full of youth and young children: I suppose the number of inhabitants, men, women and children, might amount to one thousand or fifteen hundred, as it is said they are able to muster five hundred gun-men or warriors. Their own national language is altogether or radically different from [389] the Creek or Muscogulge tongue, and is called the Savanna or Savanuca tongue; I was told by the traders it was the same or a dialect of the Shawanese.[108] They are in confederacy with the Creeks, but do not mix with them, and on account of their numbers and strength, are of importance enough to excite and draw upon them the jealousy of the whole Muscogulge confederacy, and are usually at variance, yet are wise enough to unite against a common enemy, to support the interest and glory of the general Creek confederacy.

After a little refreshment at this beautiful town, we repacked and sat off again for the Apalachucla town,[109] where we arrived after riding over a level plain, consisting of ancient Indian plantations, a beautiful landscape diversified with groves and lawns.

This is esteemed the mother town or capital of the Creek or Muscogulge confederacy: sacred to peace; no captives are put to death or human blood spilt here. And when a general peace is proposed, deputies from all the towns in the confederacy assemble at this capital, in order to deliberate upon a subject of so high importance for the prosperity of the commonwealth.

And on the contrary the great Coweta town,[110] about twelve miles higher up this river, is called the bloody town, where the Micos chiefs and warriors assemble when a general war is proposed, and here captives and state malefactors are put to death.

The time of my continuance here, which was about a week, was employed in excursions round about this settlement. One day the chief trader of Apalachucla obliged me with his company on a [390] walk of about a mile and an half down the river, to view the ruins and site of the ancient Apalachucla: it had been situated on a peninsula formed by a doubling of the river, and indeed appears to have been a very famous capital by the artificial mounds or terraces, and a very populous settlement, from its extent and expansive old fields, stretching beyond the scope of the sight along the low grounds of the river. We viewed the mounds or terraces, on which formerly stood their town house or rotunda and square or areopagus, and a little back of this, on a level height or natural step, above the low grounds is a vast artificial terrace or four square mound, now seven or eight feet higher than the common surface of the ground; in front of one square or side of this mound adjoins a very extensive oblong square yard or artificial level plain, sunk a little below the common surface, and surrounded with a bank or narrow terrace, formed with the earth thrown out of this yard at the time of its formation: the Creeks or present inhabitants have a tradition that this was the work of the ancients, many ages prior to their arrival and possessing this country.

This old town was avacuated about twenty years ago by the general consent of the inhabitants, on account of its unhealthy situation, owing to the frequent inundations of the river over the low grounds; and moreover they grew timorous and dejected, apprehending themselves to be haunted and possessed with vengeful spirits, on account of human blood that had been undeservedly *

---

* About fifty or sixty years ago almost all the white traders then in the Nation were massacred in this town, whither they had repaired from the different towns, in hopes of an assylum or refuge, in consequence of the alarm, having been timely apprised of the hostile intentions of the Indians by their temporary wives, they all met together in one house, under the avowed protection of the chiefs of the town, waiting the event; but whilst the chiefs were assembled in council, deliberating on ways and means to protect them, the Indians in multitudes surrounded the house and sat fire to it; they all, to the number of eighteen or twenty, perished with the house in the flames. The trader shewed me the ruins of the house where they were burnt.[111]

spilt in this old town, [391] having been repeatedly warned by apparitions and dreams to leave it.

At the time of their leaving this old town, like the ruin or dispersion of the ancient Babel, the inhabitants separated from each other, forming several bands under the conduct or auspices of the chief of each family or tribe. The greatest number, however, chose to sit down and build the present new Apalachucla town, upon a high bank of the river above the inundations. The other bands pursued different routs, as their inclinations led them, settling villages lower down the river; some continued their migration towards the sea coast, seeking their kindred and countrymen amongst the Lower Creeks in East Florida, where they settled themselves. My intelligent friend, the trader of Apalachucla, having from a long residence amongst these Indians acquired an extensive knowledge of their customs and affairs, I enquired of him what were his sentiments with respect to their wandering, unsettled disposition; their so frequently breaking up their old towns and settling new ones, &c. His answers and opinions were, the necessity they were under of having fresh or new strong land for their plantations; and new, convenient and extensive range or hunting ground, which unavoidably forces them into contentions and wars with their confederates and neighbouring tribes; to avoid which they had rather move and seek a plentiful and peaceable retreat, even at a distance, than to contend with friends and relatives or embroil themselves in [392] destructive wars with their neighbours, when either can be avoided with so little inconvenience. With regard to the Muscogulges, the first object in order to obtain these conveniencies was the destruction of the Yamases, who held the possession of Florida and were in close alliance with the Spaniards, their declared and most inveterate enemy, which they at length fully accomplished; and by this conquest they gained a vast and invaluable territory, comprehending a delightful region and a most plentiful country for their favourite game, bear and deer. But not yet satisfied, having already so far conquered the powerful Cherokees, as, in a manner, to force them in alliance, and compelled the warlike Chicasaws to sue for peace and alliance with them; they then grew arrogant and insatiable, and turned their covetous looks towards the potent and intrepid Chactaws, the only Indian enemy they had to fear, meaning to break them up and possess themselves of that extensive, fruitful and delightful country, and make it a part of their vast empire; but the Chactaws, a powerful, hardy, subtile and intrepid race, estimated at twenty thousand warriors, are likely to afford sufficient exercise for the proud and restless spirits of the Muscogulges, at least for some years to come, and they appear to be so equally matched with the Chactaws, it seems doubtful which of these powerful nations will rise victorious.[112] The Creeks have sworn, it seems, that they never will make peace with this enemy as long as the rivers flow or the sun pursues his course through the skies.

Thus we see that war or the exercise of arms originates from the same motives, and operates in the spirits of the wild red men of America, as it formerly did with the renowned Greeks and Ro-[393]mans or modern civilized nations, and not from a ferocious, capricious desire of sheding human blood as carnivorous savages; neither does the eager avarice of plunder stimulate them to acts of madness and cruelty, that being a trifling object in their estimation, a duffield blanket, a polished rifle gun, or embroidered mantle; no, their martial prowess and objects of desire and ambition proceed from greater principles and more magnanimous intentions, even that of reuniting all nations and languages under one universal confederacy or commonwealth.

Leaving behind the traders, Bartram and the original "company of adventurers" rode deeper into the Creek country.[113]

[396] July 13th we left the Apalachucla town, and three days journey brought us to Talasse, a town on the Tallapoose river, North East great branch of the Alabama or Mobile river, having passed over a vast level plain country of expansive savannas, groves, Cane swamps and open Pine forests, watered by innumerable rivulets and brooks, tributary to Apalachucla and Mobile; we now alter our course, turning to the left hand, Southerly, and descending near the river banks, continually in sight of the Indian plantations and commons adjacent to their towns. Passed by Otasse, an ancient famous Muscogulge town. The next settlement we came to was Coolome, where we stayed two days, and having letters for Mr. Germany, the principal trader of Coolome, I meant to consult with him in matters relative to my affairs and future proceedings.

Here are very extensive old fields, the abandoned plantations and commons of the old town, on the East side of the river, but the settlement is removed, and the new town now stands on the opposite shore, in a charming fruitful plain, under an elevated ridge of hills, the swelling beds or bases of which are covered with a pleasing verdure of grass, but the last ascent is steeper, and towards the summit discovers shelving rocky cliffs, which appear to be continually splitting and bursting to pieces, scattering their thin exfoliations over the tops of the grassy knolls beneath. The plain is narrow where the [397] town is built: their houses are neat, commodious buildings, a wooden frame with plaistered walls, and roofed with Cypress bark or shingles; every habitation consists of four oblong square houses, of one story, of the same form and dimensions, and so situated as to form an exact square, encompassing an area or court yard of about a quarter of an acre of ground, leaving an entrance into it at each corner. Here is a beautiful new square or areopagus, in the centre of the new town; but the stores of the principal trader and two or three Indians habitations, stand near the banks of the opposite shore on the site of the old Coolome town. The

Tallapoose river is here three hundred yards over, and about fifteen or twenty feet water, which is very clear, agreeable to the taste, esteemed salubrious, and runs with a steady, active current.

Being now recruited and refited, having obtained a guide to set us in the great trading path for West Florida, early in the morning we sat off for Mobile: our progress for about eighteen miles was through a magnificent forest, just without or skirting on the Indian plantations, frequently having a view of their distant towns, over plains or old fields. . . .

The path to Mobile took the travelers east of the Alabama River. Along the way, Bartram noticed a species of tall grass that exudes a resin that "[399] possesses a very agreeable fragrance and bitterish taste, somewhat like frankincense or turpentine, which is chewed by the Indians and traders, to cleanse their teeth and mouth, and sweeten their breath."[114] An abundance of wild grapes in this region also prompted him to comment.

[400] The Indians gather great quantities of them, which they prepare for keeping, by first sweating them on hurdles over a gentle fire, and afterwards dry them on their bunches in the sun and air, and store them [401] up for provisions. . . .[115]

Bartram arrived in Mobile by the end of July 1775.[116]

[404] The city of Mobile is situated on the easy ascent of a rising bank, extending near half a mile back on the level plain above; it has been near a mile in length, though now chiefly in ruins, many houses vacant and mouldering to earth; yet there are a few good buildings inhabited by French gentlemen, English, Scotch and Irish, and emigrants from the Northern British colonies. Mssrs. Swanson and M'Gillivary[117] who have the management of the Indian trade, carried on to the Chicasaws, Chactaws, Upper and Lower Creeks, &c. have made here very extraordinary improvements in buildings.

The fort Conde, which stands very near the bay, towards the lower end of the town is a large regular fortress of brick.[118]

The principal French buildings are constructed of brick, and are of one story, but on an extensive scale, four square, encompassing on three sides a large area or court yard, the principal apartment is on the side fronting the street; they seem in some degree to have copied after the Creek habitation in the general plan; those of the poorer class are constructed of a strong frame of Cypress, filled in with brick, plaistered and white-washed inside and out. . . .

[405] Not having an immediate opportunity from hence to Manchac, a

British settlement on the Mississipi, I endeavoured to procure a light canoe, with which I designed to pursue my travels along shore to the settlements about Pearl river.

August 5th, sat off from Mobile up the river in a trading boat, and was landed at Taensa bluff, the seat of Major Farmer,[119] to make good my engagements, in consequence of an invitation from that worthy gentleman, to spend some days in his family; here I obtained the use of a light canoe, to continue my voyage up the river. The settlement of Taensa is on the site of an ancient town of a tribe of Indians of that name, which is apparent from many artificial mounds of earth and other ruins. Besides Mr. Farmer's dwellings, there are many others inhabited by French families; who are chiefly his tenants. It is a most delightful situation, commanding a spacious prospect up and down the river, and the low lands of his extensive plantations on the opposite shore.

From Major Farmar's plantation, Bartram explored the region by sailboat and canoe, first investigating islands in the Mobile-Tensaw delta, north of Mobile Bay, where he saw "[406] some old uncultivated fields. . . ." Several of these evidently were French colonial farmsteads, as when he "[407] came presently to old fields, where I observed ruins of ancient habitations, there being abundance of Peach and Fig trees, loaded with fruit. . . ." Sailing up the Tombigbee River, Bartram came upon

[409] . . . an old field, and penetrating the forests surrounding, observed them to be young growth, covering very extensive old plantations, which was evident from the ridges and hillocks which once raised their Corn (Zea) Batatas, &c. I suppose this to be the site of an ancient fortified post of the [410] French, as there appears vestiges of a rampart and other traces of a fortress; perhaps fort Louis de la Mobile, but in all probability it will not remain long visible, the stream of the river making daily encroachments on it, by carrying away the land on which it stood.[120]

After returning to Major Farmar's plantation from this excursion, Bartram contracted a virulent fever, which temporarily abated, permitting him to sail eastward to Pensacola. During his brief visit to Pensacola, Bartram met West Florida Governor Peter Chester, who encouraged him to undertake extensive botanical explorations in the colony and offered to pay all his expenses. Bartram declined, but Chester gave him a formal letter of introduction, dated September 5, 1775, and permission to travel in the colony.[121]

Upon his return once again to his home base at Major Farmar's, early in September 1775, "[418] I found myself very ill, and not a little alarmed by an excessive pain in my head, attended with a high fever, this disorder soon settled in my eyes. . . ." Nevertheless, he boarded a trading boat the next day to visit the Pearl River. While there, Bartram's illness became acute; "[421] it was several weeks before I could expose my eyes to open day light, and at last I found my left eye considerably injured. . . ." Around mid-October he set off for Manchac, on the Mississippi River, then started upstream toward Baton Rouge, accompanied by a resident of that town.[122]

[429] Two miles above Manchac we put into shore at Alabama, this Indian village is delightfully situated on several swelling green hills, gradually ascending from the verge of the river: they are a remnant of the ancient Alabama nation, who inhabited the East arm of the great Mobile river, which bears their name to this day, now possessed by the Creeks or Muscogulges, who conquered the former.[123]

My friend having purchased some baskets and earthen-ware, the manufactures of these people, we left the village. . . .

Having reached Baton Rouge, they continued north to Pointe Coupée.

[433] We made our visit to a French gentleman, an ancient man and wealthy planter, who, according to the history he favoured us with of his own life and adventures, must have been very aged; his hair was of a silky white, yet his complexion was florid and constitution athletic. He said that soon after he came to America, with many families of his countrymen, they ascended the river to the Cliffs of the Natches, where they sat down, being entertained by the natives; and under cover of a strong fortress and garrison, established a settlement, and by [434] cultivating the land and forming plantations, in league and friendship with the Indians, in a few years they became a populous, rich and growing colony; when, through the imprudent and tyrannical conduct of the commandant towards the Natches, the ancients of the country, a very powerful and civilized nation of red men, who were sovereigns of the soil, and possessed the country round about them, they became tired of these comers, and exasperated at their cruelty and licentiousness, at length determined to revenge themselves of such inhumanity and ingratitude, secretly conspired their destruction, and their measures were so well concerted with other Indian tribes, that if it had not been for the treachery of one of their princesses, with whom the commander was in favour (for by her influence her nation attempted the destruction of the settlement, before their auxilaries joined them, which afforded an opportunity for some few of the settlers to escape) they would have fully accomplished their purpose, however the settlement was entirely broken up, most of the inhabitants being slaughtered in one night, and the few who

escaped betook themselves to their canoes, descending the river until they arrived at this place, where they established themselves again; and this gentleman had only time and opportunity to take into his boat one heifer calf, which he assured us was the mother of the numerous herds he now possesses, consisting of many hundred head.[124]

Bartram cut short his travels in Louisiana, due to his weakened health, and returned to Mobile.

[440] November 27th, 1777 [1775],[125] sat off from Mobile, in a large boat with the principal trader of the company, and at evening arrived at Taensa, where were the pack-horsemen with the merchandize, and next morning as soon as we had our horses in readiness, I took my last leave of Major Farmer, and left Taensa. Our caravan consisting of between twenty and thirty horses, sixteen of which were loaded, two pack-horsemen, and myself, under the direction of Mr. Tap —— y the chief trader.[126] One of our young men was a Mustee Creek, his mother being a Chactaw slave, and his father a half breed, betwixt a Creek and a white man. I loaded one horse with my effects, some presents to the Indians, to enable me to purchase a fresh horse, in case of necessity, for my old trusty slave which had served me faithfully almost three years, having carried me on his back at least six thousand miles, was by this time almost worn out, and I expected every hour he would give up, especially after I found the manner of these traders' travelling; who seldom decamp until the sun is high and hot; each one having a whip made of the toughest cowskin, they start all at once, the horses having ranged themselves in regular Indian file, the veteran in the van, and the younger in the rear; then the chief drives with the crack of his whip, and a whoop or shriek, which rings through the forests and plains, speaks in Indian, commanding them to proceed, which is repeated by all the company, when we start at once, keeping up a brisk and constant trot, [441] which is incessantly urged and continued as long as the miserable creatures are able to move forwa[r]d, and then come to camp, though frequently in the middle of the afternoon, which is the pleasantest time of the day for travelling: and every horse has a bell on, which being stopped when we start in the morning with a twist of grass or leaves, soon shakes out, and they are never stopped again during the day; the constant ringing and clattering of the bells, smacking of the whips, whooping and too frequent cursing these miserable quadrupeds, cause an incessant uproar and confusion, inexpressibly disagreeable.

After three days travelling in this mad manner, my old servant was on the point of giving out, and several of the company's horses were tired, but were relieved of their burthens by the led horses which attended for that purpose.

I was now driven to disagreeable extremities, and had no other alternative, but either to leave my horse in the woods, pay a very extravagant hire for a doubtful passage to the Nation, or separate myself from my companions, and wait the recovery of my horse alone: the traders gave me no other comfortable advice in this dilemma, than that, there was a company of traders on the road a-head of us from the nation, to Mobile, who had a large gang of led horses with them for sale, when they should arrive; and expected from the advice which he had received at Mobile before we set off from thence, that this company must be very near to us, and probably would be up tomorrow, or at least in two or three days: and this man condescended so far as to moderate a little his mode of travelling, that I might have a chance of keeping up with them until the evening of next [442] day; besides I had the comfort of observing that the traders and pack-horsemen carried themselves towards me, with evident signs of humanity and friendship, often expressing sentiments of sympathy, and saying I must not be left alone to perish in the wilderness.

Although my apprehensions on this occasion, were somewhat tumultuous, since there was little hope, on the principle of reason, should I be left alone, of escaping cruel captivity, and perhaps being murdered by the Chactaws; for the company of traders was my only security, as the Indians never attack the traders on the road, though they be trading with nations at enmity with them. Yet I had secret hopes of relief and deliverance, that cheered me, and inspired confidence and peace of mind. . . .

About the middle of the afternoon, we were joyfully surprised at the distant prospect of the trading company coming up, and we soon met, saluting each other several times with a general Indian whoop, or shouts of friendship; then each company came to camp within a few paces of each other; and before night I struck up a bargain with them for a handsome strong young horse, which cost [443] me about ten pounds sterling. I was now constrained to leave my old slave behind, to feed in rich Cane pastures, where he was to remain and recruit until the return of his new master from Mobile; from whom I extorted a promise to use him gently, and if possibly, not to make a pack-horse of him.

Next morning we decamped, proceeding again on my travels, now alert and cheerful. Crossed a brisk rivulet ripling over a gravelly bed, and winding through aromatic groves of the Illisium Floridanum, then gently descended to the high forests, leaving Deadman's creek, for at this creek a white man was found dead, supposed to have been murdered, from which circumstance it has its name.

A few days before we arrived at the Nation we met a company of emigrants from Georgia; a man, his wife, a young woman, several young children and three stout young men, with about a dozen horses loaded with their property. They informed us their design was to settle on the Alabama, a few miles above the confluence of the Tombigbe.[127]

Being now near the Nation, the chief trader with another of our company sat off a-head for his town, to give notice to the Nation, as he said, of his approach with the merchandize, each of them taking the best horse they could pick out of the gang, leaving the goods to the conduct and care of the young Mustee and myself. Early in the evening we came to the banks of a large deep creek, a considerable branch of the Alabama: the waters ran furiously, being overcharged with the floods of rain which had fallen the day before. We discovered immediately that there was no possibility of crossing it by ford-[444]ing; its depth and rapidity would have swept our horses, loads and all, instantly from our sight; my companion, after consideration, said we must make a raft to ferry over our goods, which we immediately set about, after unloading our horses and turning them out to range. I undertook to collect dry Canes, and my companion dry timber or logs and vines to bind them together: having gathered the necessary materials, and laid them in order on the brink of the river, ready to work upon, we betook ourselves to repose, and early next morning sat about building our raft. This was a novel scene to me, and I could not, until finished and put to practice, well comprehend how it could possibly answer the effect desired. In the first place we laid, parallel to each other, dry, sound trunks of trees, about nine feet in length, and eight or nine inches diameter, which binding fast together with Grape vines and withs, until we had formed this first floor, about twelve or fourteen feet in length, then binding the dry Canes in bundles, each near as thick as a man's body, with which we formed the upper stratum, laying them close by the side of each other and binding them fast; after this manner our raft was constructed: then having two strong Grape vines, each long enough to cross the river, we fastened one to each end of the raft, which now being completed, and loading on as much as it would safely carry, the Indian took the end of one of the vines in his mouth, plunged into the river and swam over with it, and the vine fixed to the other end was committed to my charge, to steady the raft and haul it back again after being unloaded; as soon as he had safe landed and hauled taught his vine, I pushed off the raft, which he drew over as quick as possible, I steadying it with [445] my vine: in this manner, though with inexpressible danger of loosing our effects, we ferried all safe over: the last load, with other articles, contained my property, with all my clothes, which I stripped off, except my breeches, for they contained matters of more value and consequence than all the rest of my property put together; besides I did not choose to expose myself entirely naked to the alligators and serpents in crossing the flood. Now seeing all the goods safe over, and the horses at a landing place on the banks of the river about fifty yards above, I drove them all in together, when, seeing them safe landed, I plunged in after them, and being a tollerable swimmer, soon reached the opposite shore; but my difficulties at this place were not yet at an end, for our horses all landing just below the mouth of a considerable branch of this river, of fifteen or twenty

100

---

*Travels
Through
North
&
South
Carolina*

feet width, and its perpendicular banks almost as many feet in height above its swift waters, over which we were obliged to carry every article of our effects, and this by no other bridge than a sapling felled across it, which is called a raccoon bridge, and over this my Indian friend would trip as quick and light as that quadruped, with one hundred weight of leather on his back, when I was scarcely able to shuffle myself along over it astride. At last having re-packed and sat off again, without any material occurrence intervening; in the evening we arrived at the banks of the great Tallapoose river, and came to camp under shelter of some Indian cabins, in expansive fields, close to the river bank, opposite the town of Savannuca.[128] Late in the evening a young white man, in great haste and seeming confusion, joined our camp, who immediately related, that being on his journey from Pensacola, it happened that the [446] very night after we had passed the company of emigrants, he met them and joined their camp in the evening, when, just at dark, the Chactaws surrounded them, plundered their camp and carried all the people off captive, except himself, he having the good fortune to escape with his horse, though closely pursued.

Next morning very early, though very cold and the surface of the earth as hoary as if covered with a fall of snow, the trader standing on the opposite shore entirely naked except a breech-clout, and encircled by a company of red men in the like habit, hailed us, and presently, with canoes, brought us all over with the merchandize, and conducted us safe to the town of Mucclasse,[129] a mile or two distant.

The next day was a day of rest and audience: the following was devoted to feasting, and the evening concluded in celebrating the nuptials of the young Mustee with a Creek girl of Mucclasse, daughter of the chief and sister to our trader's wife. The trader's house and stores formed a compleat square, after the mode of the habitations of the Muscogulges, that is, four oblong buildings of equal dimensions, two opposite to each other, encompassing an area of about a quarter of an acre; on one side of this a fence enclosed a yard of near an acre of ground, and at one of the farther corners of which a booth or pavilion was formed of green boughs, having two Laurel trees planted in front (Magnolia grandiflora.) This was the secret nuptial chamber. Dancing, music and feasting continued the forepart of the night, and towards morning the happy couple privately withdrew, and continued alone all the next day, no one presuming to approach the sacred, mysterious thalame.

[447] The trader obliged me with his company on a visit to the Alabama,[130] an Indian town at the confluence of the two fine rivers, the Tallapoose and Coosau, which here resign their names to the great Alabama, where are to be seen traces of the ancient French fortress, Thoulouse; here are yet lying, half buried in the earth, a few pieces of ordnance, four and six pounders.[131] I observed, in a very thriving condition, two or three very large Apple trees,

planted here by the French. This is, perhaps, one of the most elegible situations for a city in the world, a level plain between the conflux of two majestic rivers, which are exactly of equal magnitude in appearance, each navigable for vessels and perreauguas at least five hundred miles above it, and spreading their numerous branches over the most fertile and delightful regions, many hundred miles before we reach their sources in the Apalachean mountains.

Stayed all night at Alabama, where we had a grand entertainment at the public square, with music and dancing, and returned next day to Mucclasse, where being informed of a company of traders about setting off from Tuckabatche[132] for Augusta, I made a visit to that town to know the truth of it, but on my arrival there they were gone, but being informed of another caravan who were to start from the Ottasse town in two or three weeks time, I returned to Mucclasse in order to prepare for my departure.

On my arrival, I was not a little surprised at a tragical revolution in the family of my friend the trader, his stores shut up, and guarded by a party of Indians: in a few minutes however, the whole affair was related to me. It appeared that this son of Adonis, had been detected in an amorous in-[448]trigue, with the wife of a young chief, the day after his arrival: the chief being out on a hunt, but arrived next day, who upon information of the affair, and the fact being confirmed, he with his friends and kindred resolved to exact legal satisfaction, which in this case is cutting off both ears of the delinquent, close to the head, which is called cropping. This being determined upon, he took the most secret and effectual methods to effect his purpose. About a dozen young Indian fellows, conducted by their chief (the injured husband) having provided and armed themselves with knotty cudgels of green Hickory, which they concealed under their mantles, in the dusk of the evening paid a pretended friendly visit to the trader at his own house; when the chief feigning a private matter of business, took him aside in the yard; then whistling through his fingers (the signal preconcerted) he was instantly surrounded, knocked down, and then stripped to his skin, and beaten with their knotty bludgeons; however he had the subtilty to feign himself speechless before they really killed him, which he supposed was their intention; when he had now lain for dead, the executioner drew out his knife with an intention of taking off his ears; this small respite gave him time to reflect a little; when he instantly sprang up, ran off, leaped the fence and had the good fortune to get into a dark swamp, overgrown with vines and thickets, where he miraculously eluded the earnest researches of his enemies, and finally made a safe retreat to the house of his father-in-law, the chief of the town; throwing himself under his protection, who gave his word that he would do him all the favour that lay in his power. This account I had from his own mouth, who hearing of my return, the next morn-[449]ing after my arrival, sent a trusty messenger, by whom I found means of access to him. He farther informed me

102

*Travels
Through
North
&
South
Carolina*

that there had been a council of the chiefs of the town convened, to deliberate on the affair, and their final determination was that he must loose his ears, or forfeit all his goods, which amounted to upwards of one thousand pounds sterling, and even that forfeiture would not save his ears, unless Mr. Golphin interposed in his behalf; and after all the injured Indian declares that he will have his life. He entreated me with tears to make what speed I could to Silver Bluff, represent his dangerous situation to Mr. Golphin, and solicit that gentleman's most speedy and effectual interference; which I assured him I would undertake.

Now having all things prepared for my departure, early in the morning, after taking leave of my distressed friend the trader of Mucclasse, I sat off; passed through continued plantations and Indian towns on my way up the Tallapoose river, being every where treated by the inhabitants with marks of friendship, even as though I had been their countryman and relation. Called by the way at the beautiful town of Coolome, where I tarried some time with Mr. Germany the chief trader of the town, an elderly gentleman, but active, cheerful and very agreeable; who received and treated me with the utmost civility and friendship: his wife is a Creek woman, of a very amiable and worthy character and disposition, industrious, prudent and affectionate; and by whom he had several children, whom he is desirous to send to Savanna or Charleston, for their education, but cannot prevail on his wife to consent to it: this affair affects him very sensibly, for he has accumulated a pretty fortune by his industry and commendable conduct.

[450] Leaving Coolome, I re-crossed the river at Tuccabache, an ancient and large town, thence continuing up the river, and at evening arrived at Attasse,[133] where I continued near a week, waiting the preparations of the traders, with whom I was to join in company to Augusta.

The next day after my arrival, I was introduced to the ancient chiefs, at the public square or areopagus, and in the evening in company with the traders, who are numerous in this town, repaired to the great rotunda, where were assembled the greatest number of ancient venerable chiefs and warriors that I had ever beheld; we spent the evening and greater part of the night together, in drinking Cassine and smoking Tobacco. The great counsel-house or rotunda[134] is appropriated to much the same purpose as the public square, but more private, and seems particularly dedicated to political affairs; women and youth are never admitted; and I suppose it is death for a female to presume to enter the door, or approach within its pale.[135] It is a vast conical building or circular dome, capable of accomodating many hundred people; constructed and furnished within, exactly in the same manner as those of the Cherokees already described, but much larger than any I had seen there; there are people appointed to take care of it, to have it daily swept clean, to provide canes for fuel or to give light.

As their vigils and manner of conducting their vespers and mystical fire in this rotunda, is extremely singular, and altogether different from the customs and usages of any other people, I shall proceed to describe it. In the first place, the governor or officer who has the management of this business, with his servants attending, orders the black drink [451] to be brewed, which is a decoction or infusion of the leaves and tender shoots of the Cassine: this is done under an open shed or pavilion, at twenty or thirty yards distance, directly opposite the door of the council-house. Next he orders bundles of dry Canes to be brought in; these are previously split and broke in pieces to about the length of two feet, and then placed obliquely crossways upon one another on the floor, forming a spiral circle round about the great centre pillar, rising to a foot or eighteen inches in height from the ground; and this circle spreading as it proceeds round and round, often repeated from right to left, every revolution encreases its diameter, and at length extends to the distance of ten or twelve feet from the centre, more or less, according to the length of time the assembly or meeting is to continue. By the time these preparations are accomplished it is night, and the assembly taken their seats in order. The exterior extremity or outer end of the spiral circle takes fire and immediately rises into a bright flame (but how this is effected I did not plainly apprehend; I saw no person set fire to it; there might have been fire left on the hearth, however, I neither saw nor smelt fire or smoke until the blaze instantly ascended upwards) which gradually and slowly creeps round the centre pillar, with the course of the sun, feeding on the dry Canes, and affords a cheerful, gentle and sufficient light until the circle is consumed, when the council breaks up. Soon after this illumination takes place, the aged chiefs and warriors being seated on their cabbins or sophas, on the side of the house opposite the door, in three classes or ranks, rising a little, one above or behind the other; and the white people and red people of confederate towns in the like order on the left hand: a trans-[452]verse range of pillars, supporting a thin clay wall about breast high, separates them: the king's cabbin or seat is in front, the next back of it the head warriors, and the third or last accommodates the young warriors, &c. the great war chief's seat or place is on the same cabbin with, and immediately to the left hand of the king and next to the white people, and to the right hand of the mico or king the most venerable head men and warriors are seated. The assembly being now seated in order, and the house illuminated, two middle aged men, who perform the office of slaves or servants, pro tempore, come in together at the door, each having very large conch shells full of black drink, advancing with slow, uniform and steady steps, their eyes or countenances lifted up, singing very low but sweetly, advance within six on eight paces of the king's and white people's cabbins, when they stop together, and each rests his shell on a tripos or little table, but presently takes it up again, and, bowing very low, advances obsequiously, crossing or intersecting each other about midway: he who rested his shell before the white

Travels
Through
North
&
South
Carolina

104

———

*Travels
Through
North
&
South
Carolina*

people now stands before the king, and the other who stopped before the king stands before the white people, when each presents his shell, one to the king and the other to the chief of the white people, and as soon as he raises it to his mouth the slave utters or sings two notes, each of which continues as long as he has breath, and as long as these notes continue, so long must the person drink, or at least keep the shell to his mouth. These two long notes are very solemn, and at once strike the imagination with a religious awe or homage to the Supreme, sounding somewhat like a-hoo — ojah and a-lu — yah.[136] After this manner the whole assembly are treated, as long as the drink and light continues to hold out, [453] and as soon as the drinking begins, Tobacco and pipes are brought. The skin of a wild cat or young tyger stuffed with Tobacco is brought, and laid at the king's feet, with the great or royal pipe beautifully adorned; the skin is usually of the animals of the king's family or tribe, as the wild-cat, otter, bear, rattle-snake, &c.[137] A skin of Tobacco is likewise brought and cast at the feet of the white chief of the town, and from him it passes on from one to another to fill their pipes from, though each person has besides his own peculiar skin of Tobacco. The king or chief smokes first in the great pipe a few whiffs, blowing it off ceremoniously, first towards the sun, or as it is generally supposed to the Great Spirit, for it is puffed upwards, next towards the four cardinal points, then towards the white people in the house, then the great pipe is taken from the hand of the mico by a slave, and presented to the chief white man, and then to the great war chief, whence it circulates through the rank of head men and warriors, then returns to the king. After this each one fills his pipe from his own or his neighbours skin.

The great or public square generally stands alone, in the centre and highest part of the town, it consists of foursquare or cubical buildings, or houses of one story, uniform, and of the same dimensions, so situated as to form an exact tetragon, encompassing an area of half an acre of ground, more or less, according to the strength or largeness of the town, or will of the inhabitants; there is a passage or avenue at each corner of equal width; each building is constructed of a wooden frame fixed strong in the earth, the walls filled in, and neatly plaistered with clay mortar; close [454] on three sides, that is the back and two ends, except within about two feet of the wall plate or eves, which is left open for the purpose of a window and to admit a free passage of the air; the front or side next to the area is quite open like a piazza. One of these buildings which is properly the counsel-house, where the mico chiefs and wariors, with the citizens who have business, or choose to repair thither, assemble every day in counsel; to hear, decide and rectify all grievances, complaints and contentions, arising betwixt the citizens; give audience to ambassadors, and strangers, hear news and talks from confederate towns, allies or distant nations; to consult about the particular affairs of the town, as erecting habitations for new citizens,

105

*Travels
Through
North
&
South
Carolina*

or establishing young families, concerning agriculture &c. &c. and this building is somewhat different from the other three; it is closely shut up on three sides, that is, the back and two ends, and besides a partition wall longitudinally from end to end divides it into two apartments, the back part totally dark, only three small arched apertures or holes opening into it from the front apartment or piazza, and are little larger than just to admit a man to crawl in upon his hands and knees. This secluded place appears to me to be designed as a sanctuary * dedicated to religion or rather priest craft; for here are deposited all the sacred things, as the physic pot, rattles, chaplets of deer's hoofs and other apparatus of conjuration; and likewise the calumet or great pipe of peace, the imperial standard, or eagle's tail, which is made of the feathers of the white eagles tail † curiously formed and displayed like an [455] open fan on a sceptre or staff, as white and clean as possible when displayed for peace; but when for war, the feathers are painted or tinged with vermilion. The piazza or front of this building, is equally divided into three apartments, by two transverse walls or partitions, about breast high, each having three orders or ranges of seats or cabins stepping one above and behind the other, which accommodate the senate and audience, in the like order as observed in the rotunda. The other three buildings which compose the square, are alike furnished with three ranges of cabins or sophas, and serve for a banqueting-house, to shelter and accommodate the audience and spectators at all times, particularly at feasts or public entertainments, where all classes of citizens resort day and night in the summer or moderate season; the children and females however are seldom or never seen in the public square.

The pillars and walls of the houses of the square were decorated with various paintings[138] and sculptures; which I suppose to be hieroglyphic, and as an historic legendary of political and sacerdotal affairs: but they are extremely picturesque or caricature, as men in variety of attitudes, some ludicrous enough, others having the head of some kind of animal as those of a duck, turkey, bear, fox, wolf, buck, &c. and again those kind of creatures are represented having the human head. These designs were not ill executed, the outlines bold, free and well proportioned. The pillars supporting the front or piazza of the council-house of the square, were ingeniously formed in the likeness of vast speckled serpents, ascending upward; the Otasses being of the snake family or tribe. At this time the town was fasting, taking medicine, and I think [456] I may say praying, to avert a grevious calamity of sickness, which had lately afflicted them, and laid in the grave abundance of their citizens; they fast

---

* Sanctorium or sacred temple, and it is said to be death for any person but the mico, war-chief and high priest to enter in, and none are admitted but by permission of the priests, who guard it day and night.
† Vultura sacra.

106

————

*Travels
Through
North
&
South
Carolina*

seven or eight days, during which time they eat or drink nothing but a meagre gruel, made of a little corn-flour and water; taking at the same time by way of medicine or physic, a strong decoction of the roots of the Iris versicolor, which is a powerful cathartic; they hold this root in high estimation, every town cultivates a little plantation of it, having a large artificial pond, just without the town, planted and almost overgrown with it, where they usually dig clay for pottery, and mortar and plaster for their buildings, and I observed where they had lately been digging up this root.[139]

In the midst of a large oblong square adjoining this town (which was surrounded with a low bank or terrace) is standing a high pillar, round like a pin or needle, it is about forty feet in height, and between two and three feet in diameter at the earth, gradually tapering upwards to a point; it is one piece of Pine wood, and arises from the centre of a low circular, artificial hill, but it leans a little to one side. I enquired of the Indians and traders what it was designed for, who answered they knew not: the Indians said that their ancestors found it in the same situation, when they first arrived and possessed the country, adding, that the red men or Indians, then the possessors, whom they vanquished, were as ignorant as themselves concerning it, saying that their ancestors likewise found it standing so. This monument, simple as it is, may be worthy the observations of a traveller, since it naturally excites at least the following queries: for what purpose was it designed? its great antiquity and incorruptibility — [457] what method or machines they employed to bring it to the spot, and how they raised it erect? There is no tree or species of the Pine, whose wood, i.e. so large a portion of the trunk, is supposed to be incorruptible, exposed in the open air to all weathers, but the long-leaved Pine (Pin. palustris) and there is none growing within twelve or fifteen miles of this place, that tree being naturally produced only on the high, dry, barren ridges, where there is a sandy soil and grassy wet savannas. A great number of men uniting their strength, probably carried it to the place on handspikes, or some such contrivance.

On the Sabbath day before I sat off from this place, I could not help observing the solemnity of the town, the silence and the retiredness of the red inhabitants, but a very few of them were to be seen, the doors of their dwellings shut, and if a child chanced to stray out, it was quickly drawn in doors again: I asked the meaning of this, and was immediately answered, that it being the white people's beloved day or Sabbath, the Indians kept it religiously sacred to the Great Spirit.

Last night was clear and cold, wind North West, and this morning January 2d, 1778 [1776],[140] the face of the earth was perfectly white with a beautiful sparkling frost. Sat off for Augusta with a company of traders, four men with about thirty horses, twenty of which were loaded with leather and furs, each pack or load supposed to weigh one hundred and fifty pounds upon an average; in three days we arrived at the Apalachucla or Chata Uche river, crossed at the point towns Chehaw and Usseta; these towns almost join each other, yet speak two languages, [458] as radically different perhaps as the Muscogulge's and Chinese.[141] After leaving the river we met with nothing material, or worth particular observation, until our arrival at Oakmulge, towards evening, where we encamped in expansive ancient Indian fields, in view of the foaming flood of the river, now raging over its banks. Here were two companies of traders from Augusta, bound to the Nation, consisting of fifteen or twenty men, with seventy or eighty horses, most of which had their loads of merchandize; they crossed the river this morning and lost six horses in the attempt; they were drowned, being entangled in the vines under water at landing. But the river now falling again, we were in hopes that by next morning the waters would again be confined within the banks. We immediately sat about rigging our portable leather boat,[142] about eight feet long, which was of thick soal leather, folded up and carried on the top of a pack of deer skins; the people soon got her rigged, which was effected after the following manner. We in the first place cut down a White-Oak sapling, and by notching this at each end, bent it up, which formed the keel, stem and stern post of one piece, this being placed in the bottom of the boat, and pretty strong hoop-poles being fixed in the bottom across the keel, and, turning up their ends, expanded the hull of the boat, which being fastened by thongs to two other poles bent round, the outside of the rim forms the gunwales, thus in an hour's time our bark was rigged, to which afterwards we added two little oars or sculls. Our boat being now in readiness, and our horses turned out to pasture, each one retired to repose, or to such exercise as most effectually contributed to divert the mind. . . .

[459] The morning cool and pleasant, after reconnoitering the shores of the rivers, and consulting with our brethren in distress, who had not yet decamped, resolving to stay and lend their assistance in passing over this rapid gulph, we were encouraged to proceed, and launching our barke into the raging flood, after many successful trips ferried over all the goods, then drove in our horses altogether, and had the pleasure of seeing them all safely landed on the opposite shore; and lastly I embarked with three of our people, and several packs of leather, we then put off from shore, bidding adieu to our generous friends left behind, who re-echoed our shouts upon our safe landing.

[462] On my way down I also called at Silver Bluff, and waited on the honourable G. Golphin, Esq. to acknowledge my obligations to him, and likewise to fulfil my engagements on the part of Mr. T —— y, trader of Mucclasse. Mr. Golphin assured me that he was in a disagreeable predicament, and that he feared the worst, but said he would do all in his power to save him.

After five days pleasant travelling we arrived at Savanna in good health.

List of the towns and tribes in league, and which constitute the powerful confederacy or empire of the Creeks or Muscogulges,[143] viz.

Towns on the Talllapoose or Oakfuske river, viz.

Oakfuske, upper.
Oakfuske, lower.
Ufale, upper.
Ufale, lower.
Sokaspoge.
Tallase, great.
Coolome.
[463]
Chuaclahatche.
Otasse.
Cluale.
Fusahatche.
Tuccabatche.
Cunhutke.

These speak the Muscogulge or Creek tongue, called the Mother tongue.

Mucclasse.
Alabama.

Speak the Stincard tongue.[144]

Savannuca.

Speak the Uche tongue.

Whittumke.
Coosauda.

Speak the Stincard tongue.

Towns on the Coosau river, viz.

Abacooche.

Speak a dialect of Chicasaw.

Pocontallahasse.
Hickory ground, traders name.

Speak the Muscogulge tongue.

Natche.

Speak Muscog. and Chicasaw.

Towns on the branches of the Coosau river, viz.

Wiccakaw.

Fish pond, traders name.
Hillaba.
Kiolege.

Speak the Muscogulge tongue.

Towns on the Apalachucla or Chata Uche river, viz.

109

*Travels
Through
North
&
South
Carolina*

Apalachucla.
Tucpauska.
Chockeclucca.
Chata Uche.   Speak the Muscogulge
Checlucca-ninne.   tongue.
Hothletega.
Coweta.
Usseta.
[464]
Uche.   Speak the Savannuca tongue.
Hooseche.   Speak the Muscog. tongue.

Chehaw.
Echeta.
Occone.   Speak the Stincard.
Swaglaw, great.
Swaglaw, little.

Towns on Flint river, comprehending the
Siminoles or Lower Creeks

Suola-nocha.
Cuscowilla or Allachua.
Talahasochte.
Caloosahatche.
——Great island.   Traders name.
——Great hammock.   Traders name.
——Capon.   Traders name.
——St. Mark's.   Traders name.
——Forks.   Traders name.
With many others of less note.

The Siminoles speak both the Muscogulge and Stincard tongue.

In all fifty-five towns, besides many villages not enumerated, and reckoning two hundred inhabitants to each town on an average, which is a moderate computation, would give eleven thousand inhabitants.[145]

It appears to me pretty clearly, from divers circumstances, that this powerful empire or confederacy of the Creeks or Muscogulges, arose from, and established itself upon the ruins of that of the Natch-[465]es, agreeably to Monsieur Duprat.[146] According to the Muscogulges account of themselves, they arrived from the South-West, beyond the Mississipi, some time before the English settled the colony of Carolina and built Charleston; and their story concerning their country and people, from whence they sprang, the cause of

110

Travels
Through
North
&
South
Carolina

leaving their native land, the progress of their migration, &c. is very similar to that celebrated historian's account of the Natches, they might have been included as allies and confederates in that vast and powerful empire of red men. The Muscogulges gradually pushing and extending their settlements on their North-East border, until the dissolution of the Natches empire; being then the most numerous, warlike and powerful tribe, they began to subjugate the various tribes or bands (which formerly constituted the Natches) and uniting them with themselves, formed a new confederacy under the name of the Muscogulges.

The Muscogulge tongue being now the national or sovereign language, the Chicasaws, Chactaws, and even the remains of the Natches, if we are to credit the Creeks and traders, being dialects of the Muscogulge; and probably, when the Natches were sovereigns, they called their own the national tongue, and the Creeks, Chicasaws, &c. only dialects of theirs. It is uncertain which is really the mother tongue.

As for those numerous remnant bands or tribes, included at this day within the Muscogulge confederacy, who generally speak the Stincard language, (which is radically different from the Muscogulge) they are, beyond a doubt, the shattered remains of the various nations who inhabited the lower or maritime parts of Carolina and Florida, from Cape [466] Fear, West to the Mississipi. The Uches and Savannucas is a third language, radically different from the Muscogulge and Lingo,[147] and seems to be a more Northern tongue; I suppose a language that prevailed amongst the numerous tribes who formerly possessed and inhabited the maritime parts of Maryland and Virginia. I was told by an old trader that the Savannuca and Shawanese speak the same language, or very near alike.

Bartram spent the spring and summer of 1776 revisiting parts of Georgia and East Florida. In late October, he began the long ride home, stopping in Savannah and Charleston and finally arriving in Philadelphia in early January 1777.[148] The following discussion of the southeastern Indians comprises part 4 of *Travels*.

[481]   An Account of the Persons, Manners, Customs
and Government of the
Muscogulges or Creeks, Cherokees, Chactaws, &c.
Aborigines of the Continent of North America.

[483]   Chap. I.
Description of the Character, Customs and Persons of the American
Aborigines, from My Own Observations, As Well As from the General and

111

———

*Travels
Through
North
&
South
Carolina*

Impartial Report of Ancient, Respectable Men, Either of Their Own People, or White Traders, Who Have Spent Many Days of Their Lives Amongst Them.

Persons and Qualifications.

The males of the Cherokees, Muscogulges, Siminoles, Chicasaws, Chactaws and confederate tribes of the Creeks, are tall, erect, and moderately robust, their limbs well shaped, so as generally to form a perfect human figure; their features regular, and countenance open, dignified and placid; yet the forehead and brow so formed, as to strike you instantly with heroism and bravery; the eye though rather small, yet active and full of fire; the pupil always black, and the nose commonly inclining to the aquiline.

Their countenance and actions exhibit an air of magnanimity, superiority and independence.

Their complexion of a reddish brown or copper colour; their hair long, lank, coarse and black as a raven, and reflecting the like lustre at different exposures to the light.

[484] The women of the Cherokees are tall, slender, erect and of a delicate frame, their features formed with perfect symetry, their countenance cheerful and friendly, and they move with a becoming grace and dignity.

The Muscogulge women, though remarkably short of stature, are well formed; their visage round, features regular and beautiful; the brow high and arched; the eye large, black and languishing, expressive of modesty, difidence, and bashfulness; these charms are their defensive and offensive weapons, and they know very well how to play them off. And under cover of these alluring graces, are concealed the most subtile artifice; they are however loving and affectionate: they are I believe the smallest race of women yet known, seldom above five feet high, and I believe the greater number never arrive to that stature: their hands and feet not larger than those of Europeans of nine or ten years of age; yet the men are of gigantic stature, a full size larger than Europeans; many of them above six feet, and few under that, or five feet eight or ten inches. Their complexion much darker than any of the tribes to the North of them, that I have seen. This description will I believe comprehend the Muscogulges, their confederates, the Chactaws, and I believe the Chicasaws (though I have never seen their women) excepting however some bands of the Siminoles, Uches and Savannucas, who are rather taller and slenderer, and their complexion brighter

The Cherokees are yet taller[149] and more robust than the Muscogulges, and by far the largest race [485] of men I have seen * their complexions brighter

---

* There are however, some exceptions to this general observation, as I have myself witnessed. Their present grand chief or emperor (the Little Carpenter, Atta-kul-kulla) is a man of remarkable

112

———

Travels
Through
North
&
South
Carolina

and somewhat of the olive cast, especially the adults; and some of their young women are nearly as fair and blooming as European women.

The Cherokees in their dispositions and manners are grave and steady; dignified and circumspect in their deportment; rather slow and reserved in conversation; yet frank, cheerful and humane; tenacious of the liberties and natural [r]ights of men; secret, deliberate and determined in their councils; honest, just and liberal, and are ready always to sacrifice every pleasure and gratification, even their blood, and life itself, to defend their territory and maintain their rights. They do homage to the Muscogulges with reluctance, and are impatient under that galling yoke. I was witness to a most humiliating lash, which they passively received from their red masters, at the great congress and treaty of Augusta, when these people acceded with the Creeks, to the cession of the New Purchase; where were about three hundred of the Creeks, a great part of whom were warriors, and about one hundred Cherokees.[150]

The first day of convention opened with settling the preliminaries, one article of which was a demand on the part of the Georgians, to a territory lying on the Tugilo, and claimed by them both, which it seems the Cherokees had, previous to the opening of congress, privately conveyed to the Georgians, unknown to the Creeks, which the Georgians mentioning as a matter settled, the Creeks [486] demanded in council, on what foundation they built that claim, saying they had never ceded these lands. The Georgians answered, that they bought them of their friends and brothers the Cherokees. The Creeks nettled and incensed at this, a chief and warrior started up, and with an agitated and terrific countenance, frowning menaces and disdain, fixed his eyes on the Cherokee chiefs, asked them what right they had to give away their lands, calling them old women, and saying that they had long ago obliged them to wear the petticoat; a most humiliating and degrading stroke, in the presence of the chiefs of the whole Muscogulge confederacy, of the Chicasaws, principle men and citizens of Georgia, Carolina, Virginia, Maryland and Pennsylvania, in the face of their own chiefs and citizens, and amidst the laugh and jeers of the assembly, especially the young men of Virginia, their old enemy and dreaded neighbour: but humiliating as it really was, they were obliged to bear the stigma passively, and even without a reply.

And moreover, these arrogant bravos and usurpers, carried their pride and importance to such lengths, as even to threaten to dissolve the congress and retu[r]n home, unless the Georgians consented to annul the secret treaty with the Cherokees, and receive that territory immediately from them; as acknowledging their exclusive right of alienation, which was complied with,

———

small stature, slender, and delicate frame, the only instance I saw in the nation; but he is a man of superior abilities.

though violently extorted from the Cherokees, contrary to right and sanction of
treaties; since the Savanna river and its waters were acknowledged to be the
natural and just bounds of territory betwixt the Cherokees and Muscogulges.

113

*Travels
Through
North
&
South
Carolina*

The national character of the Muscogulges, when [487] considered in a
political view, exhibits a portraiture of a great or illustrious heroe. A proud,
haughty and arrogant race of men; they are however, brave and valiant in war,
ambitious of conquest, restless and perpetually exercising their arms, yet
magnanimous and merciful to a vanquished enemy, when he submits and seeks
their friendship and protection: always uniting the vanquished tribes in
confederacy with them; when they immediately enjoy, unexceptionably, every
right of free citizens, and are from that moment united in one common band of
brotherhood: they were never known to exterminate a tribe, except the
Yamasees, who would never submit on any terms, but fought it out to the last,
only about forty or fifty of them escaping at the last decisive battle, who threw
themselves under the protection of the Spaniards at St. Augustine.

According to their own account, which I believe to be true, after their arrival
in this country, they joined in alliance and perpetual amity, with the British
colonists of South Carolina and Georgia, which they never openly violated; but
on the contrary, pursued every step to strengthen the alliance; and their aged
chiefs to this day, speak of it with tears of joy, and exult in that memorable
transaction, as one of the most glorious events in the annals of their nation.

As an instance of their ideas of political impartial justice, and homage to the
Supreme Being, as the high arbiter of human transactions, who alone claims
the right of taking away the life of man: I beg leave to offer to the reader's
consideration, the following event, as I had it from the mouth of a Spaniard, a
respectable inhabitant of East Florida.

[488] The son of the Spanish governor of St. Augustine, together with two
young gentlemen, his friends and associates, conceived a design of amusing
themselves in a party of sport, at hunting and fishing. Having provided
themselves with a convenient bark, ammunition, fishing tackle, &c. they sat sail,
directing their course South, along the coast towards the point of Florida,
putting into bays and rivers, as conveniency and the prospect of game invited
them; the pleasing rural, and diversified scenes of the Florida coast,
imperceptibly allured them far to the south, beyond the Spanish fortified post.
Unfortunate youth! regardless of the advice and injunctions of their parents
and friends, still pursuing the delusive objects, they enter a harbour at evening,
with a view of chasing the roe-buck, and hunting up the sturdy bear, solacing
themselves with delicious fruits, and reposing under aromatic shades, when
alas! cruel unexpected event, in the beatific moments of their slumbers, they
are surrounded, arrested and carried off by a predatory band of Creek Indians,
proud of the capture, so rich a prize; they hurry away into cruel bondage the

114

———

Travels
Through
North
&
South
Carolina

hapless youth, conducting them, by devious paths through dreary swamps and boundless savannas, to the Nation.

At that time the Indians were at furious war with the Spaniards, scarcely any bounds set to their cruelties on either side: in short, the miserable youth were condemned to be burnt.

But, there being English traders in these towns, who learning the character of the captives, and expecting great rewards from the Spanish governor, if they could deliver them; they petitioned the Indians on their behalf, expressing their wishes to obtain [489] their rescue, offering a great ransom, acquainting them at the same time, that they were young men of high rank, and one of them the governor's son.

Upon this, the head men, or chiefs of the whole nation, were convened, and after solemn and mature deliberation, they returned the traders their final answer and determination, which was as follows.

"Brothers and friends. We have been considering upon this business concerning the captives. — And that, under the eye and fear of the Great Spirit. You know that these people are our cruel enemies, they save no lives of us red men, who fall in their power. You say that the youth is the son of the Spanish governor, we believe it, we are sorry he has fallen into our hands, but he is our enemy; the two young men (his friends) are equally our enemies, we are sorry to see them here: but we know no difference in their flesh and blood; they are equally our enemies, if we save one we must save all three; but we cannot do it, the red men require their blood to appease the spirits of their slain relatives; they have entrusted us with the guardianship of our laws and rights, we cannot betray them.

["]However we have a sacred prescription relative to this affair; which allows us to extend mercy to a certain degree: a third is saved by lot; the Great Spirit allows us to put it to that decision; he is no respecter of persons." The lots are cast. The governor's son was taken and burnt.

If we consider them with respect to their private [490] character or in a moral view, they must, I think, claim our approbation, if we divest ourselves of prejudice and think freely. As moral men they certainly stand in no need of European civilization.

They are just, honest, liberal and hospitable to strangers; considerate, loving and affectionate to their wives and relations; fond of their children; industrious, frugal, temperate and persevering; charitable and forbearing. I have been weeks and months amongst them and in their towns, and never observed the least sign of contention or wrangling: never saw an instance of an Indian beating his wife, or even reproving her in anger. In this case they stand as examples of reproof to the most civilized nations, as not being defective in justice, gratitude and a good understanding; for indeed their wives merit their esteem and the most gentle treatment, they being industrious, frugal, careful, loving and affectionate.

The Muscogulges are more volatile, sprightly and talkative than their Northern neighbours, the Cherokees; and, though far more distant from the white settlements than any nation East of the Mississipi or Ohio, appear evidently to have made greater advances towards the refinements of true civilization, which cannot, in the least degree, be attributed to the good examples of the white people.

115

*Travels
Through
North
&
South
Carolina*

Their internal police and family economy is what at once engages the notice of European travellers, and incontrovertibly places these people in an illustrious point of view; their liberality, intimacy and friendly intercourse one with another, without any restraint of ceremonious formality, as if they were even insensible of the use or necessity of associating [491] the passions or affections of avarice, ambition or covetousness.

A man goes forth on his business or avocations, he calls in at another town, if he wants victuals, rest or social conversation, he confidently approaches the door of the first house he chooses, saying "I am come;" the good man or woman replies, "You are; its well." Immediately victuals and drink are ready; he eats and drinks a little, then smokes Tobacco, and converses either of private matters, public talks or the news of the town. He rises and says, "I go;" the other answers, "You do!" He then proceeds again, and steps in at the next habitation he likes, or repairs to the public square, where are people always conversing by day, or dancing all night, or to some more private assembly, as he likes; he needs no one to introduce him, any more than the black-bird or thrush, when he repairs to the fruitful groves, to regale on their luxuries, and entertain the fond female with evening songs.

It is astonishing, though a fact, as well as a sharp reproof to the white people, if they will allow themselves liberty to reflect and form a just estimate, and I must own elevates these people to the first rank amongst mankind, that they have been able to resist the continual efforts of the complicated host of vices, that have for ages overrun the nations of the old world, and so contaminated their morals; yet more so, since such vast armies of these evil spirits have invaded this continent, and closely invested them on all sides. Astonishing indeed! when we behold the ill, immoral conduct of too many white people, who reside amongst them: notwithstanding it seems natural, eligible and even easy for these simple, illiterate people, to put in practice those beautiful [492] lectures delivered to us by the ancient sages and philosophers, and recorded for our instruction.

I saw a young Indian in the Nation, who when present, and beholding the scenes of mad intemperance and folly acted by the white men in the town, clap his hand to his breast, and with a smile, looking aloft as if struck with

116

---

*Travels
Through
North
&
South
Carolina*

astonishment, and wrapt in love and adoration to the Deity, as who should say, O thou Great and Good Spirit, we are indeed sensible of thy benignity and favour to us red men, in denying us the understanding of white men. We did not know before they came amongst us that ma[n]kind could become so base, and fall so below the dignity of their nature. Defend us from their manners, laws and power.

The Muscogulges, with their confederates, the Chactaws, Chicasaws, and perhaps the Cherokees, eminently deserve the encomium of all nations, for their wisdom and virtue in resisting and even repeling the greatest, and even the common enemy of mankind, at least of most of the European nations, I mean spirituous liquors.

The first and most cogent article in all their treaties with the white people, is, that there shall not be any kind of spirituous liquors sold or brought into their towns; and the traders are allowed but two kegs (five gallons each) which is supposed to be sufficient for a company, to serve them on the road, and if any of this remains on their approaching the towns, they must spill it on the ground or secrete it on the road, for it must not come into the town.

On my journey from Mobile to the Nation, just after we had passed the junction of the Pensacola [493] road with our path, two young traders overtook us on their way to the Nation. We enquired what news? They informed us that they were running about forty kegs of Jamaica spirits (which by dashing would have made at least eighty kegs) to the Nation; and after having left the town three or four days, they were surprised on the road in the evening, just after they had come to camp, by a party of Creeks, who discovering their species of merchandize, they forthwith struck their tomahawks into every keg, giving the liquor to the thirsty sand, not tasting a drop of it themselves, and they had enough to do to keep the tomahawks from their own skulls.

How are we to account for their excellent policy in civil government: it cannot derive its influence from coercive laws, for they have no such artificial system. Divine wisdom dictates and they obey.

We see and know full well the direful effects of this torrent of evil, which has its source in hell, and we know surely, as well as these savages, how to divert its course and suppress its inundations. Do we want wisdom and virtue? let our youth then repair to the venerable councils of the Muscogulges.

[494]   Chap. II
                    Of Their Government and Civil Society.

The constitution or system of their police is simply natural, and as little complicated as that which is supposed to direct or rule the approved economy of the ant and the bee, and seems to be nothing more than the simple dictates of natural reason, plain to every one, yet recommended to them by their wise and virtuous elders as divine, because necessary for securing mutual happiness: equally binding and effectual, as being proposed and assented to in the general combination: every one's conscience being a sufficient conviction (the golden rule, do as you would be done by) instantly presents to view, and produces a society of peace and love, which in effect better maintains human happiness, than the most complicated system of modern politics, or sumptuary laws, enforced by coercive means: for here the people are all on an equality, as to the possession and enjoyments of the common necessaries and conveniencies of life, for luxuries and superfluities they have none.

117

Travels
Through
North
&
South
Carolina

This natural constitution is simply subordinate, and the supreme, sovereign or executive power resides in a council of elderly chiefs, warriors and others, respectable for wisdom, valour and virtue.

At the head of this venerable senate, presides their mico or king, which signifies a magistrate or chief ruler: the governors of Carolina, Georgia, &c. are called mico; and the king of England is called [495] Ant-apala-mico-clucco * , that is the great king, over or beyond the great water.

The king although he is acknowledged to be the first and greatest man in the town or tribe, and honoured with every due and rational mark of love and esteem, and when presiding in council, with a humility and homage as reverent as that paid to the most despotic monarch in Europe or the East, and when absent, his seat is not filled by any other person, yet he is not dreaded, and when out of the council, he associates with the people as a common man, converses with them, and they with him in perfect ease and familiarity.

The mico or king, though elective, yet his advancement to that supreme dignity must be understood in a very different light from the el[e]ctive monarchs of the old world, where the progress to magistracy is generally affected by schism and the influence of friends gained by craft, bribery and often by more violent efforts; and after the throne is obtained, by measures little better than usurpation, he must be protected and supported there, by the same base means that carried him thither.

But here behold the majesty of the Muscogulge mico, he does not either publicly or privately beg of the people to place him in a situation to command and rule them. No, his appearance is altogether mysterious, as a beneficent deity he rises king over them, as the sun rises to bless the earth!

No one will tell you how or when he became their king; but he is universally acknowledged to be the greatest person among them, and he is lo-[496]ved, esteemed and reverenced, although he associates, eats, drinks and dances with them in common as another man, his dress is the same, and a stranger could

* Clucco signifies great or excellentr

118

Travels
Through
North
&
South
Carolina

not distinguish the king's habitation, from that of any other citizen, by any sort of splendor or magnificence: yet he percieves they act as though their mico beheld them though invisible. In a word, their mico seems to them, the representative of Providence or the Great Spirit, whom they acknowledge to preside over and influence their councils and public proceedings. He personally presides daily in their councils, either at the rotunda or public square: and even here his voice in regard to business in hand, is regarded no more, than any other chief or senator's, any other than in his advice as being the best and wisest man of the tribe, and not by virtue of regal prerogative. But whether their ultimate decisions require unanimity, or only a majority of voices, I am uncertain, but probably where there is a majority, the minority voluntarily accede.

The most active part the mico acts, is in the civil government of the town or tribe, here he has the power and prerogative of calling a council, to deliberate on peace and war, or all public concerns, as enquiring into, and deciding upon complaints and differences, but he has not the least shadow of exclusive executive power. He is complimented with the first visits of strangers, giving audience to ambassadors, with presents, and he has also the disposal of the public granary.

The next man in order of dignity and power, is the great war chief, he represents and exercises the dignity of the mico, in his absence in council; his voice is of the greatest weight, in military affairs: his power and authority are entirely independent [497] of the mico, though when a mico goes on an expedition, he heads the army, and is there the war chief: there are many of these war chiefs in a town or tribe, who are captains or leaders of military parties; they are elderly men, who in their youthful days, have distinguished themselves in war by valour, subtilty and intrepidity; and these veteran chiefs, in a great degree, constitute their truly dignified and venerable senates.[151]

There is in every town or tribe a high priest, usually called by the white people jugglers, or conjurers, besides several juniors or graduates. But the ancient high priest or seer, presides in spiritual affairs, and is a person of consequence; he maintains and exercises great influence in the state; particularly in military affairs, the senate never determine on an expedition against their enemy without his counsel and assistance. These people generally believe that their seer has communion with powerful invisible spirits, who they suppose have a share in the rule and government of human affairs, as well as the elements; that he can predict the result of an expedition, and his influence is so great, that they have been known frequently to stop, and turn back an army, when within a days journey of their enemy, after a march of several hundred miles, and indeed their predictions have surprized many people. They foretel rain or drought, and pretend to bring rain at pleasure, cure diseases, and exercise witchcraft, invoke or expel evil spirits, and even assume the power of directing thunder and lightning.[152]

These Indians are by no means idolaters, unless their puffing the Tobacco smoke towards the sun, [498] and rejoicing at the appearance of the new moon, * may be termed so, so far from idolatry are they, that they have no images amongst them, nor any religious rite or ceremony that I could perceive; but adore the Great Spirit, the giver and taker away of the breath of life, with the most profound and respectful homage. They believe in a future state, where the spirit exists, which they call the world of spirits, where they enjoy different degrees of tranquility or comforts, agreeable to their life spent here: a person who in this life has been an industrious hunter, provided well for his family, an intrepid and active warrior, just, upright, and done all the good he could, will, they say, in the world of spirits, live in a warm, pleasant country, where are expansive, green, flowery savannas and high forests, watered with rivers of pure waters, replenished with deer, and every species of game; a serene, unclouded and peaceful sky; in short, where there is fulness of pleasure, uninterrupted.

They have many accounts of trances and visions of their people, who have been supposed to be dead, but afterwards reviving have related their visions, which tend to enforce the practice of virtue and the moral duties.

Before I went amongst the Indians I had often heard it reported that these people, when their parents, through extreme old age, become decrepid and helpless, in compassion for their miseries, send them to the other world, by a stroke of the tomahawk or bullet. Such a degree of depravity and species of impiety always appeared to me so incred-[499]ibly inhuman and horrid, it was with the utmost difficulty that I assumed resolution sufficient to enquire into it.

The traders assured me they knew no instance of such barbarism, but that there had been instances of the communities performing such a deed at the earnest request of the victim.

When I was at Mucclasse town, early one morning, at the invitation of the chief trader, we repaired to the public square, taking with us some presents for the Indian chiefs. On our arrival we took our seats in a circle of venerable men, round a fire in the centre of the area; other citizens were continually coming in, and amongst them I was struck with awe and veneration at the appearance of a very aged man; his hair, what little he had, was as white as snow; he was conducted by three young men, one having hold of each arm, and the third behind to steady him. On his approach the whole circle saluted him, "welcome," and made way for him: he looked as smiling and cheerful as youth, yet stone-blind by extreme old age; he was the most ancient chief of the town,

* I have observed the young fellows very merry and jocose, at the appearance of the new moon, saying, how ashamed she looks under the veil, since sleeping with the sun these two or three nights, she is ashamed to shew her face, &c

119

Travels
Through
North
&
South
Carolina

1 2 0

Travels
Through
North
&
South
Carolina

and they all seemed to reverence him. Soon after the old man had seated himself I distributed my presents, giving him a very fine handkerchief and a twist of choice Tobacco; which passed through the hands of an elderly chief who sat next to him, telling him it was a present from one of their white brothers, lately arrived in the nation from Charleston: he received the present with a smile, and thanked me, returning the favour immediately with his own stone pipe [figure 14][153] and cat skin of Tobacco, and then complimented me with a long oration, the purport of which was the value he set on the friendship of the Carolinians: he said, [500] that when he was a young man they had no iron hatchets, pots, hoes, knives, razors nor guns, but that they then made use of their own stone axes, clay pots, flint knives, bows and arrows; and that he was the first man who brought the white peoples goods into his town, which he did on his back from Charleston, five hundred miles on foot, for they had no horses then amongst them.[154]

The trader then related to me an anecdote concerning this ancient patriarch, which occurred not long since.

One morning after his attendants had led him to the council fire, before seating himself he addressed himself to the people after this manner —

"You yet love me; what can I do now to merit your regard? nothing; I am good for nothing; I cannot see to shoot the buck or hunt up the sturdy bear; I know I am but a burthen to you; I have lived long enough; now let my spirit go; I want to see the warriors of my youth in the country of spirits; (bareing his breast) here is the hatchet, take it and strike." They answered with one united voice, "We will not; we cannot; we want you here."

[501]   Chap. III.
                        Of Their Dress, Feasts and Divertisements.

The youth of both sexes are fond of decorating themselves with external ornaments. The men shave their head, leaving only a narrow crest or comb, beginning at the crown of the head, where it is about two inches broad and about the same height, and stands frized upright; but this crest tending backwards, gradually widens, covering the hinder part of the head and back of the neck; this lank hair behind is ornamented with pendant silver quills, and then jointed or articulated silver plates, and usually the middle fascicle of hair, which being by far the longest, is wrapped in a large quill of silver, or the joint of a small reed, curiously sculptured and painted, the hair continuing through it terminates in a tail or tossil.

Their ears are lacerated, separating the border or cartilagenous limb, which at first is bound round very close and tight with leather strings or thongs, and anointed with fresh bear's oil, until healed; the weight of the lead, extends this

121

*Travels
Through
North
&
South
Carolina*

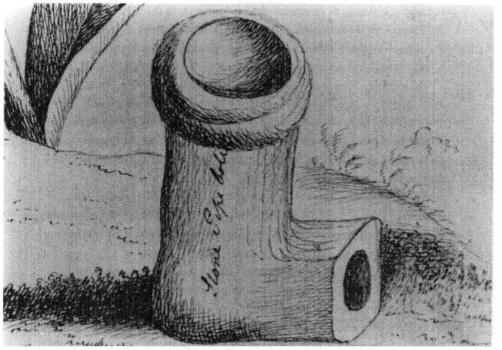

Figure 14. William Bartram's Drawing of an Indian-made Stone Pipe Bowl
(courtesy, British Museum of Natural History)

cartilage an incredible length, which afterwards being craped, or bound round
in brass or silver wire, extends it semicircularly like a bow or crescent; and it is
then very elastic, even so as to spring and bound about with the least motion or
flexure of the body; this is decorated with soft white plumes of heron
feathers.[155]

A very curious diadem or band, about four inches broad, and ingeniously
wrought or woven, and [502] curiously decorated with stones, beads, wampum,
porcupine quills, &c. encircles their temples, the front peak of which is
embellished with a high waving plume, of crane or heron feathers.

The cloathing of their body is very simple and frugal. Sometimes a ruffled
shirt of fine linen, next the skin, and a flap, which covers their lower parts, this
garment somewhat resembles the ancient Roman breeches, or the kelt of the
Highlanders; it usually consists of a piece of blue cloth, about eighteen inches
wide, this they pass between their thighs, and both ends being taken up and
drawn through a belt round their waist, the ends fall down, one before, and the
other behind, not quite to the knee; this flap is usually plaited and indented at
the ends, and ornamented with beads, tinsel lace, &c.

The leg is furnished with cloth boots; they reach from the ancle to the calf,
and are ornamented with lace, beads, silver bells, &c.

122

---

*Travels
Through
North
&
South
Carolina*

And the stillepica or moccasin defends and adorns the feet; they seem to be an imitation of the ancient buskin or sandal; these are very ingeniously made of deer skins, dressed very soft, and curiously ornamented according to fancy.

Beside this attire, they have a large mantle of the finest cloth they are able to purchase, always either of scarlet or blue colour; this mantle is fancifully decorated, with rich lace or fringe round the border, and often with little round silver, or brass bells. Some have a short cloak, just large enough to cover the shoulders and breast; this is most ingeniously constructed, of feathers woven or placed in a natural imbricated manner, usually of [503] the scarlet feathers of the flaningo, or others of the gayest colour.

They have large silver crescents, or gorgets, which being suspended by a ribband round the neck, lie upon the breast; and the arms are ornamented with silver bands, or bracelets, and silver and gold chains, &c. a collar invests the neck.

The head, neck and breast, are painted with vermilion, and some of the warriors have the skin of the breast, and muscular parts of the body, very curiously inscribed, or adorned with hieroglyphick scroles, flowers, figures of animals, stars, crescents, and the sun in the centre of the breast. This painting of the flesh, I understand, is performed in their youth, by picking the skin with a needle, until the blood starts, and rubbing in a blueish tinct, which is as permanent as their life. The shirt hangs loose about the waist, like a frock, or split down before, resembling a gown, which is sometimes wrapped close, and the waist encircled by a curious belt or sash.

The dress of the females is somewhat different from that of the men; their flap or petticoat, is made after a different manner, is larger and longer, reaching almost to the middle of the leg, and is put on differently; they have no shirt or shift but a little short waistcoat, usually made of callico, printed linen, or fine cloth, decorated with lace, beads, &c. They never wear boots or stockings, but their buskins reach to the middle of the leg. They never cut their hair, but plait it in wreathes, which is turned up, and fastened on the crown, with a silver broach, forming a wreathed top-knot, decorated with an incredible quantity of silk ribbands, of various co-[504]lours, which stream down on every side, almost to the ground. They never paint, except those of a particular class, when disposed to grant certain favours to the other sex.

But these decorations are only to be considered as indulgencies on particular occasions, and the privilege of youth; as at weddings, festivals, dances, &c. or when the men assemble to act the war farce, on the evening immediately preceding their march on a hostile expedition; but usually they are almost naked, contenting themselves with the flap and sometimes a shirt, boots and moccasins; the mantle is seldom worn by the men, except at night, in the winter season, when extremely cold, and by the women at dances, which serves the purpose of a veil, and the females always wear the jacket, flap, and buskin, even children as soon or before they can walk, whereas the male youth go perfectly naked until they are twelve or fifteen years of age.

The junior priests or students, constantly wear the mantle or robe, which is white, and they have a great owl skin cased and stuffed very ingeniously, so well executed, as almost to represent the living bird, having large sparkling glass beads, or buttons fixed in the head for eyes: this insignia of wisdom and divination, they wear sometimes as a crest on the top of the head, at other times the image sits on the arm, or is borne on the hand. These bachelors are also distinguishable from the other people, by their taciturnity, grave and solemn countenance, dignified step, and singing to themselves songs or hymns, in a low sweet voice, as they stroll about the towns.

These people like all other nations, are fond of [505] music and dancing: their music is both vocal and instrumental; but of the latter they have scarcely any thing worth the name, the tambour, rattle-gourd, and a kind of flute, made of a joint of reed or the tibia of the deers leg: on this instrument they perform badly, and at best it is rather a hideous melancholy discord, than harmony; it is only young fellows who amuse themselves on this howling instrument, but the tambour and rattle, accompanied with their sweet low voices, produces a pathetic harmony, keeping exact time together, and the countenance of the musician, at proper times, seems to express the solemn elevated state of the mind; at that time there seems not only a harmony between him and his instrument, but instantly touches the feelings of the attentive audience, as the influence of an active and powerful spirit; there is then an united universal sensation of delight and peaceful union of souls throughout the assembly.

Their music, vocal and instrumental, united, keeps exact time with the performers or dancers.[156]

They have an endless variety of steps, but the most common, and that which I term the most civil, and indeed the most admired and practised amongst themselves, is a slow shuffling alternate step; both feet move forward one after the other, first the right foot foremost, and next the left, moving one after the other, in two opposite circles, i.e. first a circle of young men, and within a circle of young women moving together opposite ways, the men with the course of the sun, and the females contrary to it, the men strike their arm with the open hand, and the girls clap hands, and raise their shrill sweet voices, answering an elevated shout of the men at [506] stated times of termination of the stanzas; and the girls perform an interlude or chorus separately.

They have songs to accompany their dances, of different classes, as martial, bacchanalian and amorous, which last I must confess, are extravagantly libidinous, and they have moral songs, which seem to be the most esteemed and practised, and answer the purpose of religious lectures.

124

———

Travels
Through
North
&
South
Carolina

Some of their most favorite songs and dances, they have from their enemy, the Chactaw;[157] for it seems this people are very eminent, for poetry and music; every town amongst them strives to excel each other in composing new songs for dances; and by a custom amongst them, they must have at least one new song, for exhibition, at every annual busque.

The young mustee, who came with me to the Mucclasses from Mobile, having Chactaw blood in his veins from his mother, was a sensible young fellow, and by his father had been instructed in reading, writing and arithmetic, and could speak English very well. He took it into his head, to travel into the Chactaw country: his views were magnanimous, and his designs in the highest degree commendable, nothing less than to inform himself of every species of arts and sciences, that might be of use and advantage, when introduced into his own country, but more particularly music and poetry: with these views he privately left the Nation, went to Mobile, and there entered into the service of the trading company to the Chactaws, as a white man; his easy, communicative, active and familiar disposition and manners, being agreeable to that people, procured him access every where, and favored his subtilty and artifice: at length, however, the Chactaws hearing of his lineage and consangui[507]nity with the Creeks, by the father's side, pronounced him a Creek, and consequently an enemy and a spy amongst them, and secretly resolved to dispatch him. The young philosopher got notice of their suspicions, and hostile intentions, in time to make his escape, though closely pursued, he however kept a head of his sanguinary pursuers, arrived at Mobile, and threw himself under the protection of the English, entered the service of the trader of Mucclasse, who was then setting off for the Nation, and notwithstanding the speed with which we travelled, narrowly escaped the ardor and vigilance of his pursuing enemies, who surprised a company of emigrants, in the desarts of Schambe, the very night after we met them, expecting to intercept him thereabout.

The young traveller, having learned all their most celebrated new songs and poetry, at a great dance and festival in the Mucclasse, a day or two after our arrival; the youth pressed him, to give out some of his new songs, he complied with their entreaties, and the songs and dance went round with harmony and eclat; their being a young Chactaw slave girl in the circle, who soon after, discovered very affecting sensations of affliction and distress of mind, and before the conclusion of the dance, many of her companions complimented her with sympathetic sighs and tears, from their own sparkling eyes. As soon as I had an opportunity, I enquired of the young Orpheus, the cause of that song being so distressing to the young slave. He replied, that when she was lately taken captive, her father and brothers were slain in the contest, and she understanding the sense of the song, called to remembrance the tragical fate of her family, and could not forbear weeping at the recital.

125

*Travels
Through
North
&
South
Carolina*

[508] The meaning of the chorus was,

> All men must surely die,
> Tho' no one knows how soon,
> Yet when the time shall come,
> The event may be joyful.

These doleful moral songs or elegies, have a quick and sensible effect on their passions, and discover a lively affection and sensibility; their countenance now dejected, or again, by an easy transition, becomes gently elevated, as if in solemn address or supplication, accompanied with a tremulous, sweet, lamentable voice; a stranger is for a moment lost to himself as it were, or his mind, associated with the person immediately affected, is in danger of revealing his own distress unawares.

They have a variety of games for exercise and pastime; some particular to the men, some to the female sex, and others wherein both sexes are engaged.

The ball play is esteemed the most noble and manly exercise; this game is exhibited in an extensive level plain, usually contiguous to the town: the inhabitants of one town play against another, in consequence of a challenge, when the youth of both sexes are often engaged, and sometimes stake their whole substance. Here they perform amazing feats of strength and agility; the game principally consists in taking and carrying off the ball from the opposite party, after being hurled into the air, midway between two high pillars, which are the goals, and the party who bears off the ball to their pillar wins the game; each person having a racquet or hurl, which is an implement of a very curious construction, somewhat resembling a ladle or little hoop-net, with a handle near three feet in [509] length, the hoop and handle of wood, and the neting of thongs of raw hide, or tendons of an animal.[158]

The foot-ball is likewise a favorite, manly diversion with them. Feasting and dancing in the square, at evening ends all their games.

They have besides, feasts or festivals almost for every month in the year, which are chiefly dedicated to hunting and agriculture.

The busk or feast of first fruits is their principal festival; this seems to end the last, and begin the new year.

It commences in August, when their new crops of Corn are arrived to perfect maturity: and every town celebrates the busk separately, when their own harvest is ready.

If they have any religious rite or ceremony, this festival is its most solemn celebration.

When a town celebrates the busk, having previously provided themselves with new clothes, new pots, pans and other household utensils and furniture, they collect all their worn out clothes and other despicable things, sweep and cleanse

126

———

Travels
Through
North
&
South
Carolina

their houses, squares, and the whole town, of their filth, which with all the remaining grain and other old provisions, they cast together in one common heap, and consume it with fire; after having taken medicine, and fasted for three days, all the fire in the town is extinguished; during this fast they abstain from the gratification of every appetite and passion whatever. A general amnesty is proclaimed, all malefactors may return to their town, and they are absolved from their crimes, which are now forgotten, and they restored to favor.

[510] On the fourth morning, the high priest, by rubbing dry wood together, produces new fire in the public square, from whence every habitation in the town is supplied with the new and pure flame.

Then the women go forth to the harvest field, and bring from thence new Corn and fruits, which being prepared in the best manner, in various dishes, and drink withal, is brought with solemnity to the square, where the people are assembled, apparelled in their new clothes and decorations. The men having regaled themselves, the remainder is carried off and distributed amongst the families of the town. The women and children solace themselves in their separate families, and in the evening repair to the public square, where they dance, sing and rejoice during the whole night, observing a proper and exemplary decorum; this continues three days, and the four following days they receive visits, and rejoice with their friends from neighbouring towns, who have purified and prepared themselves.[159]

[511]   Chap. IV.
                        Concerning Property, Agriculture,
                            Arts and Manufactures.

It has been said by historians, who have written concerning the customs and usages of the aborigines of America, that they have every thing in common, and no private property; which are terms in my opinion too vague and general, when applied to these people. From my own frequent opportunities of observation, and the information of respectable characters, who have spent many years amongst them, I venture to set this matter in a just view before my readers.

I shall begin with the produce of their agricultural labours.

An Indian town is generally so situated, as to be convenient for procuring game, secure from sudden invasion, a large district of excellent arable land adjoining, or in its vicinity, if possible on an isthmus betwixt two waters, or where the doubling of a river forms a peninsula; such a situation generally comprises a sufficient body of excellent land for planting Corn, Potatoes, Beans, Squash, Pumpkins, Citruls, Melons, &c. and is taken in with a small expence and trouble of fencing, to secure their crops from the invasion of predatory

animals. At other times however they choose such a convenient fertile spot at
some distance from their town, when circumstances will not admit of having
both together.

[512] This is their common plantation, and the whole town plant in one vast
field together, but yet the part or share of every individual family or habitation,
is separated from the next adjoining, by a narrow strip, or verge of grass, or any
other natural or artificial boundary.

In the spring, the ground being already prepared, on one and the same day,
early in the morning, the whole town is summoned, by the sound of a conch
shell, from the mouth of the overseer, to meet at the public square, whither the
people repair with their hoes and axes, and from thence proceed to their
plantation, where they begin to plant, not every one in his own little district,
assigned and laid out, but the whole community united, begins on one certain
part of the field, where they plant on until finished, and when their rising crops
are ready for dressing, and cleansing, they proceed after the same order, and so
on day after day, until the crop is laid by for ripening. After the feast of the busk
is over, and all the grain is ripe, the whole town again assemble, and every man
carries of[f] the fruits of his labour, from the part first allotted to him, which he
deposits in his own granary; which is individually his own. But previous to their
carrying off their crops from the field, there is a large crib or granary, erected in
the plantation, which is called the king's crib; and to this each family carries and
deposits a certain quantity, according to his ability or inclination, or none at all
if he so chooses, this in appearance seems a tribute or revenue to the mico, but
in fact is designed for another purpose, i.e. that of a public treasury, supplied by
a few and voluntary contributions, and to which every citizen has the right of
free and e-[513]qual access, when his own private stores are consumed, to serve
as a surplus to fly to for succour, to assist neighbouring towns, whose crops may
have failed, accommodate strangers, or travellers, afford provisions or supplies,
when they go forth on hostile expeditions, and for all other exigencies of the
state; and this treasure is at the disposal of the king or mico; which is surely a
royal attribute to have an exclusive right and ability in a community to
distribute comfort and blessings to the necessitous.[160]

As to mechanic arts or manufactures, at present they have scarcely any thing
worth observation, since they are supplied with necessaries, conveniencies and
even superfluities by the white traders. The men perform nothing except
erecting their mean habitations, forming their canoes, stone pipes, tambour,
eagles tail or standard, and some other trifling matters, for war and hunting are
their principal employments. The women are more vigilant, and turn their
attention to various manual employments; they make all their pottery or
earthen-ware, moccasins; spin and weave the curious belts and diadems for the
men; fabricate lace, fringe, embroider and decorate their apparel, &c. &c.[161]

127

*Travels
Through
North
&
South
Carolina*

128

Travels
Through
North
&
South
Carolina

Chap. V.
Of Their Marriage and Funeral Ceremonies

As to their marriage ceremonies they are very simple, yet differ greatly in the various nations and tribes. Amongst some of the bands in the Muscogulge confederacy, I was informed the mystery is performed after the following manner. When a young man has fixed his affections, and is determined to marry, he takes a Cane or Reed, such as they stick down at the hills of their Bean vines for their support: with this (after having obtained her parents or nearest relations consent) he repairs to the habitation of his beloved, attended by his friends and associates, and in the presence of the wedding guests, he sticks his Reed down, upright in the ground, when soon after his sweet-heart comes forth with another Reed, which she sticks down by the side of his, when they are married; then they exchange Reeds, which are laid by as evidences or certificates of the marriage, which is celebrated with feasting, music and dancing: each one of their relations and friends, at the wedding, contribute something towards establishing the new family. As soon as the wedding is over, the town is convened, and the council orders or recommends a new habitation to be constructed for the accommodation of the new family; every man in the town joins in the work, which is began and finished in a day's time.[162]

The greatest accomplishments to recommend a young man to his favourite maid, is to prove himself a brave warrior, and a cunning, industrious hunter.

[515] They marry only for a year's time, and, according to ancient custom, at the expiration of the year they renew the marriage; but there is seldom an instance of their separating after they have children. If it should happen, the mother takes the children under her own protection, though the father is obliged to contribute towards their maintenance during their minority and the mother's widowhood.[163]

The Muscogulges allow of polygamy in the utmost latitude; every man takes as many wives as he chooses, but the first is queen, and the others her handmaids and associates.

It is common for a great man amongst them, who has already half a dozen wives, if he sees a child of eight or nine years of age, who pleases him, and he can agree with her parents or guardians, to marry her and take her into his house at that age.

Adultery is always punished with cropping, which is the only corporal punishment amongst them, and death or out-lawry for murder, and infamy for less crimes, as fornication, theft, &c. which produces such repeated marks and reflections of ridicule and contempt, that generally ends in voluntary banishment; and these renegadoes and vagabonds are generally the ruffians who commit depredations and murders on the frontiers.

The Muscogulges bury their deceased in the earth; they dig a four square deep pit under the cabin or couch which the deceased laid on, in his house, lining the grave with Cypress bark, where they place the corps in a sitting posture, as if it were alive; de-[516]positing with him his gun, tomahawk, pipe and such other matters as he had the greatest value for in his life time. His eldest wife, or the queen dowager, has the second choice of his possessions, and the remaining effects are divided amongst his other wives and children.[164]

The Chactaws pay their last duties and respect to the deceased in a very different manner. As soon as a person is dead, they erect a scaffold eighteen or twenty feet high, in a grove adjacent to the town, where they lay the corps, lightly covered with a mantle; here it is suffered to remain, visited and protected by the friends and relations, until the flesh becomes putrid, so as easily to part from the bones, then undertakers, who make it their business, carefully strip the flesh from the bones, wash and cleanse them, and when dry and purified by the air, having provided a curiously wrought chest or coffin, fabricated of bones[165] and splints, they place all the bones therein; which is deposited in the bone-house, a building erected for that purpose in every town. And when this house is full a general solemn funeral takes place. When the nearest kindred or friends of the deceased, on a day appointed, repair to the bone-house, take up the respective coffins, and following one another in order of seniority, the nearest relations and connections attending their respective corps, and the multitude following after them, all as one family, with united voice of alternate Allelujah and lamentation, slowly proceeding on to the place of general interment, where they place the coffins in order, forming a pyramid * ; and last-[517]ly, cover all over with earth, which raises a conical hill or mount. When they return to town in order of solemn procession, concluding the day with a festival, which is called the feast of the dead.[166]

The Chactaws are called by the traders flats, or flat-heads, all the males having the fore and hind part of their skulls, artificially flattened, or compressed, which is effected after the following manner. As soon as the child is born, the nurse provides a cradle or wooden case, hollowed and fashioned, to receive the infant, lying prostrate on its back, and that part of the case where the head reposes, being fashioned like a brick mould. In this portable machine the little boy is fixed, a bag of sand being laid on his forehead, which by continual gentle compressure, gives the head somewhat the form of a brick from the temples upwards, and by these means they have high and lofty foreheads, sloping off backwards.[167] These men are not so neat in the trim of their heads, as the Muscogulges are, and they are remarkably slovenly and negligent in every part

* Some ingenious men, whom I have conversed with, have given it as their opinion, that all those pyramidal artificial hills, usually called Indian mounts were raised on this occasion, and are generally sepulchres. However I am of a different opinion.

130
———

Travels
Through
North
&
South
Carolina

of their dress; but otherwise they are said to be ingenious, sensible and virtuous men; bold and intrepid, yet quiet and peaceable, and are acknowledged by the Creeks to be brave.

They are supposed to be most ingenious and industrious husbandmen, having large plantations, or country farms, where they employ much of their time in agricultural improvements, after the manner of the white people; by which means their territories are more generally cultivated, and better inhabited than any other Indian republic that we know of; the number of their inhabitants is said to greatly exceed the whole Muscogulge confederacy, although their territories are not a fourth part as ex-[518]tensive.[168] It appeared to me from observation, and what information I could get, that the Indians entertain rational notions of the soul's immortality, and of a future state of social existence; and accordingly, in order to inculcate morality, and promote human happiness, they applaud praiseworthy actions, as commendable and necessary for the support of civil society, and maintaining the dignity and strength of their nation or tribe, as well as securing an excellent and tranquil state and degree in the world of spirits, after their decease. And they say the Great Spirit favours all good and brave men.

[519]   Chap. VI.
                     Language and Manners.

The Muscogulge language is spoken throughout the confederacy, (although consisting of many nations, who have a speech peculiar to themselves) as also by their friends and allies, the Natches. The Chicasaw and Chactaw the Muscogulges say is a dialect of theirs.

This language is very agreeable to the ear, courteous, gentle and musical: the letter R is not sounded in one word of their language: the women in particular speak so fine and musical, as to represent the singing of birds; and when heard and not seen, one might imagine it to be the prattling of young children: the men's speech is indeed more strong and sonorous, but not harsh, and in no instance guttural, and I believe the letter R is not used to express any word, in any language of the confederacy.[169]

The Cherokee tongue on the contrary, is very loud, somewhat rough and very sonorous, sounding the letter R frequently, yet very agreeable and pleasant to the ear. All the Indian languages, are truly rhetorical, or figurative, assisting their speech by tropes, their hands, flexure of the head, the brow, in short, every member, naturally associate, and give their assistance to render their harrangues eloquent, persuasive and effectual.[170]

The pyramidal hills or artificial mounts and highways, or avenues, leading from them to artificial [520] lakes or ponds, vast tetragon terraces, chunk

131

———

Travels
Through
North
&
South
Carolina

yards * and obelisks or pillars of wood, are the only monuments of labour, ingenuity and magnificence, that I have seen worthy of notice, or remark. The region lying between Savanna river and Oakmulge, East and West, and from the sea coast to the Cherokee or Apalachean mountains, North and South, is the most remarkable for their high conical hills, tetragon terraces and chunk yards; this region was last possessed by the Cherokees, since the arrival of the Europeans, but they were afterwards dispossessed by the Muscogulges, and all that country was probably many ages preceding the Cherokee invasion, inhabited by one nation or confederacy, who were ruled by the same system of laws, customs and language; but so ancient, that the Cherokees, Creeks, or the nation they conquered, could render no account for what purpose these monuments were raised. The mounts and cubical yards adjoining them, seemed to have been raised in part for ornament and recreation, and likewise to serve some other public purpose, since they are always so situated as to command the most extensive prospect over the town and country adjacent. The tetragon terraces, seem to be the foundation of a fortress, and perhaps the great pyramidal mounts, served the purpose of look out towers, and high places for sacrifice. The sunken area, called by white traders the chunk yard, very likely served the same conveniency, that it has been appropriated to by the more modern and even present nations of Indians, that is, the place where they burnt and [521] otherwise tortured the unhappy captives, that were condemned to die, as the area is surrounded by a bank, and sometimes two of them, one behind and above the other, as seats, to accommodate the spectators, at such tragical scenes, as well as the exhibition of games, shews and dances. From the river St. Juans, Southerly to the point of the peninsula of Florida, are to be seen high pyramidal mounts, with spacious and extensive avenues, leading from them out of the town, to an artificial lake or pond of water, these were evidently dignified in part, for ornament or monuments of magnificence, to perpetuate the power and grandeur of the nation, and no considerable one neither, for they exhibit scenes of power and grandeur, and must have been public edifices.

The great mounts, highways and artificial lakes up St. Juans on the East shore just at the enterance of the great Lake George, one on the opposite shore, on the bank of the Little Lake, another on Dunn's Island, a little below Charlotteville, and one on the large beautiful island just without the Capes of Lake George, in sight of Mount Royal, and a spacious one on the West banks of the Musquitoe river near New Smyrna, are the most remarkable of this sort that occurred to me; but undoubtedly many more are yet to be discovered farther

---

* Chunk yard, a term given by the white traders, to the oblong four square yards, adjoining the high mounts and rotunda of the modern Indians. — In the center of these stands the obelisk, and at each corner of the farther end stands a slave post or strong stake, where the captives that are burnt alive are bound.

132

———

Travels
Through
North
&
South
Carolina

South in the peninsula, however I observed none Westward, after I left St. Juans on my journey to little St. Juan, near the bay of Apalache.

But in all the region of the Muscogulge country, South-West from the Oakmulge River quite to the Tallapoose, down to the city of Mobile, and thence along the sea coast, to the Mississipi, I saw no signs of mountains or highways, except at Taensa, [522] where were several inconsiderable conical mountains, and but one instance of the tetragon terraces which was at the Apalachucla old town, on the West banks of that river; here were yet remaining conspicuous monuments, as vast four square terraces, chunk yards, &c. almost equalling those eminent ones at the Oakmulge fields; but no high conical mounts. Those Indians have a tradition that these remains are the ruins of an ancient Indian town and fortress. I was not in the interior parts of the Chactaw territories, and therefore am ignorant whether there are any mounts or monuments there.

To conclude this subject concerning the monuments of the Americans, I deem it necessary to observe as my opinion, that none of them that I have seen discover the least signs of the arts, sciences, or architecture of the Europeans or other inhabitants of the old world: yet evidently betray every sign or mark of the most distant antiquity.

FINIS.

CHAPTER THREE
"Observations on the Creek and Cherokee Indians"

INTRODUCTION

In 1788, the aspiring Philadelphia physician Benjamin Smith Barton posed a series of questions regarding the Creeks and Cherokees to his friend and correspondent William Bartram. Bartram's answers, completed the following year, have come to be known as his "Observations on the Creek and Cherokee Indians."[1] Barton's inquiries were detailed and extensive, covering such broad categories as tribal history, religion, government, physical characteristics, social organization and the status of women, town layout, "ancient remains," and subsistence. The thoughtfully composed queries were based on Barton's wide reading on American Indians, including Bartram's unpublished journals of his southern tour, as well as insights gleaned from correspondence and conversations with other travelers, government agents, and missionaries.

While some of the information contained in "Observations" is also found in *Travels,* Barton elicited from the reflective Bartram many new thoughts found in neither his own work nor that of others.[2] Moreover, "Observations" differs greatly in style from *Travels;* the terse, emotionally detached, manuscript responses contrast sharply with the evocative and frequently lyrical published record.

Barton sent his "Series of Questions" from Amsterdam, where he was studying medicine and natural history, enclosed in a letter to Bartram dated December 13, 1788.[3] But these were not the first such inquiries he had put to Bartram. The year before, in London, Barton published a pamphlet, *Observations on Some Parts of Natural History: To which is Prefixed an Account of Several Remarkable Vestiges of an Ancient date which have been discovered in different parts of North America, pt. 1,* in which he speculated on a

134

———

*Observations
on the
Creek
and
Cherokee
Indians*

Mexican origin of the mound builders. Writing on August 26, 1787, from Edinburgh, he recalled that Bartram had often spoken of

> several <u>artificial mounts or eminences</u>, which you saw in the course of your travels, and which were similar to those which I have described in my work: . . . I intend shortly to publish a new edition of this work, much enlarged and corrected, and as I wish to render it as perfect, as possible, I shall esteem it a great favour if you will, at your leasure, give me some account of the <u>mounts</u> which you have described, in your Journal; and I shall be happy to acknowledge the favour to <u>the Public</u>.[4]

It was evidently at this time that Barton sent a separate brief list of questions regarding "Artificial Mounts or Eminences" to Bartram for his consideration.[5] In February 1788, with as yet no reply to his letter, Barton wrote again and was ultimately successful in persuading Bartram to contribute information for his study on the origins of America's Native tribes.[6]

Bartram's answers to these inquiries were in Barton's possession by the end of the year.[7] In his letter of December 13, 1788, Barton wrote from Amsterdam that he had "received your very friendly and valuable letter containing an account of the <u>Pyramidical Eminences</u> in East-Florida, &c. I know not how to repay your goodness, and attention to my literary pursuits: but I hope you will put it in my power to be of service to you, at some future period." Unfortunately, Bartram's answers have since been lost.[8]

Barton was so encouraged by Bartram's response that he took the liberty of compiling a more extensive set of queries that resulted in the "Observations." In the letter of December 13, 1788, Barton enclosed "a <u>Series of Questions</u> to which your answers will prove a valuable acquisition to Science. I have drawn them up without much attention to method; as you will perceive. I by no means wish you to hurry yourself in answering the Queries."[9]

Bartram took nearly a year to compose his responses, during which time he suffered from a serious eye disorder. In the letter that accompanied his answers to Barton's queries, dated December 15, 1789, Bartram explained "I have been obliged to write the greater part with my eyes shut[,] and that with pain."[10] Bartram was motivated to complete his work by two factors: his regard for the inquisitive and energetic younger man and his determination to record what he had observed of the American Indians out of a sense of duty to "science."[11]

In addition, although Barton did not request this, Bartram illustrated his answers with a number of informative drawings depicting site and settle-

135

Observations
on the
Creek
and
Cherokee
Indians

ment plans, building design, and related items. Ethnologists, anthropologists, and historians should be grateful for Bartram's determination to share freely what he knew, for his illustrations and "observations and conjectures" on the southeastern Indians are among the most important ethnographic sources for the eighteenth-century Creeks and Cherokees.

In his *New Views of the Origin of the Tribes and Nations of America* (first published in 1797 and reprinted the next year), Benjamin Smith Barton only once, in passing, drew on the wealth of ethnographic detail Bartram had provided in "Observations." Characteristically, Barton continued to impose on knowledgeable informants for additional ethnographic material, but he never completed his long-planned, comprehensive volume on the American Indians. The two men remained friends and collaborated on a number of projects, medical and botanical in nature, until Barton's death in 1815.[12]

Bartram's "Observations" manuscript was somehow lost, after becoming separated from Barton's other papers after his death. By an amazing coincidence, it ultimately (sometime prior to 1842) came into the possession of Dr. Josiah Nott of Mobile, who, like Barton, was a physician with an intense interest in ethnology. To his astonishment, Nott found this important manuscript "amongst the waste paper used as stowage, in a box of books" he received "from some northern city" — undoubtedly Philadelphia.[13] Nott immediately recognized the value of the loose papers, and sent them back to that city as a present to his mentor and friend, Dr. Samuel Morton.[14]

Morton, a Philadelphia Quaker and the most influential American anatomist of the era, was a member of both the Academy of Natural Sciences and the American Philosophical Society.[15] Once in Morton's hands, Bartram's manuscript received wide notice in scientific circles. Among those eager to see it was Ephraim George Squier, an enterprising young journalist and clerk of the Ohio House of Representatives, who was collaborating with Edwin Hamilton Davis on a work documenting the antiquities of the Mississippi Valley.[16] Squier forged a friendship with Morton and obtained his permission to incorporate parts of the manuscript into his own works. Extended quotes and "reduced fac-similes of Bartram's original pen sketches" from "Observations" appeared in Squier and Davis's *Ancient Monuments of the Mississippi Valley* (1848) and Squier's *Aboriginal Monuments of the State of New York* (1850), the first two volumes published by the newly created Smithsonian Institution.[17]

At a meeting of the American Ethnological Society in September 1850, Squier proposed that the society publish Bartram's long-lost manuscript. The members agreed and directed Squier to contact Dr. Morton for permission to include "Observations" in the Society's *Transactions* series. Morton not only accepted the proposal but also volunteered to provide an introduction for the piece.[18]

The following month, Squier introduced a motion to raise money for the publication of the third volume of *Transactions,* and was appointed to the committee to oversee the effort.[19] When Samuel Morton died on May 15, 1851,[20] Squier himself determined to proceed with the project. He took over production of the introductory material, and by the June meeting of the society, publication plans were well underway.[21] Volume 3 of the *Transactions* of the American Ethnological Society appeared in 1853, featuring Bartram's "Observations on the Creek and Cherokee Indians" as the lead article, with prefatory and explanatory notes appended by Squier.

After only some twenty-five copies of the issue had been distributed, a fire at the printing house destroyed the remaining stock. As a result, the 1853 edition is exceedingly scarce. Not until its republication in 1909 did Bartram's "Observations" once again become available. However, as the 1909 edition is likewise hard to find, Bartram's "Observations" has not been widely used as a primary source by scholars.[22]

Bartram's original manuscript of "Observations" disappeared after the appearance of Squier's edition in 1853. Fortunately, two other manuscript copies transcribed prior to 1853 still exist, and these demonstrate how heavy an editorial hand Squier exercised, changing spelling, capitalization, punctuation, word choice, sequence, and even omitting some passages and illustrations. In several particularly egregious blunders, Bartram's intended meaning was distorted through careless copying. In fact, the 1853 edition differs substantially from extracts published by Squier in 1848 and 1850. Squier's edition of "Observations," though it did bring Bartram's lost work to the attention of the burgeoning anthropological community, does not meet modern standards of scholarship.

The copy of "Observations" followed here actually predates Ephraim Squier's published version, and is a byproduct of John Howard Payne's research on the southeastern Indians. Payne, best-known for his popular song "Home, Sweet Home," embarked upon an ambitious tour of the country in 1835 in order to enroll subscribers for a new periodical he planned to publish. In Alabama and Georgia he encountered Creeks and Cherokees and decided to gather material for a history of the Cherokees. He approached John Ross, the prominent Cherokee leader, who provided Payne with much ethnographic data and allowed him to copy many documents. While at Ross's home in Tennessee, Ross and Payne were kidnapped and imprisoned by the Georgia Guard, and Payne became involved in the Cherokees' struggle to retain their homeland. Payne later visited Okla-

137

Observations
on the
Creek
and
Cherokee
Indians

homa, and from his two trips produced two noteworthy articles on Native life. The first, an account of a Cherokee murder trial, was published, in two parts, in the *New York Journal of Commerce* in 1841. A meticulous account of the Creek Green Corn Dance, originally included in a letter to his sister, was eventually published in 1862 in the *Continental Monthly*. In 1841, Payne was briefly employed by the secretary of war to study treaties between the United States and the Cherokees. Although he never finished his Cherokee history, Payne accumulated many sources on the subject, including copies of some of Benjamin Hawkins's papers and a transcription of the Bartram manuscript, which Payne probably copied when it was in Morton's possession.[23]

Payne, appointed American consul to Tunis in 1842, took much of his American Indian material there with him. He died in Tunis in 1852, before completing his history. His "commonplace book" containing the copy of Bartram's "Observations" was found among his personal belongings and returned to the United States. It now resides in the Bartram Family Papers at the Historical Society of Pennsylvania.[24]

The other extant manuscript copy of "Observations" was donated to the Smithsonian Institution in 1898 by J. Woodbridge Davis. His father, Edwin H. Davis, coauthor with Squier of *Ancient Monuments of the Mississippi Valley* in 1848, had presumably acquired the manuscript from Squier during their brief collaboration.[25] This copy differs from the Payne version in many particulars, but corresponds closely to Squier's edition of "Observations," printed in 1853. Of the two extant copies, the Payne manuscript seems to preserve most fully the content of Bartram's original document. In spelling, grammar, punctuation, and style, the Payne manuscript resembles known Bartram documents much more closely than does the Davis copy. Furthermore, the Payne copy contains many words, phrases, and lines omitted from the Davis copy and the Squier edition.

Our preference for the Payne text does not, however, extend to the illustrations. Payne copied Bartram's sketches onto the heavy, white, ruled paper of his quarto composition book, while the Davis copies were made on thin tracing paper, probably taken directly from Bartram's originals. There are subtle differences in the sets of sketches (see notes), so both sets are reproduced here, along with the engravings that accompanied Squier's edition.

The fate of Bartram's original manuscript is unknown. One prominent anthropologist who searched unsuccessfully for the original document was Frank Hamilton Cushing, a member of Maj. John Wesley Powell's staff at the Smithsonian Institution's Bureau of American Ethnology. Cushing learned of the manuscript through references in Squier's works and wrote

138

———

*Observations
on the
Creek
and
Cherokee
Indians*

on January 20, 1899, to Dr. Isaac Minis Hays, librarian of the American Philosophical Society, seeking information. Cushing was anxious to "gain temporary possession of it" and even volunteered to "edit, annotate, and arrange for the publication" of the document, apparently unaware that Squier had already done so. Cushing also inquired as to the work of "an obscure individual — James Payne, Esq — relating to the Cherokees," which he had learned was "somewhere in Philadelphia." Cushing did not realize at the time that Payne's work was merely a copy of Bartram's manuscript.[26]

Our search, too, has been fruitless. Perhaps our failure will challenge others to search for the missing Bartram manuscript and discover it, if it still exists.

"Observations on the Creek and Cherokee Indians"

Queries. — [1]

1st. Have those tribes of Indians, whom you have visited, any traditions concerning their Origin, — their Progress, or Migrations, which you think worthy of notice? — If they have, what are those traditions?

2d. Which of the nations of which you have any knowledge, seem to have the most accurate, and the least suspicious, traditions concerning their Origin, Progress, &c &c.?

3d. Have you any reasons for believing, that the Cheerake, the Creeks, or any other of the Southern tribes, with whom you are acquainted, crossed the river Mississippi, in their progress to the countries which they now inhabit?

4th. If any of these tribes did cross that great river, do you think it possible to determine, with any degree of certainty, the period, or periods, when they did cross it? —

5th. Can you form a conjecture what part, or parts, of the countries bordering on the Mississippi, those tribes passed through in their migration towards the East?

Answers to the Queries, 1st, 2d, 3d, 4th & 5th. —

The Cricks, [a.] or, as they call themselves, Muscoges, or Muscogulges, [b.] is a very powerful confederacy, consisting of many tribes, or remnants of conquered nations united, perhaps above Sixty Towns; above Thirty of which speak the

---

[a.] Cricks is a name given them by the English Traders formerly, when they first began to trade amongst them, for the following reason: i:e: they observed that in their conversation, when they had occasion to mention the name of the Indian Nation, if any of the Indians were present they discovered evident signs of disgust as supposing that they were plotting some mischief against their nation &c: so they gave them this by name. [2]

[b.] Ulge signifies a nation, or people, in their language, — as Spanish Ulge, English Ulge, French Ulge, Scotch Ulge, &c. Este likewise signifies Nation, or People, but whether in another tongue, or in a more extensive sense, I know not. The white people they call Esta Hatke; the Redmen, or Indians, they call Este Chate; and so of the Spaniards who they call Yellowmen Esta Cane; or Blackmen Esta Uste; so that Este seems a specifical term of mankind comprehending the whole human race in four divisions, i:e: White, Black, Red & Yellow: Ulge seems a subdivision of nations & tribes.

140

Observations
on the
Creek
and
Cherokee
Indians

Muscogulge Tongue and are the progene or descendants of a powerful band of a nation bearing that name, who many years since, (on their nation becoming very numerous and filling their native country with inhabitants, by which game & other necessary produce of their country became scarce and difficult to procure), were induced to seperate themselves from, & go in search of new & plentiful regions. They directing their migration Eastward Leaving with great regret and difficulty their native land, relations & friends, (which was on the banks of a large & beautiful river called the Red River from great quantities of a Red Stone or Rocks being there, of which they formed their Tobacco Pipes:)[3] Their migration continued a long time under great hardships & embarrassment, being continually attacked by surrounding Indian Nations; at length they came to and crossed the Great River: i:e: Mississippi; when they began to think of establishing a permanent residence; but being yet assaulted & disturbed by surrounding nations, they yet pushed Eastward as far as the Oakmulge,[(c.)] when hearing of the settlements of white people, i.e. Spaniards at Saint Augustine, to whom they sent Ambassadors to treat with them on terms of mutual favour, but not being kindly recieved, & hearing of other nations of white people farther North East in Carolina (the English at this time were establishing the colony of South Carolina & founding Charleston) they sent deputies or Embassadors to Charleston offering their friendship & alliance to continue forever (as long as the rivers flow & the sun pursues his course). A Treaty immediately took place & they joined their arms with the Carolinians, who assisted them against the surrounding Indian Nations, which were then in the Spanish Interest, who they at length subjugated, and in the end proved the destruction of the Spanish Colony of East Florida. The Muscogulges, by uniting the remnant tribes of their conquered foes, grew strong and daily extended their empire. There are now, except the Muscogulge Towns, or those towns whose inhabitants speak that tongue, almost as many languages or dialects as there are towns.[4]

It seems apparent by this account,[(d.)] that the Muscoges crossed the Mississippi somewhere about the Chickasaw country below the confluence of the Ohio, as they mention crossing but one large River, i:e: the Mississippi, or Great River.

[(c.)] Oakmulge, southern great prong, or branch of the Alatamaha, where are to be seen at this day admirable remains of a vast town, extensive plantations, & monuments of the labour, industry, & skill of the antients, as Mounts, Terraces, Area's &c: which the present generation of the Muscogulges say is the Ruins of their Camp & first Settlement. But this I can venture to deny, & suppose it a boast of the Cricks, to aggrandize their name & nation; for these monuments discover evident signs of being of much antienter date. However, it is likely enough that the Muscoges or Cricks might have expelled the then inhabitants, took possession of the town, fortresses — & established themselves there.[5]

[(d.)] This account I had from the most antient & respectable men of the Muscogulges (by the best old Trader & good Interpreters) at different times & in various towns, & I believe to be as true as mere Tradition will allow of.

They, the Natches, Chicasaws & Chactaws, seem to be descended from the
same origin or country, as they all speak a dialect of the same country; and it is
certain they all crossed the Mississippi from the west, as they say of themselves,
and long since the Spanish invasion and conquests of Mexico; for these Indians,
i:e: Chicasaws & Chactaws say they brought with them across the river those fine
Horses called the Chicasaw & C[h]actaw Breeds. The Siminole Horses, or those
beautiful creatures bred amongst the Lower Creeks, which are of the
Andelusian Breed, were introduced by the Spaniards of St: Augustine.

As to the Cherokés, they are altogether a seperate nation from the Muscoges,
of much antiener establishment in those regions they inhabit. I made no
inquiry concerning their original descent or migrations to these parts. But I
understood they came from the West, or Sun setting. Their empire or
confederacy was once very strong & extensive. Before the league of the Cricks[e.]
and Carolinians. Their empire extended from within Forty Miles[g.] of the Sea
Coast North West to the Ohio, comprehending all the regions lying on the
waters of the Cheroke River quite to its confluence with the Ohio, and also of
the other great Eastern branches of the Ohio upwards beyond the Cunhawa,
Sante & Pede North Eastward. And it is remarkable that those great pyramidal,
or Conical Mounds of Earth,[f.] Tetragon Terraces & Cubican Yards, are to be
seen in all this vast territory. Yet it is certain that they were not the people who
constructed them, as they own themselves, nor were the people whom they
expelled when they invaded the country & took possession.

Their language is radically different from the Cricks, sounding the letter .R.
frequently; in short, there is not one word in their languages alike.

Query, 6th. —

Have you any reasons for believing that any of the tribes of Indians, whom you
have visited, are derived from either the Mexicans or the Peruvians? If you have,
what are those reasons?

Answer.

I have no reason from what I have observed myself, or information from
others, to suppose that any of these nations, or tribes, came from the Old

141

*Observations
on the
Creek
and
Cherokee
Indians*

[e.] please to observe that when I speak of the Creeks & Muscoges, I mean the same people.
[f.] The largest of these I ever saw stands on the banks of Savanna River 8 miles above Dartmouth
and about 90 miles above Augusta, which was nearly in the center of the Cherokee Empire when in
its most flourishing period.[6]
[g.] There are many artificial mounts of Earth along the Sea Coast through Carolina & Georgia,
about this distance from it & in the settlements N:W: which bear the name of Cheroké Mountains — particularly one about 10 or 12 miles from Savanna, on the road to Augusta; & many ponds
& Savannas called now Cheroke Ponds &c. Indeed there are people yet living who remember to
have seen Cheroke Towns inhabited, but a few miles above the city of Savanna and afterwards
possessed & inhabited by the Creeks.

142

Observations
on the
Creek
and
Cherokee
Indians

Mexicans, or Peruvians, unless we believe the Natches account of themselves as related to Monsieur DuPrats.[7] And that account must I should imagine be understood of New Mexico. Because the Natches account of their original country & migrations was from the west or Sun Setting, which would be west from their country on the Mississippi, near about the Lat: of St A Fee i.e. N° Lat. 34 or 35.

The Spaniards' invasion of those regions, and consequent colonising, after discovering the rich silver mines & establishing fortified posts in order to possess the country, work the mines, and extending their researches, very probably would cause many tribes of the natives to decamp in search of more peaceable abodes at a distance from such troublesome neighbours; & these nations by a N° E^n Course would likely in their opinion take them the greatest distance from those dreaded Bearded Men, their common enemy, (not yet having heard of colonies or invasions of other Bearded Men) * and thus propelling one another, as waves driven before the wind: The Chicasaws, Chactaws & Muscogulges, appear to have arrived sometime since the Natches, particularly the two former Tribes; & the Cricks last: The Natches might have come from a Region nearest to the border of the Empire of Old Mexico, ⊗ because it seems they were the most polished or civilised & had a strong tincture of the Mexican Idolatry, † superstition, complex system of legislation; and their princes were hereditary & their sovereignty absolute & power unlimited. The Natches might have arrived soon after the Spaniards had conquered the Mexican Empire, and began to extend their conquests northerly (for there is no mention of their bringing Horses with them, — these creatures not being yet so far increased, as to become wild in the country, or so plentiful as to become an article of commerce between the Spaniards & Wild Indians) ‡ for according to DuPrats, their empire had arrived to a prodigious latitude and strength some years before the French attempted to settle in their country when it appeared to be greatly on the decline; — and it must have taken many years to have so increased from so small a beginning as only a wretched fugitive band, — supposing that they had been affrightened away by the Spanish invasion & conquests.

* ⊗ See Duprat's Hist: Louisiana.

†— For although they believed in a Supreme Being (the Great Spirit) yet they adored the Sun & Planets. They had a Temple dedicated to the Sun, where they kept the Eternal Fire guarded by a High Priest, & Sacred Virgins consecrated for that purpose. And though they did not offer human victims to the Sun, nor eat human flesh sacrificed, yet they burned & otherwise put to death captives taken in war; & though it does not appear that they put to death slaves, or any other person, at the demise of their princes, sovereigns or Suns, yet their Slaves, Concubines, or Relatives, offered themselves to death in order to attend the Souls of their Sovereigns to the Other World.—[8]

‡ Wild Indians — such nations as were not conquered by the Old Mexicans, and made Tributary, which they call Chichimaches, that is Aborigines or Barbarians. —

It seems that the arrival of the Chickasaws, & Cricks, as well as Chactaws, might have been about the time that the Spaniards, French & English began their establishments in New England, Virginia, Carolina & Florida. Which I believe will appear to be about the period of the Spaniards' invasion, conquests & establishments of their power in New Mexico.

The Chactaws, I believe, came the last and in considerable force, according to DuPrats account from the Natches, who they said appeared all at once, as if they arose all at once up out of the earth. And the Cricks — have much the same idea of their arrival — like the arrival and settling of a swarm of bees, as they express themselves on that subject. Yet it is certain that all these Nations & Bands, i.e. Natches, Chicasaws, Muscogulges, and Chactaws, were derived from the same region, for they all speak dialects of the same language, generally so near alike as to converse without interpreters. Thus we may conclude that their arrival in these regions they now possess, was after one another, at so considerable a length of time intervening (perhaps a generation or two) and each contending for empire & the honor & glory of their tribes, they in part forgot and disregarded their ancient lineage & affinity. —

143

*Observations
on the
Creek
and
Cherokee
Indians*

Query, 7th.–

Have you observed among any of those tribes of Indians whom you have visited, any Paintings Superior in the execution to those of the Northern Indians, as we observe them on trees? — If you have, what did those Paintings represent? — And among what tribes of Indians did you observe these paintings? — Are any of the Indian tribes very curious in preserving the memory of events by paintings? If such Paintings are made use of by the Indians, do you know, or do you suppose, that they are acquainted with any Signs or Symbols, to denote Attributes, or Qualities, of various kinds? Thus, how would these Indians convey an idea of Courage, or of Cowardice, — of Good, or of Bad, &c: —

Answer. —

The paintings which I observed amongst the Creeks, were commonly on the clay plaistered walls of their Houses, particularly on the walls of the Four Houses composing the Publick Square, * or Ariopagus: They were, I think, Hieroglyphicks, or Mystical Writings for the same use & purpose as those mentioned by Historians to be found on the Obelisks, pyramids, and other monuments, of the Antient Egyptians; & much after the same stile & taste, extremely caricature & picturesque; & though I never saw an instance of the Chiaro Scuro, yet the outlines are bold, natural, and turned or designed to convey some meaning, passion, or admonition; & thus may be said to speak to such as can read them.

✳ See a plan of it at page [173]

144

———

*Observations
on the
Creek
and
Cherokee
Indians*

The walls are plaistered very smooth with Red Clay, then the figures or symbols are drawn with white clay paste or chalk; and if the walls are plaistered with clay of a whitish clay or stone colour, then, the figures are drawn with red, brown or bluish chalk or paste.[9]

Almost all kind of animals, sometimes plants, flowers, trees &c are the subjects. Figures of mankind in various attitudes, some very ludicrous & even obscene, & even the privates of men — but never an instance of indelicacy in a female figure.

Men are often depicted having the head & other members, of different kind of animals, as a Wolf, Buck, Horse, Buffalo, Snake, Duck, Turkey, Tiger, Cat, Crocodile &c[.] All these animals are on the other hand depicted having the human head, members &c. And animals having the head or other members of different animals, so as to appear monstrous. [a.]

But the most beautiful painting now to be found amongst the Muscogulges is in the skin on the bodies of their ancient chiefs & micos which is of a bluish, lead or indigo colour. It is the breast, trunk[,] muscul[ar] or fleshy parts of the arms & thighs & sometimes almost every part of the surface of the body that is thus beautifully depicted or wrote over with hieroglyphics — commonly the Sun, Moon & Planets occupies the breast. Zones or belts, beautiful fanciful scroles wind round the trunk of the body, thighs, arms & legs, dividing the body into many Fields or Tablets, which are ornamented or filled up with innumerable figures, as representations of animals of the chase. A sketch of a landscape representing an engagement or battle with their enemy, or some creature of the chase; & a thousand other fancies. These paintings are admirably well executed, & seem to be inimitable. It is performed by exceeding fine punctures, & seems like merzitinto or a very ingenious impression from the best executed engravings.[10]

These are no doubt hieroglyphics or mystical writings, or records of their tribe, family & memorable events &c &c.

When I was at Manchack on the Mississippi, at McGillivary & Swanson's Trading Houses, I saw several Buffaloe Hides dressed with the wool on them. The flesh side of these skins were depicted & painted very beautifully — the performance was admirable, — I may say, inimitable by the most ingenious artist amongst Europeans or people of the Old World, unless taught by the Indians. These painted hides were the work of the Illinoe Indians near Fort Chartres where the Trading Company had Ware Houses & Traders who purchased them

[a.] I am sensible that these specimens of their paintings will to us who have made such incomparable progress & refinements in arts & sciences, appear trifling & ludicrous — but as you desired me to be particular and omit nothing I hope to be excused. Yet I think they are the wretched remains of something of greater use & consequence with their ancestors.

of the Indians and sent them down here for to be sent to Europe. I was asked six dollars for one of them, which I thought cheap, considering their curiosity, but had no opportunity of conveying one home. The subjects or figures in the composition were much like those inscriptions or painting on the skin or bodies of the chiefs & warriors. Their border or verge were exceedingly ingenious & pleasing — red, black, or blue, were the colours, on a buff ground.[11]

145

Observations
on the
Creek
and
Cherokee
Indians

Query, 8th.

Which of the tribes of Indians, you have visited, are the most polished in their Religion; — in their manners; — in their language; — in their government; &c: &c: ? —

Answer. —

If adopting or imitating the manners & customs of the white people is to be termed civilization, perhaps the Cherokees have made the greater advance.

But I presume if we are to form & establish our judgment from the opinions & rules laid down by the greatest Doctors of Morality, philosophers & divines either of the Antients or Moderns — the Muscoges must have our approbation & engage our esteem.

Their Religion is perhaps as pure as that which was in the beginning revealed to the first family of Mankind. They have no notion or conception of any other God but the Great Spirit on High, the Giver & Taker Away of the Breath of Life — which is as much as to say that Eternal Supreme Being who created & governs the Universe. They worship none else.[12]

They pay a kind of homage to the Sun, Moon & Planets as the Mediators or Ministers of the Great Spirit, in dispensing his attributes for their comfort & wellbeing in this life. They have some religious rites or forms, which is managed by their priests or Doctors, who make the people believe by their cunning or craft, that they have a supernatural Spiritual communion with invisible spirits or powers, good & evil, and that they have the power of invoking the elements, and dispensing their attributes, good or bad. They make the people believe by conjuration they can bring rain, fine weather, heat, cooling breezes, thunder & lightning; — bring on or expel, & cure, sickness &ca &ca &c.

Query, 9th. —

What appear to be the great Outlines of the Governments of the Cheerake, Creeks, — and other tribes of Indians with whom you are acquainted? — Are these Governments in general, Elective, or are they Hereditary? — If Elective, is the person elected chosen for life, or only for a certain term; or so long as he shall conduct himself to the satisfaction of the people? — If Hereditary, is the

146

Observations
on the
Creek
and
Cherokee
Indians

power of the King, or Sachem, very considerable? — or is it chiefly a nominal power? — These are questions of considerable magnitude; — I should be happy; therefore, to have them, minutely, answered.

Answer. —

The government, or system of legislation, amongst all the nations of Indians I have visited seems to be exactly similar.

That is the most simple, natural & rational, that can be imagined or desired. The same spirit that dictated to Montesque the Ideas of Rational Government, seem to superintend and guide the Indians.[13] And perhaps, if I should say no more on this subject, you'll be better able to form to yourself a notion of their government.

All that I can say from my own observation, will amount to little more than conjecture & leave the subject in a doubtful situation, for at best it'll be but the apprehensions or conjectures of a traveller from cursory or superficial views, perhaps aided and perhaps led astray by the accounts given me by the Traders or other White People who have resided amongst them, who, from motives of avarice, or contempt of the Indians in general through prejudice seldom carry their observations or inquiries beyond common report (which we may be assured is against the Indians) or improving their commerce with them for their immediate private interest — Little can be depended upon from their story alone.[14]

The whole Region of the Muscogulge Empire or Confederacy comprehends a Territory of at least 500 miles * square, which consists of the Upper & Lower Cricks or Siminoles[15] comprehending the Uchés, Alabamas, Occones & many more tribes who altogether make between sixty & seventy towns and villages. Every town & village is to be considered as an independent nation or tribe, having their Mico, or King. Every individual inhabitant or citizen has an equal right to the soil to hunt & range over this region except within the jurisdiction of each town or village, which I believe seldom extends beyond the habitations and planting ground, (perhaps the Uches is to be excepted, who claim a very extensive territory over which they claim an exclusive property by right of compact or treaty when they entered into alliance & joined in confederacy with the Muscoges, but tho' they sometimes put the Cricks in mind of this privelege when their hunters make too free with their hunting grounds, yet the dispute seldom goes farther, as the Confederacy are cautious of affronting the Uches so generally yield for their common interest and safety.

The system of government in each town or tribe may be described thus:

± 500 miles square E and W. from Savana River to the Mobile, comprehending all its branches to their sources, and S. & N. from the extremity of the peninsula of E: Florida to the Cheroke or Apalachian Mountain.

First, the Mico, or King.

147

Observations
on the
Creek
and
Cherokee
Indians

Secondly, Great War Chief, Antient Warriors, or Heads of Tribes & Families that constitute the Town or Nation; And,

Thirdly, Younger Warriors & Hunters, or the Commonality.

The Mico, is considered as the First Man in Dignity & Power in the Nation or Town, and is the Supreme Civil Magistrate; yet in fact is no more than the President of the National Council in his own town or tribe, and he has no executive power independent of the Council which is convened every Day in the forenoon & held in the Public Square.

Thus the Mico, the Great War Chief who heads the army of the Tribe (and herein consists his dignity & power) — the Elder Warriors, Antient Heads of Families & Younger Warriors, composes their Divan or Daily National Council where the Mico presides. The Great War Chief being seated next to him, on the left hand, at the head of the antient & celebrated warriors, and next on his right hand (of the Mico) is the second Headman of the town at the head of Chiefs of Tribes & Families, younger Warriors, Citizens &c:

They shew the King due respect & the most profound homage, especially when assembled in the great rotunda or winter Council House. To him only they bow very low, almost to his feet, when the waiters hand him the shell of black drink, † but when out of the Council any where, they use the common civility, converse freely with him, as with a common man, he dresses no better than a common citizen, and his house is no way distinguished from another otherwise than being larger according as his ability or private riches may enable him, for he exacts no sort of tribute. He goes out to hunt with his Family & even goes to the Fields with his axe & Hoe to work every day during the season of labour.

But he has the disposal of the Corn & Fruits in the publick or National Granary. He is complimented with the First visits & gives audience to ambassadors, deputies & strangers, who come to his town or tribe, — receives presents &c. And He alone has the privelege of giving a public feast to the whole town, which is barbacued Bear (or Fat Bulls & Steers) which he must kill himself and this is called The King's Feast, or Royal Feast.[16] And when he intends this Frolick, after a successful Hunt, he sends messengers in, to prepare the Town, when they display the King's Standard at one corner, or front of his House, & hoist a Flag in the Public Square, Beats drums about the town, and the inhabitants dress, paint, and ornament themselves, for there is Dancing and frolicking all the succeeding Night. —

They have an antient High Priest & Juniors in every Town or Tribe. And the

---

‡ Black Drink, a Strong Decoction, or infusion, of the Leaves & Tender Tops of the Cassine (or Ilex Yapon.) which is Drank constantly every evening by the chief warriors in the Great Rotunda, with great Ceremony (perhaps Religious). They call this (Cassine) the beloved Tree. This infusion is perhaps the most active & powerful Diuretick of any vegetable yet known. —[17]

148

Observations
on the
Creek
and
Cherokee
Indians

High Priest is a person of great power & consequence in the State. He always sits in council & his advice in affairs concerning war is of great weight & importance; and he, or one of his disciples, always attend a war party.

It sometimes happens that the King is War Chief & High Priest, and then his power is very formidable and even dangerous to the liberty of citizens, and he must be a very cunning man, if the tomahoac or rifle dont cut his life short.[18]

And if I may be allowed in this place to venture a conjecture, the First Montezuma and Inca founders of the mighty empires of Mexico & Perue were cunning usurpers of this stamp.

As were the absolute Kings of the Antient Floridians. History mentions the King of Calos[19] in the Peninsula of Florida, assuming a communion & familiarity with powerful invisible Spirits, by which he kept his subjects in awe & to whom he sacrificed captives.

And I myself the other day was present when the Long Warrior[20] Chief King of the Siminoles assumed the Power & Dignity of a DemiGod; when at the head of his party of warriors, who, with an air of surprising arrogance & pomp, threatened Mr. McLatche if he did not comply with his requisitions, that he would command the thunder & lightning to descend upon his head & reduce his stores of goods to ashes, &c: — [21]

The power & dignity of the King is for life. They are elective. But in what manner they are chosen or appointed, I could get no satisfactory account. It appears to me the most mysterious part of the system. It is not in a publick manner, like our elections, or the Trader would have been able to inform me. Perhaps it is done in secret in the Great Rotunda, when the Whites are not admitted or in the Sanctorium or High Priests' apartment in the Publick Square.

Query, 10th.

What appear to be the great Outlines of the Religion, or Religions, of those tribes of Indians whom you have visited? Does the existence of a God appear to be generally received among those Indians? Do you remember the name, or names, by which any of the tribes, call, or designate, their God? — Does the doctrine of the Immortality of the Soul, or a doctrine, in any respect, similar to this, appear to be general among the Indian tribes you have visited? Have they any idea of the doctrine of Rewards, & Punishments, in a Future State? —

Answer. —

As I have hinted in answer to the queries of the preceding section, upon the above subject — there's little more can be said concerning their Religion.

All that I observed was that every Nation that I was amongst seemd individually to believe in a Supreme God or Creator which in their different languages they call by a name which signifies <u>the Great, or Universal Spirit</u>; <u>the Giver and Taker Away of the Breath of Life</u>; — thus the Traders all interpret the <u>word</u> or <u>words</u> & which means the <u>One Eternal Supreme Creator</u>, the Soul & Governour of the Universe.

They have no appointed times to assemble to worship the <u>Great Spirit</u>; but they frequently, in words & actions, address themselves to God in thanksgiving and adoration, as when escaping from some eminent danger, or calamity; as likewise ejaculations of praises & homage, at beholding extraordinary instances of the works & power of God in the visible creation, or the harmony & influence of his attributes in the intellectual system. —

But they worship no <u>Idols</u> either of their own formation or sublunary productions of nature.

They assemble & feast at the appearance of the New Moon, when they appear to be in great mirth & gladness, but I believe make no offerings to that planet.

They seem to do homage to the Sun as a Symbol or Minister of the Beneficence & Power of the Great Spirit. Thus at Treaties, they first puff, or blow, the smoke from the <u>Great Pipe & Calumet</u>[22] up to that planet, look upwards towards him with great reverence and earnestness; & when they confirm their talks & speeches in council as a witness of their contracts. And when they make their martial harrangues or speeches, at the head of their army when setting out or making onset — &c. —

They venerate Fire. And have some mysterious rites & ceremonies which I could never perfectly comprehend. —

They seem to keep the Eternal Fire in the Great Rotunda, which is guarded by the priests.

In their great annual Festival called <u>The Busque</u>,[23] or Feast of <u>First Fruits</u>, they put out all the fires of the Nation or Town. And then the High Priest by friction of Dry wood and adition rosin produce new fire. In the great Temple or Rotunda, from whence the whole town is Supplied; but so far are the Muscogulges from having a choir of consecrated virgins to guard & keep this fire, that the women are not allowed to step within the pale of the Rotunda, and it is death for one to enter it. None but a priest can carry any fire forth.

The Spiral Fire on the Harth or Floore of the Rotunda is very curious — It seems to light up in a flame of itself at the appointed time, but how this is effected I know not.[24]

All the Indians I have been amongst, are so confirmed in the Doctrine of the Soul's Immortality, that they would certainly judge any man to be out of his reason that should doubt of it — they also believe that every creature has a Spirit or soul that exists in a future state — Some historians have gone so far as to assert that the Indians believe that a pattern or spiritual likeness of every thing living as well as inanimate, exists in another world.

150

———

Observations
on the
Creek
and
Cherokee
Indians

They believe in rewards & punishments in a future state of existence, just in the manner we do — That virtue & merit will be rewarded with felicity, And on the contrary that vice & wickedness will be attended with infamy and misery.

They believe in visions, dreams & trances.

They relate abundance of stories of men that have been thought dead for many hours & days, who have revived again, giving an account of their transit to & from the World of Souls, and describe the condition and situation of the place, and Spirits; and these people have all returned to Life with Doctrines & admonition tending to encourage & enforce Virtue & Morality.[25]

Query, 11th. —

Which is the fairest and most comely tribe of the Southern Indians? Are the Indian women generally, fairer than the Men? Are the Indian children born with the copper tinge, or colour? — or does this colour first make its appearance, some days after birth? — We hear much, in writers, of white, and spotted, Indians, as at the Isthmus of Darien; — have you ever seen, or heard of, such white and spotted Indians, among any of the tribes, with whom you are acquainted? If you have, some account of these phenomena will be very acceptable to me. — Do you remember the names of any of the plants which the Indians, you have visited, make use of in painting, or staining their skins? — Is the Succoon (the Sanguinaria Canadensis of Linnaeus) one of the plants employed by the Northern Indians, as a pigment, — found as far South as the countries of the Cheerake, Creeks, &c. — ? –

Answer. —

The Cherokees, are the largest race of men I ever saw, and equally comely, and their complexions the brightest, being of the olive cast of the Asiaticks. This is obvious, which I suppose led the Traders to give them the by name of The Breeds, supposing them to be mixed with White People — But tho' some of them evidently are adulterated by the Traders &c, yet the national complexion is tawney.

The women are tall, slim, of a graceful figure, & have captivating features & manners, and I think their complexion rather fairer than the men's. —

The Muscogulges are in Stature nearly equal to the Cherokees, — have fine features & every way handsome men — the nose very often of the aquiline — they are well limbed, countenance upright, & their eyes brisk & fiery. But their complexions are of the dark copper colour.

Their women are very little — in appearance not much more than half the stature of the men — but they have regular & beautiful features — the eye large with high arched eyebrows — and their complexion little if any brighter than those of the men.

There are some tribes in the confederacy who much resemble the Cherokees in Stature & colour: i:e: the Uches, Savanucas and some of the Siminoles.

151

Observations
on the
Creek
and
Cherokee
Indians

I have seen Indian infants of a few weeks' old — their colour was like that of healthy male European Countryman or Labourer, of middle age, tho' a little more inclining to the red copper tinge, but they soon become of the Indian copper, I believe naturally, as I never from constant inquiry could learn that the Indians use any artificial means to change their colour.

The Indians who have commerce with the whites make very little use of colours or paints of the native production of their country, since they have neglected their own manufactures for those supplyd them cheap & in abundance from Europe — I believe they are in general ignorant themselves of the virtues of their own country productions. The Poccoon or Sanguinaria, Galium tinctorium, bark of the Acer Rubrum, Toxicodendron radicans, Rhus triphyllon and some other vegetable pigments are yet in use,[26] for the women yet amuse themselves in manufacturing some few things, as Belts & Coronets, for their Husbands, feathered cloaks, macasens, &c. —

I never saw or heard of any white, speckled or pied people amongst them.[27]

It is reasonable to conjecture that the Indians antiently were more ingenious and industrious in manufactures when necessity obliged them.

Therefore we must seek for their arts & sciences amongst nations far distant from the settlements of the White People — Or recover them by industry & experiments of our own —

There is one very remarkable circumstance, with respect to the hair of the heads of the Indians, which I don't recollect to have been observed by Travelers or Historians. —

Besides the lankness, extraordinary natural length, and perhaps coarseness, of the hair of their heads, it is of a shining black, or crow colour, shewing the same splendour & changeableness at different exposure to the light. The Traders informed me that they preserved its perfect blackness & splendour by the use of the red farinacious or fuzzy covering of the berries of the common Sumach — (Rhus Glabrum). — Over night they rub this red powder into their hair, as much as it will contain, tying it up close with a Handkerchief till morning, when they carefully comb it out, and dress their hair with clear Bear's Oil.[28]

But notwithstanding their care & assiduity, it must at last submit to old age and I have seen the hair of the extreme aged Indians as white as Cotton Wool. I have observed quantities of this red powder in their houses. —

Query, 12th. —

What is the condition of the women among those tribes of Indians whom you have visited? We are told, by many writers, that the condition, or state, of the

152

Observations
on the
Creek
and
Cherokee
Indians

Indian women is the picture of misery & oppression; — is this actually the case? — Do the Indian women ever, as far as you know, preside in the Councils of the Sachems; especially when war, or other matters of consequence, are considered in those Councils? Have you ever known, or heard of, any instance, or instances, of a woman, or of women who have presided over any nation, or nations of Indians? —

Answer.

I have every reasonable argument from my own observation as well as the accounts from the whites residing among the Indians, to be convinced that the condition of the women are as happy, compared to that of the men, as any women in any part of the world.[29] Their business, or employment, is chiefly in the house, as other women, except at the Season when their Crops of Corn &c. is growing, when they generally turn out with their Husbands or parents, but they are by no means compelled to such labour, and there is not ⅓ as many females & [i.e., as] males seen at work in their Plantations, for at this season of the year by a law of the people, they don't hunt, the game not being in season till after their crops or harvest is gathered in,[30] — so the males have little also to employ themselves, & the Indians are by no means that lazy slothful sleepy people so commonly reported to be.

Besides, you may depend on my assertion that there is no people any where who love their women more than those Indians do, or men of better understanding in distinguishing the merits of the opposite sex, or more faithful in rendering suitable compensation. They are courteous and polite to the women, gentle, tender, & fondling even to an appearance of effeminacy, tender & affectionate to their offspring. An Indian never attempts, — nay, he can't use a woman of any description amongst them with indelicacy or indecency, either in action or language.

I never saw nor heard of an instance of an Indian beating his wife or any female, or reproving them in anger or harsh language.

And indeed they make a suitable & grateful return. For they are discreet, modest, loving, faithful & affectionate to their husbands.

In the hunting season, that is, autumn & winter, the men are generally out in the forests, when the whole care of the house falls on the women[31] — Then they are obliged to undergo a deal of labour, as cutting & bringing home winter's wood, which they toat on their back or head, a great distance; especially those of antient large towns, where the commons & old fields extend some miles to the woodland, but this labour is in part alleviated by the assistance of the old men who are past their hunting days & war, remain in the towns, and likewise by the help of horses. — And the women gather in incredible quantities of Nuts and Acorns which they manufacture into Oil for annual consumption.[32] They make all the <u>Pottery</u> or Earthen Ware, which is very considerable, as some of their pots hold near a barrel & are of a tender & fragile composition — You may see mounts of fragments of Earthen Ware, round their towns, for every fragment, be it ever so small is cast into these heaps.[33]

153

*Observations
on the
Creek
and
Cherokee
Indians*

I never heard of, or knew of, any late instances of the female sex bearing rule or presiding either in council or the field; but according to report, the Cherokees & Cricks can boast of their Semiramis's, Zenobeas, & Cleopatra's. When I was passing through the Cheroke country, we came to & crossed a very fine rivulet, a branch of <u>Tugilo</u> which is called <u>Warwoman's Crick</u>. I inquired of my companion, an antient Trader the cause of so singular a name. He answered, it took its rise from a decisive battle which the Cherokees formerly gained over their enemy on the banks of this crick, through the valour & stratagem of an <u>Indian Woman</u> that was present & who afterwards was raised to the dignity of Queen or Chief of the Nation, as a reward of her superior virtues & abilities & presided in the state during her life.

The Crick to this day speak with the highest encomiums, & glory in the name of a widow of their grand chief or Mico, by whose superior wisdom, interposed in a serious dispute between these nations & the English about the time of the establishment of the Colony of Georgia (under the conduct of General Oglethorp) who restored peace betwixt them, which grew stronger and firmer every day, till the dissolution of the British Government in that region. This woman married Doct[r] Bosemoth D. D. of the new-founded colony, a very worthy man, who had as a dowry with the Queen his spouse, a large & fertile island on the coast of Georgia, together with a territory on the main. <u>If I * mistake not, Mr. Bosemoth afterward returned to England with his wife, who was even there esteemed a celebrated woman for her virtues and superior talents.</u>[34]

The Seminoles, or Lower Cricks, too, boast of a great Queen or Empress, in former days, whose empire according to their accounts must have been in E[as]t. Florida between <u>St Marys & St Juan</u>, & the Imperial City about <u>Alachua</u>. She was powerful & beneficent, and so celebrated a beauty, that all the Kings to a vast distance round about, at a certain season annually resorted to her court, with large trains of their chiefs &c, bearing presents for the Queen, not as tributary, but out of compliment & respect to her merit, where great numbers of Kings, Princes, Lords or Chiefs, continued the stated time, representing sports, feats of arms, & other divertisements, to divert & compliment this

---

* As to this latter part of this History, I am not certain whether she remained to the end of her life in Europe, or returned again to Georgia. And also I may perhaps be incorrect as to the particulars of the whole story. But the main of the History is true, as every Georgian & Indian knows, and rejoice at hearing the names of those persons mentioned. Any gentleman of Georgia will aver to its authenticity, and perhaps upon inquiry, will give you a more accurate account than I can. —

154

———

*Observations
on the
Creek
and
Cherokee
Indians*

celebrated Queen — She was carried about under a rich canopy of Feathers, on the shoulders of Princes & Nobles, &c.

Her reign, was about the time that the Europeans first visited these coasts. The Spanish Inhabitants of Et. Florida have yet a Tradition of these matters and relate accounts much like the above.[35]

Query, 13th. —

In the letter which you wrote to me concerning the mounts &c, you make mention of the Chunky=Yard of the Cheerake=Indians; — what is the nature, use &c of this Yard? — Is this Chunky=Yard confined to the Cherrake=Indians? or have you observed it among any other tribes of Indians? — A sketch of the Chunky=Yard will be very acceptable.

Answer.

The Chunky=Yard of the Cricks so called by the Traders is a cubiform Area generally in the center of the Town, because the Publick Square & Rotunda or Great Winter Council House, stands at two opposite corners of it. It is generally very extensive * , especially in the large old Towns, is exactly level and sunk, two, — sometimes, three, feet, below the banks, or terrace surrounding it, which are sometimes two — one above & behind the other, and is formed of the earth cast out of the area, at the time of its formation. These banks, or terraces serve the purpose of seats for the spectators — In the centre of the yard, there is a low, circular, mount, or eminence, in the centre of which stands erect the Chunky Pole, which is a high obelisk, or four square pillar, declining upwards to an obtuse point (in shape and proportion much resembling the antient Egyptian Obelisk) This is of wood — the heart or inward resinous part of a sound pine tree — and is very durable — generally from thirty to forty feet in height.[36] To the top of this is fastened some object to shoot at with bow & arrow or the rifle &c — at certain times appointed. Near each corner of the lower, or farther, end of the yard, stands erect a less pillar or pole, about twelve feet high — These are called Slave Posts, because to these are bound the captives condemned to be burnt; and these pillars are usually decorated with the scalps of their slain enemies; — the scalp, with the hair on them, are stretched or strained on a little hoop, usually 5 or 6 inches in width, which are suspended by a string six or seven inches in length; round about the top of the pole, where they remain as long as they last. I have seen some that have been there so long as to lose all the hair, and the skin remaining as white as paper or parchment — and the pole is usually crownd with the white dry skull of an enemy. In some of their towns, I have counted 6 or 8 scalps fluttering on one pole in these yards.[37]

—————

* The Chunky-Yards are of different sizes, according to the Largeness & Fame of the Town they belong to. — Some are 200 or 300 yards in length & of porportionable width.

155

*Observations
on the
Creek
and
Cherokee
Indians*

Thus it appears evidently enough that this area is designed for a place of publick exhibition of shows and games, and formerly some of the scenes were of the most tragical & barbarous nature; — as, torturing the miserable captives with fire, in various ways; — as, causing, or forcing, them, to run the gauntlet naked, chunked & beat almost to death with burning chunks and firebrands † &c and at last burned to ashes.

I inquired of the traders for what reason this area was called the <u>Chunky Yard</u> — They were in general ignorant, yet they all seemed to agree in a lame story of its originating from its being the place where the Indians formerly put to death and tortured their captives — Or, the interpretation of the Indian name for it, that bears such a signification.[38]

These Indians do not now torture their captives after that cruel manner as formerly, but there are some old Trader[s] who had been present at burning of captives.

I observed no Chunky Yards, Chunky Pole, or Slave Posts in use in any of the <u>Cheroke Towns</u>, & where I have mentioned in my Journal Chunky Yards in the Cheroke Country, it must be understood that I had seen the remains or vestiges of them in the Antient Ruins of Towns, for in the present Cheroké Towns that I visited, though there were Antient Mounds & signs of the Yard adjoining, yet the yard was either built on, or turn'd into a garden spot, or the like. —

And indeed I am convinc'd that the Chunky Yards now or lately in use amongst the Creeks, are of very antient date, not the formation of the present Indians, but are in most Towns clear'd out & kept in repair, being swept very clean every day & the poles kept up & decorated in the manner that I have mentioned.

<u>Query, 14th.</u> —
<u>Does there appear to be a Community of Goods among the tribes, you have visited? — Or have the members of each tribe their own exclusive Property in Lands, Produce of those lands, &ca. — ?</u>

<u>Answer.</u>
As I have already observed in answer to 9th Query, that the soil, with all its appurtenances, of the whole Muscogulge Confederacy or Empire, is equally the right and property of every individual inhabitant except within the pale or precinct of each town, where meum & tuum, or private property takes place: And tho' I believe that the Whole Territory comprehended within the claims of the confederacy is divided by lines & boundaries amongst the different Tribes, (as, for instance, the Uches as mentioned Qy 9th, and Savanucas, Alabamas &

---

‡ If we are to give credit to the accounts of Travelers & Historians concerning these matters. — [39]

156

_____

Observations
on the
Creek
and
Cherokee
Indians

other Tribes who speak the Stinkard Tongue,[40] who make perhaps One Third of the Confederacy — The Muscogulges who are the Head or Imperial Tribe & founders of the Confederacy & speak the Muscoge or National Tongue — perhaps their Towns & Villages claim the other ⅔d's of the Territory) Yet every individual citizen of the Confederacy have the same equal right to hunt and range where he pleases, in the forests and unoccupied lands, and to range stocks of cattle, horses, &ca:

All that a man earns by his labour or industry, &c, belongs to himself, who has the use and disposal of it, according to the custom & usages of the people — He may clear, settle & plant as much land as he pleases and wherever he will, within the boundaries of his Tribe.[41] There are, however, very few instances amongst the Cricks of Farms or Private plantations, out of sight of the town[42] — (I was at one belonging to a Chief of the Town of the Apalachucklas[43] about six miles from the Town, on or near the Banks of the River — I went to pay him a visit with an Old Trader my fellow pilgrim, in consequence of an Invitation to breakfast with him) He is called the Boston or Boatswain, by the Traders. As a prince he received us with politeness and most perfect good breeding. His villa was beautifully situated and constructed [figures 15–17]. There were Three oblong uniform Frame Buildings, and a Fourth Four Square fronting the principal House or Common Hall,[44] after this manner, encompassing an area: The Hall was his Lodging House, &c — large & commodious — The two wings were, — one, a Cook House, & the other Skin Houses, or Ware Houses[45] — and the large Square One was a vast Open Pavillion supporting a canopy, or cedar roof, by two rows of columns, one within the other — Between each range of pillars was a Platform, or what the Traders call Cabins, — a sort of sopha raised about two feet above the common ground & ascended by two steps. This was covered by checquered mats woven of splints of canes dyed of different colours — The middle was a four square stage, or platform, raised nine inches or a foot, higher than the cabins, and was covered with checquered mats of the same curious manufacture. In this delightful airy place we were received and entertained by this Prince. We had excellent Coffee served up in China Dishes by Young Negro Slaves[46] — We had plenty of excellent Sugar, Honey, Choice Warm Corn Cakes, Venison Steak, & Barbacued; we spent the forepart of the day with him and returned to town at evening, well pleased with the honour and distinction shewn us by that man of excellent character.

He had, near one hundred acres of fertile land in good fence, most of which is annually planted & tended by his own private family, which consists of about Thirty People, among which were about 15 Negroes, several of which were married to Indians and enjoy equal priveleges with the Indians, but they are slaves until they marry, when they become Indians, or Free Citizens.

This truly great & worthy man has acquired his riches by trading with the

157

*Observations
on the
Creek
and
Cherokee
Indians*

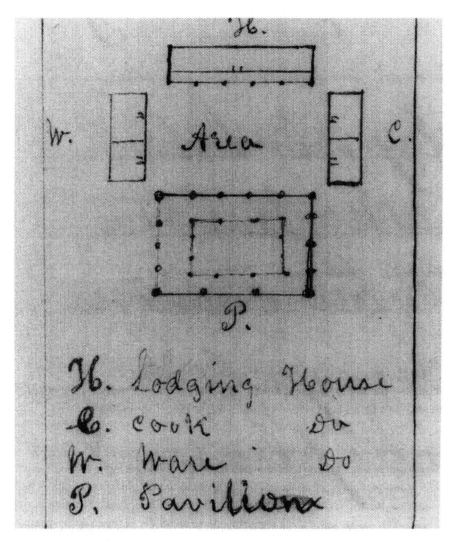

Figure 15. Edwin H. Davis's Copy of Bartram's Drawing of the Apalachicola Headman's Household (courtesy, National Anthropological Archives, Smithsonian Institution)

white people — He carries his merchandize on packhorse to the Alatamaha where having large convenient boats, he descends the River to Frederica, & sometimes continues his voyage to Sunbury and Savanna, where he disposes of his goods (i.e. Deerskins, Furs, Hides, Tallow, Oils, Honey, Wax &ca. [)] and with the net amount purchases Sugar, Coffee & every other kind of goods suitable to the Indian Markets. I have dwelt so long on this subject which may be called a digression, because I presume it may (amongst many more instances I could produce were it required of me) serve to convince those prejudiced, ignorant, obstinate people, that assert it is impossible for the Cricks to be brought over to

158

*Observations
on the
Creek
and
Cherokee
Indians*

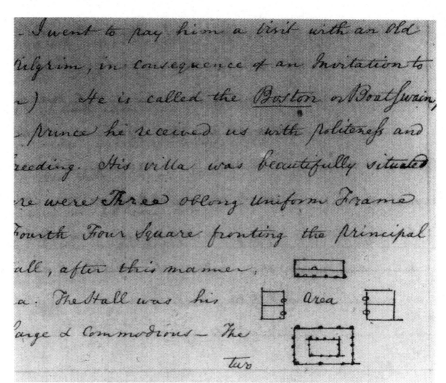

Figure 16. John Howard Payne's Copy of Bartram's Drawing of the Apalachicola Headman's Household (courtesy, Historical Society of Pennsylvania)

our modes of civil society (tho' so contrary to their notions of civilisation, & perhaps in some degree irreconcileable to right reason) —

However, I am not for leveling things down to the simplicity of Indians — Yet I may be allowed to conjecture that we might possibly better our condition in civil society by paying some more respect to, and impartially examining the system of Legislation, Morality & Œconomy of those despised, persecuted, Wild People, or as they are very learnedly called Bipedes, I suppose meaning a creature differing from Quadrupeds.

But to return to the subjects in question.

Every Town, or Community, assigns a piece, or parcels, of Land, as near as may be to the Town, for the sake of conveniency — This is called the Town Plantation, where every Family or Citizen has his parcel or share, according to desire or conveniency, or largeness of his Family — The shares are divided or bounded by a strip of grass ground, poles set up, or any other natural or artificial boundary, — thus the whole plantation is a collection of lots joining each other, comprised in one inclosure, or general boundary.

In the Spring when the Season arrives, all the Citizens as one Family, prepare the ground & begin to plant, beginning at one end or the other, as conveniency

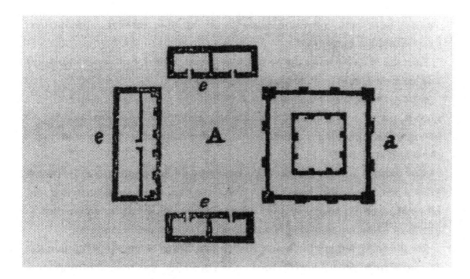

Figure 17. Ephraim G. Squier's Engraving of the Apalachicola Headman's Household (from William Bartram, "Observations on the Creek and Cherokee Indians, 1789," edited by E. G. Squier, p. 38, fig. 1)

may direct for the general good; & so continue on until finished; & when the young plants arise & require culture, they dress and husband them until their crops are ripe. The work is directed by an overseer, elected or appointed annually, I suppose, in rotation throughout the Families of the Town. He rises by day break, makes his progress through the Town, and, with a singular loud cry, awakens the people to their daily labour, who, by sunrise, assemble at the public square, each one with his hoe & axe, where they form themselves into one body or band, headed by their superintendant, who leads them to the field in the same order as if they were going to battle, where they begin their work & return at evening. The females do not march out with the men, but follow after, in detached parties, bearing the provisions for the day.

When the Fruits of their labours are ripe, and in fit order to gather in, they all on the same day repair to the plantation, each gathering the produce of his own proper lot, brings it to town & deposits it in his own crib, alotting a certain proportion for the Publick Granary which is called the King's Crib because its contents is at his disposal, tho' not his private property, but is to be considered the Tribute, or Free Contribution of the Citizens for the State, at the disposal of the King.[47]

The design of it is for the wisest & best of purposes, with respect to the condition of these people, i:e: — A Store, or Resource, to repair to in cases of necessity; — as, when a family's stores fall short, or is destroyed by accidents or otherwise; he has an equal right of assistance & supply from the Publick Granary, by applying to the King. And it furnishes aid to neighboring Towns

160

---

*Observations
on the
Creek
and
Cherokee
Indians*

that may be in want — provisions to supply their armies, travelers, or sojourners, or other publick exigencies.

Thus the Mico becomes the provider, or <u>Father of his People or of Mankind</u>, The greatest & most godlike character upon earth.

Besides this general plantation, each Habitation in the Town incloses a garden spot adjoining his House, where he plants, <u>Corn</u>, <u>Rice</u>, <u>Squashes</u>, &c, which, by early planting & closer attention, affords an earlier supply than their distant plantations.[48]

Now altho' it appears that these People enjoy all the advantages of freedom & private property, & they have Laws, Customs or Usages, which secures each one his right according to reason, justice & equity; the whole tribes seems as one Family or Community, and in fact all their possessions are in common.

For they have neither Locks nor Bars to their Doors & there is a common & continual intercourse between the families of a tribe, and indeed throughout the Confederacy they seem as one great Family, perfectly known & acquainted with each other, wherever they meet.

If one goes to anothers house and is in want of any necessary that he or she sees, and says I have need of such a thing or things, It is only a polite way of asking for it, & the request is forthwith granted, without ceremony or emotion; For he knows he is welcome to the like generous & friendly return, at any time.[49]

Indeed, they seem to consider all the Nations of the Earth as one great Family or Community who have seperated themselves, as conveniency & necessity have directed, & formed innumerable nations — climates, situations, revolutions, renovations, or other unknown causes having marked the several species, nations & tribes by different stature, colour, complexions, manners, customs & languages.

Their philanthropy and hospitality is perhaps the most universal and liberal of any people have we any account of. They hail all men, either of their own Land, or the most distant nations, by the name of <u>Brother</u>.

The Hebrews or Israelites called all of their own Nation and Religion, Brothers, or Brethren. But the Aborigines (or Red Men) of America, offers this Salutation to every Individual Man, of any Nation, Colour or Language whatever; and this is universal throughout all the Nations of this Continent, unless we are to except the <u>Uskimau's</u>, who appear to be another Race & with good reason are supposed to be derived from a European Colony much later than the colonisation of the <u>Red Men</u>, supposing these not to be absolutely Aborigines.

Such is their hospitality to Strangers, I know that a Creek Indian would not only receive in his house a Traveler or Sojourner of whatever Nation, Colour or Language, (without distinction of rank, or any other exception of person) and here treat him as a Brother or his own Child, as long as he pleases to Stay, and

161

Observations
on the
Creek
and
Cherokee
Indians

this without the least hope or thought of interest or reward, but serves you with the best of every thing his ability can afford; — he would divide with you the last grain of corn, or piece of flesh, — offer you the most valuable things in his possession that he imagines would be acceptable — nay, would part with every thing rather than contend, or let a Stranger remain or go away necessitous. And this to an Enemy who they knew, or apprehended through accident or misfortune without design of injury, came amongst them, or fell into their hands; in this case they would guard or conduct him safe beyond their frontier, & then tell him to go & take care of himself.

Even a White Man who they have very good reason to know is their most formidable, cruel, unrelenting barbarous enemy, If he came peaceably to their town, he would cherish him as long as he chose to stay, and guard him to his country — or even if he met him alone in the dreary Forests, naked, hungry, bewildered, lost, — he would give him his own only blanket, — half his provisions, — and take him to his wigwam, where he would respose securely and quietly, and in the morning conduct him safe back to his own Frontier; Tho' the day before He had been beaten, bruised and shot at, by a White Man.[50]

Thus they are hospitable, forgiving, gentle, humane, and grateful, — without precept or scholastic education — and this by nature, or some other unknown cause, without the least desire or expectation of applause or reward.

Query, 15th.

What appear to be the most common Diseases among those tribes of Indians, with whom you are acquainted? — What are their Remedies for those diseases? — Have you any reasons for believing, that the Venereal Disease was known among the North American Indians before the discovery of their countries by the Europeans? — Is it a frequent disease among those tribes with whom you are acquainted, at present? If it is, do they appear to be acquainted with any remedy, or remedies, for it? If they are, what are those remedies? —

Answer. —

The Indians seem in general Healthier than the Whites, have fewer diseases, & those they have, not so acute or contagious as the same amongst us.

The Small Pox sometimes visit them, which is the most dreaded of all diseases.[51]

Dysenteries, Pleurisy, & Intermittent Fevers, Epilepsy, & Asthma, they have at times.

The Hooping Cough is fatal among their children,[52] and Worms very frequent — But (besides their well known Remedy Spigelia anthelme) to prevent the troublesome & fatal effects of this disease, they use a strong Lexivium prepared from ashes of Bean Stalks & other vegetables, in all their

*Observations
on the
Creek
and
Cherokee
Indians*

food prepared from Corn (Zea) which otherwise they say breed worms in their Stomach.[53]

They have the Venerial Disease amongst them in some of its stages, but by their continence, temperance, powerful remedies, skill in applying them, and care, it is a disease which may be said to be uncommon; In some towns it is scarcely known, and in none arrives to that stage of virulency which we call a Pox unless sometimes amongst the White Traders who, they themselves say, as well as the Indians, that it might be eradicated if the Traders did not carry it with them to the Nations when they return with their merchandize, who contract the disorder before they set off & generally becomes virulent by the time they arrive, when they apply to the Indian Doctors to get cured.

However, I am inclined to believe that that infernal disease is the native produce of America,[54] from the Variety of Remedies found among the Indians, which are all vegetables.

And I imagine that the disease is more prevalent, as well as malignant, amongst the Northern Tribes.

The vegetables that I discovered to be used as remedies, were generally powerful cathartics. Of this class are several species of Iris, viz: Ir. versicolor, Ir. verna. And for the same purpose they have in high estimation a species of either Croton or Stillingia, I am in doubt which — I think it is unknown to the Europeans (Cr. decumbens). It is of great account in the Medicines of Doctor Howard, of No Carolina in curing the Yaws & is called Yaw Weed:[55] A great number of simple leaning stems arise from a large perennial root — These stalks are furnished with lanciolate entire leaves, both surfaces smooth; The stems terminate with spikes of Male and Female Flowers — the latter are succeeded by tricoccos seed vessells, — each cell containing a single seed — the Capsil after excluding the seed contracts & becomes of a triangular Figure, much resembling a Cocked Hat, which has given that name to the plant. i.e. Cock up Hat: — In the autumn before the stems decays, the leaves change to yellow, red & crimson colours, before they fall off.

I have been particular in the History of this plant, because it is known to possess very singular and powerful qualities. It is common on the dry, light, high lands of Carolina, Georgia & Florida.

Several species of Smilax, the woody vines of Bignonia Crucigera *, some of the Bays (Laurus) are of great account with the Indians as remedies.[56]

But the Indians in the cure of all complaints depend much on regimen and a rigid abstinence with respect to eating and drinking, as well as the gratification of other passions & appetites.[57]

The Cherokees use the Lobelia Siphilitica[58] & another plant of still greater

± [No corresponding note — eds.]

163

Observations
on the
Creek
and
Cherokee
Indians

power & efficacy, which the traders told me of, but would not undertake to show it me under Thirty Guineas Reward for fear of the Indians who endeavour to conceal the knowledge of it from the whites lest its great virtues should excite their researches for it, to its extirpation &ca &ca &ca

The vines or twining stems of this climber (Bignonia Crucigera) are equally divided longitudinally into 4 parts by 4 thin membranes somewhat resembling a piece of white tape, by which means when the vine is cut through & divided transversely, it presents to view the likeness of a cross: This membrane is of a sweet pleasant taste. The country people of Carolina chop those vines to pieces together with China Brier & Sassafras Roots & boil in their beer in the Spring for Diet Drink, in order to attenuate & purify the blood and juices. It is a principal ingredient in Howards famous infusions for curing the Yaws, &c. — the use & virtues of which he obtained from Indian Doctors.

The caustic & detergent properties of the roots of the White Nettle † of Carolina & Florida, (Tatropha urens) used for cleansing old ulcers and consuming proud flesh — And likewise the dissolvent & diuretick powers of the Root of the Convolvulus Panduratus ‡ so much esteemed as a remedy in Nephritic Complaints were discovered by the Indians to the Inhabitants of Carolina.[59]

I was informed by the people, that in order to prepare and administer both these remedies, they dig up the roots, and divide, or cut them, into thin pieces in order for their more speedy drying in the shade — and then are reduced to powder — the former being plentifully spread over the ulcer and the powder of the latter swallowed with any proper liquid vehicle. They are the more efficacious if used as fresh as possible — I suppose losing their virtues by desiccation, or being exposed to the air.

The emollient & discutient powers of the Swamp Lilly (Saururus Cernuus). And the virtues of the Hypo: or May-Apple (Podophyllum peltatum) the roots of which is a most effectual and safe emetic & also a cathartic & equally efficacious in expelling worms from the stomach.[60] The lives of many thousands of the people of the Southern States are preserved by means of this invaluable root, both of children & adults — In these countries it is of infinitely greater value than the Spanish Ipecacuanha.[61] I speak not only from my own experience, having been relieved by it, but likewise from numberless instances where I have seen its almost infallible good effects. The roots are dug up in the Autumn & Winter, spread to dry in an airy dry loft, when they are occasionally

† The White Nettle Roots are good & wholesome food when roasted or boiled. They are about the size of a large Carrot, when well grown, — but few of them are allowed to become large — the swine are so fond of them.

‡ Common field Convolvulus — grows almost every where in cleared or open grounds in Pennsylvania — The flower is large & white with a crimson, or purple, bottom or center.

164

---

*Observations
on the
Creek
and
Cherokee
Indians*

reduced to powder by the usual way of trituration (for the roots will retain their efficacy a long time when dryed) 30 gr. of the fine sieved powder is sufficient to operate on common constitutions & half that quantity on children; but a weak dose is sufficient for a cathartick — Either way never fails of clearing the stomach & intestines of worms.

In fine, I look upon this & the Saururus to be two as valuable medicinal plants as any we know of — at least in the Southern States — The virtues of them both were communicated to the White Inhabitants by the Indians.

Panax Gensang and Nondo ⊗ or White Root ⁕ (perhaps Angelica Lucida) or Belly-Ache Root[62] — These roots are of the highest esteem with the Cherokees & Creiks — The virtues of the former are well known — Of the latter, for its friendly carminitive qualities & for relieving all the painful disorders of the stomach — A dry belly-ache & disorders of the Intestines — Colick, Hysterick, &c — The patient chews the root & swallows the juice — or smokes it, when dry, with tobacco — even the smell of the roots is of good effect.

The lower Creeks in whose country it does not grow will gladly give two or three buckskins for a single root of it. —[63]

Query, Sixteenth.

Does the Food of those Indians whom you have visited, appear to be principally animal or vegetable? What are the principal vegetables employed as Food by the Indians? What vegetables do they cultivate, as Food, besides the Maize, — different species of gourds, &c —

What are the Chief Vegetables of which they make their bread? Do you think that those tribes whom you have visited, were acquainted with the use of Salt, before they became acquainted with the Europeans? — If you think they were not, what substances did they employ as substitutes to Salt? —

Answer. —

Their animal food consists chiefly of venison and Bear's Flesh, Turkeys, Hare, Wild Fowl and Domestic Poultry, and also of Domestic Kine, as Bulls, Oxen, Goats & Swine, — never Horses' Flesh, tho' they have those creatures in the greatest plenty; — Neither do they eat the Flesh of Dogs, Cats, or any such creatures as are usually rejected by the white people.[65]

⊗ The Creeks & Cherokees call it by a name which signifies White Root.

⁕ In Virginia it is called Nondo (I suppose an Indian Name) and also Belly-Ache Root — It is a plant highly worthy of cultivation — grows naturally in a good loose black moist soil, near to, and all over, the Cherokee & Apalatchian Mountains. My Father John Bartram planted it in his garden where it flourished equally as well as in its native soil. But the Ground Mice who are immoderately fond of its root as well as of that of the Gensang after several years gnaw —— [the rest of the leaf is gone — the note seems to end by a remark that the root was finally extirpated from the plantation by the ground mice.][64]

Their vegetable food consists chiefly of Corn (Zea), Rice, Convolvulus Batata, or those nourishing roots usually called Sweet or Spanish Potatoes (but in the Crick Confederacy they never plant or eat the Solanum tabrosa, or Irish Potatoe vulgo). All the species of Phaseolus & Dolichos in use among the Whites are cultivated by the Creeks, Cherokees &c: and make up a great part of their food. All the species of Cucurbita or Squashes, Pumpkins, Water Melons &c, but of the Cucumi, they cultivate none of the species, as yet, neither do they cultivate our Farinaceous grains, as Wheat, Barley, Spelts Rye, Buck Wheat &c. (not having yet the use of the plough amongst them (though it had been introduced some years ago, but the Chiefs rejected it, alledging that it would starve their Old People, who employ themselves in planting, and selling the produce to the Traders for their support and maintenance: seeing that by permitting the Traders to use the plough, one or two persons could easily raise more grain than all that the Old People in a Town could do by the Hoe).[66] Turnips, Parsnips, Sallads, &c, they have no knowledge of amongst them. Rice (Oryza) they plant on hills on high dry ground in their Gardens — By this management a few grains in a Hill (the hills about four feet apart) spread every way incredibly, & seems more prolific than if cultivated in water, as in the White settlements of Carolina — The heads or Panicles are larger & heavier & the grain is larger, firmer, or more farinaceous, much sweeter & more nourishing * — Each Family raises of this excellent grain, sufficient for family use, as for thickening their soups, ragouts, pilaus &c. —

But besides these cultivated Fruits &c above recited, together with Peaches, Oranges †, Plums (Chicasaw Plum) [,] Figs ‡ and some Apples — They have in use a vast variety of wild or native vegetable both Roots & Fruits, i.e. Diospyros, Morus rubra, Gleditsea Multiloba s. triacanthos)[67] All the species of Juglans, & Acorns (Quercus) from which they extract a very sweet oil, which enters all their cookery. Several species of Palms furnish them with a variety of agreable & nourishing food. Grapes (Vitis vinifera ⁕), too, they have in great variety & abundance, which they feed on occasionally when ripe & prepare them for keeping, which they lay up for winter & spring store. A species of Smilax

* The rice planters of Nᵒ Carolina raise very little of their rice in Flooded Lands (the natural situation of their country in general, not admitting of it) but plant in the Rich low Lands on the Banks of Rivers & Swamps, and tho' this kind of agriculture is more troublesome & expensive, yet they find their advantage, for the grain is more farinacious, substantial, and sweeter, insomuch, that their rice fetches a much higher price at foreign markets.

† Oranges & Figs are not much cultivated in the Nation, or Upper Creeks, but in the Lower Creek Countries, nearer the Sea Coast, are in great abundance, particularly the Orange, — many sorts are now become wild all over the country of East Florida.

‡ See the foregoing note.

⁕ Vitis Vinifera — I call them so, because they approach, in respect to the largeness of their Fruit, and their shape & flavour, much nearer to the grapes of Europe & Asia, of which wine is made — and are specifically different from our common Wild Grape (Vit. Labrusca) and as different from the Fox or Bull Grapes of Pennsylvania & Carolina.

165

Observations
on the
Creek
and
Cherokee
Indians

166

Observations
on the
Creek
and
Cherokee
Indians

(S. China) affords them a delicious & nourishing food, which is prepared from its vast tuberous roots.[68]

They dig up these roots, and while yet fresh & full of juice chop them in pieces — then macerate them well in wooden mortars — this substance they put in vessels, nearly filled with clean water — where being well mixed with paddles, whilst the finer parts are yet floating in the liquid, they decant it off into other vessels where it is left to settle; and after the subsidence is compleat, they cast-off the water, leaving the farinacious substance at the bottom, which being taken out and dried, is as an impalpable powder or farina, of a reddish incarnate colour. This when mixed in boiling water becomes a beautiful jelly, which, sweetened with honey or sugar, affords a most nourishing & pleasant food for children or aged people, or when mixed with fine corn flower & fryed in fresh bears' oil make excellent fritters.

I conclude these articles with mentioning a vegetable which I had but a slight opportunity of observing, just as I left the Creek country, on the waters of the Mobile River. It is a species of Palmæ[69] — It has no stalk or stem above ground — The leaves spread regularly all round, — are Flabelliform when fully expanded — otherwise cucullated — their Stipes very short — scarcely apparent at a slight view — in the centre is produced a kind of dense panicle or general receptacle of the Fruit — of the form & size of a Sugar Loaf, or of the figure of an obtuse cone — a vast collection of plums or drupes of the size & figure of ordinary plums which are covered with a fibrous farinaceous pulpy coating of considerable thickness — This substance which to the best of my remembrance resembles manna in texture colour & taste, or of the consistence of moist brown sugar, with lumps or particles of loaf Sugar mixt with it — This is a delicious & nourishing food & diligently sought after — There were several of these clusters brought in to the (Ottasse Town just before I left it, of which I ate freely with the Indians & think in substance & taste the most of any thing like manna — a little bitterish & stingy on the palate on first using it; but soon becomes familiar & desirable.

I own that I am not able to give an accurate botanical account of this very curious and valuable vegetable because it was discovered to my observation but just on my departure & tho' I saw several of the plants on the road, but being obliged to follow the mad career or manner of traveling with Pack Horses I had left the country of its native growth before I had an opportunity of leisure to examine it, which I have severely regretted. And convinced I am that it is an object of itself worth a journey to these regions, to examine and procure the plant.

Query Seventeenth.
Did you observe, in any part, or parts, of the countries through which you

travelled, any Large Teeth, or Bones, similar to those which have been found near the River Ohio, &c.? Have the Indians, as far as you know, any tradition concerning these Bones? — If they have, what is that tradition?

167

*Observations
on the
Creek
and
Cherokee
Indians*

Answer. —

Observed not the least sign or mention of any large Teeth or Bones, similar to those you mention, except some Tradition of the same story recited concerning the Big Bones on the Ohio, which stories you are well acquainted with.

I indeed frequently in the Forests of West Florida & North of Georgia observed very large Bones as those of the Thigh & Tibia, and some remarkable large grinders (Dent. Mol.) But as I was informed suppose them to belong to the Buffaloe[70] (Urus) and these were all unchanged bone, not petrified or fossil, which all the Specimens of the Great Bones I have seen appear to be.

"Thus, you have
    Sir,
        My observations and conjectures on these matters, with all the truth and accuracy, that my slender abilities will admit of, and without reserve. If they should not answer your wishes and expectations, I desire you would ascribe it to my misapprehension of the questions, or lack of knowledge, &c. &c. —

I doubt not but you'll readily excuse bad writing, composition, spelling &ca — My weakness of sight &c. I hope will plead for me, when I assure you I have been obliged to write the greater part with my eyes shut and that with pain.[71]

I do not mention this to claim any sort of obligation from you, Sir, for all that I know concerning these matters are due to you & to science.
        I remain, Sir,
        with every sentiment of respect and esteem
            Your obliged Friend,
                Wm Bartram.
Philadelphia,
    Decemb 15th, 1789.

Postscript.
    I have added the following rough Drawings of the Antient Indian Monuments, consisting of Publick Buildings, Areas, Vestiges of Towns, &c:
    Which I hope may serve in some degree to explain or illucidate my answers and conjectures.
    They are to the best of my remembrance as near the Truth as I could express; However, if I have err'd in any, I hope they may be corrected and rectified by future observation, of more accurate & industrious Travelers.

168

Observations
on the
Creek
and
Cherokee
Indians

But as time changes the face of Things, I wish they could be searched out, and faithfully recorded, before the devastations of artificial refinements, ambition & avarice totally deface those simple and most antient remains of the American Aborigines,[72] &c &c &c. — "

A View of the Antient Chunky Yard [figures 18–20][73]

A.* The great Area or Yard, surrounded by the Terrace, or banks.

B.† A circular eminence at one end, commonly 9 or 10 feet higher than the ground round about, whereon the great Rotunda or Hothouse or Winter Council House of the present Generation of Cricks stands & which probably was by the Antients who constructed it, designed and used for the same purpose.

C. Four Square Terrace or Eminence about the same height of the former or circular one: This stand at the other end of the Yard whereon stands the Publick Square of the Cricks, and was likely designed for, and put to the same use, by the Antients who rais'd it.

    b. — The Banks or Terrace round the Yard.

    c. — The Chunky Pole, or Obelisk.

    d. — The Slave Posts.

    Observ. — In the lately built, or New Towns of the Cricks, they dont raise the ground or foundation whereon their Rotunda, or Publick Square stands. But the Yard is in appearance nearly the same; & these Publick building stand in the same order and position and they retain the Obelisk & Slave Posts.

    In the Cherokee country, all over Carolina[75] and North East part of Georgia where ruins of Antient Indian Towns appear, we see, always, besides these sort of eminences, one vast conical pointed mount, which are the pyramidal mounts I have heretofore mentioned. But S° & Wᵗ of the Alatamaha I observed none of them — in no part of the Muscogulge Country; but always those lower, circular & square ones, except in the Lower Crick Country, as those vast ones observed on Rivr St Johns, Alachua, Musquito Rivr &c. &c. which however differ from those of the Cherokes, with respect to their adjuncts or appendages, particularly the Great Highway or Avenue sunk below the common level of the ground, and terminating either in a vast Savana or Natural Plain, or Artificial Pond or Lake, and sometimes both together, as of that Remarkable One of Mot Royal, from whence opens a glorious view of Lake George and its invirons. —

A. The Principal, or Council House [figures 21 and 22],[76] fronting the Area, divided transversely into three equal apartments, by a low clay wall: This

---

*†—Note both the circular & tetragon Eminences advance too far into the Yard. It was an oversight. Their limb [i.e., limit] should not intersect the line of the surrounding bank —[74] Sometimes the bank is continued unopen quite round the yard.

169

*Observations
on the
Creek
and
Cherokee
Indians*

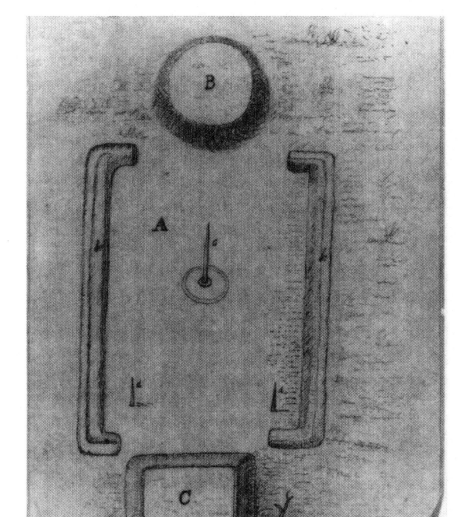

Figure 18. Edwin H. Davis's Copy of Bartram's "A view of the Ancient Chunky Yard" (courtesy, National Anthropological Archives, Smithsonian Institution)

*Observations
on the
Creek
and
Cherokee
Indians*

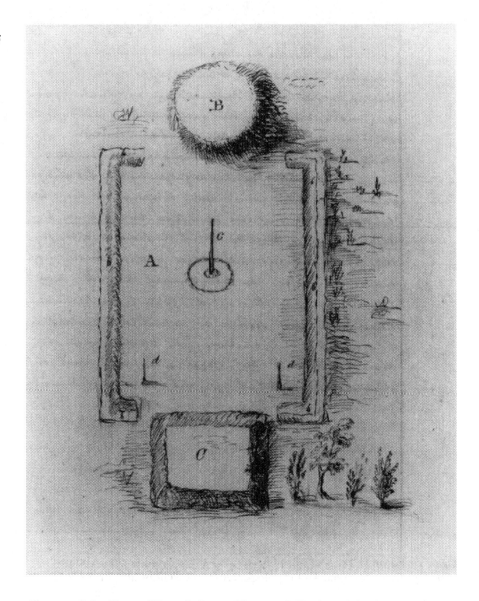

Figure 19. John Howard Payne's Copy of Bartram's "A view of the Antient Chunky Yard" (courtesy, Historical Society of Pennsylvania)

171

Observations
on the
Creek
and
Cherokee
Indians

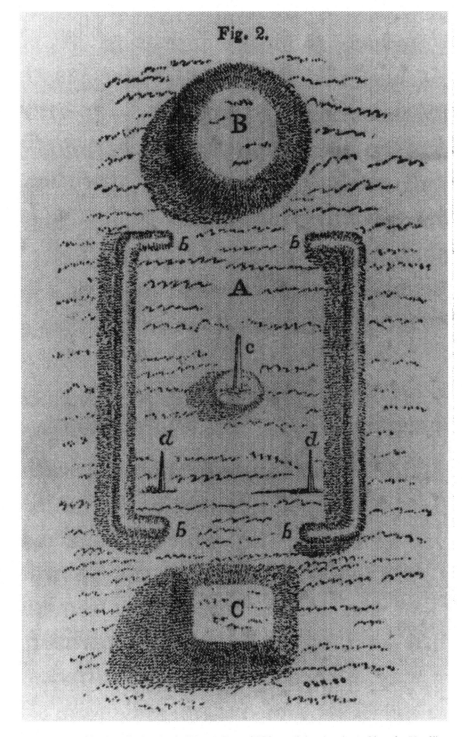

Figure 20. Ephraim G. Squier's Engraving of "Plan of the Ancient Chunky-Yard" (from William Bartram, "Observations on the Creek and Cherokee Indians, 1789," edited by E. G. Squier, p. 52, fig. 2)

172

*Observations
on the
Creek
and
Cherokee
Indians*

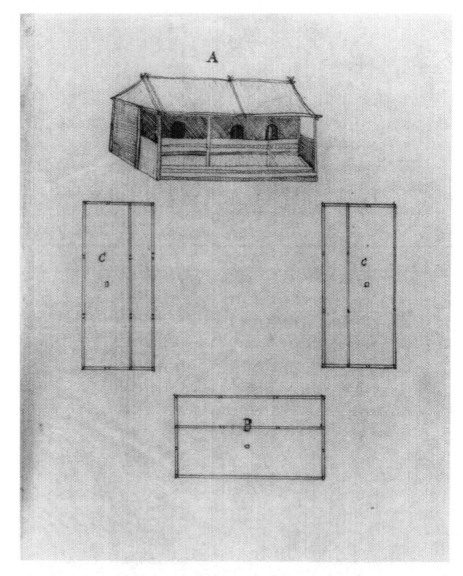

Figure 21. Edwin H. Davis's Copy of Bartram's "The Principal, or Council House" (courtesy, National Anthropological Archives, Smithsonian Institution)

building is also divided lengthwise into two nearly equal parts, — the foremost or front is an open Piazza, where are seats for the Counsil — The Middle Apartment of this is for the King (Mico) Great War Chief, Second Head Man, and other venerable & worthy Chiefs & Warriors — The two others on each side, for Warriors, Head Men, Citizens, &ca. The Back apartment of this House is

173

*Observations
on the
Creek
and
Cherokee
Indians*

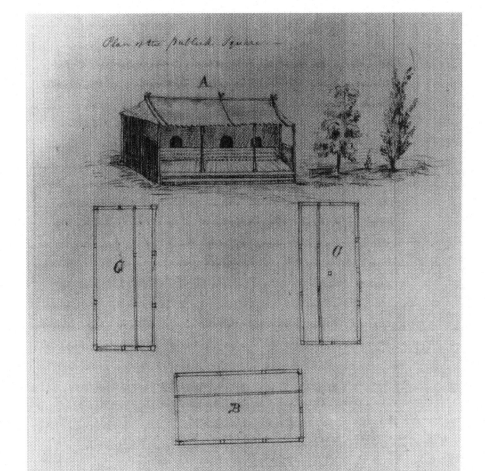

Figure 22. John Howard Payne's Copy of Bartram's "Plan of the Publick Square" (courtesy, Historical Society of Pennsylvania)

quite close and dark, except three very low arched <u>Holes</u> or <u>Doors</u> for admittance of the Priests. In this place are deposited all the most valuable Publick Things, (as the <u>Eagle Tail</u>, or National Standard) <u>Calumet & War Pipe</u>, <u>Drums</u> & all the <u>Sacred Things or Apparatus of the Priests</u> &c &c, and no person but the priests who have the care of them have admittance and it is said to be certain Death for any other Person to presume to enter.

B. The Banquetting House.

C. Halls to accommodate the People, at public times of Feasts or Festivals, &c. —

174

*Observations
on the
Creek
and
Cherokee
Indians*

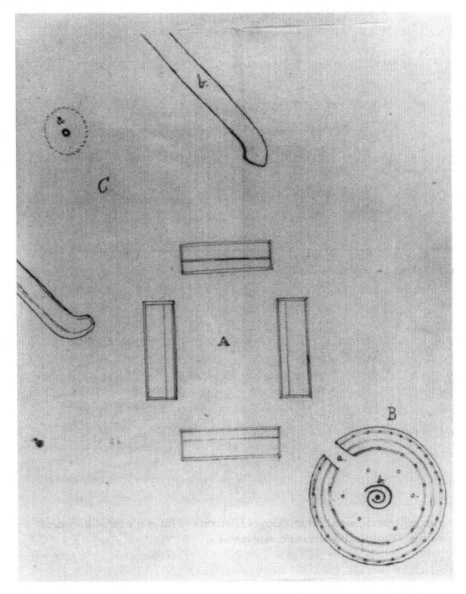

Figure 23. Edwin H. Davis's Copy of Bartram's "The Chunky Yard, Publick Square & Rotunda, of the Modern Crick Towns" (courtesy, National Anthropological Archives, Smithsonian Institution)

These three houses are nearly alike & differ from the Council House A only in not having the close back apartment.

Plan of the Publick Square. —

This is the most common plan or arrangement of the Chunky Yard, Publick Square & Rotunda, of the Modern Crick Towns [figures 23–25].[77]

175

*Observations
on the
Creek
and
Cherokee
Indians*

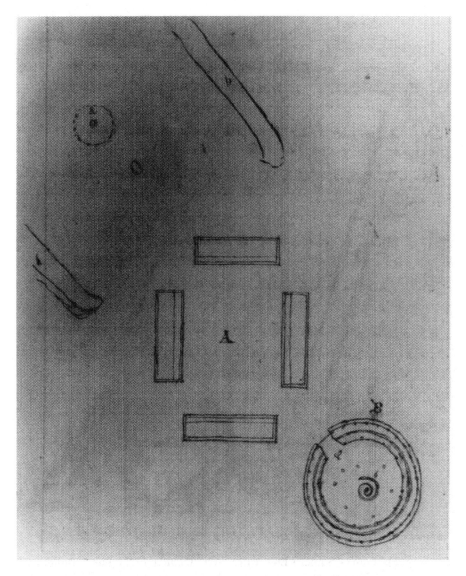

Figure 24. John Howard Payne's Copy of Bartram's "The Chunky Yard, Publick Square & Rotunda" (courtesy, Historical Society of Pennsylvania)

A. The Public Square
B. The Rotunda, a[—] the Door opening towards the Square: The three circular lines shews the two rows of cabins. (Seats or Sophas) The punctures shews the circular rows of pillars, which supports the building. b — The great center pillar or column & spiral fire, to give light to the House.
C. Part of the Chunky Yard. b. The bank or Terrace that incompasses it.

176

*Observations
on the
Creek
and
Cherokee
Indians*

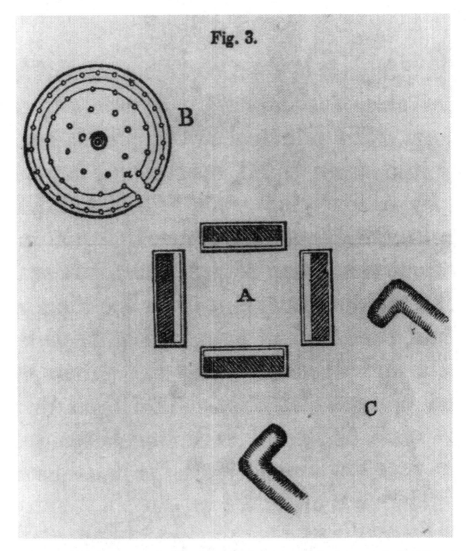

Figure 25. Ephraim G. Squier's Engraving, "Arrangement of the Public Buildings" (from William Bartram, "Observations on the Creek and Cherokee Indians, 1789," edited by E. G. Squier, p. 54, fig. 3.)

    A View of Mount Royal, near Lake George, with the Avenue, or Highway, to an Artificial Lake or Pond, on the verge of an expansive Savana, or Natural Meadow [figures 26–30].[78]

A. The Mount, about Forty feet, perpendicular height.

B. The Highway leading from the Mot. on a straight line about ½ mile to the pond.

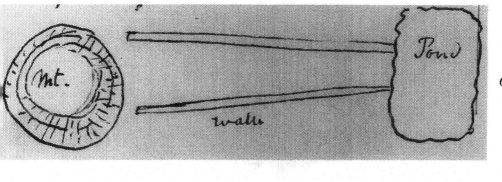

177

*Observations
on the
Creek
and
Cherokee
Indians*

Figure 27. John Howard Payne's Copy of Bartram's Sketch of the Mount Royal Site (courtesy, Historical Society of Pennsylvania)

178

---

*Observations
on the
Creek
and
Cherokee
Indians*

Figure 28. Edwin H. Davis's Copy of Bartram's "A View of Mount Royal" (courtesy, National Anthropological Archives, Smithsonian Institution)

C. Part of the Lake or Pond, of an oblong form, thus

D. Part of the Savana of many miles extent.

Qry What should be their motives for making this pond, I can't imagine, since the Mount, & the vestiges of the antient town, is situated close on the Banks of the Riv: St Juan: it could not be for conveniency of Water.

Perhaps, they rais'd the Mount with the earth taken out of it.[79]

Note. The draft of this Mount serves equally well to represent the Cheroké

¹79

*Observations
on the
Creek
and
Cherokee
Indians*

Figure 29. John Howard Payne's Copy of Bartram's "A View of Mount Royal"
(courtesy, Historical Society of Pennsylvania)

Mounts, but those last have not the Highway, but are always accompanied with
the vast Tetragon Terraces placed on one side or other:

And on the other hand, we never see the Tetragon Terraces or Eminences
accompanying the High Mounts of Et Florida.

180

---

*Observations
on the
Creek
and
Cherokee
Indians*

Figure 30. Ephraim G. Squier's Engraving of the Mount Royal Site (from William Bartram, "Observations on the Creek and Cherokee Indians, 1789," edited by E. G. Squier, p. 57, fig. 6)

The habitations of the Muscogulges or Upper Crick Towns [figures 31–33],[80] consist of Little Squares, or four oblong square houses, encompassing a square area, exactly on the plan of the <u>Publick Square</u>, — every Family however have not four of these Houses — some 3, — some 2, — and some but one, according to their circumstances, of largeness of their family, &c. — but they are situated so as to admit of four building when conveniency or necessity require it[81] — Wealthy citizens, having large Families, generally have Four Houses; and they have a particular use for each of these buildings — One serves for a <u>Cook Room & Winter Lodging House</u> — another for a Summer Lodging House & Hall for Receiving Visiters — and a 3d for a Granary, or Provision House, &c: — This is commonly two Stories high and divided into two apartments transversely — the lower story of one end being a potatoe house & for keeping such other roots & fruits as require to be kept close or defended from cold in Winter — The chamber over it is the Corn Crib[82] — The other end of this building, both lower & upper stories are open on 3 sides[83] — The lower story serves for a shed for their saddles, packsaddles, & geers & other Lumber; the loft over it is a very spacious airy pleasant Pavilion — where the Chief of the Family reposes in the hot seasons & receives his Guests, &ca. — And the Fourth House (which compleats the Square) is a Skin House or <u>Ware-house</u>, if the proprieter is a wealthy man, and engaged in Trade or Traffick — where he keeps his Deer Skins, Furs & Merchandize & treats with his Customers — Smaller or less Wealthy Families, make one, two or 3 houses serve all these purposes as well as they can.

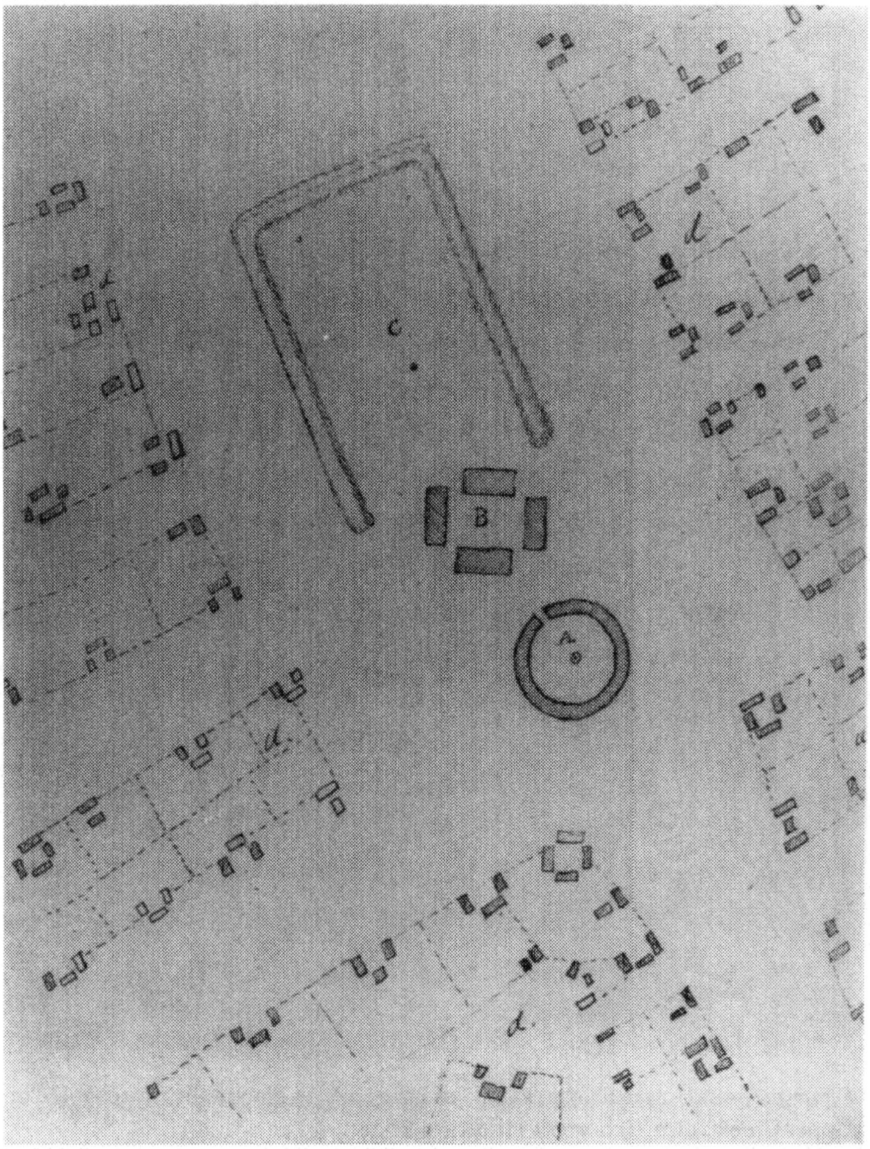

181

*Observations
on the
Creek
and
Cherokee
Indians*

Figure 31. Edwin H. Davis's Copy of Bartram's "A Plan of the Muscogulge or Upper Creek Town" (courtesy, National Anthropological Archives, Smithsonian Institution)

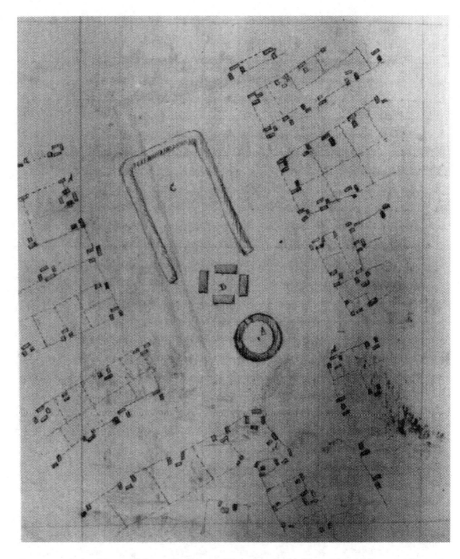

182

*Observations
on the
Creek
and
Cherokee
Indians*

Figure 32. John Howard Payne's Copy of Bartram's "A Plan of the Muscogulge or Upper Creek Town" (courtesy, Historical Society of Pennsylvania)

183

*Observations
on the
Creek
and
Cherokee
Indians*

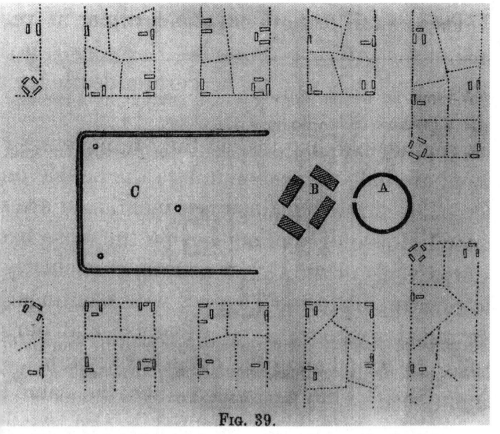

FIG. 39.

Figure 33. Ephraim G. Squier's Engraving of "Creek Towns and Dwellings" (from William Bartram, "Observations on the Creek and Cherokee Indians, 1789," edited by E. G. Squier, p. 55, fig. 4)

The Lower Creeks or Siminoles are not so regular & ingenious in their building either publick or private. They have neither the Chunky-Yard or Rotunda & the Publick-Square is imperfect — One, Two or Three Houses at farthest serve their purpose. And indeed they don't require it, for their Towns are but small, and consequently their Councils just sufficient for the government or regulation of the Town or Little Tribe, for in all great or publick matters they are influenced by the Nation (Upper Creeks).

Their Private Habitations generally consist of two buildings — One a large oblong house, which serves for Cook-Room, eating house & lodging rooms, in 3 apartments under one roof — the other's not quite so long, which is situated 8 or 10 yards distance, one end opposite the front door of the principal house, thus [figures 34 and 35.] This is two stories high, and just like & serves the same purpose of the Granary or Provision House and Loft of the Upper Creeks.

The Cherokees, too, differ greatly from the Muscogulges with respect to their Buildings — They have neither the Square or Chunky Yard. Their Summer

184

*Observations
on the
Creek
and
Cherokee
Indians*

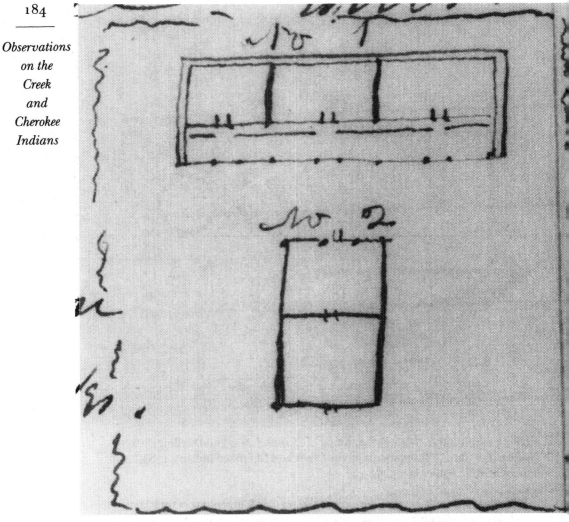

Figure 34. Edwin H. Davis's Copy of Bartram's Drawing of a Seminole "private habitation" (courtesy, National Anthropological Archives, Smithsonian Institution)

Council House, is a spacious, open loft, or pavilion, on the top of a very large oblong Building, and the <u>Rotunda</u> or <u>Great Hot-House</u> or <u>Town House</u> is the Council House in the cold Seasons.

   Their private Houses or Habitations consist of one Large Oblong-Square Log Building, divided transversely into several apartments; and a round, Hot house, stands a little distance off for a Winter Lodging House. Thus [figures 36–38][84]

William Bartram./

185

*Observations
on the
Creek
and
Cherokee
Indians*

Their private Habitations generally consist of two buildings — one a larger oblong house, which serves for Cook-Room, eating house & lodging rooms, in 3 apartments under one roof — the other not quite so long, which is situated 8 or 10 yards distance, one end opposite the front door of the principal house, this

pr. house

This is two stories high, and just like & serves the same purpose of the Granary or Provision House and Loft of the Upper Creeks.

Figure 35. John Howard Payne's Copy of Bartram's Drawing of a Seminole "private habitation" (courtesy, Historical Society of Pennsylvania)

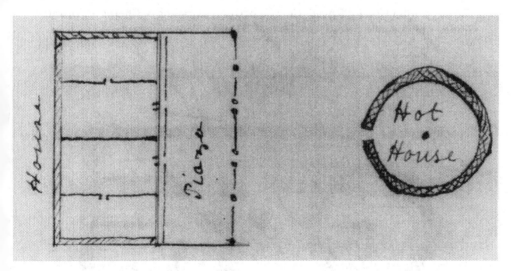

Figure 36. Edwin H. Davis's Copy of Bartram's Drawing of Cherokee "private houses or habitations" (courtesy, National Anthropological Archives, Smithsonian Institution)

186

Observations
on the
Creek
and
Cherokee
Indians

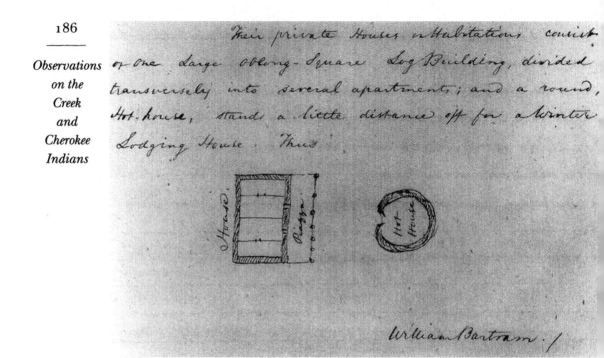

Figure 37. John Howard Payne's Copy of Bartram's Drawing of Cherokee "private houses or habitations" (courtesy, Historical Society of Pennsylvania)

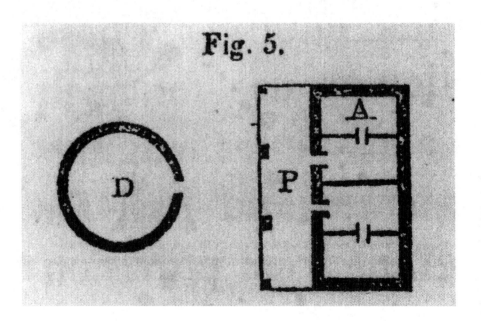

Figure 38. Ephraim G. Squier's Engraving of Cherokee "private habitations" (from William Bartram, "Observations on the Creek and Cherokee Indians, 1789," edited by E. G. Squier, p. 56, fig. 5)

"Some Hints & Observations, concerning the civilization of the Indians, or Aborigines of America"

The final document in this volume, "Some Hints & Observations . . . ," is the most mysterious of William Bartram's writings about American Indians. The original manuscript resides among the papers of Henry Knox, now housed at the Pierpont Morgan Library in New York City. Knox served as secretary of war under the Articles of Confederation and held the same office in George Washington's administration. One of his principal responsibilities in this capacity was to oversee Indian affairs, the topic Bartram addressed in this document.[1]

Though broadly titled, the paper concerns the Creeks in particular. Internal clues, such as references to the "Federal compact," indicate the piece was written after the drafting of the U.S. Constitution in 1787.[2] A tentative date ("1792?") appears in pencil at the top of the document. But judging from a reference to ongoing conflict between the Indians (in this case the Creeks) and the Americans, the document must have been composed prior to the establishment of peace between the United States and the Creeks by the Treaty of New York in 1790. The document, which is not in Bartram's hand, bears only the initials "WB." Nothing is known of the manuscript's provenance, but its style, philosophical bent, and statements of fact point conclusively to William Bartram as the author.[3]

Why Bartram wrote the piece, however, is not so readily apparent. Perhaps Henry Knox solicited the document directly, as "expert testimony" to bolster his controversial approach to federal Indian policy. Thomas Jefferson, who resided across the Schuylkill River from the Bartram garden for a time when the federal government was lodged in Philadelphia, was another possible audience. Alternatively, another person or persons might have acted as an intermediary for the retiring botanist in his appeal to federal officials. Since Bartram addressed his tract to "my Brethren," perhaps members of the Philadelphia Quaker community were his immediate audience, since they were very interested in promoting missionary activity among the American Indians, in educating them and helping extend the "benefits" of western civilization to them. In the absence of adequate records, it seems very likely that the Indian Committee of the Philadelphia Yearly Meeting, or at least another such group of interested Quakers, asked Bartram for information, which they then could have supplied to Knox.[4]

"Some Hints & Observations" is primarily an eloquent plea for equal treatment of Native Americans as brothers under God. Most important, this work set forth, in Bartram's view, the incontrovertible claim of the Natives to the land they occupied. In something of a departure from the position he espoused in *Travels*, Bartram urged that the benefits of "civilization" — the "Language, System of Legislation, Religion, Manners, Arts, & Sciences" of the dominant white society — be taught to the American Indian tribes. Once Native Americans accepted the manner of religion, work habits, and government of the United States, Bartram maintained, conflicts between whites and Indians would vanish, and the two peoples could coexist peacefully. In urging the adoption of a policy that would "banish violence & war," Bartram's discourse reflects his own pacifist nature and Quaker background.

To fully understand "Some Hints & Observations," one must consider early federal Indian policy as well as Anglo-Creek relations at the time the document was composed. Perhaps no one is so closely associated with the "civilization" argument as Thomas Jefferson, who was among the chief architects of early U.S. Indian policy. Jefferson held that the Indians were equal, in intellect and spirit, to whites. Those "deficiencies" of Native society in the realms of arts and sciences he attributed to a lack of adequate opportunities to embrace a higher culture. (In *Travels*, William Bartram argued the converse, that vices of the southeastern Indians could be traced to the foibles of white men who had come among them and corrupted their morals.)[5] To Jefferson and to scores of other philanthropists, reeducation was the key; Native American societies had to be remade in the image of enlightened white America.[6]

Philadelphia's Quaker community actively promoted "civilization" schemes, most of which aimed at reformation of the Indian economy from a hunting base to the settled life of commercial farming. The U.S. government had adopted this position as early as 1776, when the Continental Congress urged that Christianity and "civil arts" be promoted among the American Indian population. Henry Knox was one of the most influential advocates of this "civilization" theory.

After waging several costly wars against tribes in the Ohio country, Knox sought a firm peace by implementing a "moral" policy based on the acknowledgment of Native rights to land, the transfer of land only by treaty, and the transformation of the Indian way of life.[7] By July 1789, he announced that "instead of exterminating a part of the human race," the young nation should endeavor to impart "our knowledge of cultivation and the arts to the aboriginals of the country." In one of his first reports under the new government, Knox made this telling observation:

> That the civilization of the Indians would be an operation of complicated difficulty; that it would require the highest knowledge of the human character, and a steady perseverance in a wise system for a series of years, cannot be doubted. But to deny that, under a course of favorable circumstances, it could not [*sic*] be accomplished, is to suppose the human character under the influence of such stubborn habits as to be incapable of melioration or change — a supposition entirely contradicted by the progress of society, from the barbarous ages to its present degree of perfection.[8]

Among the immediate problems the Washington administration faced upon assuming office was an undeclared war then underway between the Creeks and the state of Georgia. The settlements along the Cumberland River in the Tennessee country had also felt the wrath of Creek raiding parties. Following the Revolutionary War, Georgia had negotiated three separate treaties with the Creeks, but all three were repudiated by the majority of the Creek towns. Then, led by Alexander McGillivray, the talented son of the deerskin trader Lachlan McGillivray and a prominent woman of the Wind clan, the Creeks negotiated a commercial alliance with Spanish Florida. They thereby secured trade through Panton, Leslie, and Company, a group of loyalists still economically tied to Great Britain who operated from the colony of Florida, recently restored to Spain. Guns and ammunition obtained from these trade partners were essential to the Creek campaign against American settlements in the Cumberland region and Georgia.

The Creeks were determined, in McGillivray's words, "to take arms in our defence & repel those Invaders of our Lands, to drive them from their encroachments & fix them within their own proper limits."[9] In July 1787, McGillivray claimed he had sent between 500 and 600 warriors to "ravage the Settlement of Cumberland." Incidents along the disputed border with Georgia were also common.[10] By 1789, Muscogulge war parties had killed 72 settlers, wounded 29, and taken 30 prisoner; killed 10 black slaves and captured 110; taken over 640 horses and 984 cattle, killed 387 hogs, and burned 89 houses on the disputed lands.[11] At Rock Landing, Georgia, U.S. peace commissioners acting on orders from the Washington administration met with McGillivray to settle their differences with the Creeks. The conference failed to resolve the disagreement, and the U.S. commissioners sent home recommendations for an invasion of the Creek country. All-out war seemed a distinct possibility.[12]

Under these circumstances, Bartram penned "Some Hints & Observations." Just how much influence the gentle Quaker's paper may have had on the development of U.S. policy is impossible to know. Certainly, Secretary of War Knox found considerable support for his new initiative in Bartram's treatise.

The Washington administration, faced with serious Indian problems on the northwest frontier, made one last attempt to come to terms with the Creeks. President Washington dispatched Marinus Willett to meet directly with McGillivray, iron out treaty terms, and escort a treaty delegation to New York (which then served as seat of the new government). Included among the terms suggested by Willett were provisions to implement Knox's civilization policy among the Creeks. McGillivray welcomed and may have even inspired some of the "civilization" provisions, especially the one relating to the education of selected Creek youths at the expense of the U.S. government. Once the treaty terms were agreed upon, Willett and McGillivray, accompanied by a delegation of leading Creek headmen, set out for New York.[13]

As the treaty delegation passed through Philadelphia en route to New York City, their progress was followed with keen interest by the U.S. public, and Bartram's publisher used the occasion to advertise Bartram's forthcoming *Travels*. There is no evidence that Bartram met with any members of the delegation.[14] Even so, "Some Hints & Observations" shows that Bartram had kept abreast of developments among the Creeks, perhaps through correspondence with his old friend Lachlan McIntosh.[15]

Following the successful completion of the treaty, McGillivray's nephew, Davy Tate, was left under the care of Henry Knox, who was to supervise his education under terms of the treaty.[16] Though the record is not clear on the arrangements, other Creek youths sent north for an education were entrusted by the secretary of war to the care of the Indian Committee of the Philadelphia Society of Friends Yearly Meeting. The record is silent as to whether William Bartram met with members of the 1790 treaty delegation. It is very likely that he did so, for the Creek delegation came within one mile of his home when they visited Gray's Ferry on July 17, 1790, and Bartram's friend, Benjamin Smith Barton, met Alexander McGillivray on that occasion. Likewise, there is no record that any of the Creek boys who later lived among the Philadelphia Quaker community visited Bartram, or that Bartram had contact with the Philadelphia Yearly Meeting's Indian Committee.[17]

In 1796, the U.S. government, determined to improve relations with Native Americans in the south, appointed Benjamin Hawkins, a senator from North Carolina, as "Principal Temporary Agent to the Indians South of the Ohio."[18] William Bartram, in his *Travels,* had provided the first published job description for the ideal American Indian agent:

> men of ability and virtue, under the authority of government, [should be sent] as friendly visitors, into their towns; let these men be instructed to learn perfectly their languages, and by a liberal and friendly intimacy, become acquainted with their customs and usages, religious and civil; their system of legislation and police, as well as their most ancient and present traditions and history. These men thus enlightened and instructed, would be qualified to judge equitably, and when returned to us, to make true and just reports, which might assist the legislature of the United States to form, and offer to them a judicious plan, for their civilization and union with us.[19]

Hawkins was a firm believer in the "civilization program." During his tenure as agent, from 1796 until his death in 1816, he labored diligently to transform Creek economy and society. Hawkins corresponded frequently with members of the Philadelphia Yearly Meeting Indian Committee, particularly Martha Routh, Henry Drinker, and Mrs. Elizabeth Trist, an old friend from that city.[20] It is scarcely surprising that among the books Hawkins requested to further his understanding of the Creeks was William Bartram's *Travels.* Despite the benign intentions of Knox, Bartram, the Quaker community, Hawkins, and many others, the "civilization program" was a complete disaster. Most Creeks rejected the implications of the plan, which called for changes in gender-based labor patterns, the abandonment of traditional town settlement, and the replacement of matrilineal clan authority over family matters.[21] The plan simply failed to meet the needs of the Native Americans on their own terms.

"Some Hints & Observations, concerning the civilization of the Indians, or Aborigines of America"

The Spanish settlements, in Florida, extend but a small distance from the Sea Coast: For they are very careful, not to disturb, or offend the Indians, by dispossessing them, or even hunting on their Lands.[1]

They consider them as Brethren & fellow Citizens, and use all rational means to engage their friendship, to make them good Christians & consequently good Men.

I could wish the Citizens of these States, would shew their approbation of so worthy an example, by endeavouring to conciliate the affections of the Indians, especially of those Nations within the limits of the United States. Particular notice should be taken of the tribes to the S.W. the Cherokes, * Muscogulges, Chicasa's and Chactaws. The Siminoles, although confederates to the Muscoges, are at present within the limits of the Spanish claims of Florida, and consequently, in a political view, they do not immediately concern us.[2]

The Tribes above mentioned, lay contiguous to one another, and taken collectively, comprehend a vast territory, and a very respectable number of Inhabitants, who are intrepid, and warlike. Although they are not, strictly consider'd, Aborigines of these Countries; yet they have possess'd the Soil, for some Ages past, and the Bones, and other sacred reliques of their Ancestors lie buried in the dust about their Towns.

Our Ancestors who first landed on these Coasts, were received by the Fathers, and Grandfathers of those Tribes, in the most friendly, and hospitable manner. They humanely & cheerfully treated them as wellcome Guests: But to give a stronger proof of their affection, they call'd them "Beloved Brethren" and voluntarily evacuated their Towns to accommodate them. Every necessary & conveniency, which the country afforded was brought as an inducement for our Ancestors to remain amongst them, or to repeat their Visits. The Indians regarded them with love, and reverence. Benevolence taught those natives to

* Creeks

act in the excellent characters of friends & Guardians, & to establish their White Brothers family, on their Border. The white family increased & flourished. The Spanish another more powerful family of White People, who had before settled a Plantation a little to the S^d, with envy, saw the progress of the English family. Stimulated by Rage, they determined against right, and justice, to commence hostilities & destroy them: But the natives with one hand, with one Spirit, engaged in defence of the English, and in the end expeld their envious neighbour.[3]

These instances of magnanimity & friendship, in the Natives, in my opinion, should not only recall, that gratitude which seems to have been expeld from our Breasts, but excite in us, sentiments of generosity & compassion, toward their unfortunate offspring.

Man, after he has subjugated his powerful opponent, is too apt to conclude rashly, & act tyrannically.

We unreasonably ask, to what purpose do we observe any terms, with cruel, barbarous Savages, who are continually seeking opportunities to massacre our Brethren & Relatives on the Frontiers?[4]

Wretches, who in the late glorious contest, joined our Enemy to cut our Throats![5]

Let us join as one Man, to cut them off & disposses them of those Lands, which are ours by right of conquest.

Our injustice & avarice, in pressing upon their Borders & dispossessing them of their Lands, together with the outrage committed against their Persons & encroachments made on their hunting Grounds by the Frontiers, provoke them to retaliation.[6]

Their joining, or taking part with our Enemy, during the late Contest, is I believe, understood in a too general sense. We ought at least to discriminate. I pass'd through the Muscogulge confederacy at the most critical period of the contest; that was, when a declaration of Independence was made.[7]

I endeavour'd to discover the sentiments of the Indians, with regard to it, and I found that they were nearly unanimous in reprobating the hostile proceedings, of the English, against their white Children. Mr Golphin was of the opinion, that at least two thirds of the Confederacy, were decidedly in favor of Congress; That Gentleman, had so powerful an Interest, that he displaced every British Commissary, who was amongst them, & gave those offices to the Friends of Liberty. He himself was unanimously chosen by them, as their Beloved Man, or Superintendant.[8]

I question wether there was one of the Towns, who joined their Forces with the British; if it has been the case; they were some Bands of the Lower Creeks, or Siminoles, who were far distant from the Nation, & immediately under the influence & controul, of the British, of East, and West Florida.

Now let us consider what a sacrifice, these virtuous Men, made to humanity, & honor. For fifty Years, they had constantly enjoy'd superfluous supplies of Merchandize, which were convey'd to them, from Charlston, Savana, Pensocola, and Movile. They were now entirely ignorant of any of the arts, whereby, to supply themselves with necessary clothing; they had almost forgotten how to make earthen Potts, & not one amongst them knew how to form a Stone axe, or wooden Hough. All their dependance had rested upon the Traders, who supplied them with European Manufactures; but from these, they were now entirely preculded [precluded]. Yet amidst all their difficulties, they stood firm to our advocate, Mʳ Golphin, even to the termination of the Contest. There was not a hostile Indian, who cross'd the Alatama, nor even Sᵗ Mary's, during the whole time I remained at Georgia: not one Family disturb'd altho' they were under the most alarming apprehensions. When I was at Genˡ McAntoshes, on the Alatamaha, the English attempted to invade Georgia. They advanced to the Banks of Sᵗ Mary's, possess'd themselves of it, & took Shelter in the old Indian trading House. A few Indians were in company. A Small party of the Georgians marched from the Alatamaha, to oppose them & they gain'd the banks before the Enemy had pass'd the Flood. Hostilities commenced by the Parties firing at each other across the River. The British were under cover of the evacuated trading Houses, & the Georgians sheilded themselves behind the Trees, on the Rivers Banks. The conflict had continued for some time, when the Chief of the Indians threw down his Gun & boldly stepping out from the corner of a House, he took off his Hat, & whirling it up in the Air, as he advanced to the River Side, amidst showers of Bullets, he spoke aloud to the Georgians, declaring that they were Brother's & friends & that he knew not any cause why they should spill each others Blood. Neither I (said he) nor my Companions the Red-Men, will fire another Gun. He turned about, shouted & immediately led off the Indians. This put an end to the contest at that time.[9]

In order to recover the friendship & union of our neighbouring, uncivilized nations, perhaps no more eligeble, or laudable step can be pursued, than the introduction of our Language, System of Legislation, Religion, Manners Arts & Sciences; & by the reestablishment of Trade & Commerce, in a peaceable & friendly manner, amongst them. These beget an intercourse by insensible gradations, act like facination, & while they charm & please them, we effect a revolution, & secure a permanently peaceable dominion without violence or injustice.[10]

This way of sharing a possession in those vacant & desirable Regions, is certainly, of all others, the most consistent with those divine precepts, of our holy Religion, which should guide all our actions. Those sacred Tutors, teach us that all the nations & Tribes of Men, are Brethren & the offspring of one Family: They instruct us that every nation is equally entitled to those bountiful blessings of Providence, the furniture and produce of the Earth, & the benign influence of the Planets.[11]

By them we are also commanded to banish violence & war, & sit down together in peace & goodwill toward each other; conversing & praising God.

Would we pursue those Rules, then indeed, might we sit down, in peace & full security, under the shade of the fruitful Trees. Then without the dread of resentment, from some violated & incensed foe, might the contented & cheerful Patriarchs behold their innocent Youths, sporting on the verdant Lawns, or on the verges [of] glittering Lakes. Happy should we be in our possessions, & at the return of Silent Eve, we could listen to the musick of the Lute, or behold our bleating flocks, bounding over the distant Hills.

Our Minds would then be at rest, or in rapture with the inexpressible consolation, that we had not oppos'd the will of God, nor conteracted the dictates of the moral Law, inscribed on every human Heart.

We seem not to be apprehensive of our dangerous situation, from the wisdom & superior policy, of our rival Neighbours, who surround us by Land. They practice every art & policy, to gain & secure the friendship of the Indians, and to avail themselves of the advantages arising from their intimacy: as from their Trade or Commerce, & aid in War, from their Arms.

They obtain their ends, by the most rational methods; those are the introduction of their Systems of civilisation. Were we [to] act right, we should do the same, & dissipate the dark Clouds of Prejudice, which have been hovering about our Heads from our Infancy. We ought to consider them, as they are in reality, as our Brethren & fellow Citizens, & treat them as such; notwithstanding, their manners & modes of Government are somewhat different from ours.

The People of Georgia, Virginia, Pensylvania &c, are distinct, independent States, or Tribes, with respect to their internal Legislation, & each govern'd by its own Laws, & manners; nor in these affairs will they submit to the controul of any other Sovereign Power.

But in external matters, which regard the general good of the confederacy, they acknowledge & do homage to the supreme Sovereign of the U. States, in the Federal compact.

Just in this view do the American Aborigines, comprehend the rights of homage or Sovereignty.

Every Tribe which constitutes the Muscogulge Confederacy has seperate customs & many of them different Systems of Legislation. Yet they do homage to a Sovereign Power, which is represented in their grand National Council, when very important Affairs require it; & indeed they have an Emperor, or <u>Great Mico</u> acknowledged amongst them.[12]

If we examine all the Treaties, betwixt the Indians & Europeans, from the earliest invasions[13] of the latter, down to our own times, we shall find that the

Indians, consider'd the Europeans in no other view, than as powerful, enterprising Visitants. As a mark of perfectly good breeding, they hailed them, Brothers & friends, & gave them Lands to settle on equal terms with themselves. They always consider'd the Europeans as worthy of being elected their Guardians, & Protectors & as a compliment, they call'd them Brothers, & their Kings & Governors, Fathers, elder Brothers.[14]

Surely it is very absurd to suppose they would give all their Country away, abandon their aged Parents, & consign themselves & Posterity to slavery, for the purpose of gratifying the evil & caprice of avaricious Strangers. We might almost as easily imagine that these innocent People, would tamely suffer those Strangers to cut off their Arms & Legs, or deprive them of their Members, which are necessary for procreation. We find, as they ever have been, that they now are most tenacious of their freedom, independence & other unalienable rights of Men.

Their Systems of Government, civil & Religious Customs, are in general similar to those of other Nations. Their Form, Intelects & powers of Speech the same. Their Religion or homage to the Great, or Sovereign Spirit, is the same intelectual System, as acknowledged by the wisest & most virtuous nations in the old World.

Their Ideas, with respect to the duties, & conduct of Individuals, to their Superiors, coincide with those of the most perfect Government on Earth.

Are these People not worthy of our friendship? Are they not worthy of our care? These are the abandoned Posterity, of the friends of our Progenitors; whom, some of us say, those Progenitors cut off; or drove over the Mississippi.

We now want Citizens to people hundreds of thousands of acres of Land already within our precincts.

Who has a stronger claim to this Country than the Indians? If priority of possession gives the best Right, surely they have it? But were we to think & act as just & grateful Men, & to suffer ourselves to consider that their Ancestors were the friends and Protectors of the infant states of Carolina & Georgia, we should soon find that they have a right, infinitely superior to any other claims.

We exclaim, "they are Savages & will be wild Savages: They live by hunting & War; they are idle, o[b]streperous, and predatory Vagabonds; & will never be subject to a civilized Government. They claim & hold more Land than would conveniently maintain a thousand times as many white People, as Indians; & our Children will soon want room.["]

With respect to the universal objection that they will never become civilized; I must acknowledge that I am of a different opinion from my Countrymen.

I have been among them particularly the Muscoges or Cricks, & resided some time in their Towns. I then embraced every opportunity of discovering the disposition of their Minds. I found they strongly inclined to our modes of civilization.[15]

They admire our Religion & would be pleased to have Missionaries sent, to introduce & teach it to them. They appear more sincerely religious than we ourselves, they keep strictly & I may say holy the * Sabbath Day, in all their Towns.[16]

They wish to learn our arts of spinning, weaving, Smithing, painting, & Sculpture &c: & would like to have work houses established for teaching their Youth the useful ones. It is also my opinion that nothing would please them more, than having Schools settled in their Towns, to instruct their Children in reading, writing and arithmetick.[17]

They want Sheep & horned Cattle & would be happy with our arts, and improvements in Agriculture. On their vast natural Plains, their Hills & Commons encircling their Towns, they could raise Sheep enough to supply Wool for the Manufactories of the United States, without clearing one acre of Woodland. Besides they have a natural Range for inumerable Stocks of horned Cattle & Horses; which would become articles of Commerce with us. Their climate is suitable to the culture of chochineal, & it is a business which would be agreeable to their dispositions.[18]

They might & would raise Cotton enough to clothe themselves, to satisfy the demands of the United States, & to supply foreign Markets.

Their Language is beautiful, copious & easily learned. It is adapted to our Idioms, & it would be an easy matter to translate the Bible & other useful Books, & have them printed & distributed amongst them, in their own tongue.

If such a Scheme as their civilization was seriously consider'd, & attempted with sincerity & Spirit, I believe the Patrons would gain their full reward by seeing the good fruits of their labor arrive to a State of maturity.

The most considerable obstacle would probably be their civil, & political concerns in taxes & other publick requisitions necessary for the support of Government. These things, if conducted with moderation & prudence, might by mutual concessions become conciliated. But if attempted they will require perseverance & they must be a work of time.

Let us my Brethren convince the World, that the Citizens of the United States are Men in every Sense. Let us support our dignity in all things. Let our actions, in this memorable age of our establishment, as a Nation or People, be as a Mirror to succeeding Generations. Let us leave to our Children, a monument inscribed with Lessons of Virtue, which may remain from age to age, as approved examples for their Posterity: that they, in similar cases may say to one another; see how benevolently, how gratefully[,] how nobly, our forefathers acted!

WB

* Sunday they devote to the worship of the Grt Spirit, calling it the White Man's Beloved day.

CHAPTER FIVE

The Significance of William Bartram's Writings on the Southeastern Indians

Bartram's Indian writings can be evaluated from several perspectives. Initially, as modern readers, we must critically assess the scientific accuracy of his accounts. Can his descriptions be independently verified, and how can we account for discrepancies between his statements and other evidence? Is he a reliable witness, or does his work suffer from faulty observation, deceit, lapses of memory, literary license, printer's errors, or other shortcomings?

Bartram occasionally has been suspected, over the last two centuries, of fabricating some of the more celebrated scenes in *Travels,* such as his remarkable description of alligator behavior and his encounter with a lone Seminole warrior intent on killing the first white man he found. Certainly poetry and science are closely intertwined in his portrait of

the subtle, greedy alligator. Behold him rushing forth from the flags and reeds. His enormous body swells. His plaited tail brandished high, floats upon the lake. The waters like a cataract descend from his opening jaws. Clouds of smoke issue from his dilated nostrils. The earth trembles with his thunder. When immediately from the opposite coast of the lagoon, emerges from the deep his rival champion. They suddenly dart upon each other. The boiling surface of the lake marks their rapid course, and a terrific conflict commences. They now sink to the bottom folded together in horrid wreaths. The water becomes thick and discoloured. Again they rise, their jaws clap together, re-echoing through the deep surrounding forests. Again they sink, when the contest ends at the muddy bottom of the lake, and the vanquished makes a hazardous escape, hiding himself in the muddy turbulent waters and sedge on a distant shore. The proud victor exulting returns to the place of action. The shores and forests resound his dreadful roar, together with the triumphing shouts of the plaited tribes around, witnesses of the horrid combat.[1]

Despite initial doubts, subsequent reports by zoologists and botanists eventually vindicated Bartram, confirming this and many other seemingly extraordinary observations. Today, his descriptions of the southeastern environment are still valued for their exactitude, particularly considering their early date. For example, geographers have generally confirmed Bartram's description of early hardwood-dominated forest in parts of the Georgia piedmont where now only pines are found by consulting early maps and the files of the Surveyor General.[2]

The Seminole incident, however, is not so readily corroborated. According to the chronology he presents in *Travels*, the event occurred in 1773, but Bartram's report to Fothergill, which covers that period, contains no mention of any such encounter. As has been noted repeatedly in regard to *Travels*, Bartram rather cavalierly rearranged the sequence of events that occurred in the course of his journey through the southern colonies. The published version is not a daily log or travel diary, but rather a simplified, linear account of his circuitous and sometimes repetitively rambling tour. For instance, in *Travels*, two boat trips up the St. Johns River merge, with incidents from both mingled in a single description. Other excursions through southern Georgia and northern Florida in 1776 evidently inspired scenes in *Travels*, such as the Seminole encounter, that he placed earlier in the book's chronology, along with his initial discussions of those areas. Bartram presumably felt free to alter the sequence of events in order to unify the story, improve the narrative flow, and achieve dramatic effect. In this way he also conveyed a more coherent picture of the region. After all, the human and natural inhabitants of the Southeast were his principal subjects, to which he subordinated the recital of his personal adventures.[3]

In addition to these intentional chronological alterations, though, virtually every specific date mentioned in *Travels* appears to be inaccurate, usually with the year in error. These mistakes have frequently been ascribed to Bartram's supposedly faulty memory for dates, but some are certainly printer's errors. For instance, the 1777 date of his return to Philadelphia is indicated correctly on broadsides (advertising subscriptions for the book) printed by Enoch Story in 1786 and by James & Johnson five years later, only to appear as 1778 in the published book. Another egregious misprint in *Travels* ("1788" instead of the intended "1776") appears in the first state of the Philadelphia edition but was corrected in most later editions. Bartram mentioned to an acquaintance in 1812 that "Travels had not been published under his own inspection" and that "it had always been his intention to publish a correct edition—but had neglected it until old age prevented." Scarcely any mistaken dates, exaggerations of measurements, or inaccuracies in taxonomic nomenclature occur in Bartram's manuscript report to Dr. Fothergill, an accomplishment that further suggests that an editor or the publishers were responsible for the discrepancies found in *Travels*. One can only surmise that these were among the problems Bartram had hoped to address in a revised edition.[4]

Judging from Bartram's own frequent reaffirmations of religious belief and devotion, and from testimonials to his character by highly esteemed friends and scientists such as Thomas Jefferson, it seems extremely unlikely that this Quaker scientist intentionally misrepresented or fabricated any observations presented in his writings. The physician-scientist Benjamin Smith Barton, one of Bartram's closest associates, attested to the peripatetic natural historian's "moral integrity" and "rigid veracity."[5] Moreover, Bartram's quest for objectivity led to self-examination of his work's limitations, particularly those imposed by the limited amount of time he actually spent with the American Indians, his imperfect grasp of their languages,[6] and his much-regretted reliance on white traders and interpreters for information on Indian cultures.

Bartram's omission from *Travels* of certain preeminent individuals and signal events of the era has been judged a shortcoming by some puzzled critics. Not once in the entire volume did he refer directly to the American Revolution, which prompted one scholar to suggest that Bartram harbored royalist sympathies.[7] However, a strong case has been made for the opposite conclusion, that he was passionately committed to the revolutionary cause, although he found the war deeply troubling.[8] As he wrote in an early draft of *Travels*, in a passage that was excised before publication, "I profess myself of the Christian Sect of the People called Quakers, & consequently am against War & violence, in any form or maner whatever."[9] Despite their deep-felt pacifism, though, many members of the Bartram clan openly opposed King George III. William's twin sister and three of his brothers were disowned by the Quakers for their support of the Revolution, and William signed an affirmation of "Allegiance and Fidelity" to the Commonwealth of Pennsylvania upon his return from the south.[10] If one accepts the accuracy of an 1832 biography of William Bartram, he even "volunteered and joined a detachment of men, raised by Gen. Lochlan McIntosh, to repel a supposed invasion . . . from St. Augustine by the British; he was offered a lieutenant's commission if he would remain, but the report which led him to volunteer his services having proved false, the detachment was

disbanded, and Mr. Bartram resumed his travels."[11] Francis Harper dated
the lone Seminole encounter to this period, when Bartram was staying with
the McIntoshes in the summer of 1776.[12]

Bartram clearly attempted to expunge political bias from his book. Pa-
triots and loyalists play approximately equal roles, with little or no mention
of their later partisan activities in the war. One prominent revolutionary,
Jonathan Bryan of Georgia, is scarcely mentioned in *Travels*, even though
Bartram spent considerable time visiting him and greatly admired his garden. Bryan had explored some of the same territory as Bartram, including
the Seminole village of Cuscowilla, and had attempted to secure a ninety-
nine-year lease on an enormous tract of Seminole territory encompassing
the Alachua savanna. There is no doubt that Bartram knew of Bryan's
designs on Indian lands, but in *Travels* he only obliquely alluded to Bryan's
"grand diversified schemes" for settlement and development.[13] In a private
letter to Lachlan McIntosh, Bartram acknowledged that "would those Indians part with this Land, it would admit of a very valuable Settlement
& would be a very considerable acquisition."[14] But Bartram's public reti-
cence, in this case, on the critically important conflict between U.S. expansion versus American Indian rights to land and self-determination reflects
his inability to find a satisfactory solution to a dilemma that he never personally resolved, despite considerable thought on the topic throughout his
long life. What sort of relationship should the new federal government
encourage between Natives and encroaching U.S. settlers in the aftermath of the Revolution? In order to understand his views on this matter,
and the nature of other biases that may have affected his interpretations
of Indian cultures, one must trace the origins of William Bartram's personal philosophy.

For his formal education, Bartram attended the Philadelphia Academy,
where one of his tutors was Charles Thomsen, who later became secretary
of the Continental Congress and author of a treatise on Indians that Jefferson excerpted for his own *Notes on the State of Virginia*.[15] At the heart of the
academy's curriculum were heavy emphases on the classics and the system
of moral philosophy expounded by Scottish Enlightenment philosophers,
particularly Francis Hutcheson in his treatises *An Inquiry into the Original of
Our Ideas of Beauty and Virtue* (1725) and *An Essay on the Nature and Conduct
of the Passions and Affections with Illustrations on the Moral Sense* (1728).[16] All
humans, Hutcheson argued, possess an innate moral sense of rights and
obligations that permits every individual to appreciate benevolent behavior
(what we would now call altruism) and to take delight in the order and
harmony of the universe. Hutcheson had proposed his principle of benev-

olence in response to Hobbes's and Locke's positions that moral behavior is based on reason and self-interest and, therefore, cannot be innate.

As further developed by David Hume, in his *Treatise on Human Nature* (1740) and *Enquiry Concerning the Principle of Morals* (1751), the presumed existence of an inherent moral sense in all humans provided Enlightenment writers such as Bartram with a basis for their belief in the unity of human nature. A comparison of the most rhapsodic passages from Bartram's *Travels* with Hutcheson's *Inquiry* and Edmund Burke's *A Philosophical Enquiry into the Origin of Our Ideas of the Sublime and the Beautiful* (1756) reveals how thoroughly Bartram had accepted their belief in the universality of moral sense and human emotions. "Can it be denied, but that the moral principle, which directs the savages to virtuous and praiseworthy actions, is natural or innate?"[17] Everywhere he journeyed, Bartram found people who differed only in that their unique natural environment and history had affected the particular form of their society. When he argued that "benevolence taught those natives to act in the excellent characters of friends & Guardians . . . [to] their white Brothers,"[18] Bartram echoed a democratic sentiment based on a conviction in the essential equality of all people.

Following this basic tenet of Enlightenment thought to its logical conclusion, Thomas Jefferson inferred that all humans—including American Indians—could (and would) appreciate the benefits of progress once they were exposed to civilization, and that the universality of human nature would eventually permit resolution of the persistent conflicts that had divided Indians and whites for two centuries. Bartram, on the other hand, seems to have been less certain than Jefferson of the superiority of civilization when compared with the Native ways of life he had witnessed. Perhaps his more extensive firsthand experience with other cultures also gave Bartram a greater appreciation of the formidable obstacles to directed culture change. Faced with the apparent inevitability of continuing white encroachment on Indian lands, he did occasionally mention how some particular location might prove suitable for white settlement or development. But the general tenor of his commentary suggests that he considered the Indian country of Florida entirely satisfactory as he found it, without need of the "artificial refinements" that civilization would contribute. Bartram used a narrative of Indian lifeways much as Jean-Jacques Rousseau had done, to critique the excesses of Western civilization. In contrast to many Enlightenment philosophers, though, Bartram conceived of human equality not simply as a shared potential to achieve civilized status but also as rationale to study and appreciate other lifeways for their own sake.

In his introduction to *Travels*, he wondered whether the Indians "were inclined to adopt the European modes of civil society? whether such a reformation could be obtained, without using coercive or violent means? and lastly," raising a question that occurred to virtually none of his contemporaries in England or the American republic, "whether such a revolution would be productive of real benefit to them, and consequently beneficial to the public?"[19] Despite his ambivalence, Bartram approached the position of a cultural relativist, in contrast to practically all of his countrymen, confirmed ethnocentrics, who disapproved of cultural diversity in general and savage Indians in particular. Bartram's *Travels* can be read as an extended vindication of the American Indians against the charge of savagery contained in William Robertson's *History of America* (1777) and other influential books of the period.[20]

While engaged in defending Native Americans, Bartram also clearly found fault with European and American civilization. Yet he did not wholly subscribe to the image of the "noble savage." Greed, promiscuity, and the corrupting influences of civilization are readily identified in his descriptions of white traders, but he also reported the American Indians' cruelty in warfare, and he carefully enumerated what he deemed their "vices, immoralities and imperfections," not all of which could be attributed to their contact with whites.[21] Bartram did, however, ascribe many of the Indians' virtues to their awareness and close study of nature: "we act most rationally and virtuously when our actions seem to operate from simple instinct. . . ." He may have adopted this theme of "nature as guide or teacher" from Rousseau's *Origins of Inequality Among Men* (1755), but it derives partly from his Quaker background, as well.[22]

To Quakers, God's handiwork pervaded all creation, and, in fact, God could be known only through direct, personal experience of the natural world, rather than indirectly through the scriptures and clergy of revealed religions. An individual could take delight in God by recognizing the wondrous variety and infinitely complex design of nature. To know God was to possess an "inner light" (comparable in some ways to Hutcheson's "innate moral sense"), and Quakers sought that inner light in all people. Typically their tolerance and pacifism extended particularly to American Indians, because of the Indians' especially keen appreciation and knowledge of nature. So William Bartram's willingness to accept them as moral equals undoubtedly arose partly from his religious upbringing. His father, John, differed in this regard; William's attitude might have developed partly as an act of intellectual rebellion against his father, whom he both emulated and defied.[23]

In light of his philosophical and religious background, Bartram's account of his meeting with the lone Seminole on the trail, which he placed at the beginning of his narrative, sets the tone for all of the Indian-related material to follow. The event itself is unremarkable: two travelers meet unexpectedly on a path; each eyes the other warily, uncertain of the other's intentions; the Quaker's greeting sets the Indian at ease; they part. Only later does Bartram learn that the Seminole had sworn to avenge previous humiliations at the hands of traders by killing the first white man he found. How can one explain Bartram's miraculous escape from the fate that adherents of the savage view of Indians would anticipate? According to Bartram, the Seminole possessed a moral sense, shared by all people, that guided even this wronged individual to virtue and benevolence. "The primitive state of man," he later suggested, is "peaceable, contented, and sociable."[24] Because nature was considered the emanation of a benevolent God, those who lived closest to nature, unimpeded by civilization, should behave as moral sense and Enlightenment reason predicted, and as Bartram's experience attested.[25] By reaching out to shake the hand of a stranger, an Indian, Bartram sought and found the inner light of a fellow human.

In the eighteenth century, natural history encompassed the fields we now recognize as geology, botany, zoology, anthropology, and geography. The historical exclusion of European civilizations from the purview of natural history, which occurred principally during the nineteenth and early twentieth centuries, is currently a source of hard feelings among indigenous populations of lands colonized by Europeans, populations who rightfully discern the prejudice and injustice of a system that sets one class of societies apart from and above all others.[26] It would be inaccurate, however, to attribute such an exclusionary view to William Bartram, although many of his contemporaries made the distinction. His inclusive, cohering vision of life embraced earth, plants, animals, and humans—Indians as well as whites—in a single, "morally-ordered, God-created universe."[27]

When he drew comparisons between Native Americans and whites, Bartram's purpose, in addition to simply informing his readers of little-known ways of life, invariably was to express his regret that his own society had become so disengaged from nature, a sentiment widely shared today. Several literary critics have commented on the complexity of Bartram's vision of the Southeast (as artist, moralist, scientist), which he subsumed under the guise of a seemingly straightforward travel narrative. By leaving behind the social constraints of civilization, he set out to discover through systematic observation the order of the natural world, to attain "an idea of the first appearance of the earth to man at the creation."[28] Human and natural landscapes were one, as he journeyed south in search of his own society's past.[29]

Perhaps surprisingly, given the burden of his philosophical biases, Bartram's scientific observations have largely proven precise, objective, and reliable. Although he revered the order and intricacy of nature, he did not permit his reverence to interfere with his science. In fact, he employed two very different writing styles in *Travels* to signal shifts in perspective.[30] Bartram the scientist wrote strictly descriptive passages that list physical characteristics of landscapes and their plant, animal, and human occupants and cultural modifications. As philosopher Bartram, his style indulged his artistic and moral senses with elaborate metaphors, classical allusions, and exclamations of delight in God's creation. The Indian-related material from *Travels,* included in this volume, is overwhelmingly of the first sort.

Quaker tradition encouraged critical, systematic study for the utilitarian knowledge that accrued, whether in the realms of medicine, technological invention, horticulture, or the nascent field of ethnography.[31] During his youth, Bartram had been encouraged by Benjamin Franklin, Cadwallader Colden, John Clayton, Peter Collinson, and his own father to develop his observational skills and to strive for precision in his descriptions and illustrations. His rigorous scientific training probably accounts for Bartram's awareness of differences between the southeastern tribes. The importance of his writings for modern archaeological and comparative ethnographic research is immeasurably greater because he generally avoided composite descriptions, a fault found even in such otherwise exemplary texts as James Adair's *The History of the American Indians* (1775).[32]

Much scientific exploration and description of the eighteenth century was motivated by a belief in the Chain of Being. All living things, according to this theory, were related to one another in a great linear hierarchy, from the simplest organism at one extreme to humans — assumed to be the most complex — at the other. The gradation from one immutable species to the next formed a unified sequence of life, comforting evidence of order in the universe. By means of accurate description and classification, Linnaeus and his followers hoped to discover the place of each species in the Chain, and in the process to better realize God's complete, original plan of creation.[33]

Two implications of an unqualified belief in the Chain of Being were the corollaries that no new organisms had appeared and none had become extinct since the original creation. Species were unchanging and unchangeable. Many eighteenth-century natural historians and taxonomists held this view, but one would be mistaken to assume it was universally accepted. John Bartram had corresponded with Collinson and Fothergill on the topic of species loss, fully realizing that without the efforts of American naturalists many species would disappear without record as colonists cleared large areas of forest.[34] They did not, thereby, anticipate and embrace the concept of Darwinian evolutionary change, but neither were they alone among naturalists in accepting the possibility of extinctions.

Some socially conservative Chain of Being advocates saw in their hierarchical model of the unalterable natural order a metaphor for the human condition. This they considered equally fixed, with an intellectually superior elite ruling, by moral imperative, less able classes of humanity. Some modern literary critics, amazingly and ironically, have counted among this number Thomas Jefferson and William Bartram, revolutionary proponents of democratic rights.[35] Many Enlightenment scholars, including Bartram, did not blindly accept the Chain of Being theory and all of its ramifications, at least partly because their political and religious beliefs led them to see, more clearly than many of their contemporaries, through the haze of general prejudice directed toward foreign cultures.[36] Furthermore, the comparative approach to natural history practiced by many Enlightenment scholars encouraged evolutionary interpretations of human history and cultural development.[37]

Others err by attributing to Bartram a static view of American Indian cultures: timeless customs of a people without history — an attitude held by some scientists who unquestioningly accepted the ahistorical tenets of the Chain of Being.[38] In fact, even a cursory glance at the Indian-related passages in *Travels* reveals how frequently he referred to earlier, culturally distinct times. Considering the primitive methods available to anyone of his era who endeavored to penetrate the shadows of prehistory, Bartram made a concerted effort to reconstruct the southeastern Indians' past by considering archaeological evidence, as well as oral history and mythology. He enquired about mound construction, abandoned fields and townsites, migration myths, the formation of shell middens, and material culture change. Because his own efforts yielded equivocal results, Bartram suggested that future visitors to the southeastern tribes should endeavor to learn more about "their most ancient and present traditions and history."[39]

In the final part of *Travels,* "An Account of the Persons, Manners, Customs, and Government of the Muscogulges or Creeks, Cherokees, Chactaws, &c., Aborigines of the Continent of North America," Bartram did present a summary of southeastern cultures as they existed at the time of his observations, employing in his writing what today is termed the "ethnographic present" tense. This overview of cultural behavior was clearly normative; that is, he was less interested in individual variants of behavior than in "manners and customs" that seemed to be shared by an entire society. But this approach (flawed as it is, by today's standards) was probably the only one available to him, because of his limited stay among the southeastern tribes and his necessary reliance on translators and white informants.

One other inference from the Chain of Being theory prompted a response from Bartram. Although nearly all European and colonial American thinkers of the late eighteenth century accepted a single origin for humanity (with universal descent from Adam, according to Genesis), an uncomfortably wide gap in the Chain seemed to separate known species of monkeys and apes from humans. Later, some nineteenth-century apologists for slavery and colonialism attempted to explain purported differences between geographical races of humans by positing their independent creation as distinct species. These "species" were then arrayed according to varying criteria of accomplishment to occupy the supposedly missing links in the Chain between Europeans and nonhumans. But debates in Bartram's time did not follow this course. Instead, they revolved around the presumed effects of the physical environment on human cultural diversity.[40]

George Louis Leclerc, comte de Buffon, proposed a Eurocentric theory of degeneration, in 1749, to explain the perceived inferiority of native North American animals and humans due to the effects of environment. Regarding American Indians, Buffon argued,

> Although the savage of the new world is almost of the same height as the man of our world, that is not sufficient to make him an exception to the general rule of the diminution of human nature in this whole continent; the savage is weak and small in his reproductive organs; he has neither hair nor beard, and no passion for his female . . . he is also much less sensitive, and yet more fearful and cowardly; he has no vivacity, no spiritual activity; . . . their heart is frozen, their society and authority harsh.[41]

Not surprisingly, many American colonists found this theory offensive and its supporters badly misinformed. When François Barbé-Marbois, secretary to the French legation in the United States, submitted twenty-three "queries" on America to certain prominent members of Congress, Thomas Jefferson responded with a detailed rebuttal of Buffon's argument, which he published in 1785 in his *Notes on the State of Virginia.* Jefferson's defense emphasized the equivalent moral sense possessed by Europeans, American colonists, and American Indians, which was the basis for his most cherished political principle, that all men are created equal.[42] Although he never mentioned Buffon explicitly in his public writings, William Bartram consciously phrased his descriptions of Indian sociability and mental and physical capacities also to refute the French philosopher. In his repeated demonstrations of American Indian benevolence in *Travels* and by his even-handed responses to Benjamin Smith Barton's questionnaire (modeled after Barbé-Marbois's queries to Jefferson), Bartram offered empirical evidence of the Natives' physical and moral equality to Europeans.[43]

Modern anthropologists seek the basis of our shared humanity, usually in the universality of human reason, while simultaneously accounting for the multiplicity of cultural variation, which is often attributed to historical or environmental contingency.[44] Bartram preceded by several decades any formal recognition of anthropology as a scholarly discipline. But centuries earlier there had arisen a genre of literature (the forerunner of ethnography) in which European writers described the manners and customs of unfamiliar peoples. Missionaries, travelers, and explorers — those whose occupation or inclination brought them into contact with other cultures — tabulated the characteristics that distinguished these exotic societies from their own. The systematization of scientific description that occurred in the early eighteenth century incorporated this ethnographic exercise in the broader approach of the natural historian, exemplified by William Bartram's writings.[45]

Bartram did not anticipate twentieth-century methods of "participant observation"; he wrote as a neutral, scientific observer, as an outsider reporting for the benefit of his own society. And he certainly did not understand "culture" in the current sense of the learned and shared patterns of symbolic behavior that, by their structure, permit a society to adapt and solve problems of survival posed by its environment. Consequently, he was largely unaware of (or excluded from) whole areas of southeastern Indian cultures, such as the complexities of kin relations, language, ritual, and religion. Nevertheless, because of Bartram's penetrating intellect and tolerant appreciation of human variety, he contributed significantly to the increase in ethnographic knowledge and to the development of protoanthropological method and theory.

The foremost anthropological questions of his era, in the minds of Americans of European descent, concerned the origins of the American Indians. Where had they come from, and what was their relationship to Old World peoples? Within a general consensus that all humans descended from a single creation (the theory of monogenesis), there was considerable disagreement about the settling of the New World. James Adair promoted the Lost Tribes of Israel hypothesis, whereas Benjamin Smith Barton and Thomas Jefferson found convincing evidence for a northeast Asian origin in physical and linguistic data. Instead of participating in this debate, Bartram concentrated on a related problem, the origins of the earthen mounds and other archaeological remains left by previous occupants of the Southeast.

Buffon and other chauvinistic Old World philosophers criticized the New World for a lack of history, among its many other faults. Where were the ruins of lost civilizations and past golden ages comparable to those of Europe and Asia? Bartram's litany of massive mounds, avenues, and artificial lakes, numerous abandoned fields and townsites, and Indian myths of lost tribes and ancient battles endowed the American landscape with an un-suspected antiquity.[46]

When asked about these mounds, however, "neither the Creeks nor the Cherokees, nor the nations they conquered, could render," to Bartram's satisfaction, "any account by whom or for what purposes these monuments were erected."[47] Presumably either the Indians thought that Bartram's (or his trader-interpreters') interest in ritual matters exceeded the limits of propriety, or they simply did not know the significance of some specific mounds, which were perhaps centuries-old at the time. In any case, there is considerable archaeological, ethnohistoric, and ethnographic evidence for the continuation of mound building (on a small scale) and mound symbol-ism among southeastern Indians well into the twentieth century.[48]

Despite his failure to elicit testimony of ongoing mound construction, Bartram repeatedly identified (correctly, as we now know) these sites and monuments as the work of Native Americans, rather than inferring (as some nineteenth-century theorists later did) the existence of a separate, hypothetical race of non-Indian mound builders.[49] In *Travels*, he specu-lated that some small mounds, "sepulchres or tumuli of the Yamasee" and the Choctaws, were the efforts of living Indians.[50] But his boldest argument for continuity in Native American cultural traditions of mound symbolism appeared in the "Observations" manuscript, which remained unpublished until 1853. By juxtaposing plans of abandoned and occupied Indian towns, he indicated how similar were the old and new; chunky yards were flanked by mounds in the ancient towns and by council house and square ground in the recent villages. His implication, though tacit, is still clear — the flat-topped mounds had served as platforms for these public structures, and the prehistoric and historic town plans were functionally analogous.[51]

Ever the cautious scientist, Bartram appended a disclaimer, "that the Chunky Yards now or lately in use amongst the Creeks, are of very antient date, not the formation of the present Indians. . . ."[52] Perhaps he was overly influenced by Muscogulge and Cherokee migration myths, which de-scribed their conquest of the region's original inhabitants at some unspec-ified time in the past. But the American Indians he interviewed would admit no knowledge of these old structures, so, he reasoned, they must have been constructed by the Indians' predecessors. To determine the identity of these early southeasterners, Bartram conducted some primitive archaeological excavations. The artifacts he uncovered by these probes into several mounds closely resembled the types of objects still used by living Indians. Once again analogy suggested to him that the sites had been occu-pied by Indians, although of a different sort than the present inhabitants.

Bartram's excavations, which preceded the publication of Thomas Jefferson's better-known (and more sophisticated) investigation of a Woodland burial mound in Virginia, were briefly mentioned in his report to Fothergill. On his travels through Georgia, he saw

> numbers of Indian old fields and Artificial Mounds which have antiently been Towns & Settlements of people Which The present Nations know nothing off; neither can they give any satisfactory account whenc they come or for what they raised these vast mounds of earth. But this I have observed where ever I have been on the coast of America S°. of Chesapeak Bay, between the Sea coast & the Mountains. we observe One or more of them about their old Settlements, & always find abundance of human bones[,] pieces of earthen ware[,] flint Arrow head[,] Stone Knive, Axes &^{c}. I opened some of the smaller Tumula which near the Sea coast are heaps of Oister shells; Up the Rivers, On the sides of Lakes, great Savannahs, or other convenient places for their habitations they are composed of heaps of earth; & toward the mountains are made of small Rocks & Stones heaped together; . . .[53]

This passage also indicates that Bartram, nearly alone among his contemporaries, understood the artificial origin of shell middens. In this he had been influenced by his father, who, in 1766, had described a bluff along the St. Johns River "covered with shells of oysters, which the Florida Indians fed much upon near the sea-coast."[54] Years earlier, the Bartrams had been visited by Peter Kalm, a Swedish botanist sent to North America by Linnaeus in 1748. Whether Kalm owed his interpretation to John Bartram is unknown, but he, too, commented on

> immense quantities of oysters and mussel shells piled up near the places where it is certain that the Indians formerly built their huts. This circumstance ought to make us cautious in maintaining that in all places on the seashore, or further back in the country where such heaps of shells are to be met with, that the latter have lain ever since the time when these places were overflowed by the sea.[55]

Unfortunately, despite his prescience in these matters, William Bartram had little discernible impact on the development on American archaeology until the mid-nineteenth century. In fact, his influence on the course of American anthropology in general could have been much greater if more of his writings besides *Travels* had been published in his lifetime. *Travels* itself was widely available. For instance, Benjamin Hawkins, federal Indian agent to the southern tribes, requested a copy when he took up residence among the Creeks in 1798.[56] But Bartram's other manuscripts remained unpublished for many decades.

Early in the nineteenth century, Caleb Atwater, Albert Gallatin, and other American scholars proposed a "mound builder" hypothesis, that a separate, advanced society had been responsible for the erection of America's ancient monuments. It was unclear whether the mound builders had moved north from Mexico, bringing the knowledge of pyramidal construction methods, or whether construction of mounds preceded their move to Mexico. The mound builders had, however, according to these theorists, been forcibly replaced by the less civilized, modern Indians in the fairly recent past.[57] Later in the nineteenth century, the mound builder hypothesis came to be dominated by polygenists, who believed in multiple creations and viewed the prehistoric conflict between mound builders and American Indians as a contest between superior and inferior races. They thought they saw support for their hypothesis in Bartram's allusion to mound-building predecessors of the modern Indians. A few monogenists, such as Henry Schoolcraft, understood Bartram's actual stance, that Indians themselves, though not necessarily the present-day tribes, had built the mounds.[58] But because Bartram had attributed the construction of some mounds to "an anterior race," a phrase that carried unintended connotations in the nineteenth century, he came to be associated, mistakenly, with advocates of the mound builder hypothesis.[59]

Prompt publication of the "Observations" manuscript might have helped correct the common misapprehension that all mounds were of great age.[60] When it was finally published in 1853, as a *Transaction* of the American Ethnological Society, most of the press run was destroyed in a fire. Ephraim Squier had quoted extensively from "Observations," however, and had included engravings based on several of Bartram's drawings, in several influential volumes published in 1848 and 1850.[61] In his prefatory notes to "Observations," Squier emphasized those elements of Bartram's text that supported his own beliefs (". . . our authority ascribes [mound] construction to an anterior race and assigns to them a high antiquity"), but he also acknowledged Bartram's identification of the mounds as American Indian in origin. More important, he introduced this previously unknown Bartram document to the scientific community.[62]

By the time Samuel Haven published the first historical synthesis of archaeology in the United States, in 1856, the information contained in "Observations" had been widely disseminated. Haven suggested that John and William Bartram's "careful and intelligent observation[s]" at Mount Royal may have been the earliest scientific study of an American Indian mound site.[63] Charles C. Jones, in his 1873 volume *Antiquities of the Southern Indians,* also referred extensively to both *Travels* and "Observations," making particular note of Bartram's account of Choctaw funerary mound building.[64] When Cyrus Thomas delivered a massive assault on the mound builder hypothesis in 1894, he relied heavily on evidence provided by William Bartram for his conclusion that "some of them [i.e., earthen mounds] were built by Indians and that at the first advent of the white man they were in common use among this people in the southeastern section."[65] With the mound builder hypothesis finally discredited, southeastern anthropologists could at last turn to other topics.

During the first half of the twentieth century, John Swanton, an anthropologist affiliated with the Smithsonian Institution, compiled a multivolume, encyclopedic synthesis of ethnographic and ethnohistorical references to the southeastern Indians.[66] Citations of Bartram's writings appear under nearly every subject heading; the sheer volume of his contribution to our knowledge of late eighteenth-century Native southeasterners ranks Bartram's work securely among the most important sources available from that period.

Since Swanton's day, scholarly interest has shifted away from simply cataloging cultural diversity. Now historians, anthropologists, and archaeologists are investigating cultural changes, specifically exploring the interaction of American Indians and newly arrived Europeans and Africans in the region. Faced with these questions, the Indian writings of William Bartram will continue to inform and challenge our understanding of late eighteenth-century Native Americans of the Southeast.

Notes

1. INTRODUCTION

1. The first edition of Bartram's *Travels*, printed by James and Johnson of Philadelphia in 1791, is the edition cited and quoted throughout this volume. It was the basis of the best modern edition, *The Travels of William Bartram, Naturalist's Edition,* edited by Francis Harper. The other Bartram writings that have been published are "Travels in Georgia and Florida, 1773–74: A Report to Dr. John Fothergill," annotated by Francis Harper, in *Transactions of the American Philosophical Society,* and "Observations on the Creek and Cherokee Indians, 1789," edited by E. G. Squier, in *Transactions of the American Ethnological Society;* see chapter 3 of this volume for a manuscript version of the latter.

2. A manuscript copy of "Some Hints & Observations," part of the Henry Knox Papers, is reproduced in chapter 4 of this volume. The Henry Knox Papers, formerly at the Massachusetts Historical Society, Boston, are now part of the Gilder-Lehrman Collection, on deposit at the Pierpont Morgan Library, New York City. The document is not in William Bartram's handwriting, but is initialed "WB." Internal evidence provides overwhelming proof that William Bartram was the author of the piece.

3. John Bartram, "Diary."

4. William Bartram's birthday, according to the modern calendar, is April 20. For information on William's early life, see Ernest P. Earnest, *John and William Bartram;* Edmund Berkeley and Dorothy Smith Berkeley, *Life and Travels of John Bartram,* p. 15; and Charlotte M. Porter, "Philadelphia Story," 310–23.

5. John Bartram to Peter Collinson, September 28, 1755, Bartram Family Papers, Historical Society of Pennsylvania, vol. 1, folder 35 (hereafter cited as BP, HSP; in the case of HSP, "volume" refers to box number). John Bartram made copies of letters he sent to friends and business acquaintances. Thus, many of the letters from John Bartram in this collection are drafts rather than the original received by the addressee. John Bartram's letters, as well as a considerable number of William Bartram's letters, have

been published. Where possible, we have used the original document. However, to assist the reader, we also include citations for published versions, which often vary slightly in spelling and punctuation, and occasionally in wording, from the original. The letter cited here also appears in *Correspondence of John Bartram, 1734–1777*, edited by Edmund Berkeley and Dorothy Smith Berkeley, p. 387 (hereafter cited as *Bartram Correspondence*).

6. John Bartram to Peter Collinson, April 27, 1755, BP, HSP, vol. 1, folder 35. A version of this letter is printed in *Bartram Correspondence*, pp. 381–85.

7. For instance, see *Bartram Correspondence*, pp. 384, 387, 393, 394, 404, 405, 414, 511.

8. John Bartram to Peter Collinson, April 27, 1755 (quotation), and September 28, 1755, BP, HSP, vol. 1, folder 35; Peter Collinson to John Bartram, February 1756, BP, HSP, vol. 2, folder 92. See *Bartram Correspondence*, pp. 384, 387, 393, 394, 404–5. William was tempted by an offer from Dr. Alexander Garden, a physician who was also an avid horticulturalist and naturalist, to study surgery with him in Charleston. However, John Bartram declined the proposition for his son, noting, "He longs to be with thee but it is more for ye sake of Botany then Physic or Surgery neither of which he seems to have any delight in[.] I have several books of both but can't persuade him to read A page of either[.]" John Bartram to Alexander Garden, March 14, 1756, BP, HSP, vol. 1, folder 44; printed in *Bartram Correspondence*, pp. 402–4.

9. Francis Harper, "William Bartram's Bicentennial," p. 380; Harper, ed., *Travels of William Bartram*, p. xvii; *Bartram Correspondence*, pp. 511–12, 515–16, 519, 543.

10. William Bartram to John Bartram, May 20, 1761, BP, HSP, vol. 1, folder 70; also in *Bartram Correspondence*, pp. 515–16. The passage to Cape Fear was particularly unnerving. The ship encountered two gales and William experienced a "severe attack" of seasickness. William Bartram to John Bartram, May 6, 1761, BP, HSP, vol. 1, folder 68; also in *Bartram Correspondence*, pp. 511–12.

11. John Bartram to Peter Collinson, March 4, 1764, BP, HSP, vol. 1, folder 60; also printed in *Bartram Correspondence*, pp. 621–22. Based on very limited correspondence between William Bartram and his cousin Mary, some scholars have speculated that there may have been a romantic attraction between the two during William's stay in his uncle's house. For instance, see Yvon Chatelin, *Le voyage de William Bartram*, p. 23, and Earnest, *John and William Bartram*, p. 98. However, there is absolutely no evidence that such a romance existed other than William's flowery sentiments expressed long afterwards, in a letter dated September 7, 1788, addressed to "Worthy Couz." (Gratz Collection, American Scientists, case 7, box 21, Historical Society of Pennsylvania): "Dreams by Night, or serious reveres by day, often present to my emagination striking senes of past transactions, which Occur'd to me in your delightful country; & be asured that thou my

Cousin art the formost pleasing object in these Ideal paintings; For altho
our passtimes were of the most Inocent and simple nature, such as amuse
Brothers, Sisters & Friends yet they leave sufficient impressions to be often
Recollected." Such language was routinely employed by Bartram in numerous correspondences, as well as in *Travels*, without any romantic connotations. Kenneth Marshall Anderson Jr., "The Travels of William Bartram,"
pp. 83–92, goes even further in his interpretation of such language and
states that Bartram, in writing his book, "consciously created a fictionalized
character in his work" (p. 84), a romantic lover, who "has a perpetual love
affair with the fantasized landscape that he creates" (p. 85).

12. "I should be exceedingly pleased if I could afford it, to make A
thorow search about [in margin: "not only at"] pensacola but ye coast of
florida alabamous [written above line] & ye banks of ye Misisipia." John
Bartram to Peter Collinson, March 4, 1764, BP, HSP, vol. 1, folder 60. The
term "alabamous" was the French name for the Alabama River and those
Upper Creek Indians living near the confluence of the Coosa and Tallapoosa rivers. In *Bartram Correspondence*, p. 622, the editors transcribe this
letter with the following changes: "I should be exceedingly pleased if I
could afford it, to make A thorough search not only at pensacola but ye
coast of florida alabama, Georgia & ye banks of ye Misisipi." John Bartram
had been thinking of such a venture for a long time. In a letter dated
September 30, 1763, he mentioned to Collinson the possibility of exploring "Canada & Louisiana for all natural productions convenient scituations
for manufactories & different soils minerals & vegitables ye last of which I
dare take upon my self as I know more of North American plants then any
others but this would alarm ye Indians to the highest degree all ye discoverers would be exposed to greatest Savage cruelty ye gun tomahawk
torture or revengeful devouring Jaws." September 30, 1763, BP, HSP, vol. 1,
folder 56; printed in *Bartram Correspondence*, pp. 608–9.

13. John Bartram to Peter Collinson, October 15, 1764, BP, HSP, vol. 1,
folder 53; printed in *Bartram Correspondence*, p. 641.

14. Peter Collinson to John Bartram, April 9, 1765, BP, HSP, vol. 3, folder
54; printed in *Bartram Correspondence*, pp. 644–45; see also pp. 649, 651–
52.

15. Peter Collinson to John Bartram, April 9, 1765, ibid. By September
1765, Collinson admitted that "under what Character the King is pleased
to rank thee, I do not know." Peter Collinson to John Bartram, September 19, 1765, BP, HSP, vol. 3, folder 57; printed in *Bartram Correspondence*,
pp. 654–55. John's actual claim to a title remained uncertain. Collinson
informed Thomas Lamboll that John had been appointed the "King's botanist" for the Floridas, *Bartram Correspondence*, pp. 649–50, while John told
his son William that the king had "appointed me his chief Botanist." John
Bartram to William Bartram, June 7, 1765, BP, HSP, vol. 1, folder 64;
printed in *Bartram Correspondence*, pp. 651–52. Both the elder Bartram and

his patrons felt that he had been unfairly overlooked when Queen Charlotte appointed William Young Jr. as the queen's botanist in 1766 and awarded him a large salary, £300 annually. Bartram had actually tutored Young, and the Anglo-American horticultural community rightly believed that Bartram should have received the appointment. See *Bartram Correspondence,* pp. 666, 682.

16. John Bartram to William Bartram, May 19, 1765, BP, HSP, vol. 1, folder 63; printed in *Bartram Correspondence,* p. 649.

17. John Bartram to William Bartram, June 7, 1765, BP, HSP, vol. 1, folder 64; printed in *Bartram Correspondence,* p. 652. See also Isaac Bartram to John Bartram, August 15, 1765, ibid., pp. 652–53. Charlotte M. Porter, "Philadelphia Story," pp. 313–14, states that John "used the excuse of his ailing eyes to pressure William to join him" and cites John Bartram's letter of May 19, 1765. This seems unlikely since, on May 19, 1765, John had written William, "My eye sight is so well returned, that I wrote this by candlelight & without spectacles." See *Bartram Correspondence,* p. 649. Further, Porter states that the elder Bartram implied that Collinson had ordered him to take his son, hoping thus to pressure William into joining him. But William was eager to go. William's brother Isaac wrote to his father that William "Expresses A Great desire in Going with thee"; see Isaac Bartram to John Bartram, August 15, 1765, *Bartram Correspondence,* p. 652.

18. Charles E. Bennett, *Twelve on the River St. Johns,* pp. 59, 208. *Bartram Correspondence,* p. 377.

19. Harper, ed., *Travels of William Bartram,* p. xvii. For a discussion of Bartram's early drawings, including publication data, see *William Bartram: Botanical and Zoological Drawings, 1756–1788,* edited by Joseph Ewan.

20. William's acquaintance with Laurens proved especially valuable. During William's subsequent time as a planter in Florida, in 1766, Laurens visited him, offered advice, sent supplies, and finally interceded with his father to let William give up farming and return to Philadelphia. When William went south once again, on his epic travels, Laurens remained as helpful as ever, particularly in shipping botanical collections to Dr. Fothergill in Liverpool. See *Papers of Henry Laurens* 10: 90–91. For information on Garden, see Edmund Berkeley and Dorothy Smith Berkeley, *Dr. Alexander Garden.*

21. The best account of the Bartrams' journey is Berkeley and Berkeley, *Life and Travels of John Bartram.* See pp. 226–71 and p. 234 for the meeting with John Stuart.

22. James Grant to Board of Trade, April 26, 1766, Great Britain, Public Record Office, Colonial Office, class 5, vol. 541, f. 1. (Class 5 material hereafter is cited using the following form: CO5/vol. number, folio number. Only the initial folio number is given here.)

23. The proceedings of the congress are published in full in James W. Covington, ed., *The British Meet the Seminoles.* While at Picolata, John Bar-

tram was "so weak as hard set to get up to small bed chamber & during ye meeting of ye governor & indians in ye Pavilion I was forced to sit or ly down upon ye ground, close by its side that I might observe what passed[.]" John Bartram to Peter Collinson, June 1766, BP, HSP, vol. 1, folder 49; printed in *Bartram Correspondence*, p. 669.

24. John Bartram, "Diary." For "Remarks on Yᵉ Congress Held in A Pavilion," see p. 51; the daily notations, including the description of the medals, are on p. 35.

25. James Grant to Board of Trade, April 26, 1766, CO5/541, f. 1.

26. Collinson's chief pique was that he had not seen John's manuscript previous to its publication nor received a complimentary copy of Stork's book. Said Collinson, "not the least Notice is taken of Mee." Undated letter from Peter Collinson to John Bartram, BP, HSP, vol. 3, folder 80; printed in *Bartram Correspondence*, pp. 679-80. The manuscript letter differs from the published version. Porter, "Philadelphia Story," p. 314, erroneously implies that Bartram sent his journal to London and allowed the "British Land Office to publish [his account] as part of William Stork's *Account of East-Florida*." Bartram's journal appeared in the second edition of Stork's work, *An Account of East Florida, with a Journal kept by John Bartram, of Philadelphia, Botanist to His Majesty for the Floridas; upon a Journey from St. Augustine up the River St. John's* (London: W. Nicoll & G. Woodfall, 1766). There is some question as to whether this edition appeared in 1766 or in 1767. See *Papers of Henry Laurens* 5:232, n. 9.

27. East Florida Council Journal, CO5/570, f. 13.

28. John Bartram to William Bartram, April 5, 1766, BP, HSP, vol. 1, folder 62; printed in *Bartram Correspondence*, pp. 661-62. In the same letter, John noted, "all thy friends here laments thy resolute choice to live at St Johns & leave off drawing or writeing." John Bartram to Peter Collinson, August 26, 1766, BP, HSP, vol. 1, folder 49; printed in *Bartram Correspondence*, pp. 675-76.

29. John Bartram to Peter Collinson, August 26, 1766, ibid. At the time, De Brahm's official title was surveyor general of East Florida and surveyor general for the Southern District of North America. For a brief account of De Brahm's career, see Louis De Vorsey Jr., "William Gerard De Brahm: Eccentric Genius," pp. 21-29, and *De Brahm's Report*, edited by Louis De Vorsey Jr., p. 180.

30. John Bartram to Peter Collinson, June 1766, BP, HSP, vol. 1, folder 49; printed in *Bartram Correspondence*, p. 668-69.

31. John Bartram to William Bartram, July 3, 1766, Misc. W. Bartram Collection, New York Historical Society. Also published in *Bartram Correspondence*, pp. 669-70.

32. Henry Laurens to John Bartram, August 9, 1766. The original letter is owned by the American Philosophical Society; it has been published in *Papers of Henry Laurens* 5:151-55, and *Bartram Correspondence*, pp. 670-73.

The letter can also be found in William Darlington, ed., *Memorials*, pp. 428–32; and Earnest, *John and William Bartram*, pp. 105–8.

33. Ibid. According to Henry Laurens, only two of the six slaves were skilled in field work and one of these had threatened William's life.

34. Henry Laurens to William Bartram, September 17, 1766, P. K. Yonge Library, University of Florida, Gainesville. This letter has been published in *Papers of Henry Laurens* 5:192–93; see Berkeley and Berkeley, *Life and Travels of John Bartram*, p. 267. The disposition of the slaves, land, and other property is unknown. On April 10, 1767, Collinson, writing to John Bartram, advised William to get "a Good Notable Wife . . . & return to his Estate & Sett his shoulders Heavyly to work to Improve It." BP, HSP, vol. 3, folder 67; printed in *Bartram Correspondence*, pp. 682–84.

35. On October 31, 1766, Henry Laurens sent Gov. James Grant a parcel of letters that he had received in Charleston. Included was a letter from Laurens to William Bartram, which he asked Grant to forward. If this was Laurens's letter mentioned above, dated September 17, it would mean that William could not have left his holding prior to the early part of November.

36. *De Brahm's Report*, p. 180. Bartram was also included as a planter on De Brahm's list of East Florida settlers, 1763–71, which noted that Bartram had left the province by 1771.

37. Bartram, *Travels*, pp. 144–45. "[A]bout ten years ago" was in relation to the time of his tour, approximately 1776, near the end of his journey. The New Smyrna settlement, the second largest in East Florida after St. Augustine, was the idea of Dr. Andrew Turnbull, who transported nearly 1,500 people, primarily Minorcans and some Greeks, to East Florida. The settlement was established in June 1768. For a contemporary account of life there, see Bernard Romans, *A Concise Natural History*, pp. 266–72. Bartram also mentions a visit to the "South Musquitoe River" in the introduction to *Travels* (pp. xxvi–xxvii). Characteristically, Bartram noted that the visit occurred in December but failed to cite the year. Since he does not mention the Mosquito River elsewhere in *Travels*, he was obviously referring to his trip there in December of 1766. See Harper, ed., *Travels of William Bartram*, p. 335. The biographers of John Bartram believe that William Bartram was employed by De Brahm; Berkeley and Berkeley, *Life and Travels of John Bartram*, p. 273. Porter, "Philadelphia Story," p. 317, implies that Bartram refused De Brahm's offer of employment after he abandoned his plantation. Clearly, Bartram had refused the offer prior to his plantation venture. See *Bartram Correspondence*, pp. 694, 704. Bartram's map of East Florida, which illustrated *Travels*, testifies to his cartographic skills.

38. Thomas Lamboll to William Bartram, April 28, 1767, BP, HSP, vol. 4, folder 66. [Robert M. Peck, ed.], *Bartram Heritage*, p. 79. Much of the best land had already been acquired by speculators and large landholders by 1767.

39. See *Bartram Correspondence*, pp. 694, 704.

40. Peter Collinson to John Bartram, May 28, 1766, BP, HSP, vol. 3, folder 64; printed in *Bartram Correspondence*, pp. 665–68. In this letter, Collinson praised William's botanical drawings and noted that "His Butterflies, Locust are Nature itself his yellow Fly is admirable."

41. Peter Collinson to John Bartram, April 10, 1767, BP, HSP, vol. 3, folder 67; printed in *Bartram Correspondence*, p. 682–84.

42. *Bartram Correspondence*, pp. 667, 683, 697, 699, 701, 703, 704 (second quotation), 705. The Duchess of Portland was the owner of the famous Portland vase, the finest surviving example of ancient Roman cameo glass, which inspired Josiah Wedgwood to produce his blue jasper ceramics in the late eighteenth century. See Denys E. L. Haynes, *Portland Vase*.

43. John Bartram explained to Charles Wrangel, in a letter dated July 6, 1771, "My son William is gone to North Carolina to Collect in his debts which is a difficult task in that poor Countrey." *Bartram Correspondence*, p. 743; see also p. 738. Eventually, William's brother-in-law, George Bartram, paid off his debts. John Bartram, aging and in poor health, rewrote his will, leaving his beloved garden to his son John, who had a better head for business than William. Berkeley and Berkeley, *Life and Travels of John Bartram*, pp. 283–84; Bennett, *Twelve on the River St. Johns*, p. 62.

44. John Bartram to William Bartram, July 15, 1772, copy in HSP; printed in *Bartram Correspondence*, p. 749.

45. Biographical information on Dr. Fothergill can be found in Betsy C. Corner and Christopher C. Booth, eds., *Chain of Friendship: Selected Letters of Dr. John Fothergill*. See John Fothergill to Dr. Lionel Chalmers, October 23, 1772, p. 394. John Bartram did not approve of the project and urged William to return to Philadelphia. Berkeley and Berkeley, *Life and Travels of John Bartram*, p. 285.

46. John Fothergill to John Bartram, October 29, 1768, Gratz Collection, European Physicians, HSP, case 12, box 20; printed in Corner and Booth, eds., *Chain of Friendship*, p. 289, and *Bartram Correspondence*, pp. 706–9.

47. On May 1, 1769, Fothergill wrote to John Bartram, "I am pleased that thy son William is engaged in describing the Tortoises of your country. . . . I would not limit him either in respect to time or expence. He may send me his drawings and accounts of their history as soon as he finishes them and I will pay his demands to his order." BP, HSP, vol. 4, folder 21. January 13, 1770, saw another letter from John Fothergill to John Bartram acknowledging the receipt of drawings by William, including flowers and shells for the Duchess of Portland. Fothergill wrote: "I must still desire that thy son will favour me with drawings of the rest of your American tortoises, with such remarks on them as occur to him." BP, HSP, vol. 4, folder 19. Once again, Fothergill suggested that William name his price, and urged him to be as accurate and as fast as possible at the task because he feared some species might become extinct due to human encroachment. In a letter to Hum-

phrey Marshall dated March 15, 1770, Fothergill mentioned the tortoise drawings and noted that Bartram "has a very good hand." Miscellaneous Collection, Scientists, HSP. On March 19, 1770, Fothergill wrote John Bartram, "Thy son will be kind enough to continue his drawings of any non descripts he may meet with, either plant or animals, and I shall endeavour to make him proper satisfaction." BP, HSP, vol. 4, folder 22. The above letters have been printed in *Bartram Correspondence,* pp. 710–12, 728–30, and 731–32, and in Corner and Booth, eds. *Chain of Friendship,* pp. 303–4, 317–18, 319–20, 321–22.

48. John Fothergill to John Bartram, 1772, BP, HSP, vol. 4, folder 18, and John Fothergill to William Bartram, October 22, 1772, vol. 4, folder 23. These are printed in *Bartram Correspondence,* pp. 750–51, and Corner and Booth, eds., *Chain of Friendship,* pp. 388–91, 391–93.

49. John Fothergill to William Bartram, October 22, 1772, in Corner and Booth, eds., *Chain of Friendship,* pp. 391–93.

50. John Fothergill to John Bartram, 1772, BP, HSP, vol. 4, folder 18; printed in Corner and Booth, eds., *Chain of Friendship,* pp. 389–90 (quotation is on p. 389); the letter is also printed in *Bartram Correspondence,* pp. 750–51. Fothergill also raised the possibility of supporting William on a tour of Canada in the future. To Lionel Chalmers, he confided that William was "bred to merchandise, but not fitted to it by inclination at least. He is not quite a systematic botanist. He knows plants and draws prettily. I received a letter from him this summer from Charles Town, offering his services to me in a botanical journey to the Floridas." John Fothergill to Dr. Lionel Chalmers, October 23, 1772, BP, HSP, vol. 4, folder 26; printed in Corner and Booth, eds., *Chain of Friendship,* p. 394–95.

51. John Fothergill to John Bartram, 1772, BP, HSP, vol. 4, folder 25; printed in *Bartram Correspondence,* p. 753–54, and Corner and Booth, eds., *Chain of Friendship,* pp. 391–93.

52. John Fothergill to Dr. Lionel Chalmers, October 23, 1772, BP, HSP, vol. 4, folder 26; printed in Corner and Booth, eds., *Chain of Friendship,* pp. 394–95.

53. John Fothergill to William Bartram, in care of Dr. Chalmers, September 4, 1773, BP, HSP, vol. 4, folder 27; printed in Corner and Booth, eds., *Chain of Friendship,* pp. 401–3. Fothergill's terms matched those awarded to John Bartram in 1765 by George III.

54. John Fothergill to William Bartram, October 22, 1772, BP, HSP, vol. 4, folder 23.

55. John Fothergill to Dr. Lionel Chalmers [late 1775], in Corner and Booth, eds., *Chain of Friendship,* p. 464. Bartram left Philadelphia on March 20, 1773, and did not return until January 1777.

56. John Fothergill to William Bartram, in care of Dr. Chalmers, September 4, 1773, BP, HSP, vol. 4, folder 27; printed in Corner and Booth, eds., *Chain of Friendship,* pp. 401–3.

57. Ibid.

58. John Fothergill to Israel Pemberton, July 5, 1765, in Corner and Booth, eds., *Chain of Friendship*, pp. 243–44.

59. Bartram, *Travels*, p. xxxiii.

60. The Indians arrived in late May and the treaty was signed on June 1, 1773. See *Travels*, pp. 33–46, 485–86; for Stuart's warning see Bartram, "Travels in Georgia and Florida," p. 138. Among those granted land in the New Purchase Cession was James Mendenhall, Bartram's second cousin. William's mother, Ann Mendenhall Bartram, had relatives in South Carolina, whom John Bartram had visited in 1762. Edward O. Welles Jr., "William Bartram's Trail through Nature," p. 47. See also Berkeley and Berkeley, *Life and Travels of John Bartram*, pp. 10, 208. The classic study of British boundary negotiations with the southern Indians is Louis De Vorsey Jr., *The Indian Boundary;* for the New Purchase, see pp. 161–80.

61. Bartram, "Travels in Georgia and Florida," p. 144.

62. Bartram, *Travels*, p. 55.

63. Cuscowilla, which Bartram visited, was founded by Oconees, who lived among the Lower Creeks. Oconees also participated in the 1773 uprisings.

64. Bartram probably left Savannah in March 1774; see "Conference Between Governor Sir James Wright and upper Creek Indians," in K. G. Davies, ed., *Documents of the American Revolution*, 8:90–95.

65. Allen D. Candler, Kenneth Coleman, and Milton Ready, eds., *The Colonial Records of the State of Georgia* 12:405–6.

66. The late Francis Harper, preeminent Bartram scholar, thought that part 2 of *Travels*, in which Bartram details his Florida journey, "may well be regarded as the most important section" of the book. Harper, ed., *Travels of William Bartram*, p. 348.

67. During the encounter, Long Warrior threatened to have the Great Spirit destroy a live oak tree. Bartram, *Travels*, pp. 185, 257–60 (quotation is on p. 257). Cuscowilla and Latchoway were the same town. The original location of the village was at the edge of the Alachua savanna. In the late 1760s, the villagers moved to the edge of Lake Tuscawilla, near modern Micanopy. Charlotte M. Porter, *William Bartram's Florida*, p. 11.

68. In addition to shipping specimens to Fothergill, Bartram apparently agreed to collect seeds and roots of flowering shrubs for other interested parties. See Henry Kelly to William Bartram, April 14, 1775, BP, HSP, vol. 4, folder 56. Bartram entrusted the specimens he had gathered in East Florida for Fothergill to Henry Laurens, who shipped them with his rice crop to England. The letter with instructions regarding Bartram's botanical specimens was dated March 27, 1775, so Bartram must have left Sunbury near the end of March on his way to Charleston. *Papers of Henry Laurens* 10:90–91; see also *Travels*, p. 306.

69. The only major eighteenth-century author who knew the southeast-

ern Indians better than Bartram was James Adair, an Indian trader. Adair's opinions naturally reflect his special interests as a deerskin trader and merchant. His book contains much valuable information on the south-eastern tribes, but also serves as an extended argument for a Hebrew origin of the American Indians. Modern ethnohistorians have generally failed to fully appreciate Adair's ethnographic significance because of his close asso-ciation with this discredited theory. Adair, *History of the American Indians*; Hudson, "James Adair as Anthropologist," pp. 311–28.

70. Bartram, *Travels*, p. 438.

71. Ibid., p. 493.

72. Ibid., p. 214.

73. Bartram, "Observations," chapter 3, this volume.

74. John Bartram to Peter Collinson, October 23, 1763, BP, HSP, vol. 1, folder 58; printed in *Bartram Correspondence*, p. 611–12; also quoted in Darlington, ed., *Memorials*, pp. 254–55. On August 8, 1763, the elder Bar-tram wrote Collinson, "I cant tell when ye Indians can be trusted again[.] not before they are soundly banged!" BP, HSP, vol. 1, folder 59; printed in *Bartram Correspondence*, p. 604. John Bartram and Peter Collinson had dif-fering views on the subject of Indians. For instance, see Peter Collinson to John Bartram, December 6, 1763, BP, HSP, vol. 3, folder 49; printed in *Bartram Correspondence*, p. 615–17.

75. Berkeley and Berkeley, *Life and Travels of John Bartram*, pp. 7–8.

76. John Bartram to Peter Collinson, September 30, 1763, BP, HSP, vol. 1, folder 56; printed in *Bartram Correspondence*, p. 608–9.

77. See Kerry S. Walters, "The 'Peaceable Disposition' of Animals," pp. 157–76, for a discussion of the impact of Bartram's Quaker back-ground on his attitudes toward nature, including animals.

78. Bartram, *Travels*, p. 489–90.

79. He expected charges of "partiality or prejudice" in favor of the In-dians. Harper, ed., *Travels of William Bartram*, p. xxv; Mary S. Mattfield, "Journey to the Wilderness," p. 347.

80. N. Bryllion Fagin, *William Bartram, Interpreter of the American Land-scape*, p. 57.

81. See Edward J. Cashin, " 'But Brothers, It Is Our Land,' " pp. 240–75, for a brief overview of the Revolution in Georgia and the backcountry. See also Harvey H. Jackson, *Lachlan McIntosh*.

82. John Fothergill to John Bartram, May 6, 1776, Miscellaneous Collec-tion, William L. Clements Library, University of Michigan, Ann Arbor.

83. Francis Harper, "William Bartram and the American Revolution," pp. 571–77. It is clear from his writings (see "Some Hints & Observations," this volume) that Bartram witnessed at least one skirmish along the Geor-gia–East Florida border. McIntosh was appointed colonel of the Conti-nental battalion in Georgia, and he also took charge of the militia in 1776.

Jackson, *Lachlan McIntosh*, p. 29–36. Bartram was in Charleston as late as November 1776, as he received a letter there from James Baille, dated October 30, 1776. James Baille to William Bartram, October 30, 1776, BP, HSP, vol. 1, folder 2. See Harper, ed., *Travels*, pp. 414–18, for discussion of Bartram's last months in the South.

84. Fothergill was unhappy with the infrequency of William's reports and shipments of specimens. He was especially upset that Bartram failed to send any seeds or cuttings that might be turned to profit. John Fothergill to John Bartram, July 8, 1774; printed in Corner and Booth, eds., *Chain of Friendship*, pp. 414–16, and *Bartram Correspondence*, pp. 764–65.

85. In *Travels*, Bartram dated his return to his "father's house on the banks of the river Schuylkill, within four miles of the city, January 1778." Most later writers accepted this date until Francis Harper's systematic analysis of Bartram's itinerary established the unreliability of the naturalist's published chronology. Harper decided that Bartram must have arrived in Philadelphia in January 1777 (a date that virtually everyone now accepts), but he never explicitly presented his evidence for this conclusion. An argument for a 1777 end to Bartram's journey would seem to depend on the many demonstrably inaccurate dates published in *Travels* (with months less often in error than years), the absence of any independent evidence (such as letters or diary entries written by others) that Bartram remained in the South after 1776, the title page (written in Bartram's hand) to an early manuscript version of *Travels* that mentions the inclusive dates "1773 to 1777," and the appearance of the same dates on a 1790 broadside soliciting subscribers to the Philadelphia edition of *Travels*. Bartram, *Travels*, p. 480; Harper, ed., *Travels of William Bartram*, pp. xxviii, 423; William Bartram, "Travels through the Carolinas, Georgia, and E^t. & W^t. Floridas," manuscript, 2 vols., p. 14, BP, HSP; "Proposals for Printing by Subscription . . . Travels . . . By William Bartram, Botanist, of Philadelphia, who was employed from 1773 to 1777, by the celebrated Doctor Fothergill, of London, to explore the extensive Countries above-mentioned." Thomas Jefferson Papers [June 1790], nos. 9532–3, Manuscript Division, Library of Congress.

86. Berkeley and Berkeley, *Life and Travels of John Bartram*, p. 291.

87. Harper, "William Bartram and the American Revolution," p. 572. The affirmation document is no. 5961, Miscellaneous Manuscript Collection, Library of Congress.

88. Bartram would have received more credit for his discoveries had they been properly cataloged and duly noted in the literature at the time. Unfortunately, Dr. Daniel C. Solander, the man appointed to the task by Fothergill, was preoccupied, having accompanied Capt. James Cook on his voyage around the world in 1768–71 and then traveling with Joseph Banks on his voyage to Iceland in 1772. The exotic specimens from the Pacific were given immediate attention by Solander, while Bartram's American speci-

mens were ignored. Solander died in 1782, before ever turning his full attention to Bartram's material. Thus Bartram's contribution was minimized. The drawings that Bartram sent to John Fothergill, as well as his botanical specimens, are now housed in the British Museum (Natural History). Other Bartram drawings can be found at the Historical Society of Pennsylvania, the American Philosophical Society, and Knowsley Hall, England. Some Bartram drawings, commissioned by Catherine II of Russia, are thought to be in St. Petersburg. See Charlotte M. Porter, "The Drawings of William Bartram," pp. 289–303. The Bartram drawings from the British Museum of Natural History have been reproduced in Joseph Ewan, ed., *William Bartram: Drawings*. Ewan also discusses Bartram's contributions to natural history, as well as tracing the history of his botanical specimens and illustrations; see pp. 11–12.

89. William Bartram to Mrs. M. L. [Mary Lamboll] Thomas, July 15, 1786, Misc. W. Bartram Collection, New York Historical Society, New York City.

90. Bartram suffered from an unusual malady during his stint in West Florida that left his vision impaired. Bartram, *Travels*, pp. 418–21, 436; Harper, ed., *Travels of William Bartram*, p. 407. The illness was possibly scarlet fever. Peck, "William Bartram and His Travels," p. 39. John Bartram had also been troubled by failing eyesight in his later years. In 1801, William Bartram wrote to a friend that "the exceeding painfullness and weakness in my eyes" made it impossible for him to complete drawings. William Bartram to Benjamin Smith Barton, October 25, 1801, Benjamin Smith Barton Papers, American Philosophical Society Library, Philadelphia (hereafter cited as Barton Papers, APSL).

91. William Bartram to Lachlan McIntosh, May 31, 1796, Misc. W. Bartram Collection, New York Historical Society.

92. William Bartram to Benjamin Smith Barton, undated draft of letter, Jane Gray's Autograph Collection, item 104a, Archives, Gray Herbarium, Harvard University. Characteristically, Bartram failed to record the exact date of his fall. In the letter to Barton, he noted that the fall occurred after Barton had left Philadelphia for Scotland. Since Bartram was replying to a letter dated August 1787 and since he states that he was walking by the time of his reply, after a year in bed, the accident must have taken place in 1786. Ewan, ed., *William Bartram: Drawings*, p. 12, believed the fall occurred in 1787. In the letter to McIntosh cited in n. 91, Bartram states that his fall occurred "About 4 Years after you left this country." McIntosh, who spent the waning days of the Revolutionary War in Philadelphia, left that city in July 1782. Jackson, *Lachlan McIntosh*, pp. 122–23.

93. William Bartram to Benjamin Smith Barton, March 1791, Barton Papers, APSL.

94. Porter, "Drawings of William Bartram."

95. Cornillus Macmahon Mann to William Bartram, December 17, 1812, Historical Society of Pennsylvania.

96. For information on Bartram's later years, see Fagin, *William Bartram,* pp. 11–36; Harper, ed., *Travels of William Bartram,* pp. xxviii–xxxv; and Ewan, ed., *William Bartram: Drawings,* p. 10. *Diaries of George Washington* 5:166–67, 183. Peck, "William Bartram and His Travels," p. 44.

97. Dunlap, *History of the American Theatre,* p. 170. According to his visitor, Bartram "entered into conversation with the ease and politeness of nature's noblemen." Recent archaeological excavations around Bartram's house have uncovered evidence of his family nursery business, including remnants of a greenhouse built in 1760 and thousands of broken bell jars, nursing pots, forcing pots, and watering devices; Cotter, Roberts, and Parrington, *Buried Past,* pp. 275–81.

98. Benjamin Smith Barton to William Bartram, November 30, 1805, BP, HSP, vol. 1, folder 12. A copy of this letter, not in Barton's hand, can also be found in Barton Papers, APSL.

99. William Bartram to Benjamin Smith Barton, November 30, 1805, Barton Papers, APSL. Numerous secondary sources confuse this incident and erroneously relate that Bartram was offered a position on the Lewis and Clark expedition. Perhaps this confusion arises because Barton was asked by President Jefferson to "prepare [for Lewis] a note of those on the lines of botany, zoology, or of Indian history which you think most worthy of enquiry & observation." Lewis visited Barton in Philadelphia, and it is possible that he, like many others, went to Kingsessing to pay his respects to William Bartram. Thomas Jefferson to Benjamin Smith Barton, February 27, 1803, Barton Papers, APSL. In an effort to cajole the aging naturalist, Barton asserted to Bartram that the Red River expedition "will not be fatiguing . . . a great part of it will be by water." Benjamin Smith Barton to William Bartram, November 30, 1805, BP, HSP, vol. 1, folder 12.

100. "Duty as well as gratitude impells me to offer to Your Excell^y. my most sincere thanks and acknowledgments for the distinguished honour & favour extended to me when you were pleased to select me as a suitable person for the department of Nat. History in the voyage up the Red River. The Scene was indeed flattering. But with the utmost regret I was constrained to decline it, on account of my advanced Age & consequent infirmities / being towards 70 Years of Age / and my Eyesight declining dayly." William Bartram to Thomas Jefferson, February 6, 1806, Thomas Jefferson Papers, no. 27379, Manuscript Division, Library of Congress. William Dunbar, who explored the Mississippi River with Bartram, accepted a similar offer from Jefferson and headed the exploratory team that surveyed the Ouachita River, 1804–5. Earnest, *John and William Bartram,* p. 169; Harper, ed., *Travels of William Bartram,* pp. xxviii–xxxv, 409; Fagin, *William Bartram,* pp. 11–12; cf. Ewan, ed., *William Bartram: Drawings,* p. 7. Barton also sent inquiries to Dunbar regarding the Native peoples around Natchez in 1806. Indian Materials, Barton Papers, APSL.

101. William Bartram to Gen. Lachlan McIntosh, May 31, 1796, Misc. W. Bartram Collection, New York Historical Society. Another visitor found

a permanent resting place at Kingsessing. On October 6, 1820, a Cherokee Indian named Jack Snake, who had fought against the Red Stick Creeks at the battle of Horseshoe Bend in 1814, died and was buried "in Bartram's woods"; McKinley, "End of William Bartram," p. 16, n. 95. Ralph S. Palmer, "A Biography of William Bartram," unpublished manuscript.

102. The John Bartram house and garden are now a National Historic Landmark, administered by the John Bartram Association. For information about the modern site, see Martha Wolf, "Historic Bartram's Garden."

2. TRAVELS THROUGH NORTH & SOUTH CAROLINA

Introduction

1. William Hedges, "Toward a National Literature," p. 190.

2. Douglas Anderson, "Bartram's *Travels* and the Politics of Nature," p. 3.

3. In 1783, Johann David Schoepf saw an "unprinted manuscript" in Bartram's possession "on the nations and products" of Florida. Schoepf, *Travels in the Confederation*, 1:91.

4. Harper, ed., *Travels of William Bartram*, p. xxi.

5. Benjamin Smith Barton to William Bartram, August 26, 1787, BP, HSP, vol. 1, folder 3.

6. Benjamin Smith Barton to William Bartram, February 19, 1788, BP, HSP, vol. 1, p. 4. In the letter, Barton mentioned the forthcoming work by Joseph Banks.

7. Ewan, ed., *William Bartram: Drawings*, p. 29.

8. William Bartram to Benjamin Smith Barton, undated draft of letter [1787], Jane Gray's Autograph Collection, item 104a, Gray Herbarium, Harvard University.

9. See Ewan, ed., *William Bartram: Drawings*, for a full discussion of the fate of the botanical specimens. Peck, "William Bartram and His Travels," pp. 40–42.

10. William Bartram to Mrs. M. L. Thomas, July 15, 1786, Misc. W. Bartram Collection, New York Historical Society. Previously, Mary Lamboll Thomas had shipped Bartram several plants native to the South, at Bartram's request. Mary Lamboll Thomas to William Bartram, May 11, 1785, BP, HSP, vol. 4, folder 111.

11. Robert Parrish to William Bartram, New York, 6 month 1790, Misc. Darlington Collection, New York Historical Society.

12. *Pennsylvania Packet and Daily Advertiser,* July 24, 1790. For advertisements of *Travels*, see the issues for July 30, 1790, and August 2, 1790. The St. Tammany's Society, or the Society of the Sons of Saint Tammany, also called the Columbian Order, was one of many social-political organizations that originated during the Federal period. That the Sons of Saint Tammany found Bartram's work interesting is not surprising, for they dressed like

Indians, referred to their leader as the "Grand Sachem," and called their meeting hall a "Wigwam." Donald A. Grinde and Bruce E. Johansen, *Exemplar of Liberty*, pp. 169–89.

13. Francis Harper could find "no conclusive evidence" that *Travels* was published in 1791, but he accepted the date on the verso of the title page — August 26, 1791. Harper, ed., *Travels of William Bartram*, p. xxiii.

14. Bartram evidently returned to Savannah from his excursion with the New Purchase survey team sometime in December. He stated in his report to Dr. Fothergill, "Soon after my return from the Tugilo journey to Savanah the country was alarmed by an express from Augusta, that the Indians were for war, & had actually murdered Several Families not far from Augusta. . . ." (Bartram, "Travels in Georgia and Florida," p. 144). Harper incorrectly dated this part of Bartram's journey to the fall of 1773. However, Bartram was referring to the White-Sherrill murders, which occurred in late December 1773. Bartram's description of the Altamaha is not that of the winter months. Harper assigns that part of the journey to 1776, which he dates by an eclipse of the moon described by Bartram. See Harper, ed., *Travels of William Bartram*, pp. 346, 417. Further confusing the issue, Bartram sent "one trunk and one box" of goods to East Florida in August 1773, in anticipation of a "Tour of the St. John's River." According to James Spalding, who made sure that Bartram's luggage reached East Florida, Bartram himself was expected in the area "about the month of October." Perhaps Bartram consigned the material to Spalding prior to leaving for Augusta (James Spalding to Charles McLatchy, August 15, 1773, BP, HSP, vol. 4, folder 103). At any rate, it is generally believed, as Bartram himself states in *Travels* (p. 57), that he left Savannah in March 1774 for East Florida.

15. This is documented by Bartram's letters to his father and to Lachlan McIntosh. Harper, ed., *Travels of William Bartram*, pp. 353, 361.

16. Harper, ed., *Travels of William Bartram*, p. 346. The extent of Bartram's travels between April 1773 and January 1777 is shown on the endpapers map in this volume and in figures 6–8. These maps are based on Lester J. Cappon, *Atlas of American History*, pp. 108–9; Harper, ed., "Travels in Georgia and Florida," maps 1 and 4; and Robert M. Peck, ed., *Bartram Heritage*.

17. William Bartram to Lachlan McIntosh, July 15, 1775 [1774], Dreer Collection, Scientists, Historical Society of Pennsylvania.

18. Francis Harper set the standard by which all scholars evaluate Bartram's chronology. See also Lester J. Cappon, "Retracing and Mapping the Bartrams' Southern Travels." The routes of both John and William Bartram are detailed in Cappon, *Atlas of American History*, pp. 108–9.

19. *Universal Asylum and Columbia Magazine*, vol. 1 (1792). The quotes are from the April issue, p. 267 (first quotation) and p. 266 (second quotation). Other excerpts appeared in January (pp. 8, 22), February (pp. 91–

97), March (pp. 195–97), and April (pp. 255–67). Modern zoologists have since confirmed the accuracy of Bartram's alligator account, as well as most of his other observations.

20. Quoted in Harper, ed., *Travels of William Bartram*, p. xxiv. As William Hedges has noted, Bartram's prose is characterized by "Latinate poeticisms and elaborate syntactical sonority." Hedges, "Toward a National Literature," p. 191.

21. Harper, ed., *Travels of William Bartram*, p. xxviii.

22. Harper, ed., *Travels of William Bartram*, p. xxvii. Harper thought there may have been a Dutch edition as well.

23. In a letter to Ralph Waldo Emerson, written in 1851, Thomas Carlyle recommended Bartram's work. "Do you know *Bartram's Travels?* This is one of the Seventies (1770) or so; treats of *Florida* chiefly; has a wondrous kind of floundering eloquence in it; and has also grown immeasurably *old.*" Charles Eliot Norton, ed., *Correspondence of Thomas Carlyle and Ralph Waldo Emerson, 1834–1872*, 2:198.

24. The best study of Bartram's influence on literature is Fagin, *William Bartram*, pp. 128–200. More recent examinations of Bartram's influence on literature and philosophy include Thomas V. Barnett, "William Bartram and the Age of Sensibility"; Mary S. Mattfield, "Journey to the Wilderness"; Bruce Silver, "William Bartram's and Other Eighteenth-Century Accounts of Nature"; L. Hugh Moore, "Aesthetic Theory of William Bartram" and "Southern Landscape of William Bartram"; and John Seelye, "Beauty Bare."

25. Henry David Thoreau, *A Week on the Concord and Merrimack Rivers; Walden, or Life in the Woods*, pp. 376–77.

Text

1. Nearly every date in *Travels* is in error. Consequently, those who have relied solely on the chronology contained in the many reprints based on the 1792 London edition (especially the numerous incarnations of the Van Doren edition, published in 1928, 1955, and 1988) have been led seriously astray. By tracking Bartram's movements as independently documented in his report to Dr. Fothergill and in contemporary correspondence, Francis Harper reconstructed, to a considerable extent, the correct sequence of events. We rely on his chronology throughout this work. Fagin, "Bartram's *Travels*"; Bartram, *Travels. . . : A Facsimile of the 1792 Edition*; Mark Van Doren, ed., *Travels of William Bartram*; Harper, ed., *Travels of William Bartram*, p. 336, passim.

2. Bartram had earlier described his discovery in this way: "observed a clay urn[,] the Shells being removed from it but found nothing in it but

sand & dust. it was about 18 Inches high & one foot in diameter, it was marked or carved on the outer surface in imitation of Basket work." Bartram, "Travels in Georgia and Florida," p. 135. This undoubtedly refers to stamped decoration created by impressing the surface of a clay pot with a carved wooden paddle before firing.

The shell midden sites were located on Colonel's Island, Georgia. Bartram's discussion of the origin of these shell heaps is noteworthy. Peter Kalm, a Swedish botanist who had visited the Bartrams in Philadelphia in 1748, was among the first to recognize a probable connection between Indian shellfish gathering and the presence of shell heaps along the Atlantic coast of North America. Despite Bartram's evidence of human activity at the Colonel's Island site, natural historians generally maintained that shell heaps were natural phenomena, a consensus eventually challenged by some of the earliest scientific archaeological excavations in the 1840s, when the artificial origin of most coastal shell heaps was at last widely acknowledged. Karl T. Steinen, ed., *Cultural Evolution;* Adolph B. Benson, *Peter Kalm's Travels* 1:127; Berkeley and Berkeley, *Life and Travels of John Bartram,* p. 127; Gregory A. Waselkov, "Shellfish Gathering and Shell Midden Archaeology," p. 139.

3. John Stuart served as Superintendent of Indian Affairs for the Southern Department from 1762 until his death in 1779. His career is covered in John Richard Alden, *John Stuart.* See also Kathryn E. Holland Braund, "John Stuart."

4. This incident is not mentioned in Bartram's report to Fothergill, covering the period 1773–74, leading at least one critic to suggest that the scene is a fictional literary device. Thomas V. Barnett, "William Bartram and the Age of Sensibility," p. 103, n. 6. Given his documented propensity for reordering events to achieve dramatic effect, however, Bartram has probably presented this journey to the St. Marys River out of sequence. It may have occurred during the summer of 1776, when he was evidently in Georgia. As Harper suggests, "If Bartram had been other than a Quaker, he might not have survived." Bartram, "Travels in Georgia and Florida," pp. 573–74; Harper, "William Bartram and the American Revolution," p. 574; quote from Harper, ed., *Travels of William Bartram,* p. 338.

5. Okefenokee Swamp; for a delightfully evocative portrait (in words and photographs) of the swamp in the early part of this century, see Francis Harper and Delma E. Presley, *Okefinokee Album.*

6. This tale apparently refers in a garbled fashion to the Yamasee War of 1715. After enduring a decade of increasingly abusive English trading practices, the Muscogulges (or Creeks) and many of the smaller tribes living near the colony of South Carolina, most prominently the Yamasees, attacked and nearly destroyed that colony. The Yamasees were eventually defeated and dispersed by the colonial militia and their Indian allies. Ver-

ner W. Crane, *Southern Frontier,* pp. 165–89, 242–73; Richard L. Haan, "The 'Trade Do's Not Flourish.'"

7. Bartram is describing the controversial New Purchase Cession, negotiated at Augusta during late May and early June 1773. Leading merchants and traders, with the full support of Gov. James Wright of Georgia, negotiated a cession of Cherokee and Creek lands totaling more than 2 million acres, in two tracts. In return, the traders canceled the debts of all Creeks and Cherokees. Bartram discusses the Indian speeches at the congress in greater detail on pp. 485–86 of *Travels.*

Because Creek warriors had killed several English settlers near Wrightsborough a few months earlier, John Stuart thought it was "not alltogether safe" to enter the Indian country alone; Bartram, "Travels in Georgia and Florida," p. 138. So Bartram attached himself to the survey party demarcating the boundary of the northern land cession. Louis De Vorsey Jr., *Indian Boundary,* pp. 170–72; "Indian Boundaries in Colonial Georgia," p. 75; and "Colonial Georgia Backcountry," p. 53.

8. Harper, ed., "Travels in Georgia and Florida," p. 138. Stuart was proved correct, and on Christmas Day 1773, Creek warriors murdered several white settlers on the newly ceded lands. See David H. Corkran, *The Creek Frontier,* pp. 281–83; Braund, *Deerskins and Duffels,* pp. 150–52, 159–60. Col. Barnet is actually Col. Edward Barnard.

9. Bartram has described a Mississippian town site with characteristic earthworks, dating from A.D. 1000 to 1550. This particular site, however, has not been located, despite intensive archaeological searches. By "tetragon terraces," Bartram meant truncated, flat-topped, rectangular earthworks that archaeologists refer to as substructure mounds or platform mounds. Daniel J. Elliott and Steven A. Kowalewski, "Fortson Mound, Wilkes County, Georgia," pp. 63–64; cf. Robert Silverberg, *Mound Builders of Ancient America,* p. 36.

10. The common names of these species are (1) persimmon, *Diospyros virginiana* L.; (2) honey locust, *Gleditsia triacanthos* L.; (3) Chickasaw plum, *Prunus angustifolia* Marsh.; (4) French mulberry or beauty berry, *Callicarpa americana* L.; (5) red mulberry, *Morus rubra* L.; (6) shagbark hickory, *Carya ovata* (Mill.) K. Koch; and (7) black walnut, *Juglans nigra* L. Thomas Hatley describes this as a "husbanded forest community" comprising quasidomesticated tree species preserved by Indian farmers during field clearance. Hatley, "Cherokee Women Farmers," p. 39.

11. The classic study of southeastern Indian nut oils is Herbert B. Battle, "Domestic Use of Oil."

12. Although Bartram saw no bison in the course of his travels across the Southeast, place names such as this reflect their sparse but widespread occurrence in the region during the colonial period. Erhard Rostlund, "The Geographic Range of the Historic Bison"; Robert W. Neuman, "The Buffalo in Southeastern United States."

13. At one point, near the confluence of the Tugaloo and Savannah rivers, "the Indians and Surveyors marked a Line Tree, GR. on one side for our King and the Indian Mark on the other side" (Bartram, "Travels in Georgia and Florida," p. 143). Unfortunately, few Indian-made maps of the region survive, even in the form of copies; Gregory A. Waselkov, "Indian Maps of the Colonial Southeast."

14. In his journal, Bartram said the Native American hunters carried "the Root" of the Physic Nut, *Nestronia umbellula* Raf., to attract deer. "This the Indian Doctors or Conjurers make their People believe; & for which end they hold it in high esteem & make them pay dear enough for it, this was the account I had by an Interpreter present"; Bartram, "Travels in Georgia and Florida," p. 141. See also Ewan, ed., *William Bartram: Drawings,* pl. 27, p. 65.

15. James Adair witnessed the same sort of harpoon fishing by Indians on the Savannah River. Adair, *History of the American Indians,* pp. 402–3.

16. The impressive earthen mounds at the Ocmulgee site, across the Ocmulgee River from present-day Macon, Georgia, date principally to the Mississippian era (A.D. 1000 to 1550), but several Lower Creek towns occupied the vicinity from 1690 to 1715. Excavations in the 1930s at Ocmulgee are reported in A. R. Kelly, "A Preliminary Report on Archaeological Explorations at Macon, Georgia"; Charles H. Fairbanks, *Archeology of the Funeral Mound;* Carol A. Mason, "The Archaeology of Ocmulgee Old Fields"; Halley, ed., *Ocmulgee Archaeology.*

Although Bartram does not say so, the abandoned Mississippian "Oakmulge fields" may have been ridged (as was the remnant of a thousand-year-old field found buried under mound D at Ocmulgee; Kelly, "Archaeological Explorations at Macon," pl. 1a), rather than containing the individual corn hills typical of eighteenth-century Indian fields. William E. Doolittle, "Agriculture in North America," p. 394.

17. Bartram's account of this Creek legend coincides closely with versions recounted by Chikilli in 1735 and Apatai in 1798, except that these last identify the Chattahoochee River as the place they first "sat down." However, archaeologists agree that the Mississippian occupation at Ocmulgee resulted from a migration (a "site unit intrusion," in archaeological jargon) from the west around A.D. 1100. Perhaps some glimmer of this prehistoric event was preserved in the Creeks' collective memory by the oral recitation of their migration legend. Albert S. Gatschet, *A Migration Legend of the Creek Indians* 1:222–51; *Letters, Journals and Writings of Benjamin Hawkins,* 1:326–27; also see Le Clerc Milfort, *Memoirs,* pp. 102–5; Frank T. Schnell, "The Beginnings of the Creeks."

18. This is another garbled account of the Yamasee War and its aftermath; see n. 6 and John Swanton's comments in Harper, ed., *Travels of William Bartram,* pp. 347–48.

19. Bartram recounted his frustrated attempts to travel during this pe-

riod in a letter to his father, written in Charleston on March 27, 1775. "Soon after my return to Savana in order to forward my collections to Doct^r. Fothergill, I intended to go back into the Cheroke & Creek Countries when the Alarm from the Frontiers of hostilities commencing betwen the Indians & the whites put a stop to that scheme. I then turned my views toward E^t. Florida & prepared for it I put my baggage onboard a Vessell bound from Savanah To M^r. Spaldings Store on S^t. Johns intending to go by land there, & set off accordingly got safe to the Alatamaha where I was taken Ill of a Fever of which I did not recover so as to be able to travel for near 2 Months, when I sett off again, but was turn'd back again by expresses from E^t. Florida that the Indians were up in Arms against us in that Province having killed & captivated several White People, & the Inhabitants were flying in to Augustine, & all the Indian Stores except one were robed & broken up. . . ." William Bartram to John Bartram, March 27, 1775, BP, HSP, vol. 1, p. 78.

20. James Spalding (1734–94) emigrated from Georgia to East Florida in 1763. He there joined forces with Donald McKay and Roger Kelsall and eventually established four Indian trading stores, including two stores in East Florida. Donald McKay died in 1768, and the firm continued under the name Spalding and Kelsall. This firm ultimately became the best known of all Creek trading firms, Panton, Leslie & Company. Charles McLatchy, one of Spalding and Kelsall's employees and a friend of Bartram, was one of the original partners of Panton, Leslie & Company. Kenneth E. Lewis, "The History and Archeology of Spalding's Store," pp. 25–28; William S. Coker and Thomas D. Watson, *Indian Traders of the Southeastern Spanish Borderlands*, pp. 15–30.

21. Bartram's explanation for the "Ogeechee mounts" is, no doubt, apocryphal. Originally, there were at least three shell mounds and one sand mound. The latter was excavated by Brinton and subsequently demolished during the construction of a school on the site. Daniel G. Brinton, *Notes on the Floridian Peninsula*, pp. 166–67; Harper, ed., *Travels of William Bartram*, pp. 349–50; Peck, ed., *Bartram Heritage*, pp. 86–88.

22. In his journal, Bartram explicitly states that this Indian was "a slave bro't from the Musqueto Shore," the eastern coast of modern Nicaragua. Bartram, "Travels in Georgia and Florida," p. 146.

23. Patrick Tonyn (1725–1804), a career army officer, arrived in St. Augustine on March 1, 1774, and was installed as the third, and final, governor of British East Florida on March 9, 1774. His investiture was attended by Oconee Mico, Cowkeeper, Long Warrior, and approximately a hundred other Lower Creeks and Seminoles who spent almost a week on a drinking binge celebrating the occasion. It was during this time that Tonyn met with the Seminoles and settled all outstanding breaches of the peace. Charles L. Mowat, *East Florida as a British Province*, p. 83; David H. Corkran, *The Creek Frontier, 1540–1783*, p. 283.

24. Gregory A. Waselkov and John W. Cottier, "European Perceptions of

Eastern Muskogean Ethnicity," pp 26–27. For a fuller discussion of Creek political divisions, see Braund, *Deerskins and Duffels*, pp. 5–8. East Florida governors exercised their prerogative to deal with the Lower Creeks, not just with the few detached villages in the province. Thus, major Indian conferences held in that province were attended and directed by leading Lower Creek headmen, which caused much resentment among the leading Seminoles. Perhaps the incident referred to here by Bartram occurred in January 1774, when some Lower Creeks of Tomatley town (on the Apalachicola River) robbed and killed some white people at the Bay of St. Joseph's. Even though this incident occurred in West Florida, the East Florida Seminoles may have taken over traders' stores as they fled in anticipation of British retaliation. David Taitt to John Stuart, January 2, 1774, and January 22, 1774, CO5/75, f. 45.

25. In 1766 Bartram unsuccessfully attempted to establish a 500-acre plantation on the St. Johns River, near Picolata Creek. Bernard Bailyn, *Voyagers to the West*, pp. 473–74. One year earlier he and his father had attended a congress at the old fort between British Governor Grant and the Creeks and Seminoles. According to John Bartram's account,

this day yᵉ indians & governour met to sighn yᵉ treaty[.] a great number or all of yᵉ chiefs set thair mark to two deeds to thair respective names & seals[,] one for yᵉ indians[,] yᵉ other to be kept at St[.] Augustine[.] yᵉ indin chiefs[,] according to thair dignity[,] has each A fine silver medal[—]some as big as yᵉ palm of my hand[,] others bigger than A dollar[—]hung in A fine silk ribon two yards long[,] which yᵉ governour hung about each chiefs neck[,] while yᵉ drums beat & yᵉ guns fired from yᵉ fort & vesail[.] then yᵉ governour & superint[end]ent[—] otherwise called yᵉ beloved man[—]shaked hands with them all[,] but before yᵉ delivery of yᵉ medals, smoked in yᵉ pipe of fr[i]endship[.] yᵉ governour & chiefs in georgia[,] with thair governour[,] is to meet next spring in order to settle yᵉ limits granted in georgia[,] which is much wanted. (John Bartram, "Diary," p. 35)

Forts Picolata and Pupo had been built where the "Camino Real," the path from St. Augustine to St. Marks on Apalachee Bay, crossed the St. Johns. William E. Myer, "Indian Trails of the Southeast," p. 829; John M. Goggin, "Fort Pupo."

26. Live oak acorns were widely used as an oil source by the southeastern Indians, even though they contain far less oil than hickory nuts. Benjamin Hawkins estimated that "one bushel of [red oak] acorns makes about a pint of oil." John R. Swanton, *The Indians of the Southeastern United States*, pp. 273, 279; *Letters, Journals and Writings of Benjamin Hawkins* 1:14–15.

27. This unnamed village was located at present-day Palatka (Harper, ed., *Travels of William Bartram*, p. 352). The last paragraph summarizes the state

of Seminole agriculture at this period, based on a mixture of native American and Old World domesticates. Mediterranean oranges (*Citrus aurantium* L.), Caribbean batatas or sweet potatoes (*Ipomoea batatas* [L.] Lam.), and African watermelons (*Citrullus lanatus* [Thunb.] Matsum. & Nakai) were introduced to Florida by the Spaniards. Leonard W. Blake, "Early Acceptance of Watermelon by Indians of the United States"; U. P. Hedrick, ed., *Sturtevant's Edible Plants of the World*, pp. 169–72; Mark Wagner, "The Introduction and Early Use of African Plants" pp. 117–18; see *Von Reck's Voyage: Drawings and Journal of Philip Georg Friedrich von Reck*, p. 97. Corn (*Zea mays* L.), beans (*Phaseolus* spp.), scalloped summer squash (*Cucurbita pepo* L.), and tobacco (*Nicotiana rustica* L.) had been grown in the Southeast for centuries, although by Bartram's time the southeastern Indians were obtaining the South American domesticated species, *Nicotiana tabacum* L., in trade from the Spanish and British. Crookneck squashes (*Cucurbita moschata* [Duch. ex Lam.] Duch. ex Poir.), called "pompions" or "pumpkins" by British colonists, originated in the Caribbean or Mexico. Frank G. Speck, *Gourds of the Southeastern Indians*, p. 19.

The following extended quote, on native American plant foods, is extracted from Bartram's manuscript journal to Dr. Fothergill.

> Vegitable productions which the Florideans use for food[:]
> Grenadilla, Fruit when ripe is as large as a Goose Egg, yellow, & of a very fragrant sm[ell] and an agreeable taste, the juice very sweet, inlivened with a little tartn[ess]. This fruit the Indians are very fond off, eaten singly as other fruits or prepared in this manner; When ripe they gather great quantities & throw in heaps, to mellow. when they get yellow & begin to shrivell they spread them about to air[,] then beat them with parch't corn flower, in a Mort[ar], which soon becomes like dough but continue beating till the whole is dry as flower[,] th[en] they sift it. to clear out the seeds & skins whiche being too hard & tough to marsh up with the rest[.] this flower has an agreable smell & taste, & by mixing a ve[ry] little of this meal or flower with warm water make an agreeable whole[some] kind of jelly. They like wise make Cakes or fritters of it. —
> Pumkins they use in the same manner, & barbecue them over fire & smoke[.]
> Peaches are prepared like it & barbecued. Grapes they barbecue in bunches.
> Convolvulus radice tuberora esculenta. Patates. These roots they eat boil'd & roasted, as the white People do, these they likewis[e] barbecue & keep all winter. —
> Diospyros floribus dioicis Gron. virg: Pursimmons the Indians delight to eat, they have a method of preser[ving] them by drying them; & marshing them up[,] throw^g. out the stone & mix t[he] pulp with corn

flower, bake Cakes, which will keep, a long time, & when they eat the
Cake they stew them with fat Venson & bair Oil[.]

Peaches, they slice, take out the stone, & marsh up with parch't
corn[,] beating all to dry flower, this they mix with other corn flower &
bake loaves or Cakes or barbecue the Peaches whole on hyrdles over a
gentle fire & smoke, in this manner they do Grapes, Patates, sliced
Pumkins & all other such fruites & roots & keep in dry stores, & when
they want to cook or make use of them[,] they stew them in a little water,
they plump up & look & taste as when fresh. Green Corn, Pe[ase] &
Beans they use this way &ᶜ. —

Smilax aspera nodosa, radice rubra majore. Plum. China Root vulgo.
The Indians dig up these roots, which they chop to pieces with a
hatchet, this they reduce in a wooden mortar & Pestle as fine as
posseble, and mix it with water in a large tub, stiring it about well, with a
stick, & whilst the water is thick & turgid, pour it off into another Vessell,
which when dry leaves a seddement or fine red flower or meal at the
bottom of the Vessell, This powder they keep for food, & call it Contee,
when they make use of it they mix a little of the farena with warm water
which very soon becomes a thick redish jelly, which when sweetened
with honey Or Sugar, is very agreeable & is esteamed as nourishing &
extremely coveted by the Indians[.] they make very good fritters or Pan
Cakes of this flower[,] mixing it with corn flower & fried in Bears Oil.

Glycine radice tuberosa Gron. virg. Apios americana. The Indians
gather the Roots of this Plant which they roast or boil[.] they eat like
yams or Potatoes[.] the consistence of the Root is farinacious[,] white as
snow[,] but has an earthy taste yet very wholesome and agreable enough
after being used to eat them, the Plant grows in rich low vales or
bottoms where the soil is loose & light. the roots grow in strings like
beads[,] each articulation about the size of a hens egg. The Indians
gather these Roots in the autumn after the Plant has flowered & the top
withers. they are much used by the Floridians[.] The Traders call them
Indian Patates[.]

Arum acaule, foliis hastato-cordatis acutis, angulis obtusis Hort. cliff.
Indian Turnip[.] The Floridians roast or boil the root of this plant, They
also cultivate Edoe's & Taniers, large species of Arum bro't here from
Wᵗ. Ind. Isla[nds.]

Citrus. Malus Aurantia major, Here are two sorts or varieties of
Oranges, which grow wild all over the Istmos of Florida. The large sour
Orange & the Bitter-swett both of which the Indians are emoderately
fond of, they sometimes roast the sower oranges in the ashes, which eats
something like a roasted apple.

These two species of Oranges grows, on high shell bluff on the Banks
of Rivers[,] Lakes & Ponds, & at all inlets on the Sea coast[.] they grow
in groves or copses together not commonly mixing with other Trees yet

some other sorts of Trees will grow scatteringly among them, as a fiew large live Oaks, Celtis[,] Zanthoxilon[,] Palm, Ilisium[.] they grow only on the richest high land in the country, which occ[a]tions the destruction of abundance, since this kind of soil is the most proper for the Planter to begin to clear & plant[.]

Whether the Orange Tree is an exotick, brot in here by the Spaniards or a Native to this country[,] is a question, I have inqu[ired] of some of the old spaniards at Augustine, who tell me they were first bro't in by the spaniards & spread over the Country by the Ind[ians].

Quercus foliis lanciolatis integerrimis glabris. Gron. Virg. Live Oak. The Acrons of this species of Oak is commonly used as food by the Indians of the Istmous. This fruit is as sweet & as mild as a Chesnut. The Indians beat them to flower in wooden morters, & mix with corn flower which makes good bread: they also beat the acorn to pieces then heat them in water over the fire[,] which afford a great deal of very sweet mild oil, which they use in cookery insted of Bear Oil or Butter, they roast the acorn & eat them as we do chesnuts —

Juglans cineria. The Indians hold in great esteem all kinds of sweet Hicory nuts[.] they crack the nuts, & beat them in morters, this they boil in water & save the Oil, but the most favorite dish the Indians have amongst them is Corn thin Drink seasoned with hicory nut Oil. They pick out the kernel, beat them to a paste & boil with Indian Corn flower, which being seasoned with a lixivium made of Pea straw ashes[,] gives it a consistance & taste someth^g. like cream or rich new milk & is called by the Traders hicory milk[.]

Gleditsia, spinis triplicibus axillaribus Lin. Spes. Plant. Honey Locust[.] The Indians use the fruit as food & make good beer of it[.]

Fagus

Castania Sativa. Castania pumila virginiana. Chesnut & Chinquapin[.] Both these fruites or Nuts are used for common food by the Floridian[s.] they roast & boil them & make very good Bread of them[.]

Carica, Foliorum lobis sinuatis Hort. Cleff. Papaya fructu oblong, melonis effigee. Ehret. The Floridians eat this fruite when ripe.

A Thorny evergreen shrub, calld wild limes or Tallow nuts. the fruit resembles a large yellow plumb, the pulp when ripe is of the cons[is]tance, looks & tastes like a custard having a little tartness. but very agreeable, This shrub, bears green & ripe fruit & flowers all the Year round, the Natives esteem this fruit & is the most agreable wil[d] fruit in the Itmous.

Palma, dactylifera minor. The low prickley Palmeto, bears vast quantities of oval yellow or bro[wn] sweet fruit, of the size of a Persimmon, which the Indians admire g[reatly?] they are very healthy & fatning. Cattle[,] Horses, Hog, Bears[,] dogs[,] Wolve[s], Men, birds &

almost every animal in the land feed on it & get extra fat when this fruit is ripe, it makes an excellent strong sweet d[rink] like beer, & it is emagined would yeild a good Sperit or brandy. This fru[it] is what fattens the bear in this country & I have seen seven or 8 bear siting on their breeches in view at the same time[,] feeding on [this] fruite, & the Bees collect abundance of honey from it[.]

Morus[.] Morus foliis subtus tomentosis, amentis longis dioicis. Gron. Virg. The fruit of the black mulberry is a considerable part in the food of the Indians, they dry the fruite on boards in large cakes[,] which they keep in store, & stew it with bread[,] parch't coarn flower & oil.

Besides these principle articles they eat almost all kinds of berries[,] Root & Nuts[,] Water Mellons, Musk Mellons, Squashes, Beans & Peas. (Bartram, "Travels in Georgia and Florida," pp. 169–71)

Bartram's "Granadilla" is the passion flower or maypop (*Passiflora incarnata* L.); see *Von Reck's Voyage,* p. 109; Witthoft, "Cherokee Indian Use of Potherbs," p. 253.

Other species, in the order they are listed, include sweet potato (*Ipomoea batatas* [L.] Lam.), persimmon (*Diospyros virginiana* L.), peach (*Prunus persica* [L.] Batsch), peas (possibly English peas, *Pisum sativum* L.), catbrier (*Smilax* cf. *bona-nox* L.), groundnut (*Apios americana* Medic.), arrow arum or Indian turnip (*Peltandra virginica* [L.] Schott & Endl.), bittersweet and sour oranges (*Citrus aurantium* L.), live oak (*Quercus virginiana* Miller), hickory (*Carya* spp.), honey locust (*Gleditisia triacanthos* L.), American beech (*Fagus grandifolia* Ehrh.), American chestnut (*Castanea dentata* [Marsh.] Borkh.), chinquapins (*Castanea* spp.), papaya (*Carica papaya* L.), wild lime or tallow nut (*Ximenia americana* L.), saw palmetto (*Serenoa repens* [Bartram] Small), red mulberry (*Morus rubra* L.), and cantaloupe (*Cucumis melo* L.). Catbrier: Elias Yanovsky, *Food Plants of the North American Indians,* p. 14; Frances B. King, "Plants, People, and Paleoecology," pp. 70–71. Indian turnip: Ewan, ed., *William Bartram: Drawings,* pl. 59; John H. Hann, "Use and Processing of Plants by Indians of Spanish Florida," pp. 91–93.

The introduced species were derived from the Caribbean (i.e., sweet potato, papaya, tallownut, and the two varieties of arum) and from the Old World, thanks to Spanish colonists who brought with them peaches, oranges, cantaloupes (all originally from Asia), and peas (from Europe). Archaeological remains of watermelons, cantaloupes, crookneck squash, peaches, and peas have all been found at the sixteenth-century Spanish sites of St. Augustine and Santa Elena. Elizabeth J. Reitz and C. Margaret Scarry, *Reconstructing Historic Subsistence,* p. 55.

28. Denys Rolle was a member of Parliament and one of the first British colonizers of East Florida. After his utopian attempt failed to settle petty criminals from London as white indentured servants at Charlotia (or Rollestown), he converted his grant to a plantation worked with black slave

labor. Denys Rolle, *To the Right Honourable the Lords . . .* ; Joseph Kastner, *A Species of Eternity,* p. 91; Bailyn, *Voyagers to the West,* pp. 434–36, 447–51; James M. Denham, "Denys Rolle and Indian Policy," pp. 31–44. Today the townsite is occupied by a Florida Power and Light Company generating plant. Peck, ed., *Bartram Heritage,* p. 88.

29. Bartram frequently mentioned "old fields" throughout his *Travels,* agricultural clearings abandoned—at least temporarily—by the Indians and covered with second-growth vegetation. Wild food sources, such as French mulberry (*Callicarpa americana* L.), were often seen in these old fields, where they had been planted or preserved during selective clearing by the Indians. Most later observers considered the St. Johns River shell banks to be natural, rather than cultural, in origin until the excavations of Brinton and Wyman in the 1860s and 1870s. Wyman, "Fresh Water Shell Mounds," pp. 14–15.

30. Spalding's Lower Store stood at Stokes Landing, on the west bank of the St. Johns, from 1763 until 1784. The site has been located and excavated by archaeologists. John M. Goggin, "A Florida Indian Trading Post," pp. 35–37; Lewis, "Spalding's Lower Store." The trader was probably Job Wiggens, Bartram's "old friend and benefactor" (*Travels,* p. 156).

31. John Bartram, in his journal entry for January 25, 1766, included the following description of the Mount Royal site (at modern-day Fruitland Cove).

About noon we landed at Mount-Royal, and went to an Indian tumulus, which was about 100 yards in diameter, nearly round, and near 20 foot high, found some bones scattered on it, it must be very ancient, as live-oaks are growing upon it three foot in diameter; what a prodigious multitude of Indians must have laboured to raise it? to what height we can't say, as it must have settled much in such a number of years, and it is surprizing where they brought the sand from, and how, as they had nothing but baskets or bowls to carry it in; there seems to be a little hollow near the adjacent level on one side, though not likely to raise such a tumulus the 50th part of what it is, but directly north from the tumulus is a fine straight avenue about 60 yards broad, all the surface of which has been taken off, and thrown on each side, which makes a bank of about a rood wide and a foot high more or less, as the unevenness of the ground required, for the avenue is as level as a floor from bank to bank, and continues so for about three quarters of a mile to a pond of about 100 yards broad and 150 long N. and S. seemed to be an oblong square, and its banks 4 foot perpendicular, gradually sloping every way to the water, the depth of which we could not say, but do not imagine it deep, as the grass grows all over it; by its regularity it seems to be artificial; if so, perhaps the sand was carried from hence to raise the tumulus, as the one directly faces the other at each end of the avenue; . . . here had formerly been a large Indian town; I suppose there is 50 acres of planting ground cleared and of a middling soil, a good part of which is mixed with small shells; no doubt this large tumulus was their burying-place or sepulchre: Whether the Florida Indians buried the bones after the flesh was rotted off them, as the present southern Indians do, I can't say: . . . . (John Bartram, "Diary," p. 45)

32. Bartram sketched two views of this mound site in his "Observations" manuscript (see chapter 3). According to Jeffries Wyman, the Mount Royal site remained much the same in the 1870s as it had been in Bartram's day. Clarence B. Moore excavated at this impressive Mississippian site for two seasons in the 1890s. At that time, the large mound was 4.8 meters high and the 11- to 18-meter-wide "causeway," flanked by embankments 0.75 meter high and 3.5 meters broad, extended 800 meters to the borrow pit or pond. Similar causeway and pond features are common at late prehistoric sites in the Lake Okeechobee Basin. Wyman, "Shell Mounds," p. 40; Clarence B. Moore, "Certain Sand Mounds," pp. 16–35, 130–46; Jerald T. Milanich and Charles H. Fairbanks, *Florida Archaeology*, pp. 164–65; Robert S. Carr, "Prehistoric Circular Earthworks in South Florida"; Jerald T. Milanich, *Precolumbian Florida*, pp. 270–72.

33. Harper, ed., *Travels of William Bartram*, p. 354.

34. Many Indian hunting and gathering habitats were modified and maintained at high levels of biotic productivity by routine light burning. Old fields, canebrakes, and some grasslands would have reverted to forest except for the intentional, repetitive burning that resulted in an annual regrowth of predominantly young, weedy vegetation. These plants were the favored browse of deer and other animals, and they also yielded seeds and other edible parts for human consumption. Colonial legislation frequently attempted to prevent what seemed to be indiscriminate burning. Hu Maxwell, "The Use and Abuse of the Forests"; Robin F. A. Fabel and Robert R. Rea, "Lieutenant Thomas Campbell's Sojourn among the Creeks"; Lucy L. Wenhold, "A 17th Century Letter," p. 13; *De Brahm's Report*, pp. 80–81; Gary C. Goodwin, "Cherokees in Transition," pp. 63–64; Emily W. B. Russell, "Indian-Set Fires"; *Nairne's Muskhogean Journal*, p. 52; Timothy Silver, *A New Face*, pp. 59–64; Robert Rea and Milo B. Howard, eds., *Minutes, Journals, and Acts of the General Assembly of British West Florida*, pp. 376–77.

The precise site of Spalding's Upper Store has not been determined by archaeologists, but it probably stood on the west bank of the St. Johns, about five miles above Lake George. Harper, ed., *Travels of William Bartram*, p. 354.

35. According to his original report to Fothergill, Bartram's travel companion was simply "one of the men" (which Harper took to mean a white trader), who remained with him for the entire canoe voyage. Perhaps this incident actually occurred during a later excursion on the St. Johns River. Harper, ed., *Travels of William Bartram*, p. 354.

36. Jeffries Wyman excavated part of this site, but found no "tumuli

of Yamasees." Bartram's description of the undulating ground surface resembles accounts by others of uneroded shell middens. Wyman, "Shell Mounds," pp. 33–36; Waselkov, "Shellfish Gathering," pp. 116–17.

37. The town of New Smyrna was settled in 1768 by Greek, Italian, and Minorcan immigrants lured to Florida by British land speculators. By 1777, all of the colonists had died or moved away. Bailyn, *Voyagers to the West,* pp. 451–61.

The Turtle Mound, originally known to the native Floridians as the mound of Surruque, may have been one of the largest shell middens in North America, with a height of about twenty-five meters. On the flat terrain of the east Florida coast, its huge mass served as a landmark for sailors until the late nineteenth and early twentieth centuries, when the prehistoric oyster shells were mined for construction material. Milanich and Fairbanks, *Florida Archaeology,* p. 159; Milanich, *Precolumbian Florida,* p. 257.

38. Bartram traveled as far south as modern-day Orange City, Florida. Harper, ed., *Travels of William Bartram,* p. 358.

39. As John Swanton noted, the "royal standard" can only have been the calumet, or, more specifically, the tail feathers of the southern bald eagle (*Haliaeetus leucocephalus*) attached to the cane stem of the calumet, with pipe bowl detached. Alexandre DeBatz painted an Attakapa man carrying such an artifact in 1735. John R. Swanton, "Social Organization," p. 435; Ian W. Brown, "The Calumet Ceremony," p. 312; also see Antonio J. Waring Jr., *Waring Papers.* Bartram evidently misidentified the source of the feathers, however, attributing them to his "Vultur sacra," which is identifiable as the king vulture (*Sarcoramphus papa*). He and his father were evidently the only scientists to observe this species in the Southeast. Harper, ed., *Travels of William Bartram,* p. 359.

40. This spot may have been on Tick Island, which had a sand mound, a causeway, and a huge midden of freshwater mussel and snail shells. Harper, ed., *Travels of William Bartram,* p. 360; Clarence B. Moore, "Supplementary Investigations at Tick Island"; Moore, "Certain Sand Mounds," pp. 48–63, 148–58; Otto L. Jahn and Ripley P. Bullen, "The Tick Island Site."

41. Francis Harper established that Bartram's excursions from Spalding's Lower Store, as presented in *Travels,* are out of sequence. His first trip to the Alachua savanna occurred between the end of April and the beginning of May 1774. The account of his journey up the St. Johns conflates two separate trips, which took place in May and June 1774 and in August and September 1774. Harper, ed., *Travels of William Bartram,* pp. 352, 363.

42. Bleeding a person by scratching, with rattlesnake teeth or gar scales, was a widely practiced method to cure illness and antisocial behavior. Swanton, *Indians of the Southeastern United States,* pp. 564, 782–99. Arrows tipped with gar scales were reported among the Natchez and the Cherokees. The scales must have been unmodified, because no sharpened scales that might indicate this use have ever been found in archaeological con-

texts. Ibid., pp. 573–75; Charles H. Faulkner, "The Occurrence of Gar Remains."

43. This hamlet may correspond to a site on the Santa Fe River, excavated by archaeologists in the 1950s. William H. Sears, "A–296: A Seminole Site."

44. Ahaye, or Cowkeeper, the mico of Alachua or Latchoway, was the most prominent of the eighteenth-century Seminole headmen. A Hitchiti-speaking Oconee Lower Creek, he had migrated with his people into the Alachua area in the mid-eighteenth century, and he was one of five headmen designated Great Medal Chiefs of the Lower Creeks by the British in 1765. He died during the 1790s. J. Leitch Wright Jr., *Creeks and Seminoles*, pp. 109, 126; Corkran, *Creek Frontier*, p. 246; Brent R. Weisman, *Like Beads on a String*, pp. 41, 47–48.

Ahaye was known as the Cowkeeper due to his extensive cattle herd, which thrived in the lush Alachua savanna. In a letter to Lachlan McIntosh, dated July 15, 1775, and preserved at the Historical Society of Pennsylvania, William Bartram left the following description: "the [Alachua] Savanah is computed to be 15 Miles long 6 or 7 wide & near 50 Miles round the Land about it very Good & extremely proper for Indigo, would grow good corn Etc. The whole Savanah in the Summer & Fall a meadow of very good kind of grass, & here are abundance of very large fat Cattle & Horses, 150 or 200 in droves all belonging to the Seminole's . . . would those Indians part with this Land, it would admit a very valuable Settlement & would be a very considerable acquisition." In fact, Jonathan Bryan of Georgia was attempting to acquire the property (by means of a highly irregular ninety-nine-year, personal lease of land from the Seminoles) and visited the area about the same time as Bartram. The two undoubtedly discussed the development potential of Alachua savanna when Bartram visited with Bryan later in his travels, but Bartram is strangely silent on these grandiose schemes. Bryan's speculative dealings are recounted in Alan Gallay, *The Formation of a Planter Elite*.

45. In his journal, Bartram gives this description of Cowkeeper's house: "the chiefs house was distinguished from the rest no other way than being a little larger, & by having a Flag hoisted at one Corner. Our Interpretor condu[c]ted us there. Assended an Indian Ladder, to a loft about 12 feet high where we sat down on Derr Skins." Bartram, "Travels in Georgia and Florida," p. 147.

46. In a manuscript version of *Travels*, the "Thin drink" is identified as "a cool thin hommony" (William Bartram, "A Journey from Spalding's Lower Trading House to Cuscoilla and the Great Alachua Savanna," BP, HSP, Small Bartram Volumes, p. 293), or what is called sofkee today. Charles M. Hudson, *The Southeastern Indians*, p. 305. Elsewhere Bartram described it, probably more accurately, as "a sort of grewell made of Corn flower & hicory Nut Oil & Water boild together." Bartram, "Travels in Georgia and Florida," p. 157.

47. The Alachua savanna is now known as Payne's Prairie, located imme-

diately south of Gainesville. Bartram's maps of the savanna (figures 10 and 11) show the Indian mound he passed on the trail into Cuscowilla and the "former store" on the southern border of the savanna. This may have been the store established in the area by a trader named Barnet in 1764; archaeological evidence of a store has been discovered there. *William Bartram: Drawings,* ed. Ewan, pl. 57, p. 83; Weisman, *Like Beads on a String,* p. 63.

48. For discussions of slavery in the colonial interior Southeast—Indians enslaved by Indians, Indians enslaved by the English, and Africans enslaved by Indians—see Daniel F. Littlefield Jr., *Africans and Creeks,* pp. 26–51; J. Leitch Wright, *The Only Land They Knew,* pp. 126–50; Peter H. Wood, "Indian Servitude in the Southeast," pp. 407–9; Kathryn E. Holland Braund, "Creek Indians, Blacks, and Slavery."

49. In a letter to Lachlan McIntosh, dated July 15, 1775, Bartram described this visit to the Alachua savanna, where he saw an "abundance of very large fat Cattle & Horses, 150 or 200 in droves, all belonging to the Seminole's" (Dreer Collection, Scientists, Historical Society of Pennsylvania). The most recent study of the Spanish settlements in Florida and elsewhere in the South is David J. Weber, *The Spanish Frontier in North America.*

The Seminoles picked up their knowledge of cattle raising—and undoubtedly the cattle themselves—from Spanish colonists who formerly had large ranches in north-central Florida. Charles H. Fairbanks, "The Ethno-Archeology of the Florida Seminole," p. 172; Amy Bushnell, "The Menéndez Marquéz Cattle Barony"; Charles Arnade, "Cattle Raising in Spanish Florida."

50. In an earlier version of this description, Bartram noted that the common hall doubled as a cook room "in the winter season" (William Bartram, "A Journey from Spalding's Lower Trading House to Cuscoilla and the Great Alachua Savanna," BP, HSP, Small Bartram Volumes, p. 304). According to his journal, Cuscowilla comprised forty houses, not thirty; Bartram, "Travels in Georgia and Florida," p. 147.

51. Bartram refers to "the yard belonging to each dwelling or household," not to the community's chunky yard or plaza. William Bartram, "A Journey from Spalding's Lower Trading House to Cuscoilla and the Great Alachua Savanna," BP, HSP, Small Bartram Volumes, p. 305. See figures 34 and 35 in chapter 3, this volume.

52. To those species identified in note 27, Bartram here added gourds (*Lagenaria vulgaris* Seringe) and several more types of squash and pumpkins (*Cucurbita pepo* L.), all native plant domesticates, and what he terms "Dolichos varieties," probably cowpeas or blackeyed peas (*Vigna unguiculata* [L.] Walpers) of African origin. Wagner, "African Plants," p. 114; Gregory A. Waselkov, "Seventeenth-Century Trade in the Colonial Southeast," p. 128; Kristen J. Gremillion, "Adoption of Old World Crops." The redundancy of crops—principally corn and beans—grown in both village

gardens and out-fields may have reduced risk of total crop failure by ensuring that at least a seed crop could be produced each year; Doolittle, "Agriculture in North America," p. 397.

53. The contributions to public granaries observed by Bartram were presumably a vestige of the redistributive economies of the Seminoles' prehistoric Mississippian predecessors.

54. The Camino Real, or Old Spanish Highway, reached from St. Augustine westward to St. Marks and on to Pensacola. Myer, "Indian Trails," p. 833.

55. Two informative sketches of colonial-period Indian hunting camps can be seen in *Von Reck's Voyage*, p. 117; and Charles Callender, "Shawnee," p. 625.

56. Notice again the peculiar usage of "Lower Creeks and the Nation or Upper Creeks"; see note 24.

57. A reasonable estimate places Seminole population at around 1,500 individuals in 1775. Peter H. Wood, "The Changing Population of the Colonial South," pp. 55–56.

58. Bartram undoubtedly provided his friend Benjamin Smith Barton with information on these animals for the latter's manuscript on North American mammals, which contains these passages: "The Creek Indians call this animal [Bartram's "tiger" or panther] *Causta.* . . . Some of these animals have been killed in the country of the Creek-Indians, that were nine and ten feet in length, from the nose to the end of the tail," and "In the country of the Creek-Indians *large black wolves* are common." Keir B. Sterling, ed., *Notes on the Animals of North America*, pp. 8, 41, 44.

59. On the punishment for adultery, see Hudson, *Southeastern Indians*, pp. 199–201.

60. In a single sentence, Bartram brilliantly epitomized the dilemma of ever-increasing Indian dependence on European material goods caused by the deerskin trade. See Calvin Martin, *Keepers of the Game*; Charles M. Hudson, "Why the Southeastern Indians Slaughtered Deer." For discussion of additional impacts of European trade, see Gregory A. Waselkov, "French Colonial Trade," and "Historic Creek Indian Responses to Trade."

61. Bartram discussed this journey in a letter to Lachlan McIntosh, dated July 15, 1775 [probably 1774], Dreer Collection, Scientists, Historical Society of Pennsylvania.

62. Buckskins and doeskins, in various stages of processing, served as standards of trade in the eighteenth-century Southeast. Weights ranged from one pound for a dressed doeskin to three pounds or more for a raw hide from a large buck. For an examination of the trade, see Braund, *Deerskins and Duffels.*

63. This herding dog was, almost certainly, a border collie, an ancient breed developed in Scotland.

64. Researchers have located Talahasochte at Ross Landing on the Suwa-

nee River, six miles upstream from Manatee Spring, Harper, ed., *Travels of William Bartram,* p. 372, Peck, ed. *Bartram Heritage,* p. 92.

65. Nearly 200 dugout canoes, some dating as old as 5,000 years, have been found at archaeological sites in Florida; Lee Ann Newsom and Barbara A. Purdy, "Florida Canoes." On their ocean-going canoes the Seminoles evidently used sails on masts. Wilfred T. Neill, "Dugouts of the Mikasuki Seminole" and "Sailing Vessels of the Florida Seminole." The tobacco received as a present from the governor of Cuba was *Nicotiana tabacum* L., the species originally domesticated in South America, not the native North American species.

66. Bartram's *Travels* is the only account placing the Seminoles on "the bay of Calos," or Calusahatchee Bay (at modern-day Fort Myers), during this period. A band of Indians calling themselves Calusas inhabited this area in the 1840s, but most of the surviving native Indians of Florida fled to Cuba in the 1760s to escape raids by the Muscogulges. See Swanton, *Indians of the Southeastern United States,* p. 102; Lewis, "Calusa"; Widmer, *Evolution of the Calusa;* and Hann, *Missions to the Calusa.* By the 1770s, Seminoles and Lower Creeks frequented the southern regions of the peninsula, including Tampa Bay and the Calusahatchee Bay, to trade with Cuban fishermen. Kathryn E. Holland, "The Path Between the Wars," pp. 104, 123–24, 194, 206, 222. Hawkins included "Culloosauhatche" in his 1799 list of Seminole settlements; *Letters, Journals and Writings of Benjamin Hawkins* 1:289.

67. These were the ruins of San Luis de Talimali and other Spanish missions in Apalachee, destroyed and abandoned in 1704. John H. Hann, *Apalachee: The Land Between the Rivers;* Gary Shapiro, "Archaeology at San Luis"; Richard Vernon, "Town Plan and Town Life"; Gary Shapiro and Bonnie G. McEwan, "Archaeology at San Luis."

68. Bartram's journal entry about the White King's feast differs from his description in *Travels:*

> At night a large fire was kindled in the middle of the Square, which was soon surrounded by Indians dancing & singing[.] we soon heard the Drum beat in the Square & a messenger came to invite us to eat Bear Ribs and honey, it being the Kings treat, having killd some bear[.] they never eat the Ribs when out but bring them to the Town, where they make a feast in the square to the warriors & hunters; We accordingly repared to the Square where the Men were assembling[.] they made way for us & placed us near, where the barbecued Ribs were served up in large Platters or wooden boles in One of the chief houses of the Square[.] We had kettles of honey & water, with a great wooden family Spoon in each Kettle, every one in turn took a sup or quaff, discoursing of cheerfull subjects as he liked[,] as hunting adventure, jokeing, News of love, intreagues &c., The youth & Young fellows

dancing[,] singing & wrestling about the Fire, When every one seemed
satisfied with eating & drinkin, We repared to the Fire, where the King
appeared & join'd us, in a circle seated round about the fire[.] the
Youth ceased their jollity, & with drew at some distance, the Men pass
the Pipe about the Ring, and discourse of more serious affairs with the
greatest gravity and decorum. (Bartram, "Travels in Georgia and
Florida," pp. 157–58)

69. The calumet ceremony was an elaborate greeting ritual used by many
southeastern Indians during the late seventeenth and eighteenth centuries
to help establish peaceful relations with Europeans or with other Indian
groups. The calumet itself consisted of a stone pipe bowl (usually made
of the red stone catlinite) and a cane pipe stem (*chalumeau,* in French),
painted and adorned with feathers and other attachments. Brown, "Calumet Ceremony."

John Bartram wrote an eyewitness account of a calumet ceremony performed by Seminole headmen at the Congress at Picolata for Governor
James Grant and Superintendent Stuart, on November 18, 1765:

REMARKS ON YE CONGRESS HELD IN A PAVILLION[,] which was 9 paces
long & 4 wide[,] covered over ye top with pine branches. ye back & half
of each side is walled with ye like materials: two poles is placed on each
side as far as open[,] wraped round with blankets for ye indian chiefs to
sit upon[.] ye Governour sate on ye back of ye pavilian & ye
Superintendent on his left hand[,] faceing ye open end[,] with A table
before them[.] ye indian Chiefs assembled about 150 yards distance in
ye same plain in which ye pavilian stood[,] right in front[,] to about 50
in number[,] marching in A colomn 6 in front[;] on one side too that
caried on thair arms A number[—]perhaps 20 each[—]of buckskins
dresed[,] & on ye other side 2 other chiefs[,] each carying A pipe
dressed with eagle feathers[,] by which ye interpreter marched[,] & A
rattle box: thay marched with an easy pace[,] sometimes danceing[,]
singing[,] & shouting[,] & every now & then halting. but when thay
came withing 20 paces of ye pavilian[,] thay halted 4 or 5 minits[.] then
ye 2 chiefs advanced prety fast[,] with A kind of dance[,] to ye
Governour & superindendant[,] which thay stroaked alternately all over
thair faces & heads with thair eagle feathers sorounding thair pipes,
then gently retired backward[,] danceing[,] to ye enterance of ye
pavilian[.] then returned to ye colum[,] which still halted[,] saying A
few words to them[.] then advancing with An easy pace to ye Governour
& superintendent[,] with whome thay shaked hands very friendly[,]
both standing up[.] ye 2 indians sate down & ye other succeeding chiefs
came[,] 2 or 4 at A time[,] all shakeing hands[.] then taking thair

place[,] sitting down on each side[,] & so on till all had paid thair respects that was minding[.] then ye 2 indians with dresse[d] skins on thair arms spread most of them on ye Governours & superindenants seat & ye rest before ye table[,] at each end or side of which sate one of ye grand chiefs[;] & at A 2 or 3 yard distance stood 3 interpreters: one of ye cheef indians held ye pipe of peace by ye bole while ye governour & superintendant & chief indians smoked[.] then ye superintendant opened ye affair to them. (John Bartram, "Diary," p. 51)

70. The "black drink" or "cassine" was a tea brewed from the dried stems and leaves of yaupon (*Ilex vomitoria* Ait.), a plant native to the southeastern coastal plain but transplanted widely by the Cherokees and Creeks. John Bartram, "Diary," p. 27; *Letters, Journals, and Writings of Benjamin Hawkins* 1:15. Only men consumed the black drink, partly for its high caffeine content and partly for its presumed purifying effects. Because Europeans sometimes observed Indians vomiting after taking the black drink (hence the species designation), some attributed a violent emetic effect to the tea. Europeans who themselves partook of the beverage, however, suffered no ill effects, so evidently the purgative vomiting was learned behavior associated with the achievement of purity. The black drink ceremony cleansed men of bodily and spiritual pollution and so was performed before every meeting of the council or other important town events. Hudson, *Southeastern Indians*, pp. 226–27; Charles H. Fairbanks, "The Function of Black Drink"; Hann, "Use and Processing of Plants," pp. 94–97.

Incidentally, many of the Spanish Franciscan missionaries in Florida drank the brew regularly, claiming it helped prevent kidney stones. Robert A. Matter, "The Spanish Missions of Florida," p. 135. John Bartram thought the black drink "an excellent tea, not less pleasant than oriental teas, and much more wholsome." John Bartram, "A Journey up the River Savannah," p. 168.

71. The term "Coonti" referred not only to the reddish flour procured from *Smilax bona-nox* L., as described here by Bartram, but also to flour extracted from a fern-like cycad (*Zamia floridana* A. DC.) by the Seminoles in the nineteenth and twentieth centuries. John R. Swanton, "Coonti"; Harold D. Cardwell Sr., "Coontie Root: The Dangerous Blessing."

72. Deerskins, seemingly always at hand, often provided convenient containers for liquid foodstuffs. Du Pratz described the process by which they were made. "When a deer is brought, they cut off the head, and then take off the skin whole, beginning at the neck, and rolling it down, as they cut it, like a stocking. The legs they cut off at the knee-joints, and having cleaned and washed the skin, they stop up all the holes except the neck, with a kind of paste made of the fat of the deer mixed with ashes, over which they tie several bindings with the bark of the lime-tree. Having thus provided a kind of cask, they fill it. . . ." [Antoine Simon] Le Page Du Pratz, *The History of Louisiana*, p. 249; also *Nairne's Muskhogean Journal*, p. 55.

73. Bartram's errata list for *Travels* attributes the seven young Seminoles to Caloosahatche, not Talahasochte. *William Bartram: Travels and Other Writings*, ed. by Thomas P. Slaughter, pp. 610–11. Bartram elaborated on the appearance of the "young prince" and his companions in his report to Dr. Fothergill:

> His head was shaved smooth all except a crest of hair left about an Inch long, which was cut in a circular form from the Crown reaching to the back part of his head, All his head that was shaven & his neck to his shoulders painted with Vermilion, his crest black & shone like a Raven, his head was adorned with a Diadem or Cor[o]net of Furs, which incircled his temples & went round just over the top of his fore hed, curiously wrought with Beads, & on the fore part of it waved, a high Plume of white Heron feathers, he had a large Silver gorget on his breast, & a Silver Mirror & Cross. The rest were elligantly dress & painted, with Coronets wrought ingeniously of split quills dyed of different colours & Plumes of blue Heron feathers. they had Red and blue Mantles or Match coats, fringed or laced, performed by their wives. (Bartram, "Travels in Georgia and Florida," p.160)

Bartram also described the party in a letter to Lachlan McIntosh, dated July 15, 1775 [probably 1774], Dreer Collection, Historical Society of Pennsylvania.

> We set off to return to Mr. Spaldings Stores on St. Johns In the Evening we stopt with a company of Indians who were reposing in the shade of One of these pleasant Groves or Islet commanding a prospect of a vast verdat Meadow, inameld with various Flowers & glittering Plains of Water under Spreading Oaks, Laurel & Palm Trees. They were Seven Young Seminole Fellows neatly dresst & Painted after the Indian [Fashion] tho' all were Young they seemed to be under the conduct of the oldest who affected a more grave & serious deportment & who was reclining on a Scaret Cloth Mantle. They all espress't the hightest pleasure for our visit by the most cheerful & courteous behavour, [in] these I saw simple Nature without constraint, all their movement, of body & mind, sprightly, familiar yet unstudied. These Seminole's are generally Tall well Limbed agreeable Features, they love the English.

74. Bernard Romans, *A Concise Natural History*, p. 81, observed much the same behavior among Choctaw women during his visit to that tribe in 1771.

75. Charles McLatchy, who ran James Spalding's stores on the St. Johns River, in 1783 became one of the original partners of Panton, Leslie & Company, the British firm that dominated West Florida Indian trade for several decades. Coker and Watson, *Indian Traders*, pp. 33–34.

76. The Creek-Choctaw War of 1763 to 1776, abetted by a British colonial policy that encouraged division and conflict among the militarily

powerful Indian groups of the interior Southeast, created a vast area (most of modern-day south-central and western Alabama) where intertribal warfare prevented intensive hunting. This sort of buffer zone between warring tribes acted as a deer preserve in a region where European traders exerted considerable pressure to continually harvest more deerskins and deplete the game supply. Braund, *Deerskins and Duffels;* Harold Hickerson, "The Virginia Deer and Intertribal Buffer Zones"; E. Randolph Turner, "An Intertribal Deer Exploitation Buffer Zone."

77. This reference to Bartram's "apartment in the council-house" reflects one of the functions of the public buildings in southeastern Indian towns: to serve as temporary living quarters for travelers and for those elderly or orphaned townspeople without relatives. Note, in his account farther on, that this particular council house had a back door.

78. In the southeastern Indian belief system, rattlesnakes were dangerous, anomalous creatures, associated with the underworld but living in the world of humans. Although none of the Seminoles claimed to have the "freedom or courage" to kill the snake, Bartram occupied a sufficiently ambiguous role as a guest in their society to suggest that he might be able to do so. Bartram's interest in plants, many of which had medicinal functions, paralleled the knowledge of Seminole priests and curers, who would be expected to know the ritual precautions against vengeful snake spirits. And he was an outsider, not bound by the same notions of pollution and purity, and therefore perhaps free to do what others could not. The Seminoles' response, once Bartram had dispatched the serpent, is equally instructive. By offering to scratch him, they hoped to draw off some of the excess blood that made him potentially dangerous to himself and others. His refusal to undergo a cure that any Seminole would have realized was necessary is probably once more attributable to his ambiguous relation to their society. Bartram's behavior must have puzzled his would-be curers as they went off proclaiming, probably still with some trepidation for his well-being, that "Puc-puggy was their friend."

Incidentally, his characterization of this attempt to cure him by scratching as a "ludicrous farce" has led some to maintain that Bartram thought the Indians insincere in their efforts or that he ridiculed the custom. In other contexts (such as his references to "the war farce" on pp. 263 and 504), however, Bartram used "farce" as a synonym for ritual or ceremony, not for pretense or travesty.

Bartram's drawing of the head of an eastern diamondback rattlesnake may depict this very specimen; see Ewan, ed., *William Bartram: Drawings,* p. 79, pl. 50.

A manuscript note in Bartram's handwriting contains this additional information:

I never understood that the nations of Indians I was amongst had any
Idea of the Fascinating Power of Snakes. They rather hold this animal in

a degree of Veneration & regard. It looks to me much more like the
superstition brot by the whites with them from the old World. In my
opinion The N^or. American aborigines are not Remarkable for
Superstition. But one or two small Fables or Legends of The Egyptians,
Chaldeans, Persians, Greeks or Roman even at the most Flourishing
Period & Sciences, & wisdom & Polite Learning were at their Meridian
would begger all the Superstition of the American Aborigines, together,
even admitting [?] History of the Mexicans to be true. (Indian
Materials, Barton Collection, APSL)

79. Bartram mentioned this town previously on pages 92–93 of _Travels_.
80. The dates of Bartram's movements during this period were determined by Harper, ed., _Travels of William Bartram_, pp. 379–80. In a letter to
his father, written on March 27, 1775, Bartram indicated his resolve "to
continue my travels another Year. Intend to go through the Cheroke &
Creek Countries to Pensacola where I shall send my necessary baggage, & if
it please God to spare me life & health I may go to the Missisipe River." BP,
HSP, vol. 1, p. 78.
81. John Bartram had earlier described Galphin as "an Indian trader,
who constantly employs 400 pack-horses in trading through the Creek
nations, Chicasaws, Chactaws, and other Indian tribes." "Journey up the
River Savannah," p. 167.
One of the wealthiest and most influential traders in the Southeast, and
of revolutionary sympathies, George Galphin was named in July 1775 to the
Committee of Inquiry for Indian Affairs by the South Carolina Provincial
Congress, charged with the responsibility of maintaining peaceful relations
with the Creeks. Wilfred T. Neill, "The Galphin Trading Post"; James H.
O'Donnell III, _Southern Indians in the American Revolution_, p. 20; Fritz
Hamer, "Indian Traders."
A copy of his letter of introduction for William Bartram reads as follows:

To Mssrs. Graham, Garmeny, Mossley, Carnell, Cussin, or any other
Gent^m. of my aquentins in the Creeke Contrey.
Gent^m. the berer Mr. Barteram is a gent^m. I have none a Lange time[.]
he is an onest worthey man[.] he is Imploy^d. by some of the first people
in England to procure flowers. Seeds & roots of the Diferent Spasemens
that is in amaraca to send home to them[.] any Serves you can Do him
or any Sevelty Showin him I shall Esteame it as a faver Don me[.] I am
Gent^m
Your very humbe Servent
George Galphin
Ap^le. 30 1775 (Darlington Papers, New York Historical Society)

The Mason's plantation site, possibly the largest Mississippian site along
the Savannah River, was located about a mile north of Silver Bluff before

being washed away by the floodwaters of that river in the late nineteenth century. Charles C. Jones Jr., *Antiquities of the Southern Indians,* pp. 148–57; Clarence B. Moore, "Certain Aboriginal Mounds"; David G. Anderson, *Savannah River Chiefdoms,* pp. 193–94.

82. Bartram was traveling during a very dangerous time. Many Cherokees, angered by repeated encroachments by white settlers from the Carolinas and Virginia, were calling for war against the colonial settlements. Stuart was driven from Charleston in May 1775, amidst charges of inciting the Cherokee warriors against the rebellious colonists. Two months later, George Galphin was appointed South Carolina Indian commissioner. Thus, by the time Bartram headed west along the Creek trading path in 1775, the revolutionary turmoil had reached the South, and Bartram would have been fully aware of it. In West Florida, sentiment favored the Crown. After leaving West Florida, most individuals Bartram encountered sided with the American cause.

83. Known as the Rembert Mounds group, in Elbert County, Georgia, this site was largely destroyed by flood erosion in the nineteenth century and is now submerged under a reservoir. The niches in the side of the large mound remain unexplained, but the spiral ramp (also seen on the major mound at the Lamar site near Macon) may have been created merely by cattle grazing on the mound. The Rembert Mounds dated to A.D. 1450–1650 and may have been abandoned only a century before Bartram's visit. Jones, *Antiquities,* pp. 284–85; Cyrus Thomas, "Report on the Mound Explorations," pp. 315–17; Joseph R. Caldwell, *The Rembert Mounds,* pp. 314–15; Robert Wauchope, *Archaeological Survey of Northern Georgia,* pp. 371–74; Anderson, *Savannah River Chiefdoms,* pp. 194–96. Using much the same language as he employed in his book, Bartram described these mounds to Benjamin Smith Barton in a letter preserved in the Gray Herbarium Archives, Harvard University.

84. Lochaber was Alexander Cameron's plantation on Penny Creek, a tributary of Long Cane Creek, where a treaty between the British and the Cherokees was signed on October 18, 1770. Alden, *John Stuart,* p. 279.

85. Angelica is described in some detail in Bartram's "Observations" (see chapter 3, Bartram document, note 62).

86. During the Cherokee War of 1759–61, Col. Thomas Middleton, before abandoning the campaign, was the commander of the South Carolina provincial troops who assisted Col. James Grant and his British regulars. Corkran, *The Cherokee Frontier: Conflict and Survival, 1740–62,* pp. 178–254.

87. Cherokee population estimates for this period range from 7,000 to 8,500. Wood, "Changing Population," pp. 64–66; M. Thomas Hatley, "The Three Lives of Keowee," pp. 224–27; Russell Thornton, *The Cherokees: A Population History.*

88. For a view of life at Keowee during the traumatic eighteenth century, see Hatley, "Three Lives of Keowee."

89. The Cherokees' annoyance may have been well founded. In 1743 there had been a temporary influx of prospectors from Savannah and Augusta when rumors circulated that silver had been found on Cherokee lands. Hatley, *Dividing Paths,* p. 43.

90. For a summary of the rather scant archaeological attention devoted to Lower Cherokee sites, see Michael A. Harmon, *Eighteenth Century Lower Cherokee Adaptation.*

91. Old Sticoe was near "the Dividings," where the path diverged and led to the Overhill and Middle towns. See Hatley, *Dividing Paths,* Figure 8.

92. Bartram's footnote refers to the second battle of Echoy, which took place on June 10, 1761, when Cherokees attacked an invading force of British regular and provincial troops led by Lt. Col. James Grant, who was assisted by Colonel Middleton, the provincial commander.

Archaeologists debate the nature of the stone piles seen by Bartram. They are common in central and northern Georgia along the Upper Oconee River. The excavation of one in the Lower Cherokee region yielded some eighteenth-century European trade goods, but no human bones. Other rock mounds are much older, primarily dating to the Middle Woodland period, around 2,000 years ago. Jones, *Antiquities,* p. 202; Richard W. Jeffries and Paul R. Fish, *Investigations of Two Stone Mound Localities;* Harmon, *Lower Cherokee Adaptation,* p. 21.

93. These Middle Cherokee towns are usually referred to as Echoy (Itse'yi), Nucassee (Nikwasi), Watauga (Wata'gi), Cowee (Kawi'yi), and Jore or Ihore (Ayali'yi); Goodwin, "Cherokees in Transition," pp. 122–23.

94. Bartram meant the headwaters of the Little Tennessee River.

95. See note 70, on the black drink.

96. Little Carpenter, Attakullakulla, was a leader of the pro-English faction among the Cherokees and had visited London many years before as a young man. James C. Kelly, "Notable Persons in Cherokee History."

Southeastern American Indian forms of greeting included grasping and shaking the lower arms and striking or rubbing one's own body or that of the visitor. Swanton, "Social Organization," p. 449.

97. The remains of many Cherokee structures, winter and summer domestic houses as well as their much larger public counterparts, summer and winter council houses, were excavated at the Overhill town of Chota-Tanasee. Gerald F. Schroedl, "Louis-Philippe's Journal"; Gerald F. Schroedl, ed., *Overhill Cherokee Archaeology.*

98. In a manuscript version of *Travels,* Bartram included the following additional information: ". . . there is but one outside door which is plac't on one side of the building so as to enter at the middle appartment." William Bartram, "Travels through the Carolinas, Georgia, and E^t. & W^t. Floridas," manuscript, 2 vols., p. 14, BP, HSP, Small Bartram Volumes. His description of house walls incorporating horizontal notched logs suggests some influence from European traditions of log construction.

99. This last thought is expressed differently in a manuscript version of

Travels: ". . . sometimes [the] whole roof is cover'd with earth cast over upon a layer or stratum of small brush & dry grass." Ibid., p. 15. The use of earth as a roof covering has been noted archaeologically. Roy S. Dickens Jr., *Cherokee Prehistory,* pp. 98–100; Craig T. Sheldon Jr., "Public Architecture of the Historic Creeks." A skeptical interpretation of Bartram's statement is presented by Lewis Larson, "The Case for Earth Lodges."

100. Frank G. Speck, Leonard Bloom, and Will West Long, *Cherokee Dance and Drama,* pp. 55–62.

101. The mysterious stone features observed by Bartram near Keowee may have been Mississippian stone box graves. Most stone box graves have been found in the Cumberland Valley of Tennessee, but they are also known from other regions, including this area of northern Georgia, where several were found by excavations in mounds at the Peachtree, Etowah, and Nacoochee sites. One might speculate that the unusual above-ground location of Bartram's specimens might have occurred if the stone boxes had originally been placed in an earthen mound that then eroded. Jones, *Antiquities,* p. 216; Joseph Jones, "Explorations of the Aboriginal Remains," pp. 8–9; Ian W. Brown, "A Study of Stone Box Graves," pp. 10, 13.

102. For comparative lists of eighteenth-century Cherokee towns, see Goodwin, "Cherokees in Transition," pp. 122–23; and Betty A. Smith, "Distribution of Eighteenth-Century Cherokee Settlements."

103. Bartram's "company of adventurers" probably was not a contingent of the "Company of Military Adventurers" who attempted to settle lands in the lower Mississippi Valley. The "military adventurers" were colonial veterans of the Seven Years' War, mostly from New England. Their land claims in the Yazoo region were challenged by the Choctaws, and the outbreak of the American Revolution ended this colonization effort. Bartram's travel companions may have been engaged in illegal liquor traffic in the Creek country, and he may simply have applied a phrase, commonly in use at the time, to an unrelated group of travelers. Since Bartram specifically notes that they were joined by legitimate "traders," the "company of adventurers" must have been engaged in some other activity. Their identity remains a mystery. See Robin F. A. Fabel, "Encounters Up the Mississippi," p. 102, and *Economy of British West Florida,* pp. 153–97.

104. The traders' method of equine persuasion seems to be a variant of the English practice of "twitching," whereby a rambunctious horse is made docile by pinching its lips with a rope noose. Evart Lagerweij et al., "The Twitch in Horses."

105. The movement from the Oconee River took place during or immediately after the Yamasee War of 1715; the migration to Florida probably occurred about 1750. The Oconees were the first Muscogulges to settle in Florida, becoming the first of the Seminoles. John R. Swanton, *Indian Tribes of North America,* p. 135; William C. Sturtevant, "Creek into Seminole"; Fairbanks, "Ethno-Archeology of the Florida Seminole."

The copy of the journal Bartram sent to Dr. Fothergill contains another account of the origin of the Seminoles.

I indeavoured to get a true account of the origen of the Indians of that part of Florida commonly called the Creek Nation; And being acquainted with a considerable Trader who resided for many Years amongst them, and spoke their Language perfectly well: & there being present at this time a very sensible and a very ancient Indian Chief of that People. I desired him to inquire of the old Chief, whether they who call them selves Muscogulges, were the Aborigines of Florida; He answered. That the land now inhabited by them, was, when they came to possess it[,] under the dominion of the Cherokees, or Mountainers[,] which was about the time that S°. Carolina was planted by the English, who drawing away the Savanahs or Yamases, the Indians of the lower parts of Carolina; who moved along southerly[,] took possession of the Sea Coast & small Islands, of Georgia & Florida[,] & joining with the Spaniards of Augustine drove away the Cherokes back to the Mountains. But they the Muscoges or Creeks ariving, Who they say come a long way from the Sun setting from a great River called bur[n?]tstone River, They say they are decendants from two great & powerful Nations, who became so numerous their Country was not able to contain the[m,] united in the same league to go in search of a new Country, that t[he] lower Creeks came from the head of that great River & at last the great River (messisepe)[,] they ar[riv]ed in this country; But met with opposition from the Spaniards of Augustine, who not receiving them friendly, they moved along farther & setled on the Okmulge River[,] part of the Alatamaha[,] & hearing of the English or white People Northerly, some of their Chiefs went to them, at Charlestown in S°. Carolina, who took them friendly by the hand, calling them Brothers: They were glad[,] recieving at the same time Hatchets, knives[,] Kettles[,] Guns, & Cloathing, which was very acceptable to them; having till then very fiew Necessaries[,] only Bows to kill Deer & Bear with, Flint knives & hatch[ets,] Clay potts & skins for cloathing; And that in consideration of the friendship & commerce with the whites, they made an everlasting league & allience with the English, against their enemies, the Spanierds & Yamases[,] who they say they have intirely conquered and extirpated except a small remnant of Yamasees, they have recieved amonst them[,] who dwell near the Appalatches. But inquiring farther who were the Antient Natives of E.ᵗ Florida. He said he could not tell, but, he said that, when they the Muscogulges come there, the People were very few[,] wild and wandering about the country without any setled habitations[,] living very poor & wretched[,] eating Fish[,] Oisters or what they could pick up. That the greatest part were conquered by the Spaniards[,] that there was a little Town of them, near the Bay of Calos, called Calusahatche, & this nation they called

Calosulges, Ulge in the Muscoge Tongue signifying People or Nation, there were some remnants of other different Nations[,] antients of the Itmous, & of some that were very famous & powerfull: The Names & Vestiges of their Towns still remaining[,] particularly a very powerfull & warlike Nation, called Painted People, from their painting their Bodies all over with various colours & Figures of Animals[,] Birds, Beasts[,] Frogs[,] fish, Alegators, Plants & Flowers, & another Great Nation call'd Bat Necks: some of these People were alive when we came in this land, but all These Antient People are destroy'd & carried into Slavery, except a few which the Spaniards caried away with them to Cuba; when that country was deliverd up to the English. This is the substance of the accounts I got from The Antient Chief concerning his Nation & Country. (Bartram, "Travels in Georgia and Florida," p. 171)

106. From the Oconee to Mobile, except for a detour north to Tallassee, Bartram followed trails that became the Federal Road in the early nineteenth century. Peter J. Hamilton, "Indian Trails and Early Roads," pp. 422–29; Henry D. Southerland Jr. and Jerry E. Brown, *The Federal Road*, pp. 12–14.

107. This approximate date was determined by Harper, ed., *Travels of William Bartram*, pp. 400–401.

108. Yuchi Town was situated on the Chattahoochee River, near the mouth of Uchee Creek, in present-day Russell County, Alabama. The Yuchi language was quite distinct from both Muskogee and Savanna (or Shawnee, an Algonquian language). Linguists consider Yuchi a "language isolate"; that is, it cannot presently be associated with any other language family, although some have suggested that it may be distantly related to Siouan. James M. Crawford, "Timucua and Yuchi"; J. Joseph Bauxer, "Yuchi Ethnoarchaeology," p. 372.

109. Apalachicola Town was a white, or peace, town (in contrast to those towns of the opposing Creek moiety division designated as red, or war, towns, such as Coweta), which was why no blood was supposed to be shed there. Swanton, "Social Organization," p. 252; Harper, ed., *Travels of William Bartram*, pp. 399–400.

110. Coweta Town was near modern Phenix City, Alabama.

111. This story probably refers to the "massacre" of traders during the Yamasee War, although John Swanton thought it must have occurred earlier, perhaps during a Creek and English attack on the Apalachicolas in 1707–8. However, Apalachicola and several other Chattahoochee River towns continued to be occupied between 1690 and 1715, when the majority of the population had shifted to the Oconee and Ocmulgee river valleys. Harper, ed., *Travels of William Bartram*, p. 400; also see Hann, *Apalachee*, p. 189. Bartram's site of "ancient Apalachucla" may be the Rood's Landing Site (9sw1), although it is much farther than one and a half miles from

the village of Apalachicola. Frank T. Schnell, personal communication, August 26, 1993; Caldwell, "Rood's Landing."

112. In Harper's edition of *Travels*, John Swanton stated that he was mystified as to where Bartram got "the idea that the Cherokee were dominated by the Creeks or stood in fear of them." Swanton's limited access to eighteenth-century British records and the absence of a complete history of the Creeks during the colonial era account for Swanton's confusion. Modern historians have vindicated Bartram. Harper, ed., *Travels of William Bartram*, p. 400; Corkran, *Creek Frontier;* Braund, *Deerskins and Duffels.*

113. The next two towns were located along the eastern and southern bank of the lower Tallapoosa River. Tallassee was situated just below the falls, near the mouth of Euphapee Creek. Atasi was about five miles to the southwest. Both sites are now in Macon County, Alabama. The site of James Germany's store at Old Kolumi, about five miles west of Atasi, is in Montgomery County; Kolumi of Bartram's period lay across the river, in Elmore County, but the site evidently has been destroyed by river erosion.

114. Rosin weed (*Silphium* cf. *integrifolium* Michx.) grows abundantly on the prairies of south-central Alabama.

115. These grapes probably were muscadines (*Vitis rotundifolia* Michx.). Swanton, *Indian Tribes of North America,* p. 288.

116. Harper concluded that this is the most likely date for Bartram's arrival in Mobile, although the chronology of this section of *Travels* is very confused. Harper, ed., *Travels of William Bartram,* p. 404.

117. Peter Swanson and John McGillivray were among the leading merchants of British West Florida. From their headquarters in Mobile, they controlled a large share of the trade with the Creeks, Chickasaws, and Choctaws after 1763. John McGillivray was the nephew and heir of Lachlan McGillivray, the well-known Creek trader from Augusta and a close associate of George Galphin. See Fabel, *Economy of British West Florida,* pp. 46, 55–56; John Fitzpatrick, *The Merchant of Manchac,* p. 44; Edward J. Cashin, *Lachlan McGillivray, Indian Trader;* Braund, *Deerskins and Duffels,* pp. 57–58.

118. Mobile was founded in 1702, as the first settlement in the French colony of Louisiana, at a location on the Mobile River about fifty miles north of the Gulf of Mexico. The town was removed to its present location, at the head of Mobile Bay, in 1711 and remained in French hands until the British took control in 1763. See Peter J. Hamilton, *Colonial Mobile.*

119. Maj. Robert Farmar commanded the British force that occupied Mobile in 1763. He soon obtained a plantation on the bluffs of the Tensaw River, where he resided after retirement from the army. Bartram visited Farmar in late July and August 1775, using the plantation as a home base from which he explored the Mobile–Tensaw delta by canoe. Hamilton thought the plantation was at Stockton, Alabama, but Harper placed it four miles north. The archaeological site has not been found. Robert R. Rea,

Major Robert Farmar of Mobile, pp. 135–36; Hamilton, *Colonial Mobile,* p. 194; Harper, ed., *Travels of William Bartram,* p. 404.

120. Bartram either forgot where he saw the Old Mobile site and misplaced it far up the Tombigbee River, or he may have seen a prehistoric Mississippian town site that he mistook for Old Mobile. It could not have been the site of Old Mobile and Fort Louis de la Mobile, occupied by the French from 1702 until 1711, which was at Twenty-seven Mile Bluff on the Mobile River. Hamilton, *Colonial Mobile,* pp. 299–300; Jay Higginbotham, *Old Mobile;* Gregory A. Waselkov, "Archaeology of Old Mobile."

121. Bartram's trip to Pensacola was unplanned, and once there, he states in *Travels* (p. 414), that he hoped to "conceal my avocations" from the leading citizens of the town. He was not able to do so. Whether or not Bartram's refusal of this offer had anything to do with Bartram's views of the growing conflict between Great Britain and her colonies is unknown. In any case, Chester's official letter does provide an accurate date for this part of the journey; BP, HSP, vol. 1, folder 79.

122. Bartram's companion was William Dunbar, a young planter and naturalist who had recently emigrated from Scotland. Bailyn, *Voyagers to the West,* p. 492; Harper, ed., *Travels of William Bartram,* p. 409.

123. A village of Alabama Indians accompanied the French colonists from Fort Toulouse, at the confluence of the Coosa and Tallapoosa rivers, who moved west of the Mississippi River in 1764 to escape British rule. Capt. Philip Pittman, *Present State of the European Settlements,* p. 24.

124. The Natchez destroyed the French settlements in their territory in 1729, but were themselves nearly annihilated in a long series of wars with the French. Du Pratz, *History of Louisiana;* Dunbar Rowland and Albert G. Sanders, eds., *Mississippi Provincial Archives,* vol. 1; Patricia K. Galloway, ed., *Mississippi Provincial Archives,* vol. 4.

125. As usual, Bartram's year is inaccurate; Harper, ed., *Travels of William Bartram,* p. 410.

126. "Mr. Tap——y" was John Adam Tapley, the licensed trader at Muklasa or Muccolossus and an employee of George Galphin. David Taitt, the British commissary to the Creeks, arrested the trader and sent him to Pensacola along with evidence against him for "digging up the bodies of the Coweta Indians and likewise for several felonies." The governor of West Florida, Peter Chester, ignored the charges and failed to examine either Tapley or Taitt's evidence against him. David Taitt to John Stuart, November 22, 1772, CO5/74, f. 64. Tapley, as George Galphin's agent, was the target of the British commissaries again in 1776, when Thomas Brown, head of the loyalist East Florida Rangers, attempted to arrest him for his pro-Revolutionary leanings. Tapley was freed by the Indians but was then turned over to David Taitt. Edward J. Cashin, *The King's Ranger,* p. 49.

127. These were loyalists, fleeing the war in Georgia to join other refu-

gees who were settling mainly in the Mobile and Natchez areas. Daniel H. Usner Jr., *Indians, Settlers, and Slaves*, p. 112.

128. Sawanogi, or Savannuca, was a village of Shawnees, earlier known as Savannahs. The town lay on the north bank of the Tallapoosa River, in present-day Elmore County.

129. Muklasa, also on the north bank of the Tallapoosa, was the residence of the Wolf King, one of the most prominent Upper Creek headmen.

130. The "Alabama" town visited by Bartram at the confluence of the Coosa and Tallapoosa rivers apparently was the same town later known as Taskigi or Tuskeegee. John R. Swanton, *Early History of the Creek Indians*, p. 209.

131. Fort Toulouse, a French trading entrepôt and military post, stood at this site from 1717 to 1763. Daniel H. Thomas, *Fort Toulouse*.

132. Tukabatchee, the most populous and influential Upper Creek town, was located on the west bank of the Tallapoosa River, just below the falls. Swanton, *Early History of the Creek Indians*, pp. 277–81; Vernon J. Knight Jr., *Tukabatchee*.

133. Atasi was located not upstream but downstream, a few miles below the mouth of Calebee Creek. Harper, ed., *Travels of William Bartram*, p. 412.

134. In 1936, members of the Alabama Anthropological Society excavated eight large support posts from a council house at the site of Atasi. This rotunda, which may have been the one described by Bartram, was about ninety-four feet in diameter. A series of sequentially occupied council houses has been excavated recently at the nearby site of Fusihatchee. Gregory A. Waselkov, "History of the Alabama Anthropological Society," p. 71; Craig T. Sheldon Jr., "The Council Houses of Fusihatchee."

135. Bartram clearly is in error on this matter. Creek women were excluded from participation in some specific ceremonies, since gender separation was considered a form of purification. But other visitors recorded the presence of women in council houses. Caleb Swan, "Manners and Arts in the Creek, or Muscogee Nation," p. 265; Davies, *Documents* 5:261; *Letters, Journals and Writings of Benjamin Hawkins* 1:320.

136. See note 70 for a discussion of the black drink. Bartram here describes the ritual of the black drink singer, or *Asi Yahola*. The early nineteenth-century Seminole leader Osceola held this ceremonial title. Patricia R. Wickman, *Osceola's Legacy*, p. 31.

137. These "animals of the king's family or tribe" of course are the species for which clans were named. The Bear clan was very important; Wildcat, Otter, and Snake much less so. Swanton, "Social Organization," pp. 158–62. Benjamin Smith Barton mentioned, probably on the authority of William Bartram, that "the Creek Indians call this animal [the otter] *Oó sá ná*." Sterling, ed., *Notes*, p. 29.

138. Archaeologists found a small painted portion of a council house

wall at the late Mississippian site of Toqua, in eastern Tennessee. Richard R. Polhemus, "The Toqua Site," pp. 208–9.

139. Blue flag (*Iris versicolor* L., or more likely its southern counterpart, *Iris virginica* L.) was widely employed as an effective cathartic. Lyda A. Taylor, *Plants Used as Curatives*, p. 10; Richard A. Yarnell, "Aboriginal Relationships," p. 165; Virgil J. Vogel, *American Indian Medicine*, pp. 105, 283–84; Charlotte Erichsen-Brown, *Medicinal and Other Uses of North American Plants*, pp. 228–31. Just such a pond as Bartram mentions, created by digging for clay, has been found during recent excavations by Auburn University archaeologists at the site of Fusihatchee. James Adair saw a smaller example, "a broad and shallow clay hole, contiguous to the dwelling house" at a Chickasaw town; Adair, *History of the American Indians*, p. 306.

140. The correct year is 1776. Harper, ed., *Travels of William Bartram*, p. 412.

141. The Chehaw or Chiaha are thought to have been Hitchiti speakers; Hitchiti (along with Creek, Alabama, and Koasati) was one of several distinct Muskogean languages spoken in the Creek Confederacy. Swanton, *Early History of the Creek Indians*, p. 172; Mary R. Haas, "Southeastern Languages," pp. 299–326.

142. Numerous eighteenth-century accounts mention the use of skin boats by both Indians and whites in the Southeast. Braund, *Deerskins and Duffels*, p. 95 and p. 236, note 63; N. D. Mereness, ed., "A Ranger's Report," p. 219; Davies, *Documents* 5:280; Neill, "Coracles"; Adair, *History of the American Indians*, pp. 291–92; Swan, "Manners and Arts," p. 253. Bartram's description of the traders' leather canoe suggests a European form, probably of Celtic origin.

143. Comparative lists of Creek towns are presented by Albert S. Gatschet, "Towns and Villages," and Swanton, *Early History of the Creek Indians*, pp. 434–37.

144. Muscogulges, and the European traders living with them, applied the intentionally derogatory name "stinkard" generally to any non-Muskogee speakers (as did Bartram in his list of Hitchiti speakers living on the Chattahoochee River) and specifically to the Alabamas, who joined their confederacy late in the seventeenth century. Waselkov and Cottier, "Eastern Muskogean Ethnicity," p. 26. In a similarly demeaning fashion, the Natchez elite referred to commoners in their own society as "puants" or stinkards, according to French sources.

145. The combined Creek and Seminole population in 1775 exceeded 15,000 and perhaps approached 20,000 individuals. Wood, "Changing Population," pp. 55–60; J. Anthony Paredes and Kenneth J. Plante, "Creek Indian Population Trends: 1738–1832."

146. Du Pratz, *History of Louisiana*.

147. By "Lingo" Bartram meant the "Stinking Lingua" or stinkard language (see n. 144).

148. Once again the dates of Bartram's travels are those determined by Francis Harper. Harper, ed., *Travels of William Bartram*, pp. 417, 422.

149. Stature estimates based on skeletal remains of eighteenth-century Cherokees and late prehistoric Mississippians (possibly Muscogeans), from archaeological sites in eastern Tennessee, indicate average adult heights of 5 feet 6 inches for males and 5 feet 2 inches for females. Douglas W. Owsley and Helen L. O'Brien, "Stature of Adult Cherokee Indians," p. 75; Thomas M. N. Lewis and Madeline Kneberg, *Hiwassee Island*, p. 163; Polhemus, "Toqua," p. 465.

150. In Harper's edition of *Travels*, John R. Swanton stated, "Bartram seems to have misinterpreted entirely the attitude of the Cherokee and Creeks toward each other." But Bartram's account is accurate, and his description of the New Purchase conference adds valuable details to the extant records. Harper, ed., *Travels of William Bartram*, p. 423.

151. A Frenchman, Louis LeClerc Milfort, underwent induction as *tastanagi* or war leader at Tukabatchee in 1780. Milfort, *Memoirs*, pp. 33–36, 99–102.

152. Creek *kithlas*, prophets or "knowers," were also called jugglers or "jongleurs," according to Jean-Bernard Bossu. Other ranks of shaman included medicine makers (*hilís háyaki*) and doctors (*alikchaki*). Bartram has provided us with the only detailed account of a high seer or shaman. Jean-Bernard Bossu, *Travels*, pp. 147–50; John R. Swanton, "Religious Beliefs," p. 616; Joel W. Martin, *Sacred Revolt*, pp. 123–25.

153. This pipe may be the one sketched by Bartram (figure 14). His drawing is now in the British Museum of Mankind. Ewan, ed., *William Bartram: Drawings*, p. 64, pl. 26.

154. The earliest direct trade between Charleston and the Upper Creek towns began around 1690. Bearers, particularly Apalachees and other Indians captured from the Spanish missions of northern Florida, were the mainstay of the trade until after the Yamasee War of 1715. Wright, *Only Land They Knew*, pp. 160–61; Waselkov, "Seventeenth-Century Trade," p. 118.

155. Bernard Romans's drawing of a Creek warrior with large ear hoops illustrates this fashion. Romans, *A Concise Natural History*, plate opposite p. 93.

156. This is the earliest description of Seminole music. Frances Densmore, *Seminole Music*, p. 40.

157. Songs borrowed from neighboring societies were highly prized throughout the eastern Woodlands. Jack F. Kilpatrick and Anna G. Kilpatrick, *Muskogean Charm Songs*; Howard and Levine, *Choctaw Music and Dance*.

158. Creek towns competed in the two-pole ball game described by Bartram. Another version, the single-pole ball game, pitted a single town's women, using their hands, against the men, using racquets. Mary R. Haas, "Creek Inter-town Relations," p. 89.

159. Bartram's busk seems to have been either Creek or Seminole. His information may have been obtained secondhand, as Witthoft suggested, though he may have witnessed the Cuscowilla busk in August 1774. His account of the thoroughgoing destruction of household utensils was corroborated by Milfort, writing about a busk ceremony at Otchiapofa in the 1780s. John Witthoft, *Green Corn Ceremonialism,* p. 58; Swanton, "Religious Beliefs," pp. 580–81.

160. See note 53.

161. For a more thorough, modern consideration of the topic, see Kathryn E. Holland Braund, "Guardians of Tradition."

162. The two reeds plainly represent husband and wife, who stand together to support the Creek household just as poles in the fields support the growing crops. Amelia R. Bell, "Separate People," p. 336.

163. Among southeastern tribes, children belonged to the lineage of their mother. Bartram presents no evidence that he understood the social implications of matrilineages.

164. Recent archaeological excavations at protohistoric and early historic Creek and Cherokee town sites have confirmed that graves were placed immediately beneath the raised beds or benches of domestic structures. The "sitting posture" of corpses was a semiflexed position, with knees drawn up and arms crossed over the chest or abdomen. Schroedl, "Overhill Cherokee Archaeology," pp. 32, 247, 262; cf. Adair, *History of the American Indians,* p. 186; Swanton, "Social Organization," pp. 389–93.

165. "Canes" is evidently meant, rather than "bones."

166. John Swanton gathered together most of the available historical data on Choctaw burial customs. Swanton, *Social and Ceremonial Life,* pp. 170–75.

167. Cranial deformation of infants had been practiced across the entire Southeast, but the custom was declining in popularity by Bartram's time. Hudson, *Southeastern Indians,* pp. 31–32.

168. There were, perhaps, 14,000 Choctaws in 1775. Wood, "Changing Population," p. 72.

169. Mary Haas found that Koasati men's and women's speech differed, and she speculated that other Muskogee languages once had similar gender-based dialects. In essence, Koasati men substituted sibilant ("s") endings and long vowels for women's nasalized and short vowel word endings. Haas, "Men's and Women's Speech," pp. 142–49; Geoffrey Kimball, "Men's and Women's Speech," pp. 30–38; Bell, "Separate People."

170. James Adair confirms Bartram's view: "The Indians express themselves with a great deal of vehemence, and with short pauses, in all their set speeches. . . . And in their philosophic way of reasoning, their language is the more sharp and biting, like keen irony and satyr, that kills whom it praises." Adair, *History of the American Indians,* p. 66.

Introduction

1. Neither of the two surviving manuscript copies carries a title, so we have retained the title Ephraim G. Squier applied to the 1853 edition, by which name the work is widely known. Nor do the surviving manuscript copies carry Barton's name, but evidence clearly indicates that he was the author of the questions. Perhaps most telling is a reference in Barton's *New Views of the Origin of the Tribes and Nations of America*, p. xlvi, regarding the composition of the Muscogulge Confederacy, "On the authority of my friend Wm. Bartram. M.S. *penes* me." Furthermore, three transcribed passages from Bartram's "Observations" exist among Barton's papers at the American Philosophical Society, one of which credits "Mr. William Bartram, in M.S. penes me." Squier, ed., "Observations on the Creek and Cherokee Indians," pp. 3–4; cf. Helen Gere Cruickshank, ed., *John and William Bartram's America*, p. 346.

Joseph Ewan, ed., *William Bartram: Drawings*, p. 29, thought that the "Observations" manuscript was the basis for Barton's *New Views*, although this conclusion could not have been based on a reading of either work. Barton's book on the languages and customs of Native Americans includes comparative vocabularies and other ethnographic information derived from David Zeisberger, John Heckwelder, Thomas Jefferson, and many other correspondents and authors. Francis W. Pennell, "Benjamin Smith Barton as Naturalist," p. 112.

2. Though it is widely cited, evidently few Bartram scholars have carefully read his "Observations." One described it as "an abridgement of the material contained in [*Travels*]" and another thought it had been "incorporated without major revision, as the last five chapters of the *Travels*." Fagin, *William Bartram*, p. 63; Barnett, "William Bartram," p. 127, n. 16. A recent article inaccurately identifies, as the source of Barton's queries, the American Ethnological Society, an organization founded in 1842, long after Barton's and Bartram's deaths. In 1853 the society published Ephraim Squier's edited version of Barton's queries and Bartram's responses. Charlotte M. Porter, "William Bartram's Travels."

3. Benjamin Smith Barton to William Bartram, December 13, 1788, BP, HSP, vol. 1, folder 5.

4. Benjamin Smith Barton to William Bartram, August 26, 1787, Edinburgh, BP, HSP, vol. 1, folder 3. Barton wrote several other pamphlets and books on the American Indians, but he did not revise his first publication on the subject, thinking it immature and speculative compared with his later researches. Pennell, "Benjamin Smith Barton," p. 110; Frank Spencer, "Two Unpublished Essays," p. 569.

5. This undated document is filed with Barton's letter to Bartram dated

December 13, 1788, in BP, HSP, vol. 1, folder 5. However, it has clearly been misfiled. The letter and document are not attached, and there is nothing to indicate that they belong together. The content of both the "Queries" document and various letters indicates that the document should be paired with Barton's letter to Bartram of August 16, 1787, as this is the letter in which he requests information. Moreover, in the letter of December 13, 1788, Barton acknowledges Bartram's letter regarding Indian mounds. The one-page document, addressed to "Mr. Bartram," reads:

I shall be very much obliged to you for your answers to the following Queries.
— In what particular part, or parts, of America did you meet with the Artificial Mounts or Eminences, of which you make mention in your Journal? —
— What were the general forms, and hights of these mounts? —
— Have the Indians no tradition concerning them? —
For what purpose do you suppose they were erected? —
Have you in any part of your Travels, met with any Fortifications, such as I have described in my work? or with any other Vestiges of Antiquity? —
M^r. Bartram. — [written diagonally on left margin]
— I am, with the most sincere regard and respect &c

Please to put your answers to this paper.

6. Benjamin Smith Barton to William Bartram, February 19, 1788, BP, HSP, vol. 1, folder 4. As in his previous letter, he urged Bartram to proceed with the publication of his journal.

7. An undated draft of a letter from Bartram to Barton is preserved among the Jane Gray Autograph Collection, item 104a, Gray Herbarium, Harvard University. The following annotation heads the letter: "rough draught of a letter to Dr. Barton in answer to some enquiries of his concerning Indian mounds." The letter goes on to describe the great mound on the Savannah River about Dartmouth. There are no references to East Florida mounds in this letter. However, this is clearly part of Bartram's answer to Barton's letters of August 26, 1787, and February 18, 1788.

8. Barton refers to this letter on the artificial mounds in his subsequent inquiries. See Bartram's "Observations," query 13: "In the letter which you wrote to me concerning the mounts &c. . . ."

9. Benjamin Smith Barton to William Bartram, December 13, 1788, Amsterdam, BP, HSP, vol. 1, folder 5. In the letter, Barton noted, "I feel myself so much indebted to you; you have imposed so great an obligation on me, that I beg you will let me know in what manner I can serve you: I can easily procure you seeds of many of the curious, beautiful, and valuable species of East-India plants. . . ." In the same letter, Barton boldly also

solicited a drawing, botanical description, and dried specimen of the *Frank-linia alatamaha.* He wished to publish, with Bartram's "assistance and permission," a paper on the rare tree.

10. Perhaps Bartram continued to suffer from the eye malady he contracted while exploring West Florida. See Harper, ed., *Travels of William Bartram,* p. 407, for a description of the eye troubles that afflicted him. (His father also suffered from various eye problems.) Squier began his published version of "Observations" with Bartram's letter. Actually, Bartram wrote the letter as concluding remarks upon completing Barton's questions and prior to adding a postscript and illustrations. Squier, ed., "Observations," p. 9.

11. Squier, ed., "Observations," p. 9.

12. Barton and Bartram's joint projects include Barton's *Elements of Botany, or Outlines of the Natural History of Vegetables,* 2 vols. (Philadelphia: n.p., 1803). Bartram drew the illustrations for the work, which was so popular it went through six editions. Charlotte M. Porter, *The Eagle's Nest,* p. 160. The Muskogee names found in Barton's manuscript "Notes on the Animals of North America" may have been supplied by Bartram. Porter, "Drawings of William Bartram," p. 291; Sterling, ed., *Notes.* However, Barton had other sources of information on the Creeks as well. In *New Views,* pp. xlv, xlvi, xlvii, liii, he mentions his 1790 meeting with Alexander McGillivray and cites such other sources as James Adair's *History of the American Indians,* Bernard Romans's *A Concise Natural History,* and a manuscript by an unnamed "American officer." That officer was Maj. Caleb Swan, who accompanied McGillivray and the 1790 Creek treaty delegation home from New York in 1790.

13. Squier, ed. "Observations," p. 4.

14. Josiah L. Nott to E. Squier, April 10, 1854, Ephraim George Squier Papers, Library of Congress, series I, vol. 2, part 1, reel no. 3. According to Squier's "prefatory note" to the first published edition of "Observations" (p. 4), the manuscript had been "sent to Dr. Morton from Mobile, by a gentleman whose name is forgotten." In his letter, Nott wrote: "I see you published Bartram's mss. — it was I who sent them as a present to Morton." Unfortunately, Squier's answer to Nott is lost. Since Squier spoke with Morton about the manuscript, it seems highly unlikely that Morton would have neglected to mention the name of his former pupil. At the very least, it seems unusual that Squier did not make inquiries of Nott regarding the manuscript, since they were corresponding by 1848. But, as his biographer has noted, Squier was a "master opportunist" who consistently managed to profit from the generosity of others. Squier's relationship with Edwin H. Davis, coauthor with him of *Ancient Monuments of the Mississippi Valley,* dissolved amidst an acrimonious debate over the proper credit due to each. Terry A. Barnhart, "A Question of Authorship," and "Of Mounds and Men," pp. 82–96. William Stanton, *The Leopard's Spots,* p. 87.

For information on Nott's life and work, see Reginald Horsman, *Josiah*

Nott of Mobile; for information on Morton, see *A Memoir of Samuel George Morton,* and Robert E. Bieder, *Science Encounters the Indian,* pp. 55–103.

15. Both Morton and Nott were fascinated by phrenology. Morton's cranial studies, especially his *Crania Americana,* introduced metrical analysis to American physical anthropology. Despite his presentation of overwhelming data demonstrating equivalent cranial development among different races, he remained committed to a belief in the inferior mental and physical capacities of American Indians and African Americans. Moreover, in direct contrast to William Bartram, he believed Indian cultures debased and unredeemable. Ephraim Squier, to his credit, rejected the view of nonwhites as inferior species and thought all races endowed with comparable "mental and moral" abilities. See Robert E. Bieder, *Science Encounters the Indian,* pp. 55–103, for a modern assessment of Morton's anthropological significance. More information on this topic may be found in Stanton, *Leopard's Spots,* pp. 82–121.

16. For Squier's early activities with the American Ethnological Society, see Barnhart, "Of Mounds and Men." Bieder, *Science Encounters the Indian,* pp. 104–45, provides a critical examination of Squier's entire career.

17. Jerry E. Patterson and William R. Stanton, "The Ephraim George Squier Manuscripts," p. 310. In "Observations on the Aboriginal Monuments of the Mississippi Valley," p. 120, Squier explained:

> Subsequent to the preparation of the foregoing pages for the press, and at too late a date to permit the introduction, in another connection, of the facts it embodies relating to the aboriginal monuments of the South, a manuscript work on the Southern Indians by William Bartram, was placed in the hands of the investigators, by Dr. Morton, of Philadelphia. . . . [It] serves very much to explain the character and illustrate the secondary if not the primary purposes to which the southern monuments were applied. The accompanying illustrations are reduced fac-similes of Bartram's original pen sketches.

18. Squier, ed., "Observations," p. 4.

19. *Literary World,* October 16, 1850, p. 315.

20. *Literary World,* May 31, 1851, p. 440. Squier finished editing the manuscript in July 1851; Squier, ed., "Observations," p. 7.

21. *Literary World,* June 21, 1851, p. 499. Information on Squier and the society can be found in Robert E. Bieder and Thomas G. Tax, "From Ethnologists to Anthropologists."

22. John Swanton seems to be the earliest source of the story about the 1853 fire. According to Swanton, "The issue was actually struck off in 1853, but after about 25 numbers had been distributed the remaining copies were destroyed by fire. In consequence, few were aware of the existence of

the paper in question, which did not, in fact, receive much attention until the republication of the volume in which it appeared in the year 1909, after the revival of the old society." Swanton, "Religious Beliefs," pp. 495–96; also see Earnest, *John and William Bartram*, p. 154; Hallowell, "Beginnings of Anthropology," p. 76, n. 7. In fact, Squier's liberal use in his own publications of quotes and engravings based on "Observations" ensured that Bartram's information on historic southeastern Indian architecture and mound use did receive wide readership.

Some pre-Swanton references to Bartram's "Observations" include Samuel F. Haven, *Archaeology of the United States*, p. 21, n. 1; Jones, *Antiquities*, pp. 178–81; James C. Pilling, *Bibliography of the Muskhogean Languages*, p. 8; Thomas, "Mound Exploration," p. 656; Frank Hamilton Cushing, *Exploration of Ancient Key-Dweller Remains*; David I. Bushnell Jr., *Native Villages*. A facsimile reprinting of the 1853 edition appears in William C. Sturtevant, ed., *A Creek Source Book*. The first three volumes of the *Transactions of the American Ethnological Society* have also been micropublished as publication no. 129 of *American Natural History, Based on the Bibliography of American Natural History, 1769–1865, by Max Meisel*.

23. For biographical information on Payne, see Grace Overmyer, *America's First Hamlet*, especially pp. 297–330, and Charles H. Brainard, *John Howard Payne*. Payne's relations with Ross and his involvement in the Cherokee controversy are covered in Grant Foreman, "John Howard Payne"; Payne, *John Howard Payne to His Countrymen* and "The Captivity of John Howard Payne by the Georgia Guard." For Payne's "The Green-Corn Dance," John Swanton provided an introduction and notes in *Chronicles of Oklahoma*. The account of the murder trial has also been reprinted in Grant Foreman, ed., *Indian Justice*.

Of tangential interest is some evidence for Payne's interaction with Albert Gallatin, one of the founders of the American Ethnological Society and first president of that organization, who hosted society meetings at his home and who financially supported the publication of the first two volumes of the society's *Transactions*. Gallatin obtained a Cherokee vocabulary and a description of the tribe's culture from John Ridge, a leading Cherokee. This document eventually came into Payne's possession and is now housed with the John Howard Payne Papers at the Newberry Library in Chicago. The connection between Payne, on the one hand, and Gallatin, Squier, and the American Ethnological Society, on the other, is unclear. Bieder, *Science Encounters the Indians*, pp. 30, 43.

24. Harper, ed., *Travels of William Bartram*, p. 423. Bryllion Fagin mistakenly thought the Payne manuscript was written in Bartram's hand; parenthetical references in the Payne copy noting illegible lines in the original manuscript confirm its secondary nature. Fagin, *William Bartram*, p. 58.

25. J. Woodbridge Davis to Thomas Wilson, February 11, 1898, National Anthropological Archives, Smithsonian Institution, Washington, D.C. The

letter begins: "A year or two ago at your request I made a search among my father's papers for the field notes of his survey of the mounds in the Scioto Valley and finding what is perhaps the only copy of Bartrams manuscript sent it to you. My sisters helped me in this work. . . ." See William Bartram, "Observations on the Creek and Cherokee Indians," catalog no. 173,683, accession no. 31,588, National Anthropological Archives, Smithsonian Institution, Washington, D.C.

26. Frank Hamilton Cushing to I[saac] Minis Hays, January 20, 1899, American Philosophical Society. For a look at Cushing's career, see John Sherwood, "Life with Cushing."

Text

1. The following material is handwritten, on two sheets of paper, preceding Bartram's "Observations" in the John Howard Payne manuscript; the bracketed material is in a different hand from that of the rest.

[This appears to be John Howard Payne's copy of Wm Bartram's answers to Benj Smith Barton's queries about Indians.]
This book was formerly in the possession of John Howard Payne, whose initials it bears on its back. It was found among his effects at Tunis after his death by the U.S. Consul there & by him sent to Mr. R. S. Chilton of the Department of State who presented it to Mr. George Gibbs
Mr. Payne once travelled through the South himself.
[Placed with Bartram Papers]
R.S. Chilton, Washington, D.C.
to
George Gibbs Washington Jany. 1868

2. Based on his study of English documents dating from 1690 to 1715, Verner Crane determined that the name "Creeks" originated as an abbreviated form of the expression "Ochese Creek Indians," applied to several villages of Muscogulges living along the Ocmulgee River, known as Ochese Creek during that period. Verner W. Crane, "The Origin of the Name."

3. Calumet pipe bowls made from catlinite, found in present-day Minnesota, and other fine-grained red stones were widely traded among the eastern Indians during the late seventeenth and eighteenth centuries; see Brown, "Calumet Ceremony," p. 316. The "Red River" between Minnesota and South Dakota flows near the catlinite outcrops; this migration myth may, however, have confused the northern river with its like-named southern counterpart in Arkansas and Louisiana.

4. This passage essentially reiterates the migration legend recorded in Bartram, *Travels,* pp. 53–55.

5. See chapter 2, Bartram document, note 16.

6. Bartram refers to the largest mound at the Rembert site, described in *Travels*, pp. 324–26, and in chapter 2, Bartram document, note 83. He also mentioned this mound in an undated draft of a letter to Barton in Jane Gray's Autograph Collection, Gray Herbarium Archives, Harvard University.

7. Antoine Simon Le Page du Pratz lived in the French settlement at Natchez prior to its destruction in 1729 by the Natchez chiefdom; his book is one of the principal ethnohistorical sources on those Indians; Du Pratz, *History of Louisiana*.

8. For a modern discussion of Natchez political organization and burial customs, see Hudson, *Southeastern Indians*, pp. 206–10, 255, 328–34.

9. See Bartram, *Travels*, p. 455; chapter 2, Bartram document, note 138.

10. Bartram provides one of the best descriptions of southeastern American Indian tattooing; Swanton, *Indians of the Southeastern United States*, pp. 532–36.

11. Benjamin Smith Barton, in his work on the mammals of North America, paraphrased and expanded on this portion of Bartram's "Observations": "The Creek-Indians call this animal [the bison] *Yon óu sák*. The Illinois-Indians dress the hides of the *Bison* with the hair on; and on the fleshyside they draw and paint the figures of animals, as the deer, &c. representation of the *Sun* and *Moon* and *Planets;* sketches of battles, &c. &c. Those *paintings,* I have been informed, are masterly productions, considered as the efforts of an unfortunate people, at present, in an humble form of society and improvement. Perhaps, they are the simple *Picture Annals* of this tribe, or nation, of the Americans." Sterling, ed., *Notes*, p. 27.

Painted buffalo skin robes or matchcoats appear in two drawings from the 1730s, one of a Yuchi by Philip von Reck and another by Alexandre de Batz, probably of an Atakapa. By Bartram's time, European-made cloth blankets had almost completely displaced painted skins, such as the "large painted blankets of catskin" offered to Spanish explorers in 1568. *Von Reck's Voyage*, p. 127; David I. Bushnell Jr., "Drawings of A. DeBatz," pl. 6; Hudson, *Southeastern Indians*, p. 263; Charles M. Hudson, *The Juan Pardo Expeditions*, p. 293; Morris S. Arnold, "Eighteenth-Century Arkansas Illustrated."

12. According to James Adair, fire was "their grandfather — and the supreme Father of mankind, *Esakàta-Emishe*, 'the breath master.' " Adair, *History of the American Indians*, p. 104; Corkran, *Creek Frontier*, pp. 35–36.

13. Bartram refers to the *Spirit of the Laws*, by Charles Louis de Secondat Montesquieu (published as *De L'Esprit des lois*, Paris, 1748), which specified virtue as an absolute necessity for a successful republican government. Porter, "William Bartram's Travels," p. 448.

14. In this paragraph Bartram offered a succinct, critical analysis of the opportunities he had to study the southeastern Indians, given the limitations of time and his necessary reliance on white interpreters and informants.

15. For an explanation of Bartram's unusual usage of these terms, see chapter 2, section of Bartram document tied to note 24.

16. The mico's control of the public granary and the responsibility to offer his people the "King's Feast" are, almost certainly, remnants of chiefly prerogative associated with Mississippian redistributive economies, in which the elite received food surpluses that were doled out to the populace in times of need. See chapter 2, Bartram document, note 53.

17. For a brief discussion of the black drink, see note 70 on p. 248. The caffeine content of yaupon tea produces the diuretic effect.

18. These roles continued to evolve during the colonial period, particularly among the Cherokees, who previously had had no war chiefs. Fred Gearing, "Priests and Warriors," pp. 101, 118.

19. During the sixteenth and seventeenth centuries the chiefdom of Calusa occupied the area of Calusahatchee Bay (modern Fort Myers, Florida); Spanish explorers and missionaries called the chiefs "Calos" or "Carlos," which was evidently a title of rank rather than a personal name. See Clifford M. Lewis, "The Calusa"; Randolph J. Widmer, *The Evolution of the Calusa;* John H. Hann, ed., *Missions to the Calusa.*

20. Long Warrior is unnamed in Squier's edition, where he is referred to simply as "the great warrior-chief." Squier, ed., "Observations," p. 25.

21. See Bartram, *Travels,* pp. 257–60.

22. See chapter 2, Bartram document, note 69, for comments on the calumet ceremony.

23. On the busk (*póskita* in Muskogee), or Green Corn Ceremony, see chapter 2, Bartram document, note 159. John Howard Payne witnessed a busk at Tukabatchee in 1835. Payne, "Green-Corn Dance"; Swanton, "Green Corn Dance."

24. Women were, in fact, permitted inside Creek rotundas, although at times excluded from some specific rituals held there; see chapter 2, Bartram document, note 135. According to Pope, a fire starter twirled between his palms a sassafras stick "bored into a Piece of dry Poplar." Each town's sacred fire, kept burning all year in the square ground or rotunda, was ceremoniously extinguished and rekindled anew during the busk. John Pope, *A Tour through the Southern and Western Territories,* p. 55; Hudson, *Southeastern Indians,* pp. 371–73.

25. Prior to the Creek civil war of 1813–14, Creek revitalization prophets obtained special knowledge through self-induced trance. For instance, one prophet, Captain Isaacs, gained supernatural power by "diving down to the bottom of the river and laying there and travelling about for many days and nights receiving instruction and information from an enormous and friendly serpent that dwells there and was acquainted with future events and all other things necessary for a man to know in his life." Theron A. Nuñez Jr., "Creek Nativism," p. 149.

26. These sources of vegetable pigments are pucoon or bloodroot (*Sanguinaria canadensis* L.), madder (*Galium trifidum* L., conspecific with *G. tinc-*

torium L.), red maple (*Acer rubrum* L.), poison ivy (*Rhus radicans* L.), and poison oak (*Rhus toxicodendron* L.). Ann Leighton, *American Gardens*, p. 305. Pucoon and madder roots and red maple bark were commonly used for dyes. T. N. Campbell, "Medicinal Plants," p. 287; Yarnell, "Aboriginal Relationships," p. 161; Vogel, *American Indian Medicine*, p. 213; King, "Plants, People, and Paleoecology," p. 72; Erichsen-Brown, *Medicinal and Other Uses of North American Plants*, pp. 80–81, 267–68, 318–21.

Rubia is now genus *Galium* (bedstraw, cleavers, madder), which includes many dye species. Leighton, *American Gardens*, p. 475.

Sanguinaria canadensis was also known for its emetic properties. Daniel E. Moerman, *Medicinal Plants of Native America*. In 1803, William Bartram participated in an experiment on that subject performed by William Downey, who was pursuing a medical degree at the University of Pennsylvania. Four hours after breakfast, Bartram was given some "gummous matter," powdered pucoon root dissolved in water. "In fifteen minutes a slight nausea came on with a burning at the stomach; forty, he complained of a head-ach, the nausea, at intervals, much more violent; sixty, he was vomited twice, the motions were pretty strong"; quoted in Vogel, *American Indian Medicine*, p. 354.

A manuscript by Benjamin Smith Barton contains some additional thoughts on Indian dyes. "M^r. Bartram tells me he has been informed, by the Indian Traders, that the very elegant Scarlet Colour with which the Indians die different substances is made in the following manner. — They purchase, of the Traders, the shavings, or shreds, of fine scarlet cloths: — from these shreds they extract the scarlet tinge, or colour by boiling; and the liquor extracted is mixed with the juice of the *Rubia Peregrina*, — perhaps with that of the Galium Boreale, as Forster says this plant is used by the Indians in dying their quilts, &c. &c. — " Barton Collection, Indian Materials, APSL; Hatley, *Dividing Paths*, pp. 46, 253, n. 18.

27. Benjamin Barton contributed to a debate between American and European scientists on the causes of albinism. In an essay submitted to the Royal Medical Society of Edinburgh in 1787, he distinguished "true" albinism, a condition evident at birth, from disease-triggered partial depigmentation. These conditions were thought by many to be caused by differences in the environment, which had larger implications for the argument over the origin of human races between the monogenists and polygenists. Spencer, "Two Unpublished Essays."

28. Bear oil was commonly used throughout the Southeast to cover the hair and body. William Byrd of Virginia also noted its use "by the Indians as a General Defense, against every Species of Vermin. Among the rest, they say it keeps both Bugs and Musquetas from assaulting their Persons, . . . Yet Bear's Grease has no strong Smell." Swanton, *Indians of the Southeastern United States*, pp. 526–28; William Byrd, *Histories of the Dividing Line*, p. 276; Du Pratz, *History of Louisiana*, p. 249.

Smooth or common sumac is *Rhus glabra* L.

29. European and early American writers generally agreed on the hard lot of American Indian women, especially when compared with their perceptions of the supposedly carefree, idle life of Indian men. As southeastern Indian agriculture changed in the early nineteenth century, under pressure from federal agents, and as Native women lost economic power, Indian and Euro-American gender roles began to converge. James Axtell, *The Invasion Within*, pp. 152–55; Theda Perdue, "Southern Indians"; Braund, "Guardians of Tradition"; Thomas Hatley, "Cherokee Women Farmers," pp. 37–51.

30. Deer hunting was mainly a fall and winter activity (from November to February), when hides were heaviest and bucks in rut could be lured by decoys. Gregory A. Waselkov, "Evolution of Deer Hunting."

31. Some women accompanied their husbands on long fall and winter hunts to process the deerskins, which had to be scraped clean of fat and hair before sale to English traders. The sick and elderly stayed behind in the villages. Braund, *Deerskins and Duffels*, pp. 67–68.

32. See chapter 2, Bartram document, notes 11 and 26.

33. Potsherds constitute the bulk of the artifacts recovered by archaeologists from eighteenth-century (and later) Indian village sites in the Southeast. Long after most other native manufacturing was abandoned in favor of European-made alternatives, Indian women continued to make pots in traditional forms. The largest vessels were ideally suited for a cooking style that relied on long simmering. Karl Schmitt, "Two Creek Pottery Vessels"; John M. Goggin, *Indian and Spanish: Selected Writings*, pp. 180–213; Carol A. Mason, "Eighteenth Century Culture Change"; David J. Hally, "Vessel Assemblages"; Schroedl, "Overhill Cherokee Archaeology," pp. 289–331; Knight, "Tukabatchee," pp. 79–95, 155–64, 185–233.

34. Bartram refers to Cousaponakeesa, better known as Mary Musgrove or Mary Bosomworth, niece of the preeminent Lower Creek leader Brim and daughter of an English trader. Her assistance to Gen. James Oglethorpe, as interpreter and cultural intermediary, proved critical to the success of the Georgia colony in the 1730s. E. Merton Coulter, "Mary Musgrove."

35. Bartram must be alluding to the Lady of Cofitachequi, who figures prominently in Spanish accounts of Hernando De Soto's march across the Southeast from 1539 to 1543. In his description in *Travels* of Silver Bluff, South Carolina, Bartram mentioned "[315] various monuments and vestiges of the residences of the ancients, as Indian conical mounts, terraces, areas, &c. as well as remains or traces of fortresses of regular formation, as if constructed after the modes of European military architects, and are supposed to be ancient camps of the Spaniards who formerly fixed themselves at this place in hopes of finding silver." Largely on the basis of this supposition of Bartram's, John Swanton decided that Silver Bluff must have been the location of Cofitachequi, despite the complete lack of archaeological evidence for the presence of sixteenth-century Spaniards at Silver Bluff.

Cofitachequi actually may have been on the Wateree River. Swanton, *Final Report of the De Soto Expedition Commission,"* pp. 180–83; Anderson, *Savannah River Chiefdoms,* p. 194; Charles Hudson, Marvin T. Smith, and Chester B. DePratter, "The Hernando De Soto Expedition"; Chester B. DePratter, "Cofitachequi."

36. Remnants of large, solitary poles have been found near public buildings at early Mississippian sites in the Southeast; for example, see Frank T. Schnell, Vernon J. Knight Jr., and Gail S. Schnell, *Cemochechobee,* p. 35.

37. In 1732 Alexandre De Batz painted Bride-les-Boeufs, a headman of the Tunicas, holding a staff with three scalp hoops. Jeffrey P. Brain, *Tunica Treasure,* cover illustration; Bushnell, "Drawings of A. DeBatz," pls. 2 and 5.

38. The "chunky yard" took its name from the game of chunky, which involved throwing spears or poles at a stone disc rolled across the yard. Stewart Culin, "Games of the North American Indians," pp. 485–88.

39. Squier deleted this note from his edition of "Observations."

40. See chapter 2, Bartram document, note 144.

41. Bartram overstated his point regarding agricultural fields, since matrilineages held rights to cleared fields, planted fields, and fallowed old fields.

42. Creek and Cherokee settlements became increasingly dispersed after Bartram's tour of the region in the mid-1770s. By the time of forced removal from the Southeast, in the 1830s, many town centers consisted entirely of an isolated square ground or town house, with individual affiliated households scattered over several square miles. Richard Pillsbury, "The Europeanization of the Cherokee Settlement Landscape."

43. Apalachicola Town; see chapter 2, Bartram document, note 109.

44. Bartram inserted a small drawing of the Boston's household in plan view. All three surviving versions reproduce the buildings similarly, but only the Davis copy includes Bartram's key, listing the functions of the different structures (figure 15).

45. Storehouses full of deerskins gave the Indians considerable economic leverage in dealings with colonial trade administrators, who often found such market sophistication frustrating. By withholding skins from the trade when their value was low, hunters manipulated the market to their advantage, then released skins from their stockpiles as prices rose. Hatley, *Dividing Paths,* p. 284, n. 59. Instruments of economic control—such as standard price lists and trade regulations issued in Charleston, Augusta, Pensacola, and Mobile—belied the flexibility manifested in face-to-face exchanges occurring daily in the Indian towns.

46. Black slaves had attempted to escape bondage by flight to the Indian country from their earliest days in the English colonies. The Boston of Apalachicola was unusual in owning so many black slaves, but in the mode of slavery he followed Indian norms. See chapter 2, Bartram document, note 48.

47. See Bartram, *Travels,* pp. 257–60.

48. In *Travels* (p. 85), Bartram mentioned rice (presumably *Oryza sativa* L.) grown by the Seminoles. If the Old World domesticated species of rice was raised by the Seminoles, they must have obtained it from the plantations of South Carolina, Georgia, and East Florida, perhaps from runaway black slaves.

49. Regarding this paragraph, John Swanton commented, "If Bartram could have examined actual conditions more intimately he would probably have found that this exchange took place almost entirely between members of the same clan or members of linked clans or else between individuals connected by marriage." Swanton, "Social Organization," pp. 334–35.

50. This passage obliquely alludes to an incident related in Bartram, *Travels*, pp. 20–22.

51. For discussions of the devastating effects of this introduced Old World disease among the American Indians, see Ann E. Ramenofsky, *Vectors of Death*, pp. 146–48; Marvin T. Smith, *Archaeology of Aboriginal Culture Change*, pp. 54–85; and Michael K. Trimble, *An Ethnohistorical Interpretation of the Spread of Smallpox*.

52. The bacterial infection *Bordetella pertussis*, or whooping cough, another introduced Old World disease, was known for its high infant mortality. Ramenofsky, *Vectors of Death*, pp. 150–52.

53. The Cherokees had a similar "green corn medicine." Witthoft, "Green Corn Ceremonialism," pp. 44–47. Soaking corn in lye (a solution of water and ashes) to produce hominy releases the vitamin niacin. S. H. Katz, M. L. Hediger, and L. A. Velleroy, "Traditional Maize Processing." Indian Pink (*Spigelia anthelmia* L. and *S. marilandica* L., northern and southern species) proved quite effective as a vermifuge and was intensively harvested by Indians for sale to European colonists. Hatley, "Three Lives of Keowee," pp. 233–35; Romans, *A Concise Natural History*, p. 52; Taylor, *Plants Used As Curatives*, p. 51; Vogel, *American Indian Medicine*, pp. 348–49; Moerman, "Medicinal Plants," p. 467.

54. Abundant skeletal evidence supports the conclusion that syphilis originated in the New World. Brenda J. Baker and George J. Armelagos, "The Origin and Antiquity of Syphilis."

55. Bartram's writings (see chapter 2, Bartram document, note 139) are the earliest references to the use of these species as cures for syphilis. His list includes blue flag (*Iris virginica* L.), dwarf iris (*I. verna* L.), and queen's delight (*Stillingia* cf. *sylvatica* Gard.), all of which were considered to have other medicinal functions. Taylor, *Plants Used As Curatives*, pp. 10, 36; Yarnell, "Aboriginal Relationships," p. 165; Vogel, *American Indian Medicine*, pp. 105, 283–84; King, "Plants, People, and Paleoecology," p. 60; Moerman, "Medicinal Plants," pp. 237–38, 469–70; Erichsen-Brown, *Medicinal and Other Uses of North American Plants*, p. 229.

56. These plants are catbrier (*Smilax* spp.), cross vine (*Anisostichus capreolata* L., Bartram's *Bignonia crucigera*), and bays (*Persea* spp.), although

Bartram included sassafras (*Sassafras albidum* [Nuttal] Nees.) in the same genus. Leighton, *American Gardens*, p. 301; Taylor, *Plants Used As Curatives*, pp. 8, 24–25, 57–58; Campbell, "Medicinal Plants," p. 289; Moerman, "Medicinal Plants," pp. 93, 444–45, 459.

57. Squier, in his edition of "Observations" (p. 45), altered the phrase "a rigid abstinence with respect to eating and drinking," substituting "a rigid abstinence in respect to exciting drinks," which conveys quite a different meaning. Southeastern Indians believed most ill health was caused either by inadvertently offending an animal spirit or by violating some social rule or prescribed avoidance. For example, Bartram's encounter with the rattlesnake at Cuscowilla (*Travels*, pp. 260–63) offended the spirits of all snakes. His friends' effort to scratch him was intended to assuage the snake spirits' displeasure, which otherwise might cause illness. Bodily pollution could also lead to illness, the cure being avoidance of the source of pollution, such as certain types of food and drink, and purification of the patient. Hudson, *Southeastern Indians*, pp. 340–51.

58. European colonists first learned of the blue cardinal flower or great lobelia (*Lobelia siphilitica* L.) from the Iroquois, who thought it a cure for syphilis and a vermifuge. Vogel, *American Indian Medicine*, pp. 330–32; Moerman, "Medicinal Plants," p. 268; Erichsen-Brown, *Medicinal and Other Uses of North American Plants*, pp. 243–44.

59. Bartram's "White Nettle" is now known as tread-softly (*Cnidoscolus stimulosus* [Michx.] Engelm. & Gray); it is not the introduced European stinging nettle (*Urtica urens* L.). The wild potato vine (*Ipomoea pandurata* [L.] Meyer), also known as wild jalap or "man-root," was also a food source. Yanovsky, "Food Plants," p. 53; Vogel, *American Indian Medicine*, pp. 324–25.

60. Lizard's tail or swamp lily (*Saururus cernuus* L.) seems to have been used mainly as a poultice on wounds. The poisonous mandrake or may apple root (*Podophyllum peltatum* L.) is an effective vermifuge, and, more recently, a source of an antileukemia drug. Taylor, *Plants Used As Curatives*, p. 11; Moerman, "Medicinal Plants," pp. 446, 354–55; Vogel, *American Indian Medicine*, pp. 334–35; Erichsen-Brown, *Medicinal and Other Uses of North American Plants*, pp. 324–28.

61. Bartram refers to the South American ipecac (*Cephaelis ipecacuanha*).

62. Ginseng (*Panax quinquefolium* L.) was *hilis hatki*, white medicine, to the Creeks. Swanton, "Religious Beliefs," p. 657; Taylor, *Plants Used As Curatives*, p. 44; Alvar W. Carlson, "Ginseng"; Moerman, "Medicinal Plants," pp. 322–23. Francis Harper identified Bartram's "Nondo or White Root (perhaps Angelica lucida) or Belly-Ache Root," or what the Creeks called *notosa*, as lovage (*Ligusticum canadense* [L.] Britt.). But it may actually have been a species of *Angelica* (cf. *atropurpurea* L.). Squier gave the plant yet another name, "norida," in his edition of "Observations" (p. 46). Swanton, "Religious Beliefs," p. 325; Harper, ed., *Travels of William Bartram*, p. 438;

Witthoft, "Cherokee Indian Use of Potherbs," p. 252; Vogel, *American Indian Medicine,* pp. 272–73; Moerman, "Medicinal Plants," pp. 37–38; Erichsen-Brown, *Medicinal and Other Uses of North American Plants,* pp. 246–48.

63. Barton posed further queries to Bartram on the "Materia Medica" in 1792. Bartram's response is now preserved among the Benjamin Smith Barton Collection at the American Philosophical Society Library:

To B. S. Barton, M.D., Philadelphia
Kingsess Decemb^r. 29th, 1792.
My ingenius worthy Friend
. . . I wish it were in my Power to answer, to thy satisfaction, thy usefull queries concerning the Materia Medica of the Creeks and other Nations of Red Men, a perfect knowledge of which would be very interesting to Human Society.

I think I have observed that they have few Complaints, or bodily ailments in comparison to what Afflict the inhabitants of the Old Continent, or the White People of this.

Yet sometimes they have Mortal diseases, very calamitous, even to the depopulation of Towns, & almost extermination of whole Tribes, but these Awfull visitations happen but seldom, but when they do come it baffles the skill of their Physicians, Then they resign themselves to their fate. These scourges of Mortality seem to fall grieviously on their Children, in Hooping Coughs, & Sore Throat which they have no remidy for as I was informed. A grievious distemper called Pleurisy in the Head which is contagious and sweeps away the Adult, particularly Hearty Men. The <u>Fall Fever</u> or inflamatory Fever, sometimes destroy many of their Adults & the Small pox destroys all in its way, few escaping with their Life, & those are miserably disfigur'd. I believe the pestilential, or putrid contagious Fevers, by which I mean the <u>Yellow & Spotted Fevers</u> have not yet reach't them. The <u>Ague</u> is very common.

I do not know what particular remedy they use against each disorder, but I believe that most if not all their Remedies are Vegetables, applyed in various ways, particularly Emetics, Cathartics, Sudorificks, & Diureticks. The infusion or decoction of the leaves & tender young shoots of the <u>Ilex Casine</u> is perhaps the most powerful & effecacious vegetable Diuretick yet known, for its effects are almost instantanious after the draught; which I have experienced often; This famous decoction (called Black Drink) is consider'd rather as a preventative, than a Medicine, & I do not recollect that it is properly amongst their Physick Plants, Yet held in divine estimation, supposd to be ordaind for the preservation of their health. The Indian Physicians, injoin the patient strictly to regimen during their attendance on them and the Stove or Sweat houses are in constant practice.

They use Phlebotomy, by Scratching, & I believe Cuping, or at least sucking the blood out of the scarifications.

The Lower Creeks, Siminoles in particular, live perhaps in the lowest, & most inundated country on the Globe, yet appear to be healthyer & have fewer disorder than the Upper Creeks, whether they derive their advantages from the natural food & Air of the Country, I know not.

It is my opinion, from frequent observation, that a wet country, in a Hot & even temperate Climate, is more favourable to health & longivity, to Mankind, than a Dry country in those Climates.

Perhaps the unhealthiness of the People in the lower Region of the Carolina's & Georgia is more owing to the intemperate use of Ardent Spirits, fermented Liquors, high seasoned & Flesh food &c than to the Native Air they breathe & water which nature furnishes them with for cooling Drink. . . .

    I can assure Thee I am thy
      Sincere Friend
      W^m. Bartram

64. John Howard Payne added the sentence in square brackets when he transcribed Bartram's manuscript.

65. Although they began raising horses in the early eighteenth century, southeastern American Indians only gradually adopted Old World domesticated animal species for food use. Their reluctance may have been due to the abundance of meat available as a byproduct of the deerskin trade and to the labor investment in fences around their crops that animal husbandry required. Chickens were commonly raised by the 1750s, while hogs and cattle became commonplace during the 1770s and 1780s. Arthur E. Bogan, "A Comparison of Subsistence Strategies."

Benjamin Smith Barton, in his manuscript on North American mammals, added the following information, undoubtedly on the authority of his "ingenious friend Mr. William Bartram": "Our common *Wild Rabbit* is called by the Cheeroke, whose country it inhabits, *Chistow*." Additionally, "[the groundhog] inhabits the whole extent of the country of the Cheeroke-Indians, who call it Oconnee." Sterling, ed., *Notes*, pp. 36, 38, 44.

66. In the Creek towns, widows and other needy women supplied fresh vegetables to traders in exchange for trade goods. For this reason, the Creeks vehemently opposed the importation and use of plows and slaves by resident traders to produce their own food. In the nineteenth century, American agent Benjamin Hawkins touted the plow as a means to increase agricultural output, but his attempt to convert the Creeks to commercial farming was a dismal failure, ending abruptly with the Creek War of 1813–14. Braund, *Deerskins and Duffels*, pp. 75, 174–86. Hawkins's career is traced in Florette Henri, *The Southern Indians and Benjamin Hawkins*.

67. For a discussion of most of these species, see chapter 2, Bartram document, notes 10 and 27.

68. See chapter 2, Bartram document, note 71.

69. Bartram probably tasted the ripe, purplish, pulpy fruit of the Spanish

bayonet (*Yucca aloifolia* L.); cf. Swanton, *Indians of the Southeastern United States*, p. 287.

70. See chapter 2, Bartram document, note 12.

71. Bartam's eye problems began with a fever (perhaps scarlet fever) contracted in Mobile on his travels. Harper, ed., *Travels of William Bartram,* p. 407.

72. Here, and elsewhere, Bartram explicitly drew a direct connection between the earthworks he saw on his travels and Indians living in the same region.

73. Bartram's descriptions in *Travels* (pp. 390, 522) of the mound complex he saw at Apalachicola Old Town closely match the view depicted in these versions of his sketch of the "Antient Chunky Yard." The close similarity of all three copies suggests that they accurately portray the essence of Bartram's original. His observation of contemporary Creek rotundas on mounds such as these testifies to the continuity of southeastern Indian belief systems from the prehistoric to historic periods. Vernon J. Knight Jr., "Symbolism of Mississippian Mounds."

74. Squier deleted the first three sentences of this note in his edition of "Observations." His "reduced fac-simile" of the figure, however, incorporates the correction that Bartram expresses here. Squier, ed., "Observations," p. 52.

75. In his transcription John Howard Payne noted: "Here something is obliterated in the MSS."

76. A representation of the council house was not reproduced by Squier and, to our knowledge, has never before been published. The copies of the Bartram drawing once again match in most particulars, except that Davis seems to have omitted a few posts from the back wall of floor plan B, whereas Payne appears to have added an extra post to the back wall of the right floor plan. Davis's copy suggests that these structures were constructed with gable ends. Since twentieth-century Creek square ground structures have shed roofs, Bartram's depiction of double-pitched roofs with gable ends indicates an earlier architectural form, one that no other observer recorded. There are additional trees and other embellishments on Payne's version and several other of his copies.

Bartram saw many square grounds such as this in the course of his travels. His descriptions of the Cuscowilla and Talahasochte square grounds bear comparison; see *Travels,* pp. 191, 257. Craig T. Sheldon Jr., "Public Architecture of the Upper Creeks."

77. Bartram's plan of the typical arrangement of Creek public architecture contained a detailed floor plan of a Creek rotunda, which has been interpreted differently by our three copyists. Payne placed the hearth, with its spiral fire, and the central support posts off center. And no two agree on the number of central supports; Davis shows six, Payne seven, and Squier eight. Several historic-period rotundas or council houses have been exca-

vated by archaeologists, and they assist in interpreting Bartram's written descriptions and the copies of his sketch. He is the only firsthand observer to record a central support column, around which the spiral fire burns in the drawing. Since this feature has not been found archaeologically, Bartram may have recorded an unusual instance, perhaps an attempt at repair that involved the use of a central prop to maintain a sagging roof. He is also unique in the description and depiction of two concentric outer rows of posts. The innermost of these two rows may have upheld the raised beds used for seating, but no independent evidence suggests that those intermediate posts were necessary for structural support.

For further comparative information, see Bartram, *Travels,* pp. 450–53; Swanton, "Social Organization," pp. 176–79; Schroedl, ed., "Overhill Cherokee Archaeology," pp. 263–65; Sheldon, "Council Houses of Fusihatchee"; Shapiro and McEwan, "Archaeology at San Luis," pp. 1–70.

78. Although Bartram's text mentions only one "Plan of Mount Royal" at Lake George, both surviving copies of his document include two plans: a sketch and a finished drawing. Another version is an engraving of Bartram's sketch that was published by Squier and Davis in *Ancient Monuments* (p. 122) but not included in Squier's edition of "Observations." The three versions of the sketch differ enormously in scale and perspective. Bartram's finished drawing underwent considerable reinterpretation as well, judging by a comparison of the generally similar Davis and Payne copies with the two published versions, found in Squier and Davis's *Ancient Monuments* (p. 122) and in Squier, ed., "Observations," (p. 57). This site was obviously a favorite of Bartram's; see *Travels,* pp. 99–100, for one of his descriptions.

79. Borrow pits, as archaeologists term the ponds created when dirt was dug for construction fill, occur at many sites in proximity to mounds.

80. Squier's engraving of Bartram's Creek town plan has undoubtedly been reproduced more often than any other Creek ethnographic illustration, so the Davis and Payne manuscript copies may seem startlingly different from the engraving at first glance. Both show the town plan from a different viewpoint and in much greater detail, but the well-known Squier engraving captured the essential nature of Creek settlement patterns in the 1770s. Bartram did not, unfortunately, tell us whether this plan represents a particular town. But he did mention that all of these drawings were done from memory, so the layout of domestic structures and fences is probably not precise. Furthermore, archaeological research suggests that the households were more dispersed than Bartram has indicated here.

81. Compare this passage with his description in *Travels,* p. 191–92.

82. Squier inexplicably transcribed "Corn Crib" as "*council*" for his published edition, p. 56.

83. In Squier's edition of "Observations," "3 sides" appears as "their sides," p. 56.

84. Bartram included these tiny sketches of Cherokee house plans at the

end of his text. Once again, the Davis copy seems to have been drawn with more care, but all three reproductions show the same basic features. They differ principally in the number of posts in the front wall of the rectangular summer house. The Davis copy of this drawing was reproduced in Pillsbury, "Europeanization of the Cherokee Settlement Landscape," p. 64, the only one (to our knowledge) of these manuscript sketches to have been previously published.

4. "SOME HINTS & OBSERVATIONS"

Introduction

1. Gen. Henry Knox of Maine (1750–1806) saw active duty in the Revolutionary War. He was named the second secretary of war by the Confederation Congress in 1785 and held the same office under the Washington administration until 1795.

2. A number of studies have attempted to demonstrate the influence of American Indian government, primarily that of the Iroquois, on the framing of the U.S. Constitution. The argument is, as yet, unconvincing; while the framers may have employed Native American imagery and terminology, they rarely admired Native modes of government. See Donald A. Grinde Jr., and Bruce E. Johansen, *Exemplar of Liberty;* Bruce E. Johansen, *Forgotten Founders;* Bruce A. Burton, *Forgotten Founders;* Jack Weatherford, *Indian Givers.* This controversial topic is debated in Elisabeth Tooker, "The United States Constitution and the Iroquois League"; Bruce E. Johansen, "Native American Societies"; and Elisabeth Tooker, "Rejoinder to Johansen."

Though a number of the delegates to the Constitutional Convention, held in Philadelphia, visited Bartram at his garden, there is no evidence that he had any impact on the proceedings. Kenneth M. Anderson Jr., "The Travels of William Bartram," pp. 177–78, speculates that the adoption of the Constitution had an impact on Bartram's choice of words in his description of Indian government in *Travels.*

3. After 1787 Bartram produced a number of other similar discourses, all of which are incomplete and untitled. The first, cataloged as an "article on Morality," is found in BP, HSP, vol. 1, p. 81. An essay on slavery can be found on the reverse of an oversize "Catalogue of American Trees, Shrubs and Herbacious Plants . . . in John Bartram's Garden, near Philadelphia," Broadside Collection, Historical Society of Pennsylvania. One author mistakenly thought this to be an address by Bartram to the U.S. Congress. Peck, ed., *Bartram Heritage,* pp. 17, 54, note 49, 144. Two other similar essays are found in the Simon Gratz Collection, Historical Society of Pennsylvania. In one, an essay on birds, Bartram divided families of birds into tribes. The other work, incomplete "reflections or notions" on the relationship be-

tween "Reason" and "Senses," was written in 1795 and addressed to
"A. Laribore."

The longest essay, which has captured the attention of Bartram scholars,
is the incomplete, four-page, untitled draft found in BP, HSP, vol. 1, p. 83.
This essay concerns the moral sensibility of "brute creation," or animals,
and contains the following observations on Indians:

Thus it appears I think that we act most Rationally & virtuously when
our Actions seem to operate from simple instinct, or approach nearest
to the manners of the Animal creation. For if we examen minutely the
Morality Or Manners of Animals, & compare them with Those nations
of tribes of the human Race who yet remain in the simple state of
primitive Nature As Our Indians, who have had but little intercourse
with white people, we shall find but little difference between their
manners & the Animal creation in general

having resided some considerable time amongst several of these
Nations, I can give a pretty concise view, both of their Arts & sciences, &
their Morality.

In the first place, The male & female united [?] in reciprocul Love &
affection for the purpose of reproduction, the female shews the greatest
tenderness & solicitude for the young offspring, & both contribute to
rear them up to a state of maturity, & dont abandon them untill they are
old enough & able to mantain & defend themselves; they Build Houses,
retreats or castles, for defending themselves from the injury of the
Elimants, & for the defence & preservation of their Lives & their
offspring; to hoard up provision against a time of necessity, & to have it
convenient. They risque their Lives in defense of their persons &
property & likewise to obtain & defend their beloved mate or consort;
they comfort, defend, feed & protect their aged & decripid parents
Relations & friends. Being born with a naked & defencless skins, natural
Instinct, Intuitive Knowledge, or Reason tells them so & That the
Creator hath form'd them, with Members after such maner & form as to
inable them to fabricate natural Materials of which, Instinct, knowledge,
or Reason directs them how to form these manufactures into Cloths to
cover their Skin, to defend them from the scorching Sunbeams in the
South & the rigorous, chilling Winds & biting frosts in the North, or to
make use of furred Skins of Animals, for the same purpose. This same
comprehends most of the wisdom Knowledge & understanding of
Nations in simple state of nature, In their Attitude & expressions of
homage to the great Spirit the Almighty they look aloft to that awful [?]
upon uttering a Voice of ejaculation. When in a state of rest &
tranquility, or when their heart is warmed & animated with gratitude &
Love, they sing Hymns & Odes, Or when the Heart Throbs with sorrow,
& the whole frame agitated, with pain & anguish, either through bodily

disease or conflict of passion & affections, for the Death of a parent
Friend or Child, We need not ask them or converse with them by words,
to know the cause or meaning of all their various actions, operations, &
affections they speak themselves, they commune with the Achetypal
system of Ideas in each one of us. we know without asking a single
question. Tho we observe it in a nation we never saw or heard of
before. . . .

For a discussion of this essay, see Walters, "The 'Peaceable Disposition' of
Animals."

4. For information on Quaker efforts among the American Indians, see
Rayner W. Kelsey, *Friends and the Indians, 1655–1917,* and Sydney V. James,
A People among Peoples.

5. For example, see Bartram, *Travels,* p. 492.

6. The foremost study of Jeffersonian policy on Native Americans is Bernard W. Sheehan, *Seeds of Extinction.*

7. Francis Paul Prucha, *American Indian Policy,* p. 40; Reginald Horsman,
"United States Indian Policies," p. 32.

8. *American State Papers.* Vol. 1, class 2, *Indian Affairs,* p. 53.

9. McGillivray to O'Neill, March 28, 1786, in John W. Caughey, *McGillivray of the Creeks,* p. 104.

10. McGillivray to O'Neill, July 10, 1787, in Caughey, *McGillivray,* p. 155.

11. *American State Papers.* vol. 1, *Indian Affairs,* p. 77. See also Caughey,
McGillivray, pp. 119–20.

12. Lucia Burk Kinnaird, "The Rock Landing Conference of 1789." The
most accessible copies of the commissioners' reports are found in Linda De
Pauw, ed., *Senate Executive Journal and Related Documents,* pp. 188–99, 210–
41.

13. The Creek contingent was the first American Indian delegation to
travel to the seat of the new nation's government. For information on the
treaty, see J. Leitch Wright Jr., "Creek-American Treaty of 1790."

14. The Creek delegation arrived in Philadelphia on July 17, 1790, and
according to Willett, saw an "exhibition" at "Gray's gardens." Gray's Ferry
Gardens was a public garden on the Schuylkill River, not far from Bartram's
home. There is no entry in Willett's journal for Sunday, July 18, but on
Monday the delegation went sightseeing in Philadelphia and was visited
by a contingent of Quakers. That evening, the Creeks were treated to a
public dinner and attended the theater. The delegation left Philadelphia
on July 20, 1790. William M. Willett, ed., *A Narrative of the Military Actions of
Colonel Marinus Willett,* p. 112.

15. McIntosh served as the Georgia commissioner at the Treaty of Hope-
well with the Cherokees in 1785 and as commissioner to the southern
Indians in 1789.

16. Young Tate accompanied the delegation to New York and then ap-

parently returned to Philadelphia. He later spent time in Scotland under the tutelage of his grandfather, loyalist Lachlan McGillivray, who had been a partner of George Galphin prior to the war. *Pennsylvania Packet and Daily Advertiser,* July 15, 1790; Cashin, *Lachlan McGillivray,* p. 308.

17. Kathryn E. Holland Braund, "The Creeks and the Quakers." Barton, *New Views of the Origin of the Tribes and Nations of America,* pp. xlv, xlvii, liii. Barton also had access to a diary kept by Maj. Caleb Swan, who accompanied the Creek delegation on their return home from New York (p. xv). A portion of Swan's manuscript is preserved at the American Philosophical Society Library. For the published version, see "Manners and Arts in the Creek, or Muscogee Nation."

18. Hawkins's job proved permanent. The most recent account of his career is Henri, *Southern Indians and Benjamin Hawkins.*

19. Bartram, *Travels,* p. xxxiv.

20. *Letters, Journals and Writings of Benjamin Hawkins* 1:104–5.

21. Internal conflict among the Creeks, due in large part to disagreements over the "civilization program," resulted in a bloody civil war in 1813–14. See Henri, *Southern Indians and Benjamin Hawkins.*

Text

1. Manuscript initialed "WB" at the end of the document; Henry Knox Papers, Pierpont Morgan Library, New York City, vol. 47 (1793–95), p. 51. The notation by "W.B." also appears under the title in a different pen.

2. Here Bartram adopted the more conventional usage of "Muscogulges" for Upper and Lower Creeks and reserved the term "Seminoles" for the Native American inhabitants of Florida. It is clear from this passage, as well as many following, that Bartram kept informed on events in the South.

3. Perhaps Bartram refers to the Spanish attack on the first English traders at Coweta in 1685. See Corkran, *Creek Frontier,* pp. 50–51.

4. This is a reference to the depredations by the Creeks in Georgia and the Cumberland region.

5. Many Creeks did join the British in the American Revolution, on both the Georgia–East Florida front and in West Florida. Most of the Indian participation was confined to forages and joint skirmishes with loyalist or royal troops and was not aimed at civilians. See Corkran, *Creek Frontier,* 288–325.

6. This was the explanation promulgated by Alexander McGillivray for the Creek action against U.S. settlements and is largely true.

7. Bartram's only documented trip through the Creek towns occurred in 1775. However, it is possible that he made another journey to the towns in 1776, as he does not account adequately for much of his time during the last year of his travels.

8. George Galphin (1709–80) was named by the South Carolina Provi-

sional Congress as one of three Creek commissioners in July 1775. Later that summer, he was nominated to the Continental Indian Commission for the Southern District, which attempted to persuade the Lower Creeks to remain neutral during the war. In the Upper Towns, there was more widespread support for the British.

9. According to Bartram's chronology in *Travels* (as reconstructed by Harper, ed., *Travels of William Bartram*), this incident must have taken place sometime during 1776. The details cannot be verified in the extant records, but Native Americans did participate in most of the raids. For information on the vicious border warfare in the St. Mary's–Altamaha region, see Martha Condray Searcy, *The Georgia-Florida Contest*, and Cashin, *King's Ranger.*

10. These two sentences summarize the aims of the "civilization program."

11. Compare this sentence with the following from Bartram's introduction in *Travels*, p. xiv: "This world, as a glorious apartment of the boundless palace of the sovereign Creator, is furnished with an infinite variety of animated scenes, inexpressibly beautiful and pleasing, equally free to the inspection and enjoyment of all his creatures."

12. There was no "National Council" among the Creeks when Bartram toured their towns in the 1770s. The National Council was created later by Alexander McGillivray in an attempt to systematize the irregular, usually crisis-oriented meetings of the Creek headmen. See Michael D. Green, "Alexander McGillivray." See Braund, *Deerskins and Duffels,* for a look at Creek political organization during the time Bartram visited the Creek towns.

13. Bartram is virtually alone in his use of the word "invasions" rather than "explorations" or "settlements" during the eighteenth century. Today, the usage is common.

14. Bartram's assessment is correct and was repeated by the Indians themselves at every treaty involving the transfer of land during the British colonial period.

15. Bartram greatly overestimated the desire of the Indians to adopt Euro-American agricultural practices, which was the essence of "civilization" from the viewpoint of white Americans of the period. Perhaps he was convinced this was the Creek view by his conversations with deerskin traders, such as James Germany, who lived among the Creeks and who had Indian wives and families. Those traders and their offspring were practically the only ones who desired such "improvements." The call for Christian missionaries was virtually nonexistent, and when missionaries finally arrived in the early nineteenth century, they were usually ignored.

16. Bartram got this impression from a trader when he visited Atasi; *Travels,* p. 457. Very few traders — and fewer Muscogulgees — observed the Sabbath. The reason for their strange behavior at Atasi is unknown. Perhaps it was respect for Bartram.

17. Perhaps Bartram got this idea from James Germany, who lamented to Bartram that his Creek wife would not allow her son to leave the Indian country to attend school; Bartram, *Travels*, p. 449.

18. See Bartram, *Travels* (p. 234) for a reference to cochineal in West Florida. Bernard Romans also suggested that parts of Florida would be suitable for the production of the cacti upon which the cochineal insect feeds. The body of the female produced a dye used in the wool trade. Romans, *A Concise Natural History* (p. 157), believed that cochineal production would fare better in East Florida. There were attempts to produce the commodity in British West Florida; Fabel, *Economy of British West Florida*, p. 119. But Bartram was overly optimistic in believing that the insect could be raised in the Creek towns.

5. THE SIGNIFICANCE OF BARTRAM'S WRITINGS

1. Bartram, *Travels*, p. 118; Harper, ed., *Travels of William Bartram*, p. 355.

2. De Vorsey, "Early Maps," pp. 26–28.

3. Mattfield, "Journey to the Wilderness," p. 350; Barnett, "William Bartram," p. 52. Alexander von Humboldt similarly admitted several decades later to having "arranged the facts" of his American voyage "not successively in the order in which they have presented themselves, but according to the relations which they have between themselves," quoted in Padgen, *European Encounters*, p. 48. The chronological disorder of *Travels* has misled many later readers, such as Pamela Regis, *Describing Early America*, p. 42.

4. Harper, ed., "Travels in Georgia and Florida," p. 130. Quote from Darlington, ed., *Reliquiae Baldwinianae*, p. 235.

5. Barton, *Elements of Botany*, vol. 1, pp. x–xi; Pennell, "Benjamin Smith Barton," p. 113.

6. By his own admission, Bartram spoke no Cherokee, but was able to make himself understood in Muskogee. Bartram, "Travels in Georgia and Florida," p. 160; *Travels*, p. 362.

7. According to Wright (*Creeks to Seminoles*, p. 132), "The reader [of *Travels*] . . . is almost unaware that a momentous revolution was in progress. Such vagueness may have been because Bartram was a Quaker. Most American Quakers were lukewarm for independence. . . . In 1791 Bartram may not have wanted to explain why during the Revolution he was consorting with Tory Indian countrymen and merchants who encouraged Creeks to take patriot scalps."

8. Harper, "William Bartram and the American Revolution."

9. William Bartram, "A Journey from Spalding's Lower Trading House to Cuscoilla and the Great Alachua Savanna," p. 338, BP, HSP.

10. Harper, "William Bartram and the American Revolution," p. 572.

11. Cited in Harper, ibid., p. 573.

12. Ibid., pp. 573–74.

13. For information on Bryan, see Gallay, *Jonathan Bryan*, p. 94; Bartram,

Travels, pp. 148, 469–70; Harper, ed., *Travels of William Bartram,* pp. 345–46. Joel Martin considers it "telling that even a thinker as sympathetic and responsive to the Muskogees as this Quaker naturalist could not refrain from engaging in a fantasy of English settlement and commercial development." Martin, *Sacred Revolt,* pp. 89–90.

14. William Bartram to Lachlan McIntosh, July 15, 1775, Dreer Collection, Scientists, Historical Society of Pennsylvania. Bartram's letters home extolling the agricultural potential of the Indian country may have led James Mendenhall, a second cousin of William's, to obtain a grant of land in the Georgia New Purchase in December 1773. Welles, "William Bartram's Trail Through Nature."

15. Harper, "William Bartram and the American Revolution," p. 572; Peck, comp., *Bartram Heritage,* p. 43; Thomas Jefferson, *Notes on the State of Virginia.*

16. Francis Hutcheson, *An Inquiry into the Original of Our Ideas of Beauty and Virtue* (1725) and *An Essay on the Nature and Conduct of the Passions and Affections with Illustrations on the Moral Sense.* 3d ed. (London: A. Ward et al., 1728). See Henry F. May, *The Enlightenment in America,* pp. 81–84; Garry Wills, *Inventing America: Jefferson's Declaration of Independence,* pp. 176–96, 294; Barnett, "William Bartram," pp. 7–23.

17. Bartram, *Travels,* p. 22; cited in Patricia M. Medeiros, "Three Travelers," p. 205; for discussions of Edmund Burke's influence on Bartram's writings, see Richard M. Gummere, "William Bartram, a Classical Scientist"; and Regis, *Describing Early America,* pp. 42, 64–65.

18. Bartram document, "Some Hints and Observations," chapter 4, this volume.

19. Bartram, *Travels,* p. xxxiii.

20. Wayne Franklin, *Discoverers, Explorers, Settlers,* p. 48; Robert F. Berkhofer Jr., *The White Man's Indian,* pp. 48–49; Mattfield, "Journey to the Wilderness," p. 334; Pagden, *European Encounters,* p. 132.

21. Barnett, "William Bartram," pp. 83, 88–90; Bruce G. Trigger, *A History of Archaeological Thought,* pp. 65–66; Medeiros, "Three Travelers," p. 205.

22. Quoted in Fagin, *William Bartram,* p. 46, and in Larry R. Clarke, "The Quaker Background of William Bartram's View of Nature," p. 445; Silver, "Accounts of Nature," pp. 600–602; Trigger, *History of Archaeological Thought,* pp. 65–66; Kerry S. Walters, "The 'Peaceable Disposition' of Animals," pp. 161–63. Bartram firmly rejected William Robertson's position that Indians viewed nature "without curiosity or attention. . . . he is unacquainted with all the ideas which have been denominated *universal,* or *abstract,* or *of reflection*"; Robertson, *History of America,* p. 312, quoted in Pagden, *European Encounters,* p. 132.

23. Barnett, "William Bartram," pp. 59–67; Clarke, "Quaker Background," pp. 437–45.

24. Bartram, *Travels,* p. 71.

25. Gummere, "William Bartram," p. 168; Arthur O. Lovejoy, *The Great Chain of Being,* pp. 288–89; Sheehan, *Seeds of Extinction,* p. 32; Franklin, *Discoverers, Explorers, Settlers,* p. 68; Barnett, "William Bartram," pp. 20–22.

26. Regis, *Describing Early America,* pp. 5–6.

27. Quote from Medeiros, "Three Travelers," p. 204; also see Gummere, "William Bartram," p. 170; Mattfield, "Journey to the Wilderness," p. 346. Regis, *Describing Early America,* p. 73, shares this anticolonial indignation and castigates Bartram equally with his contemporaries. Ironically, Bartram's view of an environment comprehending both human and natural components resembles the modern holistic perspective advocated by ecologists and anthropologists.

28. Bartram, *Travels,* p. 3; cited by Mattfield, "Journey to the Wilderness," p. 348.

29. Gummere, "William Bartram," p. 170; Mattfield, "Journey to the Wilderness," pp. 348–50; Sheehan, *Seeds of Extinction,* p. 110; Silver, "Accounts of Nature," p. 603; Franklin, *Discoverers, Explorers, Settlers,* pp. 68–70; Clarke, "Quaker Background," p. 439; Pagden, *European Encounters,* pp. 117–18.

30. Silver, "Accounts of Nature," p. 598.

31. Clarke, "Quaker Background," p. 442; May, *Enlightenment in America,* p. 217.

32. Fagin, *William Bartram,* pp. 55, 68.

33. Lovejoy, *Great Chain of Being,* p. 186; Stephen J. Gould, *The Flamingo's Smile,* pp. 281–83.

34. Darlington, ed., *Memorials,* p. 254; Corner and Booth, eds., *Chain of Friendship,* p. 318.

35. Peck, ed., *Bartram Heritage,* pp. 32–33; according to one, "The stiff, immutable world that men like Jefferson, Peale, and Bartram constructed was their rhetorical invention; it was a figure for social stability." Christopher Looby, "The Constitution of Nature," p. 257; also pp. 253, 260.

36. Gould, *Flamingo's Smile,* p. 269.

37. Trigger, *History of Archaeological Thought,* p. 59.

38. Pamela Regis maintains that Bartram's "indigenous peoples are relocated in separate chapters as if in textual homelands or reservations, pulled out of time to be preserved, contained, studied, admired, detested, pitied, mourned." Regis, *Describing Early America,* pp. 22–23. In addition to the anachronistic inappropriateness of her references to homelands and reservations, Regis's characterization ignores Bartram's considerable efforts to explore the American Indians' past, through both archaeological speculation and elicitation of myths from people who, in fact, had no written history. Bartram certainly cannot be faulted for relegating references to Native Americans to separate chapters; Indian references are pervasive in *Travels,* as chapter 2 of this book demonstrates.

39. Bartram, *Travels*, p. xxxiv.

40. Berkhofer, *White Man's Indian*, pp. 38–39; Stanton, *The Leopard's Spots*.

41. Quoted in Jefferson, *Notes on the State of Virginia*, p. 88.

42. Jefferson, *Notes;* "We shall probably find that they are formed in mind as well as in body, on the same module with the Homo sapiens Europaeus," p. 62.

43. Bartram possessed a copy of the 1781 London edition of Buffon's *Natural History* and jotted a critique of Buffon's thesis in his treatise "On Morality." Robert McCracken Peck, "Books from the Bartram Library," p. 47; Dumas Malone, *Jefferson and the Rights of Man*, p. 101; Stephen Kunitz, "Benjamin Rush on Savagism and Progress," p. 33; Wills, *Inventing America*, pp. 284–85; Porter, *Eagle's Nest*, pp. 7–8, 19.

44. For discussions of the dynamic tensions between these two goals, see Earnest Gellner, *Relativism and the Social Sciences*, p. 84; Bruce G. Trigger, "Early Native North American Responses to European Contact"; and Anthony Pagden, *The Fall of Natural Man*.

45. Regis, *Describing Early America*, pp. 75–76; I. C. Jarvie, *Rationality and Relativism*, pp. 29–30; Trigger, "Early Native North American Responses," pp. 1196–98; Gordon R. Willey and Jeremy A. Sabloff, *A History of American Archaeology*, p. 29.

46. Waring, *Waring Papers*, p. 288; Peck, *Bartram Heritage*, pp. 40–41; cf. Barnett, "William Bartram," pp. 95–96, and Regis, *Describing Early America*, pp. 36–37.

47. Bartram, *Travels*, p. 518.

48. Swanton, "Religious Beliefs," pp. 498–99; James H. Howard, *The Southern Ceremonial Complex and Its Interpretation* pp. 130–32; Knight, "Symbolism of Mississippian Mounds," p. 289, n. 4.

49. Bartram, *Travels*, pp. 168–72, 367, 390, 522; Silverberg, *Mound Builders*, p. 41.

50. Bartram, *Travels*, pp. 139, 514–16.

51. Joffre L. Coe, "Cherokee Archeology," pp. 53–54; Waring, *Waring Papers*, p. 55; Knight, "Symbolism of Mississippian Mounds," p. 285. Marvin D. Jeter, ed., *Edward Palmer's Arkansaw Mounds*, p. 8. Ian Brown has argued that Bartram's analogy is the earliest known application of the direct historical approach, a method of anthropological interpretation popularized in the mid-twentieth century to determine the function of archaeological remains by tracing the origin of similar artifacts or structures of known historic function, by moving "from the known historic into the unknown prehistoric." Ian W. Brown, "William Bartram and the Direct Historical Approach"; Trigger, *History of Archaeological Thought*, p. 69.

52. Bartram document, *Observations*, chapter 3, this volume.

53. Harper, ed., "Travels in Georgia and Florida," p. 142. Jeffries Wyman detected some uncertainty in Bartram's implication that all shell heaps were produced by humans. "He does not, however, seem to have inferred, as one would naturally suppose from the facts he would, that the mounds were artificial, for, in another part of his narrative, he says he cannot pretend to conjecture the cause of them." Wyman, "Shell Mounds," pp. 14–15, citing *Travels*, pp. 94, 165.

54. John Bartram, "Diary," p. 47. Further indication of John Bartram's archaeological interests is found in a letter to Hans Sloane, dated November 14, 1742: "I have procured an indian pipe made of soft stone intire: it was dug by chance out of an ould indian grave ye figure & dimensions see below this I esteem as A great Curiosity & if I knowed that thee had none of this kind I should endeavour to give thee an opertunity of seeing it & calling it thy own." Berkeley and Berkeley, eds., *Correspondence of John Bartram*, pp. 207–8.

55. Benson, ed., *Peter Kalm's Travels*, p. 127.

56. On December 7, 1798, Hawkins wrote "I pray you to send me some groceries, Adair's *History of the American Indians*, Bartram's *Travels* and any other book on Indian transactions." *Letters, Journals and Writings of Benjamin Hawkins* 1:227. Though Hawkins corresponded regularly with Philadelphians, particularly Elizabeth Trist and the Quaker community, he did not, as far as the record indicates, correspond directly with Bartram. Ibid., pp. 85–86.

57. Caleb Atwater, "Description of the Antiquities"; Albert Gallatin, "A Synopsis of the Indian Tribes"; Trigger, *History of Archaeological Thought*, pp. 104–6.

Advocates of various explanations of the origin of earthen mounds formed three camps: one — which included Bartram and Jefferson — championed autochthonous development, or in-place evolution of Indian cultures; the second favored a Mexican inspiration; and the third promoted much more distant sources, migrations by Phoenicians, Atlanteans, Egyptians, Vikings, "Hindoos" (this was Atwater's choice), and so on. Stephen Williams, *Fantastic Archaeology*, pp. 28–60, and "Fantastic Archaeology: Another Road Taken by Some."

58. Henry R. Schoolcraft, *Information Respecting the History, Condition and Prospects of the Indian Tribes*, part 5, pp. 110, 115.

59. John Swanton claimed that *Travels* threw "an atmosphere of mystery" around the origin of southern earthworks, and he gave credence to the mound builder theory. Swanton, "Religious Beliefs," p. 495; Fagin, *William Bartram*, p. 58.

60. Silverberg, *Mound Builders*, p. 39.

61. John Swanton, "The Interpretation of Aboriginal Mounds by Means of Creek Indian Customs," pp. 495–96; A. Irving Hallowell, "The Begin-

nings of Anthropology in America," p. 76, note 7; Squier and Davis, "Ancient Monuments," pp. 120–23; figs. 23–25; Squier, "Observations on the Aboriginal Monuments," pp. 131–207; Squier, *Aboriginal Monuments,* pp. 135–41, figs. 136–40.

62. Squier and Davis, *Ancient Monuments,* p. 123; Squier, *Aboriginal Monuments,* pp. 139–40.

63. Haven, "Archaeology of the United States," pp. 20–21.

64. Jones, *Antiquities,* pp. 123–25, 130–31, 178–81; Bartram, *Travels,* pp. 516–17.

65. Thomas, "Mound Explorations," pp. 315, 597, 654–56. Some archaeologists continued to battle the mound builder hypothesis for several decades; e.g., M. R. Harrington, "Cherokee and Earlier Remains," p. 275.

66. Among Swanton's better known works on the Creeks are *Early History of the Creek Indians*; "Religious Beliefs"; "Social Organization"; *Indians of the Southeastern United States.* See Green, *American Science,* pp. 348–50, on Swanton's interpretation of Bartram's writings.

Bibliography

MANUSCRIPT SOURCES

American Philosophical Society Library, Philadelphia.
    Benjamin Smith Barton Papers.
    Barton-Delafield Collection.
    Society Collection.
British Museum of Natural History, London.
    Fothergill Album.
William L. Clements Library, Ann Arbor, Michigan.
    Miscellaneous Collections.
Great Britain, Public Record Office.
    Colonial Office. American and West Indies. Indian Affairs. Class 5, vols. 65–
    82, 541, 570.
Historical Society of Pennsylvania, Philadelphia.
    Bartram Family Papers.
    Dreer Collection, Scientists.
    Etting Papers, Scientists.
    Simon Gratz Collection.
Library of Congress, Manuscript Division, Washington, D.C.
    Ephraim George Squier Papers.
    Miscellaneous Manuscript Collection.
    Thomas Jefferson Papers.
Pierpont Morgan Library, New York City.
    Henry Knox Papers, Gilder-Lehrman Collection.
National Anthropological Archives, Smithsonian Institution, Washington, D.C.
    Copy of William Bartram manuscript "Observations on the Creek and Cher-
    okee Indians," J. Woodbridge Davis Papers.
New York Historical Society, New York City.
    Miscellaneous Darlington Collection.
    Miscellaneous William Bartram Papers.

P. K. Younge Library, University of Florida, Gainesville.
Miscellaneous Manuscripts.

NEWSPAPERS

The Literary World, 1850–51.
Pennsylvania Gazette, 1790.
Pennsylvania Packet and Daily Advertiser, 1790.
Universal Asylum and Columbia Magazine, 1792.

PUBLISHED PRIMARY SOURCES

Adair, James. *The History of the American Indians.* Edited by Samuel Cole Williams. London: Edward & Charles Dilly, 1775. Reprint. Johnson City, Tenn.: Watauga Press, 1930.

American State Papers: Documents, Legislative and Executive, of the Congress of the United States, from the First Session of the First to the Third Session of the Thirteenth Congress, Inclusive: Commencing March 3, 1789, and Ending March 3, 1815. Vol. 1, class 2, *Indian Affairs.* Edited by Walter Lowrie and Matthew St. Clair Clarke. Washington, D.C.: Gales & Seaton, 1832.

Bartram, John. *The Correspondence of John Bartram, 1734–1777.* Edited by Edmund Berkeley and Dorothy Smith Berkeley. Gainesville: University Presses of Florida, 1992.

———. "Diary of a Journey Through the Carolinas, Georgia, and Florida, from July 1, 1765, to April 10, 1766." Edited by Francis Harper. *Transactions of the American Philosophical Society,* new series, vol. 33, part 1. Philadelphia: APS, 1942.

———. "An Extract of Mr Wm. Bartram's Observations in a Journey up the River Savannah in Georgia, with his Son, on Discoveries." *Gentleman's Magazine* 37 (1767): 166–69.

Bartram, William. "Observations on the Creek and Cherokee Indians, 1789, with Prefatory and Supplementary Notes by E. G. Squier." *Transactions of the American Ethnological Society,* vol. 3, part 1, pp. 1–81. New York: AES, 1853.

———. "Travels in Georgia and Florida, 1773–74: A Report to Dr. John Fothergill." Annotated by Francis Harper. *Transactions of the American Philosophical Society,* new series, vol. 33, part 2. Philadelphia: APS, 1943.

———. *Travels of William Bartram.* Edited by Mark Van Doren. New York: Macy-Masius, 1928. Reprint. New York: Dover, 1955.

———. *The Travels of William Bartram, Naturalist's Edition.* Edited by Francis Harper. New Haven: Yale University Press, 1958.

———. *Travels Through North and South Carolina, Georgia, East and West Florida: A Facsimile of the 1792 Edition.* Introduction by Gordon DeWolf. Savannah: Beehive Press, 1973. Reprint. Charlottesville: University of Virginia Press, 1980.

———. *Travels Through North and South Carolina, Georgia, East and West Florida, the Cherokee Country, the Extensive Territories of the Muscogulges, or Creek Confederacy, and the Country of the Chactaws.* Introduction by James Dickey. New York: Viking Penguin, 1988.

———. *Travels Through North & South Carolina, Georgia, East & West Florida, the Cherokee Country, the Extensive Territories of the Muscogulges, or Creek Confederacy, and the Country of the Chactaws; Containing an Account of the Soil and Natural Productions of Those Regions, Together with Observations on the Manners of the Indians.* Philadelphia: James & Johnson, 1791.

———. *William Bartram: Botanical and Zoological Drawings, 1756–1788.* Edited with an introduction and commentary by Joseph Ewan. Memoirs of the American Philosophical Society, vol. 74. Philadelphia: APS, 1968.

Benson, Adolph B., ed. *Peter Kalm's Travels in North America: The English Version of 1770.* 2 vols. New York: Dover, 1966.

Bossu, Jean-Bernard. *Jean-Bernard Bossu's Travels in the Interior of North America, 1751–1762.* Translated and edited by Seymour Feiler. Norman: University of Oklahoma Press, 1962.

Boyd, Julian P., ed. *The Papers of Thomas Jefferson.* 21 vols. Princeton, N.J.: Princeton University Press, 1950–.

Byrd, William. *Histories of the Dividing Line Betwixt Virginia and North Carolina.* Reprint. New York: Dover, 1967.

Candler, Allen D., Kenneth Coleman, and Milton Ready, eds. *The Colonial Records of the State of Georgia.* 28 vols. Atlanta: C. P. Byrd, 1904–16. Athens: University of Georgia Press, 1974–76.

Corner, Betsy C., and Christopher C. Booth, eds. *Chain of Friendship: Selected Letters of Dr. John Fothergill of London, 1735–1780.* Cambridge, Mass.: Belknap Press, 1971.

Covington, James W., ed. *The British Meet the Seminoles: Negotiations Between British Authorities in East Florida and the Indians, 1763–68.* Contributions of the Florida State Museum, Social Sciences, no. 7. Gainesville: University Press of Florida, 1961.

Darlington, William, ed. *Memorials of John Bartram and Humphrey Marshall, with Notices of Their Botanical Contemporaries.* Philadelphia: Lindsay and Blackiston, 1849.

———, *Reliquiae Baldwinianae: Selections from the Correspondence of the Late William Baldwin, M.D.* Philadelphia: Kimber and Sharpless, 1843.

Davies, K. G., ed. *Documents of the American Revolution, 1770–1783.* 20 vols. Dublin: Irish University Press, 1972–79.

De Brahm, William Gerard. *De Brahm's Report of the General Survey in the Southern District of North America.* Edited by Louis De Vorsey Jr. Columbia: University of South Carolina Press, 1971.

De Pauw, Linda Grant, ed. *Documentary History of the First Federal Congress of the United*

States of America, March 4, 1789 — March 3, 1792. Vol. 2, *Senate Executive Journal and Related Documents.* Baltimore: Johns Hopkins University Press, 1974.

Du Pratz, [Antoine Simon] Le Page. *The History of Louisiana.* Facsimile reproduction of the 1774 London edition. Baton Rouge, La.: Claitor's Publishing, 1972.

Fitzpatrick, John. *The Merchant of Manchac: The Letterbooks of John Fitzpatrick, 1768–1790.* Edited by Margaret F. Dalrymple. Baton Rouge: Louisiana State University Press, 1978.

Foreman, Grant, ed. *Indian Justice: A Cherokee Murder Trial at Tahlequah in 1840 as Reported by John Howard Payne.* Oklahoma City: Harlow Publishing, 1934.

———. "John Howard Payne and the Cherokee Indians." *American Historical Review* 37 (1932): 723–30.

Galloway, Patricia K., ed. *Mississippi Provincial Archives, French Dominion.* Vol. 4, *1729–1748.* Originally collected, edited, and translated by Dunbar Rowland and Albert G. Sanders. Baton Rouge: Louisiana State University Press, 1984.

Hawkins, Benjamin. *Letters, Journals and Writings of Benjamin Hawkins.* Edited by C. L. Grant. 2 vols. Savannah: Beehive Press, 1980.

Laurens, Henry. *The Papers of Henry Laurens.* Edited by Philip M. Hamer et al. 13 vols. Columbia: University of South Carolina Press, 1968–.

McGillivray, Alexander. *McGillivray of the Creeks.* Edited by John W. Caughey. Norman: University of Oklahoma Press, 1938.

Milfort, Le Clerc. *Memoirs or a Quick Glance at My Various Travels and My Sojourn in the Creek Nation.* Edited and translated by B. C. McCary. Savannah, Ga.: Beehive Press, 1972. (Originally published as *Mémoir du coup d'oeil rapide sur mes differens voyages et mon séjour dans la Nation Creek.* Paris: Giguet et Michaud, 1802.)

Morton, Samuel G. *A Memoir of Samuel George Morton, M.D., late president of the Academy of Natural Sciences of Philadelphia, read November 6, 1851.* Philadelphia: T. K. and P. G. Collins, 1851.

Nairne, Thomas. *Nairne's Muskhogean Journal: The 1708 Expedition to the Mississippi River.* Edited by Alexander Moore. Jackson: University Press of Mississippi, 1988.

Norton, Charles Eliot, ed. *The Correspondence of Thomas Carlyle and Ralph Waldo Emerson, 1834–1872.* 2 vols. London: Chatto & Windus, 1883–84.

Nuñez, Theron A., Jr. "Creek Nativism and the Creek War of 1813–1814" [including reproduction of George Stiggins Manuscript]. *Ethnohistory* 5 (Winter 1958): 1–47, 131–75, 292–301.

Payne, John Howard. "The Captivity of John Howard Payne by the Georgia Guard." *North American Quarterly Magazine* 7 (January 1836): 107–24.

———. *John Howard Payne to His Countrymen.* Edited with an introduction by Clemens de Baillou. University of Georgia Libraries Miscellanea Publications, no. 2. Athens: University of Georgia Press, 1961.

Pittman, Capt. Philip. *The Present State of the European Settlements on the Mississippi, with a Geographical Description of that River Illustrated by Plans and Draughts.* London, 1770.

———. "A Ranger's Report of Travels with General Oglethorpe, 1739–1742." In *Travels in the American Colonies,* edited by Newton D. Mereness, pp. 213–36. New York: Antiquarian Press, 1961.

Rea, Robert R., and Milo B. Howard, eds. *Minutes, Journals, and Acts of the General Assembly of British West Florida.* Tuscaloosa: University of Alabama Press, 1979.

Rolle, Denys. *To the Right Honourable the Lords of His Majesty's Most Honourable Privy Council, the humble petition of Denys Rolle, esq, setting forth the hardships, inconveniencies, and grievances, which have attended him in his attempts to make a settlement in Florida.* Facsimile reproduction of the 1765 edition. Gainesville: University Presses of Florida, 1977.

Romans, Bernard. *A Concise Natural History of East and West Florida.* Facsimile reproduction of the 1775 edition. Gainesville: University Presses of Florida, 1962.

Rowland, Dunbar, and Albert G. Sanders, eds. and trans. *Mississippi Provincial Archives, French Dominion.* Vol. 1, *1729–1740.* Jackson: Mississippi Department of Archives and History, 1927.

Schoepf, Johann D. *Travels in the Confederation [1783–1784].* Translated by Alfred J. Morrison. 2 vols. Cleveland: Arthur H. Clark, 1911.

Sturtevant, William C., ed. *A Creek Source Book.* New York: Garland, 1987.

Swan, Caleb. "Position and State of Manners and Arts in the Creek, or Muscogee Nation in 1791." In vol. 5 of *Information Respecting the Condition and Prospects of the Indian Tribes of the United States,* edited by Henry Rowe Schoolcraft, pp. 251–83. Philadelphia: J. B. Lippincott, 1852–57.

Taitt, David. "David Taitt's Journal to and Through the Upper Creek Nation." In *Documents of the American Revolution, 1770–1783.* Vol. 5, *Transcripts, 1772,* pp. 251–82. Edited by K. G. Davies. Dublin: Irish University Press, 1974.

Von Reck, Philip Georg Friedrich. *Von Reck's Voyage: Drawings and Journal of Philip Georg Friedrich von Reck.* Edited by Kristian Hvidt. Savannah, Ga.: Beehive Press, 1980.

Washington, George. *The Diaries of George Washington.* Edited by Donald Dean Jackson and Dorothy Twohig. 6 vols. Charlottesville: University of Virginia Press, 1976–79.

Wenhold, Lucy L. "A 17th Century Letter of Gabriel Diaz Vara Calderón, Bishop of Cuba, Describing the Indians and Indian Missions of Florida." *Smithsonian Miscellaneous Collections* 95 (1936): 1–14.

Willett, William M., ed. *A Narrative of the Military Actions of Colonel Marinus Willett, Taken Chiefly from His Own Manuscript.* 1831. Reprint. New York: New York Times, 1969.

Bibliography Adams, Percy G. "Notes on Crèvecoeur." *American Literature* 20 (1948): 327–33.

Alden, John R. *John Stuart and the Southern Colonial Frontier: A Study of Indian Relations, War, Trade, and Land Problems in the Southern Wilderness, 1754–1775.* University of Michigan Publications in History and Political Science, no. 15. Ann Arbor: University of Michigan Press, 1944. Reprint. New York: Gordian, 1966.

American Natural History, Based on the Bibliography of American Natural History, 1769–1865 by Max Meisel. Vol. 129. New Haven, Conn.: Research Publications, 1974.

Anderson, David G. *The Savannah River Chiefdoms: Political Change in the Late Prehistoric Southeast.* Tuscaloosa: University of Alabama Press, 1994.

Anderson, Douglas. "Bartram's *Travels* and the Politics of Nature." *Early American Literature* 25 (1990): 3–17.

Anderson, Kenneth Marshall, Jr. "The Travels of William Bartram." Ph.D. diss., Columbia University, 1971.

Arnade, Charles W. "Cattle Raising in Spanish Florida, 1513–1763." *Agricultural History* 35 (1961): 116–24.

Arnold, Morris S. "Eighteenth-Century Arkansas Illustrated." *Arkansas Historical Quarterly* 53 (1994): 119–36.

Atwater, Caleb. "Description of the Antiquities Discovered in the State of Ohio and Other Western States." *Archaeologia Americana: Transactions and Collections of the American Antiquarian Society* 1 (1820): 105–267.

Axtell, James. *The Invasion Within: The Contest of Cultures in Colonial North America.* New York: Oxford University Press, 1985.

Bailyn, Bernard. *Voyagers to the West: A Passage in the Peopling of America on the Eve of the Revolution.* New York: Vintage Books, 1986.

Baker, Brenda J., and George J. Armelagos. "The Origin and Antiquity of Syphilis." *Current Anthropology* 29 (1988): 703–37.

Barnett, Thomas V. "William Bartram and the Age of Sensibility." Ph.D. diss., Department of English, Georgia State University, 1982.

Barnhart, Terry A. "A Question of Authorship: The Ephraim George Squier–Edwin Hamilton Davis Controversy." *Ohio History* 92 (1983): 52–71.

———. "Of Mounds and Men: The Early Anthropological Career of Ephraim George Squier." Ph.D. diss., Department of History, Miami University, 1989.

Barton, Benjamin Smith. *Elements of Botany, or Outlines of the Natural History of Vegetables.* 2 vols. Philadelphia: 1803.

———. *New Views of the Origin of the Tribes and Nations of America.* Philadelphia: John Bioren, 1797.

Battle, Herbert B. "The Domestic Use of Oil among the Southern Aborigines." *American Anthropologist* 24 (1922): 171–82.

Bauxer, J. Joseph. "Yuchi Ethnoarchaeology, Parts I–V." *Ethnohistory* 4 (1957): 279–301, 369–464.

Bell, Amelia R. "Separate People: Speaking of Creek Men and Women." *American Anthropologist* 92 (1990): 332–45.

Bennett, Charles E. *Twelve on the River St. Johns.* Gainesville: University Presses of Florida, 1989.

Berkeley, Edmund, and Dorothy Smith Berkeley. *Dr. Alexander Garden of Charles Town.* Chapel Hill: University of North Carolina Press, 1969.

———. *The Life and Travels of John Bartram: From Lake Ontario to the River St. John.* Gainesville: University Presses of Florida, 1982.

Berkhofer, Robert F., Jr. *The White Man's Indian: Images of the American Indian from Columbus to the Present.* New York: Vintage Books, 1978.

Bieder, Robert E. *Science Encounters the Indian, 1820–1880: The Early Years of American Ethnology.* Norman: University of Oklahoma Press, 1986.

Bieder, Robert E., and Thomas G. Tax. "From Ethnologists to Anthropologists: A Brief History of the American Ethnological Society." In *American Anthropology: The Early Years,* edited by John V. Murra, pp. 11–22. Proceedings of the American Ethnological Society for 1974. St. Paul, Minn.: West Publishing, 1976.

Blake, Leonard W. "Early Acceptance of Watermelon by Indians of the United States." *Journal of Ethnobiology* 1 (1981): 193–99.

Bogan, Arthur E. "A Comparison of Late Prehistoric Dallas and Overhill Cherokee Subsistence Strategies in the Little Tennessee River Valley." Ph.D. diss., Department of Anthropology, University of Tennessee, 1980.

Brain, Jeffrey P. *Tunica Treasure.* Papers of the Peabody Museum of Archaeology and Ethnology, vol. 71. Cambridge: Peabody Museum, Harvard University, 1979.

Brainard, Charles H. *John Howard Payne: A Biographical Sketch of the Author of "Home, Sweet Home" with a Narrative of the Removal of His Remains from Tunis to Washington.* Washington, D.C.: George A. Coolidge, 1885.

Braund, Kathryn E. Holland. "The Creek Indians, Blacks, and Slavery." *Journal of Southern History* 57 (1991): 601–36.

———. "The Creeks and the Quakers: From Wrightsborough to Philadelphia." Paper presented at the Ninth Annual Meeting of the Society for Historians of the Early American Republic, Philadelphia, July 1987.

———. *Deerskins and Duffels: Creek Indian Trade with Anglo-America, 1685–1815.* Lincoln: University of Nebraska Press, 1993.

———. "Guardians of Tradition and Handmaidens to Change: Women's Roles in Creek Economic and Social Life During the Eighteenth Century." *American Indian Quarterly* 14 (1990): 239–58.

———. "John Stuart." In vol. 2 of *The American Revolution, 1775–1783: An Encyclopedia,* edited by Richard L. Blanco, pp. 1597–98. New York: Garland Publishing, 1993.

Brinton, Daniel G. *Notes on the Floridian Peninsula, Its Literary History, Indian Tribes and Antiquities.* Philadelphia: J. Sabin, 1859.

Brown, Ian W. "The Calumet Ceremony in the Southeast and Its Archaeological Manifestations." *American Antiquity* 54 (1989): 311–31.

———. "A Study of Stone Box Graves in Eastern North America." *Tennessee Anthropologist* 6 (1981): 1–26.

———. "William Bartram and the Direct Historical Approach." In *Archaeology of Eastern North America,* edited by James B. Stoltman, pp. 277–82. Mississippi Department of Archives and History, Archaeological Report 25. Jackson: MDAH, 1993.

Burton, Bruce A. *Forgotten Founders: How the American Indian Helped Shape Democracy.* Boston: Harvard Common Press, 1982.

———. "Iroquois Confederate Law and the Origins of the U.S. Constitution." *Northeast Indian Quarterly* (1986): 4–9.

Bushnell, Amy. "The Menéndez Marquéz Cattle Barony at La Chua and the Determinants of Economic Expansion in Seventeenth-Century Florida." *Florida Historical Quarterly* 56 (1978): 407–31.

Bushnell, David I., Jr. "Drawings of A. DeBatz in Louisiana, 1732–1735." *Smithsonian Miscellaneous Collections* 80 (1927): 1–14.

———. *Native Villages and Village Sites East of the Mississippi.* Smithsonian Institution, Bureau of American Ethnology Bulletin 69. Washington, D.C.: Government Printing Office, 1919.

Caldwell, Joseph R. "Investigations at Rood's Landing, Stewart County, Georgia." *Early Georgia* 2 (Summer 1955): 22–49.

———. *The Rembert Mounds, Elbert County, Georgia.* River Basin Survey Paper no. 6. Smithsonian Institution, Bureau of American Ethnology Bulletin 154. Washington, D.C.: Government Printing Office, 1953.

Callender, Charles. "Shawnee." In *Northeast,* edited by B. G. Trigger, pp. 622–35. Vol. 15 of *Handbook of North American Indians.* Washington, D.C.: Smithsonian Institution Press, 1978.

Campbell, T. N. "Medicinal Plants Used by Choctaw, Chickasaw, and Creek Indians." *Journal of the Washington Academy of Science* 41 (1951): 285–90.

Campbell, William Bucke. *Old Towns and Districts of Philadelphia.* Philadelphia: City History Society of Philadelphia, 1942.

Cappon, Lester J., ed. *Atlas of American History: The Revolutionary Era, 1760–1790.* Princeton, N.J.: Princeton University Press, 1976.

———. "Retracing and Mapping the Bartrams' Southern Travels." *Proceedings of the American Philosophical Society* 118 (1974): 507–13.

Cardwell, Harold D., Sr. "Coontie Root: The Dangerous Blessing." *Florida Anthropologist* 40 (1987): 333–35.

Carlson, Alvar W. "Ginseng: America's Botanical Drug Connection to the Orient." *Economic Botany* 40 (1986): 233–49.

Carr, Robert S. "Prehistoric Circular Earthworks in South Florida." *Florida Anthropologist* 38 (1985): 288–301.

Cashin, Edward J., Jr. " 'But Brothers, It Is Our Land We Are Talking About': Winners and Losers in the Georgia Backcountry." In *An Uncivil War: The Southern Backcountry During the American Revolution,* edited by Ronald Hoffman, Thad W. Tate, and Peter J. Albert, pp. 240–75. Charlottesville: U.S. Capitol Historical Society by the University Press of Virginia, 1985.

——, ed. *Colonial Augusta "Key of the Indian Country."* Macon: Mercer University Press, 1986.

——. *The King's Ranger: Thomas Brown and the American Revolution on the Southern Frontier.* Athens: University of Georgia Press, 1989.

——. *Lachlan McGillivray, Indian Trader: The Shaping of the Southern Colonial Frontier.* Athens: University of Georgia Press, 1992.

Clarke, Larry. "The Quaker Background of William Bartram's View of Nature." *Journal of the History of Ideas* 46 (1985): 435–48.

Coe, Joffre L. "Cherokee Archeology." In *Symposium on Cherokee and Iroquois Culture,* edited by William N. Fenton and John Gulick, pp. 53–60. Smithsonian Institution, Bureau of American Ethnology Bulletin 180. Washington, D.C.: Government Printing Office, 1961.

Coker, William S., and Thomas D. Watson. *Indian Traders of the Southeastern Spanish Borderlands: Panton, Leslie & Company, and John Forbes & Company, 1783–1847.* Gainesville: University Presses of Florida, 1986.

Corkran, David H. *The Creek Frontier, 1540–1783.* Norman: University of Oklahoma Press, 1967.

Cotter, John L., Daniel G. Roberts, and Michael Parrington. *The Buried Past: An Archaeological History of Philadelphia.* Philadelphia: University of Pennsylvania Press, 1992.

Coulter, E. Merton. "Mary Musgrove, 'Queen of the Creeks.' " *Georgia Historical Quarterly* 11 (1927): 1–30.

Crane, Verner W. "The Origin of the Name of the Creek Indians." *Mississippi Historical Review* 5 (1918): 339–42.

——. *The Southern Frontier, 1670–1732.* Ann Arbor: University of Michigan Press, 1929. Reprint. New York: W. W. Norton, 1981.

Crawford, James M. "Southeastern Indian Languages." In *Studies in Southeastern Indian Languages,* edited by J. M. Crawford, pp. 1–120. Athens: University of Georgia Press, 1975.

——. "Timucua and Yuchi: Two Language Isolates of the Southeast." In *The Languages of Native America,* edited by L. Campbell and M. Mithun, pp. 327–54. Austin: University of Texas Press, 1979.

Cruikshank, Helen Gere, ed. *John and William Bartram's America.* New York: Devin-Adair Company, 1957.

Culin, Stewart. "Games of the North American Indians." In *Twenty-Fourth Annual Report of the Bureau of American Ethnology.* Washington, D.C.: Government Printing Office, 1907.

Cushing, Frank H. *Exploration of Ancient Key-Dweller Remains on the Gulf Coast of Florida.* Proceedings of the American Philosophical Society, vol. 35, no. 153. Philadelphia: American Philosophical Society, 1897. Reprint. New York: AMS for Peabody Museum of Archaeology and Ethnology, Harvard University, 1973.

Denham, James M. "Denys Rolle and Indian Policy in British East Florida." *Gulf Coast Historical Review* 7 (1992): 31–44.

Densmore, Frances. *Seminole Music.* Smithsonian Institution, Bureau of American Ethnology Bulletin 161. Washington, D.C.: Government Printing Office, 1956.

DePratter, Chester B. "Cofitachequi: Ethnohistorical and Archaeological Evidence." In *Studies in South Carolina Archaeology,* edited by A. C. Goodyear and G. T. Hanson, pp. 133–56. Columbia: University of South Carolina, Institute of Archaeology and Anthropology, 1989.

De Vorsey, Louis, Jr. "The Colonial Georgia Backcountry." In *Colonial Augusta: "Key to the Indian Countrey,"* edited by Edward J. Cashin, pp. 3–26. Macon, Ga.: Mercer University Press, 1986.

———. "Early Maps as a Source in the Reconstruction of Southern Indian Landscapes." In *Red, White, and Black: Symposium on Indians in the Old South,* edited by Charles M. Hudson, pp. 12–30. Southern Anthropological Society Proceedings, no. 5. Athens: University of Georgia Press, 1971.

———. "Indian Boundaries in Colonial Georgia." *Georgia Historical Quarterly* 54 (1970): 63–78.

———. *The Indian Boundary in the Southern Colonies, 1763–1775.* Chapel Hill: University of North Carolina Press, 1966.

———. "William Gerard De Brahm: Eccentric Genius of Southeastern Geography," *Southeastern Geographer* 10 (1970): 21–29.

Dickens, Roy S., Jr. *Cherokee Prehistory: The Pisgah Phase in the Appalachian Summit Region.* Knoxville: University of Tennessee Press, 1976.

Doolittle, William E. "Agriculture in North America on the Eve of Contact: A Reassessment." *Annals of the Association of American Geographers* 82 (1992): 386–401.

Dunlap, William. *A History of the American Theatre.* New York: J. & J. Harper, 1832.

Earnest, Ernest P. *John and William Bartram, Botanists and Explorers.* Philadelphia: University of Pennsylvania Press, 1940.

Elliott, Daniel J., and Steven A. Kowalewski. "Fortson Mound, Wilkes County, Georgia." *Early Georgia* 17 (1989): 50–75.

Erichsen-Brown, Charlotte. *Medicinal and Other Uses of North American Plants.* New York: Dover Publications, 1989.

Fabel, Robin F. A. *The Economy of British West Florida, 1763–1783.* Tuscaloosa: University of Alabama Press, 1988.

Fabel, Robin F. A., and Robert R. Rea. "Lieutenant Thomas Campbell's Sojourn among the Creeks, November, 1764–May, 1765." *Alabama Historical Quarterly* 36 (1974): 97–111.

Fagin, N. Bryllion. "Bartram's *Travels*." *Modern Language Notes* 46 (1931): 288–91.

———. *William Bartram: Interpreter of the American Landscape*. Baltimore: Johns Hopkins University Press, 1933.

Fairbanks, Charles H. *Archeology of the Funeral Mound, Ocmulgee National Monument, Georgia*. U.S. Department of the Interior, National Park Service, Archeological Research Series 3. Washington, D.C.: National Park Service, 1956.

———. "The Ethno-Archeology of the Florida Seminole." In *Tacachale: Essays on the Indians of Florida and Southeastern Georgia During the Historic Period*, edited by Jerald Milanich and Samuel Proctor, pp. 163–93. Gainesville: University Presses of Florida, 1978.

———. "The Function of Black Drink among the Creeks." In *Black Drink: A Native American Tea*, edited by Charles M. Hudson, pp. 120–49. Athens: University of Georgia Press, 1979.

Faulkner, Charles H. "The Occurrence of Gar Remains on Tennessee Archaeological Sites." *Tennessee Anthropological Association Newsletter* 17 (1992): 5–8.

Franklin, Wayne. *Discoverers, Explorers, Settlers: The Diligent Writers of Early America*. Chicago: University of Chicago Press, 1979.

Gallatin, Albert. "A Synopsis of the Indian Tribes Within the United States East of the Rocky Mountains and in the British and Russian Possessions in North America." *Archaeologia Americana: Transactions and Collections of the American Antiquarian Society* 2 (1836): 1–422.

Gallay, Alan. *The Formation of a Planter Elite: Jonathan Bryan and the Southern Colonial Frontier*. Athens: University of Georgia Press, 1989.

Gatschet, Albert S. *A Migration Legend of the Creek Indians*. Vol. 1. Brinton's Library of Aboriginal American Literature, no. 4. Philadelphia: D. G. Brinton, 1884. Reprint. New York: AMS Press, 1969.

———. "Towns and Villages of the Creek Confederacy in the XVIII and XIX Centuries." *Alabama Historical Society Publications, Miscellaneous Collections* 1 (1901): 386–415.

Gearing, Frederick O. *Priests and Warriors: Social Structures for Cherokee Politics in the Eighteenth Century*. American Anthropological Association, memoir 93. Menasha, Wis.: AAA, 1962.

Gellner, Ernest. *Relativism and the Social Sciences*. Cambridge: Cambridge University Press, 1985.

Goggin, John M. "A Florida Indian Trading Post, circa 1763–1784." *Southern Indian Studies* 1 (1949): 35–37.

———. "Fort Pupo: A Spanish Frontier Outpost." *Florida Historical Quarterly* 30 (1951): 139–92.

———. *Indian and Spanish: Selected Writings.* Coral Gables, Fla.: University of Miami Press, 1964.

Goodwin, Gary C. *Cherokees in Transition: A Study of Changing Culture and Environment prior to 1775.* University of Chicago, Department of Geography, Research Paper 181. Chicago: University of Chicago Press, 1977.

Gould, Stephen Jay. *The Flamingo's Smile: Reflections in Natural History.* New York: W. W. Norton, 1985.

Green, Michael D. "Alexander McGillivray." In *American Indian Leaders: Studies in Diversity,* edited by R. David Edmunds, pp. 41–63. Lincoln: University of Nebraska Press, 1980.

Greene, John C. *American Science in the Age of Jefferson.* Ames: Iowa State University Press, 1984.

Gremillion, Kristen J. "Adoption of Old World Crops and Processes of Cultural Change in the Historic Southeast." *Southeastern Archaeology* 12 (1993): 15–20.

Grinde, Donald A., Jr., and Bruce E. Johansen. *Exemplar of Liberty: Native America and the Evolution of Democracy.* Los Angeles: UCLA American Indian Studies Center, 1991.

A Guide to the Lions of Philadelphia. Comprising a Description of the Places of Amusement, Exhibitions, Public Buildings, Public Squares, &c. In the City; and of Places of Public Resort and Objects of Interest and Curiosity in the Environs. Philadelphia: Thomas T. Ash & Co., 1837.

Gummere, Richard M. "William Bartram, a Classical Scientist." *Classical Journal* 50 (1955): 167–70.

Haan, Richard L. "The 'Trade Do's Not Flourish As Formerly': The Ecological Origins of the Yamassee War of 1715." *Ethnohistory* 28 (1982): 341–58.

Haas, Mary R. "Creek Inter-town Relations." *American Anthropologist* 42 (1940): 479–89.

———. "Men's and Women's Speech in Koasati." *Language* 20 (1944): 142–49.

———. "Southeastern Languages." In *The Languages of Native America,* edited by Lyle Campbell and Marianne Mithun, pp. 299–326. Austin: University of Texas Press, 1979.

Hallowell, A. Irving. "The Beginnings of Anthropology in America." In *Selected Papers from the American Anthropologist, 1888–1920,* edited by Frederica de Laguna, pp. 1–104. Washington, D.C.: AAA, 1960.

Hally, David J. "Vessel Assemblages and Food Habits: A Comparison of Two Aboriginal Southeastern Vessel Assemblages." *Southeastern Archaeology* 3 (1984): 46–64.

———, ed. *Ocmulgee Archaeology, 1936–1986.* Athens: University of Georgia Press, 1994.

Hamer, Fritz. "Indian Traders, Land and Power: A Comparative Study of George

Galphin on the Southern Frontier and Three Northern Traders." M.A. thesis, Department of History, University of South Carolina, 1982.

Hamilton, Peter J. *Colonial Mobile.* Boston: Houghton-Mifflin, 1897; revised, 1910.

————. "Indian Trails and Early Roads." *Alabama Historical Society, Miscellaneous Collections* 1 (1901): 422–29.

Hann, John H. *Apalachee: The Land Between the Rivers.* Gainesville: University Presses of Florida, 1988.

————. *Missions to the Calusa.* Gainesville: University of Florida Press, 1991.

————, ed. "The Use and Processing of Plants by Indians of Spanish Florida." *Southeastern Archaeology* 5 (1986): 91–102.

Harmon, Michael A. *Eighteenth Century Lower Cherokee Adaptation and Use of European Material Culture.* South Carolina, Institute of Archaeology and Anthropology, Volumes in Historical Archaeology, no. 2. Columbia: SCIAA, 1986.

Harper, Francis. "The *Vultur sacra* of William Bartram." *Auk* 53 (1936): 381–92.

————. "William Bartram and the American Revolution." *Proceedings of the American Philosophical Society* 97 (1953): 571–77.

————. "William Bartram's Bicentennial." *Scientific Monthly* 48 (1939): 380.

Harper, Francis, and Delma E. Presley. *Okefinokee Album.* Athens: University of Georgia Press, 1981.

Harrington, M. R. *Cherokee and Earlier Remains on Upper Tennessee River.* Heye Foundation, Museum of the American Indian, Indian Notes and Monographs. New York: Museum of the American Indian, 1922.

Hatley, M. Thomas. "Cherokee Women Farmers Hold Their Ground." In *Appalachian Frontiers: Settlement, Society, & Development in the Preindustrial Era,* edited by Robert D. Mitchell, pp. 37–51. Lexington: University Press of Kentucky, 1991.

————. *The Dividing Paths: The Encounters of the Cherokees and the South Carolinians in the Southern Mountains, 1670–1785.* Oxford: Oxford University Press, 1993.

————. "The Three Lives of Keowee: Loss and Recovery in Eighteenth-Century Cherokee Villages." In *Powhatan's Mantle: Indians of the Colonial Southeast,* edited by P. H. Wood, G. A. Waselkov, and M. T. Hatley, pp. 223–48. Lincoln: University of Nebraska Press, 1989.

Haven, Samuel F. *Archaeology of the United States. Smithsonian Contributions to Knowledge,* vol. 8, part 2. Philadelphia: T. K. and P. G. Collins, 1856.

Haynes, Denys E. L. *The Portland Vase.* London: Trustees of the British Museum, 1964.

Hedges, William. "Toward a National Literature." In *Columbia Literary History of the United States,* edited by Emory Elliott. New York: Columbia University Press, 1988.

Hedrick, U. P., ed. *Sturtevant's Edible Plants of the World.* New York: Dover Publications, 1972.

Henri, Florette. *The Southern Indians and Benjamin Hawkins, 1796–1816.* Norman: University of Oklahoma Press, 1986.

Hickerson, Harold. "The Virginia Deer and Intertribal Buffer Zones in the Upper Mississippi Valley." In *Man, Culture and Animals,* edited by Anthony Leeds and Andrew P. Vayda, pp. 43–65. American Association for the Advancement of Science, Publication 78. Washington, D.C.: AAAS, 1965.

Higginbotham, Jay. *Old Mobile: Fort Louis de la Louisiane, 1702–1711.* Mobile, Ala.: Museum of the City of Mobile, 1977.

Holland [Braund], Kathryn E. "The Path Between the Wars: Creek Relations with the British Colonies, 1763–1774." M.A. thesis, Department of History, Auburn University, 1980.

Horsman, Reginald. *Josiah Nott of Mobile: Southerner, Physician, and Racial Theorist.* Baton Rouge: Louisiana State University Press, 1987.

———. "United States Indian Policies, 1776–1815." In *History of Indian-White Relations,* edited by Wilcomb E. Washburn, pp. 29–39. Vol. 4 of *Handbook of North American Indians.* Washington, D.C.: Smithsonian Institution Press, 1988.

Howard, James H. *The Southern Ceremonial Complex and Its Interpretation.* Missouri Archaeological Society Memoir no. 6. Columbus: Missouri Archaeological Society, 1968.

Howard, James H., and Victoria Lindsey Levine. *Choctaw Music and Dance.* Norman: University of Oklahoma Press, 1990.

Hudson, Charles M. "James Adair as Anthropologist." *Ethnohistory* 24 (1977): 311–28.

———. *The Juan Pardo Expeditions: Explorations of the Carolinas and Tennessee, 1566–1568.* Washington, D.C.: Smithsonian Institution Press, 1990.

———. *The Southeastern Indians.* Knoxville: University of Tennessee Press, 1976.

———. "Why the Southeastern Indians Slaughtered Deer." In *Indians, Animals, and the Fur Trade,* edited by Shepard Krech III, pp. 155–76. Athens: University of Georgia Press, 1981.

Hudson, Charles M., Marvin T. Smith, and Chester B. DePratter. "The Hernando De Soto Expedition: From Apalachee to Chiaha." *Southeastern Archaeology* 3 (1984): 65–77.

Hutcheson, Francis. *An Inquiry into the Original of Our Ideas of Beauty and Virtue.* N.p.: 1725.

Jackson, Harvey H. *Lachlan McIntosh and the Politics of Revolutionary Georgia.* Athens: University of Georgia Press, 1979.

Jahn, Otto L., and Ripley P. Bullen. *The Tick Island Site, St. John's River, Florida.* Florida Anthropological Society Publications no. 10. Gainesville: Florida Anthropological Society, 1978.

James, Sydney V. *A People among Peoples: Quaker Benevolences in Eighteenth Century America.* Cambridge: Harvard University Press, 1963.

Jarvie, I. C. *Rationality and Relativism: In Search of a Philosophy and History of Anthropology.* London: Routledge & Kegan Paul, 1984.

Jefferson, Thomas. *Notes on the State of Virginia.* London: John Stockdale, 1785.

Jeffries, Richard W., and Paul R. Fish. *Investigations of Two Stone Mound Localities, Monroe County, Georgia.* University of Georgia, Department of Anthropology, Laboratory of Archaeology, Report 17. Athens: University of Georgia, Department of Anthropology, 1978.

Johansen, Bruce E. *Forgotten Founders: Benjamin Franklin, the Iroquois and the Rationale for the American Revolution.* Ipswich, Mass.: Gambit, 1982.

Jones, Charles C., Jr. *Antiquities of the Southern Indians, Particularly the Georgia Tribes.* New York: D. Appleton and Co., 1873.

Jones, Joseph. *Explorations of the Aboriginal Remains of Tennessee.* Smithsonian Contributions to Knowledge no. 259. Washington, D.C.: Smithsonian Institution, 1876.

Kastner, Joseph. *A Species of Eternity.* New York: Alfred A. Knopf, 1977.

Katz, S. H., M. L. Hediger, and L. A. Valleroy. "Traditional Maize Processing Techniques in the New World." *Science* 184 (1974): 765–73.

Kelly, A. R. *A Preliminary Report on Archeological Explorations at Macon, Ga.* Smithsonian Institution, Bureau of American Ethnology, Bulletin 119, pp. 1–68. Washington, D.C.: Government Printing Office, 1938.

Kelly, James C. "Notable Persons in Cherokee History: Attakullakulla." *Journal of Cherokee Studies* 3 (1978): 2–34.

Kelsey, Rayner W. *Friends and the Indians, 1655–1917.* Philadelphia: Associated Executive Committee of Friends on Indian Affairs, 1917.

Kilpatrick, Jack F., and Anna G. Kilpatrick. *Muskogean Charm Songs among the Oklahoma Cherokees.* Smithsonian Institution, Contributions to Anthropology, vol. 2, no. 3. Washington, D.C.: Government Printing Office, 1967.

Kimball, Geoffrey. "Men's and Women's Speech in Koasati: A Reappraisal." *International Journal of American Linguistics* 53 (1987): 30–38.

King, Frances B. *Plants, People, and Paleoecology.* Illinois State Museum, Scientific Paper 20. Springfield: Illinois State Museum, 1984.

Kinnaird, Lucia Burke. "The Rock Landing Conference of 1789." *North Carolina Historical Review* 9 (1932): 349–65.

Knight, Vernon J., Jr. "Symbolism of Mississippian Mounds." In *Powhatan's Mantle: Indians in the Colonial Southeast,* edited by P. H. Wood, G. A. Waselkov, and M. T. Hatley, pp. 279–91. Lincoln: University of Nebraska Press, 1989.

———. "Tukabatchee: Archaeological Investigations at an Historic Creek Town, Elmore County, Alabama, 1984." Office of Archaeological Research, Alabama State Museum of Natural History, Report of Investigations 45. Tuscaloosa: University of Alabama, 1985.

Kunitz, Stephen. "Benjamin Rush on Savagism and Progress." *Ethnohistory* 17 (1970): 31–42.

Lagerweij, Evart, Pieter C. Nelis, Victor M. Wiegant, and Jan M. van Ree. "The Twitch in Horses: A Variant of Acupuncture." *Science* 225 (1984): 1172–74.

Larson, Lewis. "The Case for Earth Lodges in the Southeast." In *Ocmulgee Archaeology, 1936–1986*, edited by D. J. Hally, pp. 105–15. Athens: University of Georgia Press, 1994.

Leighton, Ann. *American Gardens in the Eighteenth Century: "For Use or for Delight."* Boston: Houghton Mifflin, 1976.

Lewis, Clifford M. "The Calusa." In *Tacachale: Essays on the Indians of Florida and Southeastern Georgia During the Historic Period*, edited by J. Milanich and S. Proctor, pp. 163–93. Gainesville: University Presses of Florida, 1978.

Lewis, Kenneth E., Jr. "History and Archeology of Spalding's Lower Store (PU-23), Putnam County, Florida." M.A. thesis, Department of Anthropology, University of Florida, 1969.

Lewis, Thomas M. N., and Madeline Kneberg. *Hiwassee Island: An Archaeological Account of Four Tennessee Indian Peoples*. Knoxville: University of Tennessee Press, 1946.

Littlefield, Daniel F., Jr. *Africans and Creeks, from the Colonial Period to the Civil War.* Westport, Conn.: Greenwood Press, 1979.

Looby, Christopher. "The Constitution of Nature: Taxonomy and Politics in Jefferson, Peale, and Bartram." *Early American Literature* 22 (1987): 252–73.

Lovejoy, Arthur O. *The Great Chain of Being*. Cambridge: Harvard University Press, 1973.

McKinley, Daniel. "The End of William Bartram, Naturalist, Traveler, Philosopher: But Where Was He Buried?" *1993 Centennial Celebration and Bartram Family Reunion, Sixth Month 25, 26, & 27, 1993*. Philadelphia: Historic Bartram's Garden, 1993.

Malone, Dumas. *Jefferson and His Time*. 6 vols. Boston: Little, Brown & Co., 1948–77.

Martin, Calvin. *Keepers of the Game: Indian-Animal Relationships and the Fur Trade*. Berkeley: University of California Press, 1978.

Martin, Joel W. *Sacred Revolt: The Muskogees' Struggle for a New World*. Boston: Beacon Press, 1991.

Mason, Carol A. "The Archaeology of Ocmulgee Old Fields, Macon, Georgia." Ph.D. diss., Department of Anthropology, University of Michigan, 1963.

——. "Eighteenth Century Culture Change among the Lower Creeks." *Florida Anthropologist* 16 (1963): 65–80.

Matter, Robert A. "The Spanish Missions of Florida: The Friars Versus the Governors in the 'Golden Age,' 1606–1690." Ph.D. diss., Department of History, University of Washington, 1972.

Mattfield, Mary S. "Journey to the Wilderness: Two Travelers in Florida, 1696–1774." *Florida Historical Quarterly* 45 (1967): 327–51.

Maxwell, Hu. "The Use and Abuse of the Forests by the Virginia Indians." *William and Mary Quarterly* 19 (1910): 33–103.

May, Henry F. *The Enlightenment in America.* New York: Oxford University Press, 1976.

Medeiros, Patricia M. "Three Travelers: Carver, Bartram, and Woolman." In *American Literature, 1764–1789: The Revolutionary Years,* edited by Everett Emerson, pp. 195–211. Madison: University of Wisconsin Press, 1977.

Milanich, Jerald T. *Archaeology of Precolumbian Florida.* Gainesville: University Press of Florida, 1994.

Milanich, Jerald T., and Charles H. Fairbanks. *Florida Archaeology.* New York: Academic Press, 1980.

Moerman, Daniel E. *Medicinal Plants of Native America.* 2 vols. University of Michigan, Museum of Anthropology, Technical Report 19. Ann Arbor: University Museum of Anthropology, 1986.

Mooney, James. "Myths of the Cherokee." In *Nineteenth Annual Report of the Bureau of American Ethnology,* pp. 3–576. Washington, D.C.: Government Printing Office, 1900.

Moore, Clarence B. "Certain Aboriginal Mounds of the Savannah River." *Journal of the Academy of Natural Sciences of Philadelphia* 11 (1898): 162–72.

———. "Certain Sand Mounds of the St. John's River, Florida." *Journal of the Academy of Natural Sciences of Philadelphia* 10 (1894): 5–246.

———. "Certain Shell Heaps of the St. John's River, Florida, Hitherto Unexplored." *American Naturalist* 26 (1892): 912–22; 27 (1893): 8–13, 113–17, 605–24, 709–33; 28 (1894): 15–26.

———. "Supplementary Investigations at Tick Island." *American Naturalist* 26 (1892): 568–79.

Moore, L. Hugh. "The Aesthetic Theory of William Bartram." *Essays in Arts and Sciences* 12 (1983): 17–35.

———. "The Southern Landscape of William Bartram: A Terrible Beauty." *Essays in Arts and Sciences* 10 (1981): 41–50.

Morton, Samuel G. *Crania Americana.* Philadelphia: Dobson, 1839.

Mowat, Charles L. *East Florida as a British Province, 1763–1784.* University of California Publications in History, vol. 32. Berkeley: University of California Press, 1943.

Myer, William E. "Indian Trails of the Southeast." In *Forty-Second Annual Report of the Bureau of American Ethnology,* pp. 727–857. Washington, D.C.: Government Printing Office, 1928.

Neill, Wilfred T. "Coracles or Skin Boats of the Southeastern Indians." *Florida Anthropologist* 7 (1954): 119–26.

———. "Dugouts of the Mikasuki Seminole." *Florida Anthropologist* 6 (1953): 77–84.

———. "The Galphin Trading Post Site at Silver Bluff, South Carolina." *Florida Anthropologist* 21 (1968): 42–54.

———. "Sailing Vessels of the Florida Seminole." *Florida Anthropologist* 9 (1956): 79–86.

Neuman, Robert W. "The Buffalo in Southeastern United States Post-Pleistocene Prehistory." In *Southeastern Natives and Their Pasts,* edited by D. G. Wyckoff and J. L. Hofman, pp. 261–80. Oklahoma Archaeological Survey, Studies in Oklahoma's Past, no. 11. Norman: OAS, 1983.

Newsom, Lee Ann, and Barbara A. Purdy. "Florida Canoes: A Maritime Heritage from the Past." *Florida Anthropologist* 43 (1990): 164–80.

O'Donnell, James H., III. "Bartram's *Travels* as Promotional Literature." In *Threads of Tradition and Culture along the Gulf Coast,* edited by Ronald V. Evans, pp. 58–77. Proceedings of the Gulf Coast History and Humanities Conference, vol. 10. Pensacola: Gulf Coast History and Humanities Conference, 1986.

———. *Southern Indians in the American Revolution.* Knoxville: University of Tennessee Press, 1973.

Owsley, Douglas W., and Helen L. O'Brien. "Stature of Adult Cherokee Indians During the Eighteenth Century." *Journal of Cherokee Studies* 7 (1982): 74–78.

Pagden, Anthony. *European Encounters with the New World: From Renaissance to Romanticism.* New Haven: Yale University Press, 1993.

———. *The Fall of Natural Man: The American Indian and the Origins of Comparative Ethnology.* Cambridge: Cambridge University Press, 1982.

Palmer, Ralph S. "A Biography of William Bartram." Unpublished manuscript.

Paredes, J. Anthony, and Kenneth J. Plante. "A Reexamination of Creek Indian Population Trends: 1738–1832." *American Indian Culture and Research Journal* 6 (1983): 3–28.

Patterson, Jerry E., and William R. Stanton. "The Ephraim George Squier Manuscripts in the Library of Congress: A Checklist." *Papers of the Bibliographical Society of America* 53 (1959): 309–26.

Payne, John Howard. "The Green-Corn Dance." *Continental Monthly* 1 (1862): 17–29.

[Peck, Robert M., comp.] *Bartram Heritage: A Study of the Life of William Bartram.* Montgomery, Ala.: Bartram Trail Conference, 1979.

Peck, Robert M. "Books from the Bartram Library." In *Contributions to the History of North American Natural History,* edited by Alwyne Wheeler, pp. 46–50. London: Society for the Bibliography of Natural History, 1983.

———. "William Bartram and His Travels." In *Contributions to the History of North American Natural History,* edited by Alwyne Wheeler, pp. 35–45. London: Society for the Bibliography of Natural History, 1983.

Pennell, Francis W. "Benjamin Smith Barton as Naturalist." *Proceedings of the American Philosophical Society,* vol. 86, part 1 (1942), pp. 108–22.

Perdue, Theda. "Southern Indians and the Cult of True Womanhood." In *The Web of Southern Social Relations: Women, Family, and Education*, edited by W. J. Fraser Jr., R. F. Saunders Jr., and J. L. Wakelyn, pp. 35–51. Athens: University of Georgia Press, 1985.

Pilling, James C. *Bibliography of the Muskhogean Languages*. Smithsonian Institution, Bureau of American Ethnology, Bulletin 9. Washington, D.C.: Government Printing Office, 1889.

Pillsbury, Richard. "The Europeanization of the Cherokee Settlement Landscape Prior to Removal: A Georgia Case Study." *Geoscience and Man* 23 (1983): 59–69.

Polhemus, Richard R. *The Toqua Site: A Late Mississippian Dallas Phase Town*. University of Tennessee, Department of Anthropology, Report of Investigations 41. Knoxville: UT, Department of Anthropology, 1987.

Pope, John. *A Tour Through the Southern and Western Territories of the United States of North-America*. Richmond, Va.: J. Dixon, 1792.

Porter, Charlotte M. "The Drawings of William Bartram (1739–1823), American Naturalist." *Archives of Natural History* 16 (1989): 289–303.

———. *The Eagle's Nest: Natural History and American Ideas, 1812–1842*. Tuscaloosa: University of Alabama Press, 1986.

———. "Philadelphia Story: Florida Gives William Bartram a Second Chance." *Florida Historical Quarterly* 71 (1993): 310–23.

———. *William Bartram's Florida, A Naturalist's Vision: The Teacher's Manual*. Gainesville: Florida State Museum, 1988.

———. "William Bartram's Travels in the Indian Nations." *Florida Historical Quarterly* 70 (1992): 434–50.

Prucha, Francis Paul. *American Indian Policy: The Indian Trade and Intercourse Acts, 1790–1834*. Lincoln: University of Nebraska Press, 1962.

Ramenofsky, Ann F. *Vectors of Death: The Archaeology of European Contact*. Albuquerque: University of New Mexico Press, 1987.

Rea, Robert R. *Major Robert Farmar of Mobile*. Tuscaloosa: University of Alabama Press, 1990.

Regis, Pamela. *Describing Early America: Bartram, Jefferson, Crèvecoeur, and the Rhetoric of Natural History*. DeKalb: Northern Illinois University Press, 1992.

Reitz, Elizabeth J., and Margaret C. Scarry. *"Reconstructing Historic Subsistence with an Example from Sixteenth-Century Spanish Florida."* Society for Historical Archaeology, Special Publication 3. Ann Arbor, Mich.: SHA, 1985.

Robertson, William. *History of America*. 2 vols. London: W. Strahan and T. Cadell, 1777.

Rostlund, Erhard. "The Geographic Range of the Historic Bison in the Southeast." *Annals of the Association of American Geographers* 50 (1960): 395–407.

Russell, Emily W. B. "Indian-Set Fires in the Forests of the Northeastern United States." *Ecology* 64 (1983): 78–88.

Sargent, Winthrop, and Benjamin Smith Barton. *Papers Relative to Certain American Antiquities.* Philadelphia: Thomas Dobson, 1796.

Schmitt, Karl. "Two Creek Pottery Vessels from Oklahoma." *Florida Anthropologist* 3 (1950): 3–8.

Schnell, Frank T. "The Beginnings of the Creeks: Where Did They First 'Sit Down'?" *Early Georgia* 17 (1989): 24–29.

Schnell, Frank T., Vernon J. Knight Jr., and Gail S. Schnell. *Cemochechobee: Archaeology of a Mississippian Ceremonial Center on the Chattahoochee River.* Gainesville: University Presses of Florida, 1981.

Schroedl, Gerald F. "Louis-Philippe's Journal and Archaeological Investigations at the Overhill Cherokee Town of Toqua." *Journal of Cherokee Studies* 3 (1978): 206–20.

———, ed. "Overhill Cherokee Archaeology at Chota-Tanasee." University of Tennessee, Department of Anthropology, Report of Investigations 38. Knoxville: UT, 1986.

Searcy, Martha Condray. *The Georgia-Florida Contest in the American Revolution, 1776–1778.* Tuscaloosa: University of Alabama Press, 1985.

Sears, William H. "A-296 — A Seminole Site in Alachua County." *Florida Anthropologist* 12 (1959): 25–30.

Seelye, John. "Beauty Bare: William Bartram and His Triangulated Wilderness." *Prospects* 6 (1981): 37–54.

Shapiro, Gary. "Archaeology at San Luis: Broad-scale Testing, 1984–1985." *Florida Archaeology* 3 (1987): 1–271.

Shapiro, Gary, and Bonnie G. McEwan. "Archaeology at San Luis, Part One: The Apalachee Council House." *Florida Archaeology* 6 (1992): 1–77.

Sheehan, Bernard W. *Seeds of Extinction: Jeffersonian Philanthropy and the American Indian.* Chapel Hill: University of North Carolina Press, 1973.

Sheldon, Craig T., Jr. "The Council Houses of Fusihatchee." In *Archaeological Excavations at the Early Historic Creek Indian Town of Fusihatchee (Phase I, 1988–1989),* by G. A. Waselkov, J. W. Cottier, and C. T. Sheldon, pp. 45–76. Report to the National Science Foundation, 1990. Grant no. BNS-8718934.

———. "Public Architecture of the Historic Creeks." Paper presented at the Southeastern Archaeological Conference, Mobile, Alabama, 1990.

Sherwood, John. "Life with Cushing: Farewell to Desks." *Smithsonian* 10 (1979): 96–113.

Silver, Bruce. "William Bartram's and Other Eighteenth-Century Accounts of Nature." *Journal of the History of Ideas* 39 (1978): 597–614.

Silver, Timothy. *A New Face on the Countryside: Indians, Colonists, and Slaves in South Atlantic Forests, 1500–1800.* Cambridge: Cambridge University Press, 1990.

Silverberg, Robert. *Mound Builders of Ancient America: The Archaeology of a Myth*. Greenwich: Conn. New York Graphic Society, 1968.

Smith, Betty A. "Distribution of Eighteenth-Century Cherokee Settlements." In *The Cherokee Indian Nation*, edited by D. H. King, pp. 46–60. Knoxville: University of Tennessee Press, 1979.

Smith, Marvin T. *Archaeology of Aboriginal Culture Change in the Interior Southeast: Depopulation During the Early Historic Period*. Gainesville: University of Florida Press, 1987.

Southerland, Henry D., Jr., and Jerry E. Brown. *The Federal Road Through Georgia, the Creek Nation, and Alabama, 1806–1836*. Tuscaloosa: University of Alabama Press, 1989.

Speck, Frank G. *Gourds of the Southeastern Indians*. Boston: New England Gourd Society, 1941.

Speck, Frank G., Leonard Bloom, and Will West Long. *Cherokee Dance and Drama*. Norman: University of Oklahoma Press, 1983.

Spencer, Frank. "Two Unpublished Essays on the Anthropology of North America by Benjamin Smith Barton." *Isis* 68 (1977): 567–73.

Squier, Ephraim George. *Aboriginal Monuments of the State of New York*. Smithsonian Institution, Contributions to Knowledge, vol. 2. New York: Edward O. Jenkins, 1850.

———. "Observations on the Aboriginal Monuments of the Mississippi Valley." *Transactions of the American Ethnological Society* 2 (1848): 131–207.

Squier, Ephraim George, and Edwin Hamilton Davis. *Ancient Monuments of the Mississippi Valley*. Smithsonian Institution, Contributions to Knowledge, vol. 1. Washington, D.C.: Smithsonian Institution, 1848.

Stanton, William. *The Leopard's Spots: Scientific Attitudes Toward Race in America, 1815–59*. Chicago: University of Chicago Press, 1960.

Steinen, Karl T., ed. *The Cultural Evolution and Environment of Colonels Island, Georgia*. Carrollton: West Georgia State College, 1978.

Sterling, Keir B., ed. *Notes on the Animals of North America*, by Benjamin Smith Barton. New York: Arno Press, 1974.

Sturtevant, William C. "Creek into Seminole." In *North American Indians in Historical Perspective*, edited by E. B. Leacock and N. O. Lurie, pp. 92–128. New York: Random House, 1971.

Swanton, John R. "Coonti." *American Anthropologist* 15 (1913): 141–42.

———. *Early History of the Creek Indians and Their Neighbours*. Smithsonian Institution, Bureau of American Ethnology Bulletin 73. Washington, D.C.: Government Printing Office, 1922.

———. *Final Report of the United States De Soto Expedition Commission*. 76th U.S. Congress, 1st session, House Document 71.

———. "The Green Corn Dance." *Chronicles of Oklahoma* 10 (1932): 170–95.

———. *The Indians of the Southeastern United States.* Smithsonian Institution, Bureau of American Ethnology Bulletin 137. Washington, D.C.: Government Printing Office, 1946.

———. *The Indian Tribes of North America.* Smithsonian Institution, Bureau of American Ethnology Bulletin 145. Washington, D.C.: Government Printing Office, 1952.

———. "The Interpretation of Aboriginal Mounds by Means of Creek Indian Customs." In *Forty-First Annual Report of the Bureau of American Ethnology*, pp. 495–506. Washington, D.C.: Government Printing Office, 1927.

———. "Modern Square Grounds of the Creek Indians." *Smithsonian Miscellaneous Collections* 85 (1931).

———. "Religious Beliefs and Medical Practices of the Creek Indians." In *Forty-Second Annual Report of the Bureau of American Ethnology*, pp. 473–672. Washington, D.C.: Government Printing Office, 1928.

———. "Social Organization and Social Usages of the Indians of the Creek Confederacy." In *Forty-Second Annual Report of the Bureau of American Ethnology*, pp. 23–472. Washington, D.C.: Government Printing Office, 1928.

———. *Source Material for the Social and Ceremonial Life of the Choctaw Indians.* Smithsonian Institution, Bureau of American Ethnology Bulletin 103. Washington, D.C.: Government Printing Office, 1931.

Taylor, Lyda A. *Plants Used as Curatives by Certain Southeastern Tribes.* Cambridge: Harvard University, Botanical Museum, 1940.

Thomas, Cyrus. "Burial Mounds of the Northern Sections of the United States." In *Fifth Annual Report of the Bureau of Ethnology*, pp. 3–119. Washington, D.C.: Government Printing Office, 1887.

———. "Report on the Mound Explorations of the Bureau of Ethnology." In *Twelfth Annual Report of the Bureau of Ethnology*, pp. 3–742. Washington, D.C.: Government Printing Office, 1894.

Thomas, Daniel H. *Fort Toulouse: The French Outpost at the Alabamas on the Coosa.* Introduction by Gregory A. Waselkov. Tuscaloosa: University of Alabama Press, 1989.

Thoreau, Henry David. *A Week on the Concord and Merrimack Rivers; Walden, or Life in the Woods; The Maine Woods, and Cape Cod.* Library of America. New York: Viking Press, 1985.

Thornton, Russell. *The Cherokees: A Population History.* Lincoln: University of Nebraska Press, 1990.

Trigger, Bruce G. "Early Native North American Responses to European Contact: Romantic Versus Rationalistic Interpretations." *Journal of American History* 77 (1991): 1195–1215.

———. *A History of Archaeological Thought.* Cambridge: Cambridge University Press, 1989.

Trimble, Michael K. *An Ethnohistorical Interpretation of the Spread of Smallpox in the Northern Plains Utilizing Concepts of Disease Ecology.* Lincoln, Neb.: J. & L. Reprint Co., 1986.

Turner, E. Randolph. "An Intertribal Deer Exploitation Buffer Zone for the Virginia Coastal Plain–Piedmont Regions." *Archeological Society of Virginia Quarterly Bulletin* 32 (1978): 42–48.

Usner, Daniel H., Jr. *Indians, Settlers, and Slaves in a Frontier Exchange Economy: The Lower Mississippi Valley Before 1783.* Chapel Hill: University of North Carolina Press, 1992.

Vernon, Richard. "Town Plan and Town Life at Seventeenth-Century San Luis." *Florida Archaeological Reports,* no. 13. Tallahassee: Dept. of State, 1989.

Vogel, Virgil J. *American Indian Medicine.* Norman: University of Oklahoma Press, 1970.

Wagner, Mark. "The Introduction and Early Use of African Plants in the New World." *Tennessee Anthropologist* 6 (1981): 112–23.

Walters, Kerry S. "The 'Peaceable Disposition' of Animals: William Bartram on the Moral Sensibility of Brute Creation." *Pennsylvania History* 56 (1989): 157–76.

Waring, Antonio J., Jr. *The Waring Papers: The Collected Works of Antonio J. Waring, Jr.* Edited by Stephen Williams. Papers of the Peabody Museum of Archaeology and Ethnology, vol. 58. Cambridge: Peabody Museum, Harvard University, 1977.

Waselkov, Gregory A. "Archaeology of Old Mobile, 1702–1711." *Gulf Coast Historical Review* 6 (1990): 6–21.

———. "Evolution of Deer Hunting in the Eastern Woodlands." *Midcontinental Journal of Archaeology* 3 (1978): 15–34.

———. "French Colonial Trade in the Upper Creek Country." In *Calumet and Fleur-de-Lys: Archaeology of Indian and French Contact in the Midcontinent,* edited by John A. Walthall and Thomas E. Emerson, pp. 35–53. Washington, D.C.: Smithsonian Institution Press, 1992.

———. "Historic Creek Indian Responses to Trade and the Rise of Political Factions." In *Ethnohistory and Archaeology: Approaches to Postcontact Change in the Americas,* edited by J. Daniel Rogers and Samuel M. Wilson, pp. 123–31. New York: Plenum Press, 1993.

———. "A History of the Alabama Anthropological Society." *Southeastern Archaeology* 13 (1994): 64–76.

———. "Indian Maps of the Colonial Southeast." In *Powhatan's Mantle: Indians in the Colonial Southeast,* edited by P. H. Wood, G. A. Waselkov, and M. T. Hatley, pp. 292–343. Lincoln: University of Nebraska Press, 1989.

———. "Seventeenth-Century Trade in the Colonial Southeast." *Southeastern Archaeology* 8 (1989): 117–33.

———. "Shellfish Gathering and Shell Midden Archaeology." In *Advances in Archae-*

ological Method and Theory, edited by Michael Schiffer, pp. 93–210. New York: Academic Press, 1987.

Waselkov, Gregory A., and John W. Cottier. "European Perceptions of Eastern Muskogean Ethnicity." In *Proceedings of the French Colonial Historical Society, 1984,* edited by P. P. Boucher, pp. 23–45. New York: University Press of America, 1985.

Wauchope, Robert. *Archaeological Survey of Northern Georgia with a Test of Some Cultural Hypotheses.* Memoirs of the Society for American Archaeology, no. 21. Salt Lake City: Society for American Archaeology, 1966.

Weatherford, Jack. *Indian Givers: How the Indians of the Americas Transformed the World.* New York: Crown Publishers, 1988.

Weber, David J. *The Spanish Frontier in North America.* New Haven: Yale University Press, 1992.

Weisman, Brent R. *Like Beads on a String: A Culture History of the Seminole Indians in North Peninsular Florida.* Tuscaloosa: University of Alabama Press, 1989.

Welles, Edward O., Jr., "William Bartram's Trail Through Nature." In *Into the Wilderness,* edited by Robert L. Breeden, pp. 34–63. Washington, D.C.: National Geographic Society, Special Publications Division, 1978.

Wickman, Patricia R. *Osceola's Legacy.* Tuscaloosa: University of Alabama Press, 1991.

Widmer, Randolph J. *The Evolution of the Calusa: A Nonagricultural Chiefdom on the Southwest Florida Coast.* Tuscaloosa: University of Alabama Press, 1988.

Willey, Gordon R., and Jeremy A. Sabloff. *A History of American Archaeology.* San Francisco: W. H. Freeman, 1974.

Williams, Stephen. *Fantastic Archaeology: The Wild Side of North American Prehistory.* Philadelphia: University of Pennsylvania Press, 1991.

———. "Fantastic Archaeology: Another Road Taken by Some." Paper presented at the American Association for the Advancement of Science Annual Meeting, Boston, 1993.

Wills, Gary. *Inventing America: Jefferson's Declaration of Independence.* Garden City, N.Y.: Doubleday & Co., 1978.

Wissler, Clark. "The American Indian and the American Philosophical Society." *Proceedings of the American Philosophical Society* 86 (1942): 189–204.

Witthoft, John. "Cherokee Indian Use of Potherbs." *Journal of Cherokee Studies* 2 (1977): 250–55.

———. *Green Corn Ceremonialism in the Eastern Woodlands.* University of Michigan, Museum of Anthropology, Occasional Contributions, no. 13. Ann Arbor: UM, 1949.

Wolf, Martha. "Historic Bartram's Garden." In *Celebration of Travels 1791: Proceedings of the Bartram Trail Conference and Symposium, November 8–9, 1991,* edited by Eliott O. Edwards Jr., pp. 14–18. Savannah, Ga.: Bartram Trail Conference, 1993.

Wood, Peter H. "The Changing Population of the Colonial South: An Overview by Race and Region, 1685–1790." In *Powhatan's Mantle: Indians of the Colonial Southeast,* edited by P. H. Wood, G. A. Waselkov, and M. T. Hatley, pp. 35–103. Lincoln: University of Nebraska Press, 1989.

———. "Indian Servitude in the Southeast." In *History of Indian-White Relations,* pp. 407–9. Vol. 4 of *Handbook of North American Indians,* edited by Wilcomb E. Washburn. Washington, D.C.: Smithsonian Institution Press, 1988.

Wright, J. Leitch, Jr. "Creek-American Treaty of 1790: Alexander McGillivray and the Diplomacy of the Old Southwest." *Georgia Historical Quarterly* 51 (1967): 379–400.

———. *Creeks and Seminoles: The Destruction and Regeneration of the Muscogulge People.* Lincoln: University of Nebraska Press, 1986.

———. *The Only Land They Knew: The Tragic Story of the American Indians in the Old South.* New York: Free Press, 1981.

Wyman, Jeffries. "Fresh Water Shell Mounds of the St. John's River, Florida." *Memoirs of the Peabody Academy of Sciences* 1 (1875): 1–94.

Yanovsky, Elias. *Food Plants of the North American Indians.* U.S. Department of Agriculture, Miscellaneous Publication 237. Washington, D.C.: USDA, 1936.

Yarnell, Richard A. *Aboriginal Relationships Between Culture and Plant Life in the Upper Great Lakes Region.* University of Michigan, Museum of Anthropology, Anthropological Paper 23. Ann Arbor: UM, 1964.

Index

The Caddo Chiefdoms
Caddo Economics and Politics, 700–1835
By David La Vere

Keeping the Circle
American Indian Identity
in Eastern North Carolina, 1885–2004
Christopher Arris Oakley

Choctaws in a Revolutionary Age, 1750–1830
By Greg O'Brien

Cherokee Women
Gender and Culture Change, 1700–1835
By Theda Perdue

The Brainerd Journal
A Mission to the Cherokees, 1817–1823
Edited and introduced by Joyce B. Phillips and Paul Gary Phillips

The Cherokees
A Population History
By Russell Thornton

Buffalo Tiger
A Life in the Everglades
By Buffalo Tiger and Harry A. Kersey Jr.

American Indians in the Lower Mississippi Valley
Social and Economic Histories
By Daniel H. Usner Jr.

Powhatan's Mantle
Indians in the Colonial Southeast
Edited by Peter H. Wood, Gregory A. Waselkov, and M. Thomas Hatley

Creeks and Seminoles
The Destruction and Regeneration of the Muscogulge People
By J. Leitch Wright Jr.

CPSIA information can be obtained at www.ICGtesting.com
Printed in the USA
LVOW03s1127030615

440994LV00006B/35/P